Planned
Urban
Environments

Ann
Louise
Strong

Planned
Urban
Environments

Sweden
Finland
Israel
The
Netherlands
France

The Johns Hopkins Press

Baltimore and London

Copyright © 1971 by The Johns Hopkins Press
Manufactured in the United States of America

The Johns Hopkins Press, Baltimore, Maryland 21218
The Johns Hopkins Press Ltd., London

Library of Congress Catalog Card Number 73-134204
ISBN-0-8018-1245-3

Contents

Illustrations

Finland

Israel

Tables

Acknowledgments

Ever since I simultaneously began to explore some of the weaknesses of American planning implementation and to learn of European planning accomplishments, I have wanted to bring some knowledge of European planning methods to the growing body of Americans concerned with the widening gulf between our planning aspirations and achievements. Given the size and complexity of the task, it is not one which I could possibly have carried out alone. Financial support, cooperation in providing information and interpretation of information in each of the countries studied, technical assistance, and critical review all were vital to the research and writing of the book. To all of those mentioned here, and to many others who gave of their time and ideas, I extend my gratitude, as well as my hope that our efforts may be rewarded through the wider sharing of knowledge concerning significant European planning achievements.

The U.S. Public Health Service awarded the grant (EF 00674-01) which enabled me to make an initial nine-week trip to nine European countries in search of ideas and information. Two subsequent trips for additional information followed, but without public support. The Public Health Service grant, supplemented by support from the University of Pennsylvania's Institute of Legal Research and Institute for Environmental Studies, has made it possible to complete the work.

For reasons discussed in the Introduction, the scope of this book is limited to five of the nine countries which I chose originally for study. I wish to acknowledge the help of several people in the other countries and to assure them that the materials and ideas which they offered so generously are of continuing value to me and my students in the course on European planning offered annually in the Department of City and Regional Planning, University of Pennsylvania.

In Denmark, Mrs. Eva Siesby of the Danish Ministry of Building offered and has continued to offer information about, and interpretations of, Danish planning programs and laws.

Hans B. Barbe, of Seiler and Barbe in Zurich, Switzerland, and his wife, Verena, offered gracious hospitality, advice, and personal introductions to many of Zurich's leading planners.

In Great Britain, so many people were so kind, giving of their time, ideas, and knowledge, that I fear to offend by omission. However, I must acknowledge the assistance of Desmond Heap, solicitor of the City of London and acknowledged master of the British town and country planning laws; Dennis Kirby, general manager of the East Kilbride Development Corporation; J. D. Jones, then deputy secretary of the Ministry of Housing and Local Government; G. R. B. MacGill, general manager of the Cumbernauld Development Corporation; and Sir Frederic J. Osborn, dean of British planning.

Professor Luis F. Negron Garcia of the University of Puerto Rico was most cordial; his lucidity in explaining the Puerto Rican context of the extremely important *Rosso* decision, a landmark decision on the right of the public to take land for new development, was of great assistance.

In Sweden, Finland, Israel, the Netherlands, and France, a number of planners have been of continuing help since we first met in 1964. In addition, there are many others whom I have interviewed, corresponded with, or asked to criticize draft manuscripts. Again, as in the other European countries, the information they have provided is an important resource for planning students at the University of Pennsylvania. Without this information, and without the interpretations, explanations, and comments of those whose help I now acknowledge, this book could not have been written.

In Sweden, Harry Bernhard, deputy director-general of the National Housing Board, and Mrs. Ella Ödmann of the National Board of Building and Town Planning were the first to give me particular assistance in gathering and interpreting information on Swedish planning. Subsequently, Göran Sidenbladh, director of the City Building and Planning Office, Stockholm, and architect-planner Thomas Atmer, also of the City Building and Planning Office, provided much further information and help, including review and criticism of the text pertaining to Sweden.

Because of Heikki von Hertzen, a chapter on Finnish planning was considered essential. The new town of Tapiola is his vision and his creation. Von Hertzen has given unsparingly of his time and of himself to communicate his goals for Tapiola and his concept of the relationship of man and nature in the urban environment. To understand Tapiola, it is first necessary to explore the Finnish setting and character and to learn of the nature and direction of Finnish planning. Arno Hannus, secretary-general of the Ministry of the Interior, has, from 1964 to the present, willingly taken the time to present and explain his government's approach to planning and its response to the challenge of Tapiola. Pekka Sivula, director of the Turku City Planning Agency, offered a different viewpoint in explaining Finnish planning.

In Israel, Professor M. Dennis Gouldman of the Institute for Legislative Research and Comparative Law, Hebrew University, responded with immediate enthusiasm to my undertaking and has been a most constructive correspondent ever since. Morris Hill, a former colleague at the University of Pennsylvania and now associate professor of Architecture and Town Planning at Technion in Haifa, offered suggestions at the outset of this enterprise as well as a final critique of the chapter on Israel. Jacob Dash, chief planner in the Ministry of the Interior, contributed advice and a careful review of the chapter.

Two gentlemen in the Netherlands have devoted extraordinary care and patience to the review of the Dutch chapter. To them is due special thanks and appreciation for the time and trouble taken to ensure the accuracy and timeliness of the chapter. Jacques P. Thysse, former director of the Institute for Social Studies, The Hague, and, too briefly, former visiting professor in the Department of City and Regional Planning at the University of Pennsylvania, and Jasper Vink, former director of the Government Physical Planning Service, began providing reports and comments in 1964; together, they are responsible for most of what I now know about planning in the Netherlands. B. Fokkinga, director of the Rotterdam Town Planning Department, offered comments concerning the planning process in Rotterdam.

French planning is as complex and multi-faceted as the French people. For that reason, many people were able to explain with precision and clarity the role of their particular agency, but few were in a position to provide a synoptic view. Roger Macé, then director of urban development in the Ministry of Construction, was one of the exceptions, as was my friend and helpful critic, Max Falque, planner of the Company for the Provence Canal. Jean Canaux, director of the Center of Urban Research, and his staff reviewed the French text and offered helpful comments and corrections. Pierre Reynaud, director of the Interministerial Mission for Languedoc-Roussillon, graciously reviewed the discussion of that project.

The contributions of these planners were essential; so too was the assistance of staff and students at the University of Pennsylvania. Translations, research assistance, graphic materials, typing, and editorial aid were the work of planning, architecture, and economics graduate students and the staff of the Institute for Environmental Studies.

Geert de Koning, a graduate of the Department of City and Regional Planning, translated much-needed material from Dutch to English. Christoph M. J. Brôzek, another graduate of the Department of City and Regional Planning, translated Swiss materials from German to English and also conducted a number of interviews in Zurich. Andrew Reschovsky, a doctoral student in economics, was of great assistance in assembling and interpreting economic materials from France. Jean-Paul Loevenbruck, a student in the Department of City and Regional Planning, gave freely of his time to discuss the structure and operation of French planning.

Three students prepared the maps, graphs, and illustrations. Ashgar Minai, a doctoral student in architecture, did most of the work for the chapters on Finland and Sweden. Philip Loukissas, a student in the Department of City and Regional Planning, prepared the largest share of the graphics, working with great skill and accuracy; he is responsible for a portion of the work for the chapters on Finland and Sweden, all of the graphics for the chapters on Israel and the Netherlands, and part of the graphics for the chapter on France. A student in architecture, Frederico Valda, completed the graphic work for France. Frosso Vassiliades prepared the index.

Beatrice Solomon and Laura Kessler of the Institute for Environmental Studies have borne with remarkable patience and good humor the work of preparing the several drafts of each chapter. Mrs. Solomon, administrative assistant of the Institute for Environmental Studies, has been of immense help—with editorial assistance, organization, and typing—while Mrs. Kessler has shared the extensive task of typing and proofreading.

My husband, Michael L. Strong, took many of the photographs which illustrate the book. Much more important, he accompanied me on all of my trips; without his company and insights, I would have learned far less.

One delightful result of undertaking this study has been the friendships made with men and women named here, as well as with many more. The hospitality offered to my husband and me has been warm and generous. We are grateful for what we have learned. I hope that this book communicates the ideas of our European friends and will stimulate readers to develop new planning concepts for the United States.

Ann Louise Strong

Introduction

The United States must make a commitment to national environmental planning, both for urban development and resource management.

We can no longer encourage exploitation of our land and our people for the benefit of a few. We have thought it patriotic as well as exciting to push back the frontier and turn to profit this land's vast resources. In nearly two centuries as a nation, we have despoiled and laid waste vast areas once bountiful and beautiful. We have farmed heedlessly, creating dustbowls and eroded hillsides. Good topsoil now chokes our rivers with mud. Our human and industrial wastes befoul our shorelines and waters. We have slaughtered, and often exterminated, many species of birds and animals. We have become the richest nation in the world, but at a terrible cost in destruction and consumption of resources. We are living off capital as well as income, and have reinvested little to assure future income.

Starting with the subjugation of the Indian, many of us have sanctioned, or conveniently overlooked, the mistreatment of our fellow men that has enabled a few to profit inordinately. The foundations of our society are being rent because the equality of opportunity promised in the United States Constitution is but a cruel hoax.

Our European forefathers shared a respect for the land and an awareness of man's interdependence with it; this sense of a bond between man and the land did not survive the sea voyage to the New World. Whereas harmony had been the goal there, the conquest of nature became the goal here. Perhaps the clues to our aggressive, spendthrift approach to the land lie in the nature of those who chose to be pioneers and frontiersmen. No doubt, too, the vastness of this land and its resources, compared with the paucity of its settlers, made it inconceivable that destruction of species and despoliation of the land could occur here. Nonetheless, the freedom to explore, to choose a homesite, was transmuted for many into a freedom to use land as one saw fit, regardless of the consequences to others. Just as the bond with the land was loosed, so was the bond between man and other men, in which the limits of space and resources constrained each to consider the effects of his acts upon others. Ours became a society of "me first" and "the devil take the hindmost." Self-sufficiency and independence, not harmony and interdependence, were our models for behavior.

Now that the effects of our depredation of the natural environment and neglect of our fellow men are writ so large as to be incontrovertible and inescapable, now that our frontier has in effect vanished and our urban areas are as densely packed as those of Europe (see Map 1, *a* and *b*), will we learn from those who have been less richly endowed than we?

At last, and hopefully not too late, Americans are awakening to the decline of our environment and to the despair of large sectors of our society. If we

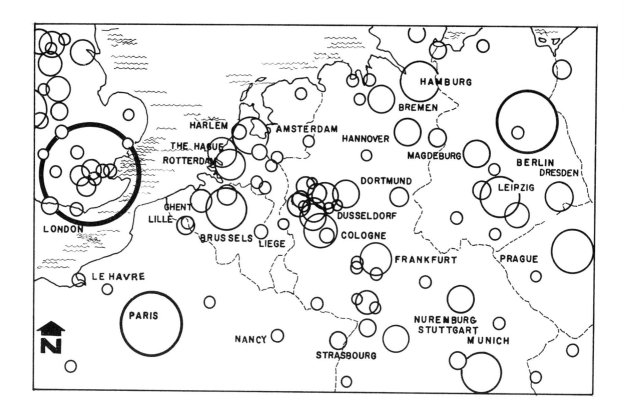

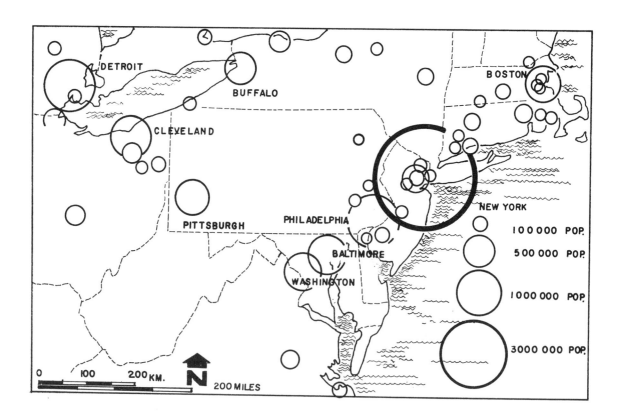

Map 1. Density of Settlement: (*a*) Northwestern Europe; (*b*) the Northeastern
United States

are to start again, if we are to create a society in which all men can flourish, nothing less than a national commitment of our resources can suffice. To sustain life, we must control our population size and distribution, manage our resource base, and restore the quality of our air, water, and soil. To offer liberty, all people must have the opportunity to partake of the nation's resources. In the pursuit of happiness, we must explore, then create, the congeries of living patterns—density, mobility, variety, choice, and size—which are most satisfying to men. As a government, we must officially re-establish our goals as a nation and then plan for the commitment of our resources to the fulfillment of those goals. We also must create a process for continually re-evaluating our goals and the comparative effectiveness of the programs followed in realizing them.

There are positive signs that we are ready for such a national planning program, ready to renew an effort which has lain dormant since the 1930s, when the demise of the National Resources Planning Board and the abandonment of the greenbelt towns program occurred.

■ In his January, 1970, State of the Union message, President Nixon proposed that the United States "develop a national growth policy" and that the "Federal government . . . assist in the building of new cities." He reinforced this commitment in his introduction to *Environmental Quality*,[1] the first annual report of the new Council on Environmental Quality, stating: "I believe that the problems of urbanization . . . , of resource management, and of land and water use generally can only be met by comprehensive approaches which take into account the widest range of social, economic, and ecological concerns. I believe we must work toward development of a National Land Use Policy."

■ Other public officials of both parties have articulated the need for national planning of land use. As Robert C. Weaver, secretary of housing and urban development in the Johnson administration, said, "It is distressing to realize that this country is one of the few Western nations that does not have a clearly defined national land use policy."[2] The concluding report of the Public Land Law Review Commission recommended similar action. Congressman Ashley, Senator Jackson, and others have introduced bills directed toward these objectives. As of autumn, 1970, however, the administration had yet to offer a specific proposal.

■ National aid for population planning, anathema to the Eisenhower administration, now is politically acceptable. In 1970, Congress and President Nixon authorized the appointment of a Commission on Population Growth and the American Future. The commission will report, in March, 1972, on (1) the probable course of growth and migration by the year 2000; (2) the nature and extent of the public resources which will be required to accommodate this growth; (3) the effects of growth on government; (4) the impact of growth on the natural environment; and (5) "the various means appropriate to the ethical values and principles of this society by which our nation can achieve a population level properly suited for its environmental, natural resources, and other needs."[3]

■ We are moving toward a national new towns program. Enactment of the new communities provisions of the Housing Act of 1968 was a step, albeit a small one. It was an initial recognition of the crippling handicaps under which new towns ventures entirely dependent on private capital must labor. Leading congressmen, governors, and mayors have recommended a federal loan and loan guarantee program for new cities for people of all incomes. The proposed Housing Act of 1970 may take another small step. Several states are considering new towns programs; New York's Urban Development Corporation already is at work on new communities. In May of 1969, the National

Commission on Urban Growth recommended that federal assistance be provided for the construction, by the year 2000, of 100 new towns with populations of 100,000 each, and 10 new cities of one million people each. Were we to reach that target, 7 percent of our population would be living in new towns by 2000.

■   Environmental protection legislation is proliferating. We now have created a national Council on Environmental Quality, which will occupy a position comparable to the Council of Economic Advisers, and an Environmental Protection Agency to bring under one roof many of the federal pollution control agencies. Congress is allocating funds for environmental programs; in 1969, for instance, the appropriation for water pollution control more than trebled the administration's request. The National Environmental Policy Act of 1969 promises improved coordination and communication and provides new legal bases for executive and judicial decisions concerning the nation's resources. The act also sets forth new statements of national policy: "It is the continuing policy of the Federal Government . . . to use all practicable means . . . to foster and promote the general welfare, to create and maintain conditions under which man and nature can exist in productive harmony, and [to] fulfill the social, economic, and other requirements of present and future generations of Americans." Further, it is the "continuing responsibility of the Federal Government" to act so that the nation will "attain the widest beneficial uses of the environment without degradation . . . and maintain, wherever possible, an environment which supports diversity and variety of individual choice."[4]

■   Public power to condemn land for new development has been affirmed. The U.S. Supreme Court, by denying certiorari in the *Rosso* case,[5] upheld the right of a public body, namely the Puerto Rican Land Authority, to condemn undeveloped land for resale or lease for development in accordance with public plans. President Nixon's Commission on Urban Housing has recognized the advantages of public landownership by calling for new powers for the Department of Housing and Urban Development to lease rather than sell land for subsidized housing and related community facilities.

■   Congress has stated the national dimensions of housing need and has fixed a timetable for programs to eliminate substandard housing. The Housing Act of 1968 contains a statement of intent to build or rehabilitate 26 million dwelling units in the next ten years. As yet, however, the intention has not been matched by appropriation of anywhere near adequate funds.

If the climate for national planning is improving, is there experience in Europe from which we might learn? After studying planning in a number of European countries, as well as in Israel, my conclusion is that there is a broad range of experience, many elements of which are transferable to the United States. The history of the commitment to planning and the means of achieving planning objectives vary widely from country to country. The recognition of the need for planning and the nature of planning goals vary far less.

Common planning objectives in Europe today are: wise management of the natural environment; provision of adequate housing for all, without social discrimination against the needy; creation of communities offering residents a choice of jobs, housing, leisure activities, and social contacts; widespread sharing of the profits from development; development of convenient, attractive mass transportation; distribution of population to limit urban density and size and to promote national economic development; and dedication to the creation and preservation of environmental amenities.

Differences in national circumstance—history, politics, resources, and culture—contribute to the development of different routes to, and different conceptions of, the above planning objectives. My criteria for selecting countries to discuss were variety, novelty, and achievement—variety among the countries, the novelty of their planning approaches to Americans, and achievement in terms of actual implementation of planning objectives. Using these criteria, I chose Sweden, Finland, Israel, the Netherlands, and France.

The sole reason for excluding Great Britain was that such a distinguished company—including Colin Buchanan, Peter Hall, Sir Desmond Heap, Nathaniel Lichfield, Sir Frederic J. Osborn, Wyndham Thomas, and, from the United States, Daniel Mandelker and Lloyd Rodwin—already has described British planning and British planning achievements so authoritatively. For example, for an understanding of the evolution of British new town development, with milestones such as Letchworth and Welwyn, Harlow and Stevenage, East Kilbride and Cumbernauld (see Figures 1–10), one must look to *The New Towns*.[6]

Turning to compensation and betterment (one of the most instructive areas of the British experience), who could do without, or improve upon, Sir Desmond Heap's many books and articles? Because so many superior accounts of British planning already exist, I decided that it would be more useful to focus on other European planning, about which information is less readily available, particularly to an English-speaking audience. What, then, were the particular elements of variety, novelty, and achievement which led to the choice of Sweden, Finland, Israel, the Netherlands, and France?

The most notable achievements in Swedish planning are those of the city of Stockholm, which has successfully engaged in long-term planning and plan implementation for many decades. National planning and regional planning now are coming to the fore, but, historically, municipal planning has been of greater significance in shaping the character of urban growth. Modern Stockholm, with its efficient and attractive public transit system, its rationally organized network of neighborhoods and satellite communities, and its economic allocation of development resources, could not have been built without long-term advance planning. The foresight which, fifty or more years ago, guided the city in the acquisition of vast tracts of land has enabled today's municipal planners to control both when this land comes into development and how it is developed. Most significantly, it has permitted less costly development, for no speculative gains in land are realized by the private market. While municipal land-banking is customary in much of Europe, its economic benefits are most evident in Stockholm, where thorough planning long has accompanied it.

Stockholm's planners have established the transit system as the structure about which urban growth will occur and then have related the location of community centers, housing, and open space, the density of housing, and the location and character of the highway network to this system. As each new satellite community, beginning with Vällingby, has been completed, plans for the next have been revised to meet the observed shortcomings of those already built.

Stockholm's success in carrying out a rational planning program now is likely to be duplicated at the regional level. With the creation of a regional planning process, as well as a regional political process, in which Stockholm participates, the region is moving toward a cooperative program of public land acquisition, long-range planning, public construction of the communications network and infrastructure, and private development in accordance with public plans.

The chronic national housing shortage, particularly acute in Stockholm, has led to an emphasis—in the satellite centers as well as elsewhere—on the construction of multi-family industrialized housing. The growing market demand for single-family detached housing has been largely unmet, except

Figure 1. Typical Residential Area, East Kilbride, Near Glasgow

Figure 2. Neighborhood High School, East Kilbride

Figure 3. Low-Density Housing, East Kilbride

Figure 4. Neighborhood Shops, East Kilbride

Figure 5. The Town Center, East Kilbride

Figure 6. Access to the Town Center, Cumbernauld, Near Glasgow

Figure 7. Housing at Cumbernauld

Figure 8. Housing at Cumbernauld

Figure 9. Housing at Cumbernauld

Figure 10. Housing at Cumbernauld

through proliferating summer houses. With the national government responding to public pressure for more, and more spacious, housing, however, and with a national housing program under which the number and types of dwellings to be built are allocated annually to each municipality, there is a means as well as a policy for eliminating the housing shortage. An indicator of success is that, during the 1960s, Sweden's rate of housing construction far outstripped the rate of population increase.

Tapiola, Finland, is my personal choice as the finest new town yet created. It is true—and in this Heikki von Hertzen fully concurs—that many of the new cities of the future must be far larger than Tapiola's planned 17,000. For the United States, a reasonable target population might be from ten to twenty times the size of Tapiola. Nevertheless, for its scale, there is little to find fault with at Tapiola and much in which to delight. There is also much for Americans to learn before embarking on new cities ventures.

Tapiola was built by Asuntosäätiö, a non-profit private enterprise which regularly substituted talent, imagination, and fortitude for the private and public funds that were in such short supply. Finland is not a rich country, and her postwar burdens would have been unmanageable by a less determined people. At the time that Asuntosäätiö committed itself to build Tapiola, many bankers and government officials thought it an impossible dream. No government money helped launch Tapiola, and in later years only the modest public funds available to any other developer were granted the new town. The land was assembled privately, planned privately, and the initial financing was private. Despite financial constraints at least as severe as those which have hobbled or ruined new town projects in the United States and the rest of Europe, Tapiola succeeded. Today it is almost complete. Tapiola is beautiful and spacious; it is economically and socially integrated. Man lives in harmony with nature and his fellow man. In the test of the market place, no one moves out and everyone wants to move in. While one could point to Tapiola as a private enterprise success in a country with a tradition of few public controls on land use—and so, seemingly, as a model for the United States—it is not this which I wish to stress. Given Tapiola's handicaps of the lack of long-term financing and the absence of land-assembly and land-use control powers, I believe that only an exceptional organization could have succeeded. Because such a combination of talent and organizational commitment is a rarity, either here or in Finland, Tapiola must be disqualified as a model for success. Instead, it is my hope that Americans will learn from Tapiola's physical and social design, so that in building new cities we will retain a sense of the pre-existing natural environment and will design structures and systems which derive from and accentuate the unique characteristics of the site, and further, that we will create a living environment hospitable to all elements of society.

Israel's people have many of the better attributes of our pioneers: optimism, vitality, courage, and strength. Their confident belief in their country and its future is reminiscent of a spirit we have lost. The analogy to an earlier America ends there. The Israelis are builders, not plunderers. They have not had the luxuries of space, climate, and resources enjoyed by our ancestors. They have taken a barren and inhospitable, backward and lightly populated land and, with the resources of brains and money, have transformed it into a productive and, absent war, almost self-supporting economy for more than 2.5 million people. Israel has a national physical master plan and, under it, has shaped the settlement of people, the allocation of land to agriculture or development, and the management of scarce resources, particularly water. To an even greater extent than Great Britain (given their comparative population bases), Israel has built and populated a hierarchy of new towns from Ashdod, with an anticipated population of 350,000, down to scores of farm villages. In the process, Israel has learned much about new town size and structure. People, whether rural or urban residents, want access to the variety and range of services and activities which only a city can offer. As incomes have risen and mobility has increased, Israelis have eschewed the villages and small towns for the cities, new and old. Of the new towns, the larger have grown more rapidly than anticipated, while the smaller have either grown slowly or stagnated. Even with the powerful economic weapons of jobs and housing, Israel has been unable to deflect as much growth as desired from her three principal metropolitan areas. The 10 percent of the land in private ownership lies in the metropolitan areas and, there, private speculation and development have proceeded apace, in disregard of government planning.

Israel's development experience also yields valuable social insights. While the population is extremely heterogeneous, it can be broadly categorized as European developed or Afro–Middle Eastern underdeveloped. Those of European origin have been dominant politically, economically, intellectually, and culturally. Despite a planning commitment to mix the population, the Europeans have congregated in the larger metropolitan areas, where they have prospered and risen to positions of prominence. Many of the African and Middle Eastern immigrants have continued their rural agricultural life style. Disparities of income and position have developed which are related to the cultural heritage of the people. Recognizing this, the government has redoubled its efforts to provide an equal level of services and cultural opportunities to people in the outlying and urban areas and to develop, through the schools and military service, a common level of training for all. Combined with this desire to guarantee equal opportunity is a recognition of the desirability of encouraging people to sustain that which is unique in their cultural heritages. Immigrants are settled in neighborhoods with others from the same country or who speak the same language and are encouraged to sustain their language and culture as well as to assimilate the Hebrew language and predominant Israeli culture. Unlike France, where the approach to planning is intellectual and complex, Israel started with a relatively simple theoretical structure, built a country as rapidly as possible (substituting pragmatism for theory in many instances), and now is reconsidering theory in light of experience.

Israeli and Dutch physical planning have rested on the same theories of Christaller regarding the optimum hierarchical form of settlement. Experience in the new towns of the polders has paralleled that in Israel: as people gain mobility, they abandon the small town for the city. Given new systems of travel and communication, the traditional formulation of the theory no longer is valid.

The Dutch are a thorough, practical people. What the French may have divined through insight, the Dutch will have determined through controlled experimentation. Over the centuries—five, at least—the Dutch have developed a system of national physical planning which is highly democratic and which has worked well for them, partly because their survival depended on it, but at least equally because they are an unusually responsible people. They believe that the welfare of each is contingent upon the good of all; from this belief they have built responsible local participation into the national planning process. Today, this cornerstone of Dutch planning faces its first major challenge in the conflicting goals of Rotterdam. The national physical plan places first priority on a good life for all, including comfortable housing, adequate living space, convenient access to job and leisure activities, and location near a clean and attractive natural environment. This vision of the good life carries within it the implication that metropolitan growth, in density and extent, may have to be restricted. In fact, the plan envisions a polynuclear national urban structure in which no one center is dominant. Today's challenge to national planning principles comes from the Rotterdam metropolitan area, which already is a growth over-achiever from the national planning viewpoint. The Rotterdam area's economic boosters seek further growth, urging that this is essential in order to be competitive on the international economic front. Yet greater growth will drain development from other areas of the country and will diminish many of the opportunities for the good life endorsed in the national plan. In the past, plans have been implemented by voluntary local action. Agreement has been reached, the national government has undertaken its share of the task, and local governments, in conjunction with private enterprise, have proceeded to discharge their responsibilities. Because plans have evolved slowly, with full participation and discussion, there has been little need for *force majeure*. The next few years will show whether Rotterdam and the national government can reach an accommodation.

France is outstanding as one of the few nations which has an official national economic plan as well as a national environmental plan. Not only are there plans, but government financing is tied to them effectively. The French people are at least as individualistic and as suspicious of government intervention as Americans, yet, after World War II, they recognized the need for national planning and adopted their first medium-term economic plan. The five-year Fifth Plan terminated in 1970. This plan was developed with regional as well as national inputs and, upon adoption, was divided into regional sectors for effectuation. The Fifth Plan was the first of the economic plans to be coordinated with a national environmental plan.

The French are a shrewd, ingenious people, and their mechanisms for implementing these plans offer a wealth of exportable ideas. There are the ZUP, ZAD, and ZAC, through which national and local governments, acting in concert, can tie up land planned for development, spread out payment for the acquisition of land over a period of from four to twelve years, and direct all development in a metropolitan area to land so designated. There are programs for new towns, for strengthening regional centers, and for deflecting growth from Paris. There are schemes for reallocating inefficient parcels of land. There is a capital gains tax designed to foil the would-be tax evader. Savings funds are tapped to provide low-interest funds to support government programs. There are housing subsidy and housing finance programs galore, including housing funds created from required contributions by employers of ten or more people. Many sectors—labor, business, elected officials, technicians—participate on regional and national planning commissions. Most development is in the hands of public-private companies, in which different levels of government, private corporations, chambers of commerce, other mixed corporations (such as housing corporations), unions, and private individuals hold varying percentages of stock. The Languedoc-Roussillon project for developing six new towns and 120 miles of Mediterranean coast is being carried out by six such public-private companies. Think of a novel approach to financing development; in all likelihood the French thought of it first.

Public landownership has been a crucial element of almost all successful European planning. Tapiola is a major exception, although public acquisition of land prior to development is common in Finland. Stockholm's satellite centers, the British and Israeli new towns, the polder new towns in the Netherlands, Rotterdam's port development and urban expansion, and the Languedoc-Roussillon resort towns and coastal development share the common element of public land acquisition in advance of development. In most of these instances, as well as in much of the European planning of which they are illustrative, the land is leased rather than sold for development. If the desired use of the land changes over time, the public can secure the altered use—as well as increments in land values—through negotiation of new lease terms.

In the United States, there is an antipathy to public landownership and a conviction that the increment in land value accruing from increased development potential should go to the successful speculator rather than to the public at large to offset public development costs. We have been ready to compensate the landowner damaged by public planning decisions, but, unlike the Europeans, we have refused to charge the landowner benefited by such decisions. Given the increasing attribution of incidences of development value to public decisions and investments, the irrationality of our current posture is ever more costly to us as a nation, and to us as individual taxpayers. It is yet another example of squandered capital, but of public funds rather than of our soil or oil. Faced with urgent demands for the tax dollar—for the elimination of substandard housing and malnutrition, for the abatement of air and water pollution, and for the development of adequate education programs for all, it is an ideological quirk we no longer can afford to indulge. Nor need we fear that the public retention or capture of development value through public acquisition of land in advance of development, taxation, and enforcement of public plans spells doom for the American Way of Life. Public landownership is thoroughly American; it has yet, in our history, to prove a harbinger of communism. The public domain was created when the Articles of Confederation were ratified, when all land held by the thirteen colonies under charter from Great Britain was ceded to Congress. Except for Texas and Hawaii, all additional lands were acquired as part of the public domain of the United States. From colonial times onward, the government has sold or given away land in the public domain, but even today 700 million acres remain of the original public domain. The government of the United States still holds, as owner or trustee, 35 percent of all land within the nation. Most of this land is in the West; as seen in Map 2, 95 percent of Alaska and 86 percent of Nevada are federally owned. Unfortunately, in terms of the utility of this land for urban expansion, most of it is far from existing urban areas.

States and municipalities also own significant amounts of land. As of 1960 the states owned 80 million acres; municipalities owned 17 million acres, for a combined total of 5 percent of all land in the United States. About one-third of the land in our cities is publicly owned. Altogether, public lands total approximately 40 percent of the land area of the United States (see Figure 11).

The public lands present a superb opportunity for new city development; without new investments in land and without the need for new land-use control legislation, we can plan and build our conception of beautiful, efficient cities for all U.S. citizens. By 1961, Israel had built new towns and cities for 13 percent of her population; in Great Britain the current total is a more modest 2 percent of the population after two decades of the new towns program. Might the United States set a target for each remaining decade of this century so that, by the year 2000, 10 percent of our population—or 30 million people—will be living in new or newly expanded cities?

We need not continue to crowd into the existing metropolitan areas; we have the luxury of space. New Jersey, for instance, may have a density comparable to that of the Netherlands, but, with a national density of almost ten acres per person, we have options already foreclosed in the Netherlands. New Jersey need not grow further; we could offer sufficient differential in incentives to encourage people and industries to settle in new or expanded cities in less densely settled states, thereby affording New Jersey the opportunity to cope with the present ravages of man's development. Such a choice

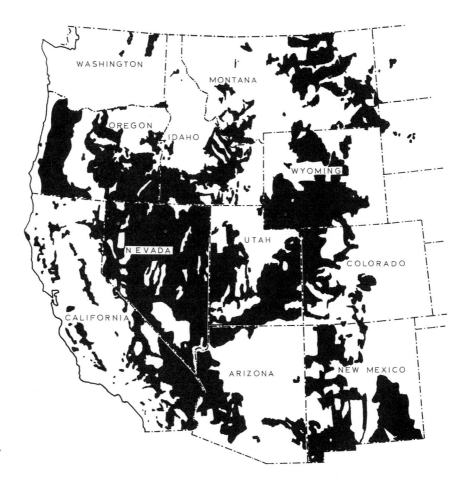

Map 2.
Public Land under
the U.S. Bureau of
Land Management,
1964

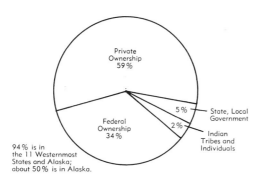

Landownership in the United States

Private
Ownership
59%

5% — State, Local
Government

2% —

Federal
Ownership
34%

Indian
Tribes and
Individuals

94% is in
the 11 Westernmost
States and Alaska;
about 50% is in Alaska.

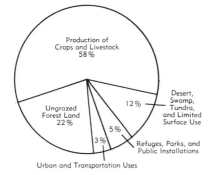

Land Use in the United States
Total Acres in the 50 States—2.3 Billion

Production of
Crops and Livestock
58%

12% — Desert,
Swamp,
Tundra,
and Limited
Surface Use

Ungrazed
Forest Land
22%

5% —

3% —

Refuges, Parks, and
Public Installations

Urban and Transportation Uses

Figure 11.
Landownership
and Land Use in
the United States

could offer all of us—those remaining in megalopolis and those moving to new urban areas—the possibility of a better balanced and more enjoyable urban and natural environment.

Such goals require long-range planning, both to specify environmental objectives and economic priorities and to create a process for translating them into realities. In this time of public outcries for inclusion in the decision process, we can look to the French system of environmental and economic planning and to the French approach to financing and development for imaginative experimentation with the involvement of all public and private sectors.

Meeting the long-standing legislative mandate of a decent home for every American family must be an essential element of U.S. national planning. The 1968 congressional statement of intent to build or rehabilitate 26 million dwelling units by 1978 must be matched by adequate financing. When compared to our acknowledged need or to European achievements, our record here is pathetic. In 1967, only 2 percent of all residential construction received any subsidy; in the five countries studied, between 37 and 66 percent of residential construction was subsidized. The lack of subsidy funds contributed to a lower rate of construction; in 1967 the United States built only 6.7 dwelling units per 1,000 population, less than any of the five countries studied, and 50 percent less than Sweden's construction rate. Given our vaunted Gross National Product, does this not suggest a reordering of priorities?

Urban and rural Europe offer many lessons. If we have the will to learn from the successes and failures there, if we have the commitment to meet the needs of all of our people, and if we can rekindle a land ethic, we may yet create a healthy and richly satisfying environment. We must acknowledge the perils of the present as the legacy of past misadventures. We must change course and reorder our priorities today. Have we the wisdom and the will?

Notes

1. (Washington, D.C., 1970), p. xiii.
2. "Natural Resources and Tomorrow's Cities" (Speech presented in Houston, Texas, March 11, 1968).
3. Public Law 91-213, March 16, 1970.
4. Public Law 91-190, January 1, 1970, sec. 101(a) and (b).
5. *Commonwealth of Puerto Rico v. Jorge I. Rosso and wife Carmen Descartes*, opinion 67-172, El Tribunal Supremo de Puerto Rico, December 7, 1967; *cert. denied*, 393 U.S. 14 (Sup. Ct. 1969).
6. Sir Frederic J. Osborn and Arnold Whittick (New York: McGraw-Hill, 1963).

I | Sweden

Stockholm:
Physical
Planning
Realized

Hotorget, a New Transit and Commercial Hub for Stockholm

Contents

The National Setting

Sweden today is prosperous, modern, and stable. More than a century and a half of neutrality, some thirty years' investment in social welfare programs, abundant natural resources, and the world's lowest national birth rate[1] all have contributed to Sweden's high standard of living.

Spurred by industrialization, urbanization began midway through the nineteenth century. In 1870, almost 75 percent of the people were farmers; today, almost 75 percent live and work in the cities.[2] Current migration is from farms and small towns to the larger urban areas, as is the case throughout the world. This migration pattern is encouraged by a national economic policy of concentration of growth in a few urban areas. Sweden's economic planners want to place their country in the best competitive position with neighboring European countries (see Map I-1). They believe that only very large urban areas can compete as major trade centers. Given Sweden's population and resources and the probable level of competition from other nearby metropolitan areas, it has been proposed that Sweden should encourage concentration of her urban growth in the Stockholm area, or possibly in and near Gothenburg and Malmö in addition to Stockholm.

Of course, this economic policy has considerable physical and social planning implications. If one or a few urban areas are to have very large populations for agglomeration advantages, these advantages cannot be dissipated through inefficient transportation and communication and unsatisfactory living conditions. The recent and continuing development of metropolitan Stockholm shows how the planners are meeting the challenge of creating a large, functional, and competitive urban area. An excellent public transportation system links satellite centers, located inside and outside the city limits, to the center city and to one another. The satellite centers have a high density and offer a range of shops and cultural facilities clustered about transit stops, all of which are within easy walking distance of most residences.

Because most of the land being developed in the Stockholm area is publicly owned, and because the state and municipalities exercise considerable control over the construction industry, plans, once they are approved by the legislative bodies, generally are carried out as approved. Stockholm's satellite centers therefore afford an unusual opportunity to observe the physical realization of publicly adopted urban development objectives and to evaluate whether those objectives have been achieved.

Natural Environment

Sweden, with an area of 173,600 square miles, is similar in size and shape to California (see Map I-2). Her climate, like Finland's, is benefited by the flow of the Gulf Stream along the coast of Norway. The lower third of

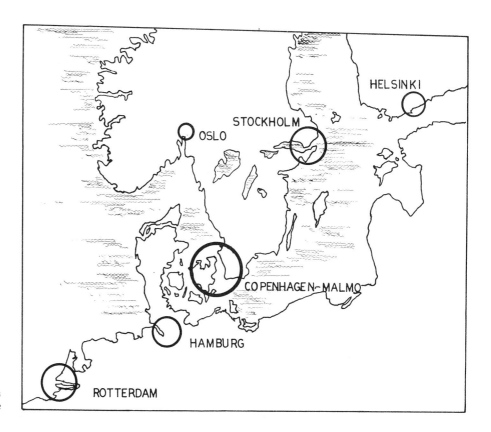

Map I-1.
Metropolitan Areas
of Northern Europe

Sweden is more southerly than any part of Finland and so enjoys a more temperate climate, a longer summer, and a shorter winter. Here the mean daily temperature is 32° F. in winter and 61° F. in summer. The three largest cities—Stockholm, Gothenburg, and Malmö—all are located in the southern third of the country, as is the best agricultural land.

Traveling north, the rolling farmland gives way to forests, and they in turn bow to the tundra and glaciers of the Arctic. Rivers rise in the mountains along the Norwegian border and flow southeast to the coastal plain. Some 100,000 lakes dot the mainland, while archipelagos of thousands of islands lie offshore.

The total area of Sweden is divided as follows: lakes and rivers, 9 percent; forests, 55 percent; cultivated land and pasture, 10 percent; urbanized land, 6 percent; miscellaneous, 20 percent.

Sweden lacks coal and petroleum and, as of 1967, met 79 percent of her energy requirements through imports (see Table I-1). The fast-flowing rivers provide an inexpensive source of hydroelectric power, however, and are used to generate 17 percent of the country's electricity. Large shale deposits rich in uranium are being mined, and the uranium is processed, partly as an additional source of power. Farsta, one of Stockholm's newer satellite centers, is supplied with electricity and heat by nuclear power plants.

Sweden's other important natural resources are her forests and iron ore deposits. After felling, timber is floated downstream or trucked to the pulp mills, saw mills, and processing factories located along the northeast coast. The largest and most important iron ore deposits are located in Lappland, although some deposits, as well as most steel mills, are in central Sweden. Other minerals, including copper, gold, and lead, are found in sufficient quantities to meet most or all domestic requirements.

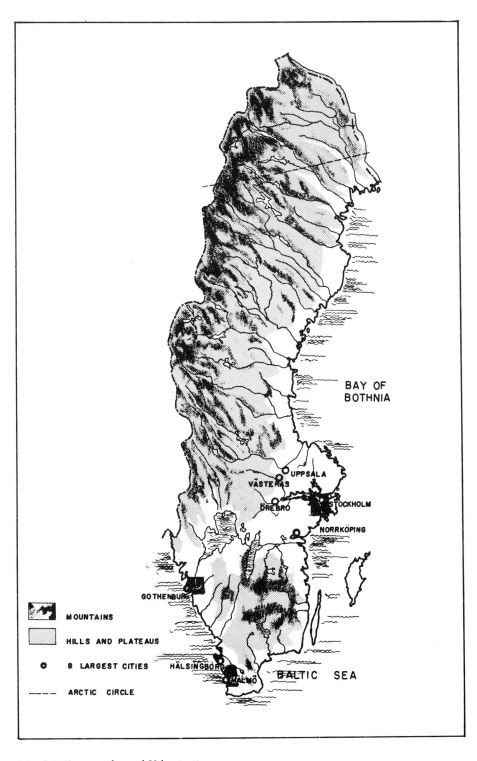

Map I-2. Topography and Urbanization

Table I-1.
Sources of Energy

Source	Year			
	1950	1955	1962	1967
Domestic				
Hydroelectric power	28%	28%	36%	17%
Other resources	18	12	6	4
Total	46	40	42	21
Imported				
Coal and coke	30	19	9	8
Gasoline and motor oil	8	11	12	11
Fuel oils	16	30	37	59
Hydroelectric power	—	—	—	1
Total	54	60	58	79

SOURCES: The Swedish Institute, *Facts About Sweden* (Stockholm, 1964); Stockholms Enskilda Bank, *Some Data About Sweden* (Stockholm, 1968).

The Government

The present parliamentary democracy dates back to 1809, the year in which Sweden deposed her authoritarian monarch and adopted the present constitution; it was the same year in which Sweden surrendered Finland to Russia. In 1810 the French marshal Jean Bernadotte was elected heir to the throne; his male descendents have continued the reign to the present day. Legislative power has been exercised by the bicameral Parliament, or Riksdag, while executive power rests with the cabinet. In 1970 the two legislative houses merged to form a unicameral Parliament. On September 20, 1970, general elections were held for the new 350-seat Parliament, and once again the Social Democrats won a plurality, although they ran almost 4 percent behind their share of the 1968 vote. With 166 seats they do not have a majority and therefore are looking to the Communists, with 17 seats, for support in a coalition. The Center party gained in the 1970 election and now holds 73 seats. The Liberals and the Conservatives hold the remaining 94 seats. As a result of a constitutional reform which bars parties gaining less than 4 percent of the vote from Parliament, there will be no splinter-party representation in the new Parliament.

The Social Democrats—the labor party—have been in power, either alone or in coalition with other parties, continuously since 1932, except for one six-month period. Although Sweden is termed socialist by some, 90 percent of the economy is privately owned, and 90 percent of the labor force works for private firms. However, Prime Minister Palme is committed to naming government officials to the boards of the twenty largest firms in order to better coordinate public and private planning.

The king appoints as prime minister the leader of the majority party; he in turn selects seventeen cabinet members, of whom thirteen are ministry heads and four serve without portfolio. The ministries are relatively small and are concerned principally with the development of the government's over-all executive policies.

The Swedish executive branch is unusual in that there is, and traditionally has been, a marked separation between the policy-making function, lodged in the ministries, and policy implementation, which is the responsibility of more than fifty central administrative boards. These boards are headed by civil servants with permanent tenure and they vary in size, form of organization, and operating procedures. They are responsible to the cabinet as a whole rather than to the particular ministry to which they have been assigned for organizational purposes. The boards have a substantial degree of independence from the ministries.

The twenty-four counties, or provinces, and Stockholm, which is classed separately as a county corporate, are administrative units of the state. The provincial governors and their staffs are state appointed, while the provincial council is elected. The central administrative boards have provincial employees who occupy a position (vis-à-vis the governor and his staff) comparable to that of the boards to the cabinet at the state level.

There are 1,037 local governments or communes—133 cities and 904 rural communes. To achieve more efficient administration, the state is pressing for voluntary consolidation, which would reduce the total number of local governments to about 300, each with a population of at least 8,000.[3] The communes are governed by elected councils, which operate through committees; the latter include an executive committee, a financial committee, and a planning and building committee, each of which may be served by professional staff. The communes have a high degree of autonomy with regard to local government functions. Where programs of state concern and state funding are delegated to the communes for implementation, considerable control over the programs is retained by the state and exercised directly or through the provincial governments.

The People

Sweden's 7.7 million people are concentrated in the urban areas dotting the seacoast and bisecting the southern part of the country from Stockholm to Gothenburg. There is an enormous range in population density—from eight persons per square mile in the north to 338 persons per square mile in the southwest. The average density of 45 persons per square mile is not much less than the United States average density of 50.5 persons per square mile in 1960.[4]

The urban-rural distribution of the population is described by the Swedes as 75 percent urban, 25 percent rural (see Figure I-1). Because communities with as few as 200 people are classed as urban, this definition should be kept in mind when comparing Sweden with other countries. Applying a different measure, 40 percent of the population lives in cities of 50,000 or more people or in their suburbs. The shift of the population from rural to urban areas has been particularly rapid during the past quarter-century and is continuing. Each year 30,000 people leave the farms for the cities. In 1939, 3.5 million people, or 55 percent of the population, lived in rural areas; today, fewer than 2.0 million people live there. In 1960 the predicted rate of annual urban population growth to 1980 was 1.25 percent (see Figure I-2).[5] It has been predicted that, during those twenty years, the total population will increase by 1.0 million, while the population of urban areas will rise by 1.7 million (the result of migration as well as of natural increase). If this occurs, 86 percent of the total population will be urban.[6]

In 1960, more than half of the urban population lived in the hundreds of small towns and cities which have fewer than 50,000 inhabitants; the remainder lived in twelve cities with from 50,000 to 800,000 inhabitants (see Table I-2).

Stockholm, with about 783,000 people, is the largest Swedish city. It is almost twice as large as Gothenburg, the second largest city. The Greater Stockholm area (including the city) had a 1965 population of 1,230,000. The older part of the city began to decline in population in the 1940s; the total

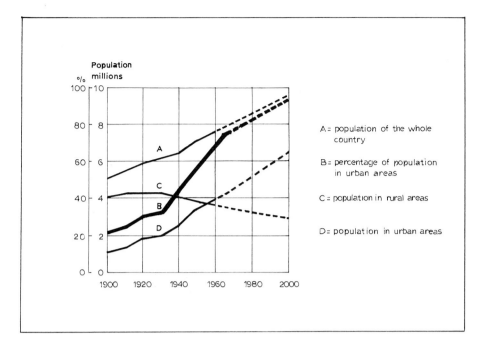

Figure I-1.
Urban-Rural
Population
Distribution

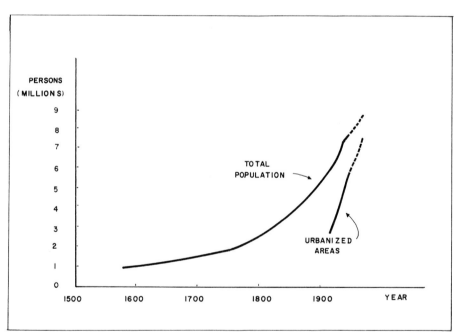

Figure I-2.
Population Growth
in Sweden

Table I-2.
Urban Population Distribution, 1960

Number of Inhabitants	Number of Urban Areas	Total Number of People
200–499	889	283,000
500–1,999	625	600,000
2,000–9,999	230	967,000
10,000–49,999	65	1,286,000
50,000–99,999	9	880,000
100,000–999,999	3	1,438,000

SOURCE: Sweden, National Road Board, *The Question of Pure Water in Sweden*, Water and Sewerage Series, Pu 8.3 (Stockholm, 1964).

city population recently passed its peak and has begun to decline. It is expected that the suburban areas will continue their rapid growth and that, by 1990, 20 percent of the Swedish population will live in Greater Stockholm (see Figure I-3).

Continuing migration to urban areas will assist the government in carrying out its agricultural program for merger of the present 250,000 farms into 50,000 farms. As the rural population decreases, however, the problem of providing adequate community resources for those people remaining on the farms and in small villages will become more acute.

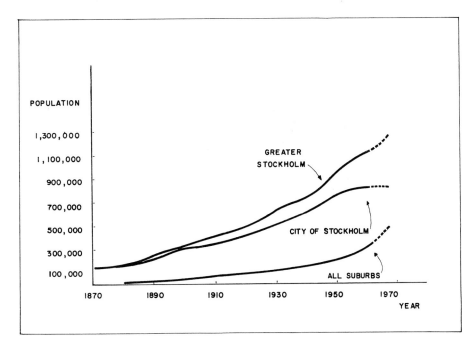

Figure I-3. Population Trends of Greater Stockholm

The Economy

A healthy economy, with full employment and a steady increase in real income, enables Swedes to enjoy a high standard of living, and prospects are excellent for a continuing rise in the standard of living. People now work a forty- to forty-five-hour week with four weeks' paid vacation. Most no longer work on summer Saturdays. Most homes have radios, television, telephones, and a variety of electric appliances. In Sweden, there are 450 telephones per 1,000 people; in the United States, telephones number 478 per 1,000. One of every eight Swedish families has a summer house. Every fourth person[7]—and every second family with children—owns a car. As seen in Table I-3, the average budget for a family with children shows a smaller allocation for housing than is usual in the United States and a fairly substantial share devoted to nonessentials.

To earn the salaries to buy these goods and services, 36 percent of the labor force works in industry, 27 percent in trade, transportation, and communications, 12 percent in agriculture, and 25 percent in other occupations. One in three wives works part or full time to provide added family income.

After World War II, Sweden's Gross National Product increased at an average annual rate of 3.5 percent, and from 1960 to 1980 it is expected to increase at an average annual rate of 4 percent. Industry contributed about 40 percent to the postwar Gross National Product; distribution and communications, 22 percent; building, 9 percent; agriculture and forestry, 8 percent; private services, 10 percent; and other services, 11 percent. The 1964 Gross National Product was $19 billion,[8] of which more than 30 percent was used for public and private investments, including a 6.6 percent investment in housing. As seen in Table I-4, the share of the Gross National Product devoted to both state and local investment and consumption has been rising steadily.

Wood and wood-related industries, such as paper and wallboard, furniture, and organic chemicals, provide the largest share of Swedish income. Recognizing the importance of the timber crop to the economy, the government has enacted laws requiring proper forest management, including the replanting of harvested areas.

Since the nineteenth century, Sweden has been the world's major exporter of iron ore. The world's largest underground mine is an iron mine at Kiruna, in Lappland. The manufacture of steel and of iron and steel machine goods is of considerable importance today. The other major industries of Sweden are machine products, food manufacturing, and textiles.

Exports, combined with foreign income from shipping, are balanced by imports. As seen in Table I-5, iron, steel, and wood products dominate exports, while fuel, manufactured goods, and machinery are the major imports. Other European countries, the United Kingdom and West Germany in particular, are Sweden's principal trading partners (see Table I-6).

Sweden has for some time used its tax policy, together with other fiscal, monetary, and regulatory measures, to regulate the business cycle, and to a greater extent than most other countries in the West.

Direct taxation of personal and corporate income and of property (net wealth) yields 35 percent of total tax revenues; the remainder is raised through many indirect taxes, the most important of which are the sales and excise taxes. The state income tax is highly progressive, while local governments levy a flat rate which averages 15 percent. A maximum of 80 percent of an individual's net income may be taken in direct taxes, state and local. State revenues in 1964 were spent primarily for welfare programs (29 percent), defense (17 percent), and education (14 percent).[9]

Table I-3.
Average Family Budget, 1958

Expenditure	Percentage of Income
Food	30
Eating out	4
Wines and liquors	2
Tobacco	2
Housing (including fuel)	14
Clothing	11
Furniture and household equipment	8
Transportation	10
Medical and personal care	5
Recreation	2
Gifts	1
Other	11
Total	100
Average annual income	$3,200

SOURCE: The Swedish Institute, *Facts About Sweden* (Stockholm, 1964).

Table I-4.
Allocation of Gross National Product, 1938–64

Allocation	Percentages		
	1938/39	1950	1964
Consumption			
Private	66.2	62.1	53.0
Public			
State	3.3	4.6	5.8
Local	4.6	5.6	8.3
Total	74.1	72.3	67.1
Investment			
Private	17.5	17.9	18.5
Public			
State	4.2	5.5	6.8
Local	2.6	4.3	7.0
Total	24.3	27.7	32.3
Net of trade and changes in stocks	1.6	—	0.6
Total	100.0	100.0	100.0

SOURCES: Per Holm, "Sweden: Balance of Resources, 1964" (Stockholm, 1965); The Swedish Institute, *Facts About Sweden* (Stockholm, 1964).

Table I-5.
Exports and Imports, 1962

Product	Percentage by Value	
	Exports	Imports
Foodstuffs, beverages, tobacco, etc.	3	12
Raw materials (except fuel), including timber products, pulp, iron ore	27	7
Fuel	—	13
Chemical products, mineral and vegetable oils	4	8
Manufactured goods, including iron and steel, paper, textiles	26	22
Machinery and transportation equipment	36	29
Finished products, including furniture, clothing, instruments	4	9
Total	100 ($2.8 billion)	100 ($3.1 billion)

SOURCE: The Swedish Institute, *Facts About Sweden* (Stockholm, 1964).

Table I-6.
Exports and Imports, 1967, by Country

Country	Percentage by Value	
	Exports	Imports
EFTA	43.6	35.2
United Kingdom	13.3	14.7
Norway	11.9	6.0
Denmark	9.4	7.0
Finland	5.1	2.8
Switzerland	2.2	2.5
Austria	1.2	1.5
Portugal	0.5	0.7
EEC	26.8	35.2
West Germany	11.0	19.3
France	4.7	4.8
The Netherlands	4.3	4.9
Italy	3.6	3.8
Belgium, Luxembourg	3.2	2.4
United States	7.3	9.3
Spain	1.7	0.8
Canada	1.4	0.7
Soviet Union	1.3	1.9
Australia	1.0	0.3
Mexico	1.0	—
Japan	0.9	1.4
Brazil	0.8	1.3
All Others	14.2	13.9

SOURCE: Stockholm Enskilda Bank, *Some Data About Sweden* (Stockholm, 1968).

Housing

Demand versus Supply

Despite the highest rate of housing construction in Swedish history—12.5 dwelling units per 1,000 population in 1965—the urban housing shortage remains acute. An often-told anecdote concerns a young man who complains that he and his fiancé have had to postpone their marriage year after year because they cannot obtain an apartment. When asked why they have not moved in with his parents, he replies: "Because they're still living with my grandparents."

Municipal agencies register people in need of housing and establish queues. Applicants are divided into two major subgroups: those, both renters and owners, who have their own home but wish to move, and those who lack their own home, including newlywed couples, people living with other families, and people wishing to move into the municipality. The size of the queue and the waiting period between registration and the allocation of a home are the best indicators of the shortage. In Greater Stockholm, where the shortage is most severe, the queue has numbered about 100,000 households for some years. The waiting period for a young couple is about ten years.[10] In 1961, in the seventy-eight municipalities reporting a shortage, 332,000 people were in the queues. Multiplying this figure by average family size indicates that 10 percent of the population in these municipalities is seeking better housing.[11]

The shortage can be traced back at least to the 1930s. At that time, typical urban housing for one family consisted of one room and a kitchen, plus rudimentary, often-shared bathroom facilities. Low incomes kept people from demanding better housing. As the country emerged from the depression, some government loan programs acted as a slight stimulus to construction. Then, in 1939, the outbreak of World War II paralyzed housing construction. Sweden remained neutral throughout the war, and the government instituted programs to start construction again. By the war's end, production had reached the prewar high. That, however, was not high enough, particularly in light of the increased demand, the pre-existing shortage, and the low production during the war.

Today, housing quality is good, but space standards are way below what people demand and can afford. The demand for single-family houses is far in excess of the supply. Most people who would like a single-family house have the expectation of only a larger apartment. The housing demand in urban areas is a product of full employment, high wages, and migration from rural areas.

The Present Stock

As of 1960, the distribution of dwelling units by number of rooms was as follows:[12]

One room and kitchen	17%
Two rooms and kitchen	32
Three rooms and kitchen	23
Four or more rooms and kitchen	19
Other (including one or more rooms without kitchen)	9

Nationally, the average age of all housing is twenty-five years, while in towns two-thirds of the housing is less than twenty-five years old.

In the country, timber or timber and stone houses predominate. Urban areas are a mix of three-story brick apartment buildings dating back to the 1930s and 1940s and more recent low-, medium-, and high-rise apartment buildings of lightweight concrete, precast concrete, and brick. Little single-family housing is built in urban areas. Builders and government housing officials claim that Swedish building techniques, combined with current mortgage provisions, make multi-family construction cheaper than single-family construction.[13]

Sweden long has been concerned with the provision of housing for retired people. Many apartment buildings—consisting of efficiency, one-bedroom, and a few two-bedroom units, plus common areas such as central kitchens and dining rooms or recreation rooms—have been built for pensioners. In recent years, however, there has been a trend away from apartment buildings solely for the retired; instead, apartments designed for this segment of the population have been included in buildings also accommodating families.

Housing is well equipped; in 1955, 90 percent of all dwelling units had running water, 65 percent had central heat, 60 percent had toilets, 40 percent had bathrooms, and 40 percent had refrigerators.[14]

There are 3 million dwelling units in Sweden; with a population of 7.8 million, this means that there is an average of 2.6 people per unit. This average is somewhat misleading, for it masks a distribution which includes a substantial number of people living alone and, at the opposite end of the scale, many large households, often composed of two families doubled up. Today, one in four households consists of one individual; this is a higher ratio than exists in any other country. In addition, half of all households consist of two or three people.[15] For a comparison of household sizes in Sweden, the United States, England, and the Netherlands, see Table I-7.

More significantly, as of 1960, 9 percent of all households and 38 percent of households with three or more children were living in overcrowded conditions.[16] Overcrowding remained constant in the decade after World War II but has declined considerably since then as new construction has enabled many elderly persons and young couples with children to move into their own homes.

New Construction

Given the fact that from 90 to 95 percent of all housing is built with government financial assistance, the government, through its annual allocation of funds for housing, determines how many units of what types will be built (see Table I-8). Of course, housing competes with other types of construction for government support (see Figure I-4).

The National Housing Board, the agency charged with carrying out the government's housing policy as well as with making policy proposals to the government, has recommended that the number of housing starts per year be increased from the 1964 level of 85,000 to 100,000, and that construction be concentrated in areas of greatest need, especially Greater Stockholm.[17] Because rural interests are powerful in Parliament, the large cities have in the past been shortchanged in the allocation of housing units. About half of the nation's need is in the large cities, but they have been allocated only about one-sixth of the housing units. In the budget for 1967–68, Parliament set the number of housing starts at 92,000. Despite the demand for single-family houses, about 70 percent of the dwelling units built continue to be in multi-family buildings.[18]

After the war there was a trend away from the traditional three-story walk-up apartment buildings toward taller and taller elevator apartment

Table I-7.
Household Size

Number of Persons	Percentage of Households			
	Sweden 1960	U.S. 1950	England 1951	The Netherlands 1950
1	21	10	11	5
2	28	29	28	40
3	22	23	25	
4	18	19	19	
5	7	10	10	55
6	3	5	4	
7 or more	1	4	3	

SOURCES: Statens Offentliga Utredningar, *Konsumtionsmönster På Bostadsmarknaden* (Stockholm, 1964); the Netherlands figures are taken from Ernest Michanek, *Housing Standards and Housing Construction in Sweden*, prepared for The Swedish Institute (Stockholm, 1965).
NOTE: The figures for Sweden are for densely populated areas only.

Table I-8.
Housing Construction, 1958–64

Construction	1958	1959	1960	1961	1962	1963	1964
Total number of dwelling units	62,200	69,300	68,300	73,800	75,100	81,400	87,200
Number of one- and two-family houses	17,400	17,900	17,300	20,400	21,600	23,200	27,000
Percentage of all dwelling units	28	26	25	28	29	29	31
Percentage of units receiving government financial aid	93.8	95.5	94.7	93.8	94.1	92.6	?
Number of dwelling units per 1,000 population	8.4	9.3	9.1	9.8	9.9	10.7	11.3

SOURCE: Just Gustavsson, "The Organizational Structure of Swedish Housing Administration, Financing of Housing, and the Role of Physical Planning in Housing Programmes in Sweden," mimeographed, prepared for the National Planning Board (Stockholm, 1964).

Figure I-4.
Government
Investment in
Construction, 1964

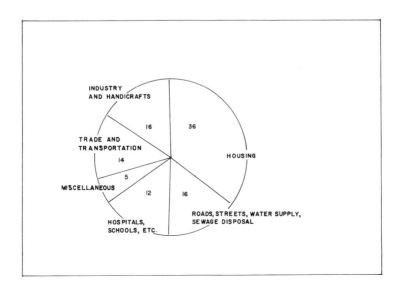

buildings, referred to as point towers. There has been some dissatisfaction with point towers, particularly in their capacity as homes for families with young children. An increasing number of apartments are being built which provide as many units as the point towers but which are of moderate height and great length. There are those who question whether high gross density may not be as undesirable as excessive height. "On the whole one can today observe a fondness for very big building units in the municipal planning work. Among planners and architects and from the side of the daily press of people in common there begins however to grow an opinion against the big scale."[19]

Housing units currently under construction have more and larger rooms and are better equipped than ever before. Units completed in 1963 had the following distribution by number of rooms:[20]

One room and kitchen	7%
Two rooms and kitchen	19
Three rooms and kitchen	30
Four or more rooms and kitchen	31
Other (including one or more rooms without kitchen)	13

Construction of an even larger proportion of housing units of three or more rooms is needed.

Standards issued by the National Housing Board are applicable to all new construction. These standards require dwelling units to have an average of five hours of sunshine per day.[21] Minimum space standards are set; for example, a unit of two rooms plus kitchen must have at least 590 square feet, one of three rooms plus kitchen at least 700 square feet. In each unit the living room must measure 215 square feet, and the master bedroom 130 square feet. Standards also have been set for bathroom and kitchen equipment, parking space, and elevators and other facilities used in common by apartment dwellers.[22]

Costs

The average household head spends 14 percent of his income for housing, including utilities and a summerhouse (if he has one). In the 1930s the same percentage of total income would have paid for one room and a kitchen. Today, it will cover the cost of three rooms and a kitchen. Large families and the elderly receive government subsidies for housing. The subsidy for the elderly depends on their income and may cover all housing costs. Families with two or more children and with below-average or average incomes receive a subsidy of about 25 percent of their housing costs.[23]

The executive branch of the Swedish government is well aware of the need to build more and larger housing, particularly in expanding urban areas. Migration to the urban areas will continue. People's desires for larger homes and for single-family homes are expected to increase with their ability to pay more for housing. The National Housing Board's recognition of these factors has resulted in its recommendation for an increase in construction to 100,000 dwellings per year and for making government loans available to all enterprises willing and able to undertake single-family housing construction.

The legislative branch of the government has recognized the need for housing, as evidenced by its authorization of a rate of construction which is the highest in Sweden's history and one of the highest for any country. Doubling-up and overcrowding are declining. Nonetheless, the vast numbers of people in the queue are testimony to the pressure for an even greater allocation of the national budget to housing construction.

Government Programs and Policies for Urban Development

The Swedish government exercises considerable control over when and where urban development occurs. Parliament annually determines how many housing units are to receive state mortgage aid in the ensuing year, how much money is to be provided for such aid, and how construction is to be divided between single- and multi-family housing. Following this determination, the National Housing Board is responsible for allocating the total number of authorized housing units among the provincial housing boards, each of which in turn allocates its housing units to the municipalities within its territory. If a municipality is not prepared to accept its quota of housing, the units must be reallocated to municipalities able to build them.

Given the fact that between 90 and 95 percent of all housing construction is dependent on receipt of government mortgage assistance, these allocations of housing units effectively limit the volume and location of housing construction which a given community may undertake. They do not, however, assure that construction consistent with the allocations will occur. Because housing allocations are determined in part by the availability of labor and in part by national economic decisions to encourage or discourage growth, urban housing construction directly reflects national development policy. Further control is imposed by the national requirement that each large municipality submit annually a five-year proposal for housing development which indicates the capability of the municipality to assure the availability of land and utilities for such development. The allocation of housing units will not exceed this municipal proposal. In addition, municipalities may permit dense development only in areas covered by an approved municipal plan.

To date, national housing policies have been more clearly articulated and more closely adhered to than planning policies. At the local and regional level, however, a few cities—Stockholm most notably—have implemented their enunciated planning goals precisely, through development and redevelopment.

National Government

Structure and Organization

Several ministries have policy responsibilities that touch on urban development. The Ministry of the Interior is charged with proposing recommendations covering most areas of housing policy, as well as labor market and employment policies. The Ministry of Social Affairs makes housing subsidy proposals. The Ministry of Communications has planning and transportation policy responsibilities. The Ministry of Finance makes budgetary policy recommendations, including those for the allocation of national revenues to support housing construction and housing subsidies. Nature conservation and water resource management are among the Ministry of Agriculture's responsibilities.

The national boards, as well as the ministries, prepare policy recommendations for Parliament, but their principal role is to implement policies adopted by Parliament. While each national board is under the supervision of a specific ministry, the boards enjoy considerable autonomy. They develop links with other ministries and boards sharing common concerns. Among the boards whose regulations, plans, and standards have a substantial effect on urban development are the National Housing Board and the National Labor Market Board under the Ministry of the Interior; the National Building and Town Planning Board, the National Highways and Waterways Board, and the National Railway Board under the Ministry of Communications; the National Board of Social Welfare under the Ministry of Social Affairs; and the Swedish Nature Conservancy Board under the Ministry of Agriculture.

The operation of the National Housing Board is illustrative of each of these boards. The board's six members are appointed by the government; of these members, only the chairman is a full-time employee, acting also as director-general or chief executive officer of the staff. The board acts directly and through its twenty-four subsidiary provincial housing boards. It develops and promulgates housing standards, develops prototype housing designs, controls the approval of construction costs, prepares housing production statistics, and estimates future housing needs and construction costs. Its studies are coordinated with those of other boards, such as those concerned with the allocation of the labor force or the development of mass transit. Although the provincial housing boards and the municipalities are responsible for approving housing loans and subsidies, appeals from their decisions can be taken to the National Housing Board.

Planning

Planning in Sweden dates back to the sixteenth century, when plans for new development in towns had to be ratified by the king before building could start. These plans were directed toward promoting the health, wealth, and safety of town residents and toward establishing good traffic patterns. In 1874 the first national building law was passed, making planning compulsory.[24] Cities were required to develop town plans, which established requirements for street width, adequate light and air, and private and public open spaces, and to build pursuant to the plan. Many cities lacked the inclination or the money to enforce the act, however, so it exerted only a slight influence on urban development. The Planning Law of 1907 was passed to help meet this problem.

Subsequent legislation over the years incrementally extended public control over development. Today, the principal laws regulating planning at the local and regional levels are the Building Act of 1947 and the Building Statutes of 1959. These laws distinguish between dense and sparse development and establish the requirements for planning prior to dense development. Dense development is defined as development requiring streets, sewers, and public water.[25]

National planning consists of the work of the various national boards in the development of standards and, in a few instances, in the preparation of national plans covering the board's particular area of responsibility. There is increasing talk about the desirability of preparing a national land-use plan, but little action has yet been taken in this direction. Concern over the manifestations of a higher standard of living—increasing urbanization and the concomitant depopulation of the countryside, rapidly rising car ownership, greater leisure time, and the expanding conflict between demands for coastal land for summer houses,[26] for industry, and for public open space—underlies the growing interest in national planning. Those interested in conservation and the protection of natural resources advocate national planning to provide a basis for deciding between the conflicting demands of nature and the city. "... It is necessary to have ... *national planning* to which the various exploiting undertakings would have to subordinate themselves. Otherwise we shall soon be in a position where everything of value is destroyed or is encroached on by roads, buildings, power lines, etc."[27]

Among specific national planning efforts, the housing standards promulgated by the National Housing Board already have been mentioned. The National Building Board has issued "Recommendations and Directions for Master Planning" and, in collaboration with the National Road Board, "Parking Standards." The Board of Education has issued a series of circulars establishing guidelines for school location and size. Similarly, other boards have set standards on a nationwide basis which affect specific aspects of urban development, including noise, air pollution, fire protection, medical centers, and childrens' centers.[28]

The most detailed national planning has been that for transportation. In 1959 Parliament approved a national plan for major highways. The National Board of Railroads plans on a continuing basis for the railroads, most of which are state owned. Similarly, the National Board of Civil Aviation plans for domestic civil aviation. In another area of public responsibility, a national plan for the location of regional hospitals was completed in 1958.

In 1964 the cabinet considered two proposals which, if enacted by Parliament, would place Parliament more strongly in the role of establishing location policies. One proposal would require decentralization of 185 state administrative offices and would result in the moving of about 100,000 people away from the Stockholm area. The other proposal would provide state subsidies for industrial location in areas where 1.25 percent of the work force is unemployed. These proposals have generated considerable debate at the national level.[29] Until now, it has been the policy of the National Labor Market Board to seek to persuade industry to move to the north and to other areas of population decline. Its objectives have been twofold: to slow the growth of Stockholm, Gothenburg, and Malmö, and, in smaller towns, to retain populations large enough to support community services. The board estimates that, for a degree of regional independence, a given area would need a population of 30,000. It has defined regions of this potential minimum size.

As an incentive to implement its policy, the board has a fund with which to underwrite part of industrial relocation costs. The controversy brought to a head by the proposal in Parliament is between those who concur with the board's policy of defining minimum standards for viable small communities, and then manipulating taxes and incentives to sustain or build such communities, and those who believe that growth should be focussed in a few very large metropolitan areas. So far, the argument has been largely economic: is a healthy national economy fostered better by emphasizing the maintenance of a substantial number of economically sound small communities or by promoting the growth of a few centers to a size commensurate with the major metropolitan areas of nearby countries? It has been suggested that Sweden needs "plans that are 'anti-urban,' to 'de-develop' towns and regions which in the long run cannot be economically attractive."[30] To date, Parliament's rural bias has led it to prefer measures which support the smaller communities; moreover, this bias has not allowed an evaluation of the impact of this preference on the national economy.

There has been little sociological evaluation in terms of the impact of too small or too large urban areas on people, or of people's environmental preferences. "It is not too much of an exaggeration to say that we have been so overwhelmed by the intense demand for housing in relation to the weak supply that the aspects of people's preferences really have not been much considered."[31]

Control of Land Use

Through a complex network of laws and regulations the national, provincial, and local governments together have powers which enable them to control most land use, whether or not the land is subject to a plan. These powers applicable to unplanned areas often are not exercised, and much sparse development occurs as the individual landowner wishes, and without planning permission.

If there is a detailed plan, primary control of land use is exercised by the municipality. If a detailed plan is in preparation, the provincial government can issue prohibitions forstalling changes in land use pending completion of the plan. In areas where no detailed plan exists or is in preparation, the national and provincial governments have a number of means of controlling land use, including, at the provincial level, categorization of a proposed use as dense development, issuance of prohibitions, shoreline regulations, and, at the national level, designation of nature monuments. Many of these controls have aesthetic objectives.

The national government is empowered to designate as nature monuments areas of botanic, geologic, or scenic importance. Through the use of this designation, more than 300 sites, totaling 7,500 acres, have been protected. Lakes, trees, bird habitat, views, and marshes, located on private and crown lands, are subject to use restrictions because of their classification as nature monuments.[32] Usually no compensation is paid a private landowner when some or all of his property is designated a nature monument. "Up to now the landowners have been proud to have nature monuments on their ground, and they have themselves been very interested to have some areas protected, so usually we have not had to pay anything for these areas, but I think this will change. . . . However, I think our real problem is that so many small farms are reforested that we will have a darker and not so beautiful land in about thirty to forty years. About 2.5 million acres will be planted in the next ten years. We can't stop this."[33]

The individual's right to use his land as he pleases is somewhat impinged on by the traditional right ("all men's right") of the public to enter and enjoy private property as long as no direct harm results. People can swim in lakes and rivers, hike, pick wild berries and mushrooms, pitch a tent for a night, and build campfires. A license is needed for hunting or fishing. Only the garden and lawn immediately adjoining a house are exempt from these public recreation rights.[34]

Condemnation

Before briefly considering the status of Swedish condemnation law as it affects undeveloped land, it is important to reiterate that ownership of land carries with it no inherent development rights. "Beyond doubt the most important basic principle of the Town Planning Act is that landowners do not enjoy an unconditional right to open their properties to dense development. It is assumed that this opportunity will depend on community growth and not on anything that the landowner does. Accordingly, if land is to be used for dense development, the necessary condition is that planners and municipal planning committees find this to be in the public interest."[35] The landowner has the right to build for his own use, although even this right may be circumscribed. Therefore, the landowner has no grounds for legal action if, under a plan or prohibition, his land is limited to farming or some other very low-density use. There would be a public taking of the fee only if the public action caused the owner a total loss. If the public action prohibited the owner from building himself a house but permitted other economic uses of the land, such as farming or forestry, there would be a public taking of the right to build. Both takings would be compensable through condemnation proceedings.[36] In a fee taking of undeveloped land, the measure of damages is (1) the market value of the land for sparse development, plus (2) damages caused by the taking of the owner's remaining land, if any, minus benefits accruing to such land from the taking, plus (3) personal damages such as loss of business or moving expenses.

A national commission on expropriation is at work to develop proposals for the amendment of existing laws. Of particular concern is the fact that at present there is no means by which the government can capture the unearned increment accruing to landowners because of planning decisions permitting dense development. Under today's law, plans affect landowners inequitably: some receive no right to develop and no compensation, while others, because a plan grants them the right to develop, are assured considerable gain. Note, however, that the developer must give the municipality all land needed for streets and parks and also must pay for building streets and sewerage systems. One approach being debated is the provision of funds by the state to the municipalities to enable them to buy land many years in advance of its need for development. The municipalities then would lease the land, first on an interim basis, then on long-term leases for development. This approach has been highly successful in Stockholm, but many municipalities have no source of funds sufficient to allow them to make large-scale land purchases. To be most effective, it is possible that provision of funds for municipal land acquisition should be accompanied by a grant of power to municipalities to expropriate land outside their boundaries, provided that the planned long-term use accords with regional plans.

Development Financing

The government assists housing construction by granting third mortgages at moderate interest rates and by subsidizing part of the interest rate of private market first and second mortgages. The government mortgage program is applicable to all types of housing and all types of ownership, although rates and terms differ. Government mortgages are available for commercial development on terms less favorable than those for housing. With 95 percent of all housing construction dependent on government mortgage assistance, the state is able to influence what is built and by whom. Present government mortgage programs favor multi-family housing built by municipalities.

The government also influences the time when construction takes place. Direct subsidy funds to cover higher construction costs are offered to encourage wintertime construction as an offset to seasonal unemployment.

In a capital market where demand exceeds supply, the government guarantees the availability of private funds sufficient to permit financing of the annual housing production program as adopted by Parliament by circumscribing the authorization of lenders to extend credit for other purposes. "Control over the issuance of bonds has to a certain extent directed long-term capital into mortgage banks. Liquidity and placement quotas have been used to affect the commercial banks' lending and to direct capital into the housing sector."[37]

A housing developer—be it a private enterprise, a cooperative, or a municipality—which requires government assistance may not break ground until its application for a government mortgage has been approved. The application is filed with the municipality and is forwarded by it, with its recommendations, to the provincial housing board for decision. The application must show that the housing would meet government standards for such factors as density, room size, utilities, sunlight, parking, and accessibility to play areas and community facilities. "Another consideration in weighing a government loan is whether the dwellings and the area are going to represent a sound milieu, whether the immediate surroundings will reasonably meet the needs of those living in the houses."[38] In addition, if there is a plan for the area, the housing must conform to it. The price to be paid for the land must be adjudged "reasonable," there must be enough labor available in the area to build the housing, and the housing must be within the quota allotted to the municipality.[39]

Once the application is approved and the government is committed to participation in the permanent financing, the developer can proceed. There is no government assistance for construction financing. Funds, called building credits, are obtained from commercial banks. As of 1964, these rates were 1 percent for the total amount of the building credit for the entire construction period, plus 7 percent on funds as they are drawn by the developer.

Permanent financing consists of private primary and secondary mortgages and a government third mortgage. Private lenders include the commercial, savings, and special mortgage banks, life insurance companies, and organizations such as the agricultural credit associations and the cooperative credit associations. As seen in Figure I-5, the first mortgage customarily is for 60 percent of the loan basis; in 1964, interest was 5.75 percent, with a thirty-year term and no amortization of principal. The second mortgage usually is for 10 percent of the loan basis; in 1964, interest was 6.25 percent, with a thirty-year term and amortized principal. At the time of negotiating the first and second mortgages, the borrower is guaranteed that the interest rates will remain fixed throughout the term of his loan. The government guarantees that, if the market rate rises, it will pay the lender the difference between the guaranteed interest rate and the market rate. For housing built in 1962, the government was paying an interest subsidy of 4 percent in 1965, a fact which reflects the rapid rise in market rates during the past few years.

Figure I-5.
Financing for
Multi-Family
Housing

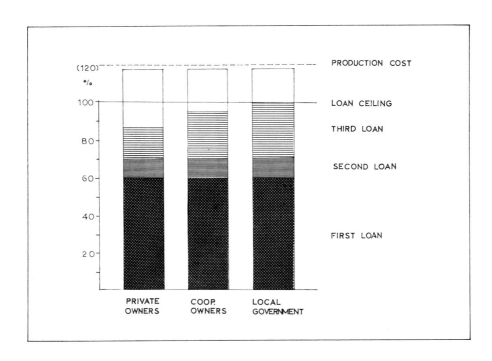

The percentage of loan basis granted by the government on the third mortgage depends on the category of borrower. As seen in Figure I-5, local governments receive 30 percent, cooperatives 25 percent, and private builders 15 percent.[40] This differential in support has contributed to the decline of housing construction by private builders. In 1949 they built 34 percent of all units; by 1963 their share had declined to 22 percent.[41] The private builder also is subject to rent controls on housing covered by a government mortgage.[42] The provincial housing boards set the rents, which are calculated to cover the builder's costs and provide him with what is considered sufficient profit. The third mortgage carries a guaranteed interest rate of 4 percent (5 percent for the non-residential portion of a development) and is amortized in equal installments over a period of thirty years. The third mortgage may cover a larger percentage of the loan basis when primary and secondary commitments are not available up to the usual percentage.

The builder frequently must put up additional funds because building costs regularly exceed the loan basis. The loan basis is a standard computation developed by the National Housing Board and is adjusted for different locales and for shifts in the value of the krone. Included in the computation are land acquisition and clearance costs; construction costs, computed on gross floor area, height, type of construction, and type of dwelling unit; wage rates; street and utility construction costs; and landscaping. It is the intent of the government, in calculating the loan basis, to assure that building is carried out economically; however, it often is impossible for production costs to be held down to the loan basis. In the Stockholm area, especially, where land is scarce and prices high, building costs regularly exceed the loan basis. Members of a cooperative, for instance, may be required to make a 10 percent down payment—5 percent to cover the difference between the mortgages and the loan basis and an added 5 percent to enable the builder to recover production costs.[43]

Financing the private construction of a single-family house is similar to that just described, but terms are somewhat less favorable. First, government mortgages are available only when the house does not exceed 1,250 square feet. There is a first mortgage for 70 percent of the loan basis, amortized over a period of fifty years, and a government mortgage of 20 percent.

In fiscal 1963–64, the government's housing program—including mortgage loans, interest subsidies, housing allowances, and administration—cost $213 million, or 5.2 percent of total government expenditures for that year.[44]

Taxation

State revenues are derived principally from income and net wealth taxes, as well as from sales and excise taxes; municipalities are financed by the municipal income tax. Parliament sets the legislative framework for the municipal and state tax structures but leaves the responsibility for fixing the annual tax rate to each municipality.

The state income tax is highly progressive for individuals, estates, and trusts but is levied at a fixed rate on business enterprises. The tax on net wealth is a progressive tax levied annually on individuals, estates, and trusts; in 1965 the first $15,000 of net wealth was exempt and the rate ranged from 0.5 percent for property worth $15,000 to 1.8 percent for net wealth in excess of $200,000. There is no national real property tax as such, although an individual's real property is included in his wealth for net wealth tax purposes. Also, income from real property is imputed at the rate of 2.5 percent of assessed value and is included in income for income tax purposes. If a person's actual income from his property is greater, this amount is taxed. Property sold less than ten years after acquisition is subject to a special capital gains tax. No individual is taxed more than 80 percent of his net income in direct taxes.

The municipal income tax is levied at a flat rate, which in recent years has ranged from 13 to 19 percent of net income. Although the municipality determines its own tax rate, the decision is strongly influenced by state requirements regarding services which must be provided. "It is estimated that 70 percent of municipal expenditures are more or less determined by state commitments."[45] As development increases, so too do the level of services required and the revenues required to provide these services. "Money is needed for financing municipal investment, and this means higher municipal taxes. You have to pay for more schools, more libraries, more everything. Nevertheless, the increase is small compared with the higher standard of living and the better municipal services provided."[46]

Provincial Government

Exercising many powers delegated to them by the state, the provinces are largely creatures of the state. The provincial governor and each provincial board are appointed by the state government, and the board structure at the provincial level parallels that at the national level. The provincial housing boards, for instance, consist of a chairman and five members. The chairman often is the provincial governor, and one of the members also is the chief provincial housing officer. The staffs of the provincial housing boards, numbering 350 nationwide, have a range of skills similar to that of the National Housing Board staff.

In addition to the appointments made by the state government, there is an elected provincial council.

Control of Land Use

The provinces now exercise considerable control over urban development. Since 1960 the provincial boards of the National Board of Building and Town Planning have had final authority to approve municipal detailed development plans. Since 1963 the provincial boards of the National Housing Board have processed municipal applications for housing loans and subsidies. Some of the activities of the provincial boards of the National Board of Building and Town Planning are illustrative of the extensive and powerful role now filled by the provinces.

Although dense development is defined as development requiring public utilities and roads, the provincial planning offices, with the approval of the National Board of Building and Town Planning, have on occasion denied an application for a building permit for a single house. Their ground for this is that such construction would be dense development, either because this was only the first of a contemplated group of houses, or because the house would be an intrusion in a beautiful landscape. The courts have supported the latter interpretation of dense development to the extent of requiring people who disregard the provincial planning office and build houses deemed to detract from a beautiful landscape to remove them.[47]

Under the Scenic Preservation Law, the provincial planning offices are empowered to establish prohibitions barring specified uses of land which in their opinion would be detrimental to the enjoyment of the landscape.

Under the Building Act of 1947 and the Nature Protection Act of 1952, such land uses as quarrying, billboard advertising, and building construction have been restricted or prohibited on the ground that they would deface the landscape.

The Natural Beauty Act of 1965 recognized nature as a national asset to be protected by all levels of government. A fund of $900,000 was established to compensate landowners who were denied building permission through the application of provisions of the act.

As much as half of the land in a few provinces and almost all of the land in the Province of Stockholm is subject to some form of use prohibition.[48] These prohibitions are used with increasing frequency to bar summerhouse construction in particularly scenic locations. Anyone wishing to build in an area subject to prohibitions must request a building permit; if refused, he can appeal to the Ministry of Communications.

The Foreshores Act of 1952, modeled after similar Danish legislation, authorizes the provinces to prohibit or restrict development and to provide for public use of the shores of lakes, rivers, and the ocean 1,000 feet inland from the high-water mark. This authorization is applicable only to areas not subject to a detailed plan. Under the Foreshores Act, compensation is payable where the prohibitions bar all building. In such an instance, through its prohibition and subsequent denial of a building permit, the province is said to have condemned the owner's right to build. Compensation is computed as the difference between the market value of the land before and after enactment of the prohibition. The act created a fund of $150,000 for the initial year of the program's operation to cover compensation costs. Evidence of the cautiousness with which the provinces have applied the act is seen in the fact that by 1964 only $35,000 of this amount had been spent. Only limited areas have been regulated and, even within these areas, property owners frequently gain permission to build houses on what the provincial government decides is the least objectionable site.[49] The Foreshores Act has a considerable unrealized potential; possibly it will be used more extensively as concern over the development of shorelines mounts.

Local Government

Sweden has a tradition of strong local government. Perhaps in all of Europe only Switzerland has more powerful local government. Today, despite centralization of many government functions, much control over planning and development rests with the municipalities.[50] This control is limited by the power of the state to withhold financial assistance if local programs fail to satisfy state standards. "If, for instance, a municipality wants to build a school building and the National Board of Education, in scrutinizing the drawings, finds that the building will be unnecessarily big and luxurious they may demand that the municipal authorities change the drawings. Of course, the same thing will happen if the building is too small. Thus the state through its economic aid, which of course is wanted by all municipalities, holds a controlling hand over almost the whole field of municipal activity."[51]

Among the responsibilities of the municipality are: planning the production of housing to meet the needs of all residents of the municipality; assuring that an adequate supply of land is available for housing; supplementing state aid by subsidizing housing for special groups in the population; acquiring land for and construction of utilities, schools, and transportation systems; and administering housing loan and subsidy applications.

Planning

Under the Building and Planning Act of 1947, a municipality's planning responsibilities are placed with a planning and building committee. This committee, which usually consists of members of the municipal council, is responsible for planning, and for supervising construction. Municipal real estate activities are the responsibility of another committee. The planning committee is served by a professional staff, which may include architects, planners, engineers, and building inspectors. The planning duties of the committee include preparation of a master plan and a detailed plan, and, if so ordered by the Ministry of Communications, participation with one or more other municipalities in the development of a regional plan.

The state government can require two or more municipalities to undertake regional planning when it foresees that the need for intergovernmental coordination of development will not be met through municipal planning alone. Municipalities may create a regional planning association voluntarily; however, all but one of the nine so far established have been formed in response to government orders. The regional planning association consists of a representative named by each constituent municipality and a chairman and vice-chairman named by the government. The state contributes 50 percent of the cost of preparing the plan; the municipalities divide the remainder of the cost.

The purpose of a regional plan is to make general locational decisions for industry, residences and commerce, for major highways, water and sewerage systems, and for protection of the shoreline. Two regional plans—one for Stockholm and one for Borås—have been completed and ratified by the regional planning association and the government. The regional plan for Borås, a textile center of western Sweden, provides for major recreation areas, protection of certain farmlands, four different sizes of commercial centers, and sites for urban expansion. Once ratified, the regional plan is supposed to serve as a framework for municipal planning; however, the plan is advisory only. The regional planning association has no power to implement it, and it is not binding on the constituent municipalities. Of course, this results in a situation whereby the municipalities accept those parts of the plan which suit them and reject those which do not. "We say that they just pick all the icings off the cake."[52]

All municipalities are required to have a master plan. The function of the master plan is to look ahead fifteen or twenty years and indicate future locations of roads, water and sewerage lines, greenbelts, and urban development. The municipal planning and building committee consults informally with the provincial planning and building office as work on the master plan proceeds. When the plan is finished, either it can be filed with the government and used by the municipality as a general guide for detailed planning or it can be adopted officially by the municipality and submitted to the government for approval, in which case it becomes binding and can be used as the basis for prohibition of uses contrary to its intentions. Municipalities almost **never** choose the second alternative.

> This plan is usually not binding, and we are now discussing the possibility of making it more binding. It can be sanctioned by the government, but the communities don't want to have it sanctioned. They just want to keep it in the drawer so nobody knows about it. Even if it's official and published they don't want to have it sanctioned, because they would be forced to follow the intentions in the plan.[53]

Thus, while the requirement to prepare a master plan is followed, the resulting plan often is of limited influence.

Detailed plans are a prerequisite to dense development. They need **not** cover an entire municipality, but only those areas where dense development is anticipated. The detailed plan is called a town plan if it is prepared for an urbanizing area of a municipality, a building plan if it is prepared for a small development in a rural area, such as a cluster of summerhouses. The only significant difference between a town plan and a building plan is that, once officially adopted, the town plan places on the municipality the responsibility for land acquisition and development of community facilities and amenities such as streets, parks, and market places. Condemnation may be used, if necessary. Execution of the building plan is the responsibility of the land-owners, not the municipality.

The initiative for preparing detailed plans can come from a municipality, from a province having before it an application for housing loans or sub-sidies, or from a developer. The work of preparing the plan is carried out by the municipal planning and building committee and its staff. The detailed plan is just that: not only does it indicate the general location of all uses, including streets, parks, and houses, but it specifies, for housing for instance, the type of house, its height, the number of stories, and how the house shall be sited. The plan discusses the sequence in which development is to proceed, how it is to be carried out, approximately what it will cost, and whether condemnation is likely to be necessary. Under a detailed plan, the developer has little freedom with regard to the arrangement or mix of buildings. For large developers, the municipality sometimes prepares an elastic town plan,[54] which, for a given area, sets certain maximums for height, floor area, and ground coverage and allows the developer to design the composition of the area within the limits set by these maximums. The developer's plan must be approved by the planning and building committee before he is granted a building permit.

When completed, a detailed plan is submitted to the municipal council for approval. During its preparation, and prior to approval of the plan, the coun-cil may request the province to place prohibitions on development of the area to be included in the plan. On approval, the plan automatically becomes a municipal prohibition on development until a building permit is granted.

Planning Standards

Following the exhortation contained in the Building Statutes of 1949, the national boards have developed many standards, some specific, some general, governing urban development.

Detailed plans are reviewed for inclusion of these standards. For open space, for instance, the standards take the form of general recommendations. In implementing the spirit of these recommendations, Stockholm requires that on land leased from the city

... the planning of the plot shall be so carried out that a good relationship is established with existing conditions in the matter of the original terrain and vegeta-tion and that due consideration is taken to the general effect of streets, gardens and landscape. Trees which stand at a distance of more than two meters [6 feet] from a building may not be removed without special permission from the Office of Real Estate. Pedestrian paths should have a minimum width of two meters. Apart from the seats which should always be found around play spaces, there is need for some sheltered and quiet seats for older people. Where possible, these seats should be arranged preferably in the vicinity of flower beds.[55]

Land Acquisition for Plan Implementation

Sweden has a long tradition of municipal landownership. When chartered by the crown, some towns were granted land by the crown for municipal development.[56] The towns thus owned most of the land, which they leased rather than sold. By the beginning of the twentieth century, municipalities no longer were accustomed to investing proceeds from land leases in new land acquisition, and much land in municipalities was privately owned. Neverthe-less, many cities continued to buy large tracts of land far in advance of the anticipated time of development. The customary practice was to buy land, lease it for farm use until development was imminent, and then lease it for development under a sixty-year term. Also around 1900, and inspired by British legislation, the Swedish government decided that cities should buy land, install the infrastructure, and then sell or lease the land for construction of low-income housing.

Today, the foresight of the early twentieth-century city fathers is widely praised but insufficiently emulated. It is said that sound economic growth and the provision of good housing for people of modest income can be assured only when the municipality controls land prices and land availability. The executive arm of the national government encourages municipalities to engage in regular land-buying programs. Parliament, however, with its many rural members cool to the needs of the cities, has yet to provide help. Pressure now is growing for the state to offer low-interest loans to aid municipal purchase some ten years in advance of development. "Part of the problem of financing housing is control of continual increase in land prices. We are interested in stimulating the municipalities to buy land in abundance so that they always have control over the supply of land and the price of land. It's always easy to get an acceptable price if you buy ten years in advance."[57]

At present, the municipalities are buying little land for future development and have developed or leased for development most of that which they already own. Many local officials favor municipal land acquisition programs but plead lack of funds and an inability to compete with private developers for choice sites. Although there are a few administrative and legal difficulties, the main impediment to municipal land acquisition is lack of money.

Municipalities may buy land from willing sellers within or without the municipal boundaries. If land within their borders cannot be purchased through voluntary agreement at a reasonable price, municipalities may acquire it by eminent domain under several circumstances: if the land is needed for construction of streets or for other public uses; if rights in land are needed, as for utility lines or subway tunnels; to obtain reasonably priced land for dense development; and if the land is planned for dense development but the owner is not expected to develop it within a reasonable time.[58] Before bringing an expropriation action, the municipality must have the approval of the provincial planning office and of the Ministry of Communications. Municipal expropriation[59] can be demanded by a landowner as a right if a plan causes him a total loss in the value of his land.

After land is acquired, either by voluntary purchase or eminent domain, the municipality usually leases it to a developer for a sixty-year term. The lease is likely to provide for the renegotiation of rents at twenty-year intervals and for renewal at the expiration of the term.

Condemnation. Municipalities are responsible for street and utility construction, as well as for the provision of parks and public facilities, in all areas planned for dense development. The infrastructure is installed before dense development is permitted. If the land or rights in land required for this municipal construction cannot be acquired by voluntary purchase, the municipalities resort to the use of eminent domain.

Agreements granting municipalities rights in land for utility or subway construction contain provisions for payment of damages caused by the public use. For example, noise and the shaking of buildings or an increase in the cost of foundations caused by a subway system are compensable damages.[60] The cost of street and sewerage construction is recovered from those whose property fronts on the street. Users of water, gas, electricity, and other utilities are charged for installation and operating costs.[61]

The eminent domain provisions permitting municipalities to condemn land planned for dense development if there is an inadequate supply of reasonably priced land available for development,[62] or if the owner is unwilling or unable to develop the land within a reasonable time,[63] do not define "reasonable time." However, for specific sites, a municipality can request the provincial planning office to set a time limit within which the private owner must begin development. If the owner does not act within this time, the municipality may condemn his land.

Private owners also have limited rights to condemn other privately owned land in the same plot in order to realize a plan. If an area planned for dense development and subject to a plot plan is in multiple ownership, the owner of the most valuable tract has one year after ratification of the plot plan to acquire, either voluntarily or by eminent domain, all other tracts within the area of the plot plan.[64]

Open space, other than that designated for public parks or other active use, can be preserved by excluding land from areas proposed for dense development. Because a landowner has no right to develop his land other than the right created by inclusion of his land in a plan for dense development, there is no right to compensation if his land is to remain in farm or low-density use. If, however, as a result of the plan, a property owner suffers a total loss in the value of his land and can neither use it nor sell it, then the municipality must purchase the land.

Municipalities are reluctant to use their right of eminent domain because its enforcement is expensive and slow. Because the municipality must pay the condemnee's court costs, the condemnee is not loathe to incur expenses or to take appeals from the Expropriation Court to the Court of Appeals and then to the Supreme Court. The period between the bringing of an expropriation action and a final decision by the Supreme Court is often as much as five years. If the condemnee accepts the decision of the Expropriation Court, the proceedings still take up to two years.

The Expropriation Court has three values to set in computing the condemnee's compensation: (1) the market value of the land, as indicated by recent sales of comparable land; (2) damages for encroachments on any land retained by the condemnee, minus benefits contributed by the condemnor's action; and (3) personal damages, such as loss of business or the cost of moving.[65] In an area covered by a detailed plan, market value is the value of the use shown in the plan. This method of valuation can result in a windfall to the condemnee and is yet another factor contributing to municipal reluctance to use eminent domain.

Extraterritorial Land Acquisition. Municipalities wishing to buy land in a neighboring municipality can use eminent domain only if the land is to be used for recreation purposes. Therefore, in most instances they must compete for land with private developers and cooperatives. They may negotiate through straw parties to conceal their identity. Gothenburg, for instance, recently bought land totaling more than half the total area of each of several nearby municipalities. The city acted secretly, through an intermediary. Had it become known that the city was in the land market, prices would have skyrocketed.

Social, more than political or economic, motives appear to be the driving force behind extraterritorial land acquisition by the large cities. Once the land within a city's boundaries is fully built up, it is primarily a sense of obligation to provide adequate housing for the city's residents, rather than expansionist aims or a search for a more lucrative tax base, which leads the city to seek land within neighboring boundaries. Pressures for metropolitan government and for a reduction in the number of local governments emanate primarily from the state.

Extraterritorial land that is purchased and developed by a city is not annexed to the city without the consent of the municipality where the land is located. Usually, the land remains under the political jurisdiction of the neighboring municipality, and the city is treated like any private landowner.

The city will agree with the other municipality that a given percentage of all housing units built on the city's land will be offered first to people on the city's housing queue. Stockholm's agreements with its neighboring municipalities set the figure at 75 percent. Without such an arrangement, the housing outlook for many residents of the larger cities would be bleak. Huge queues, the absence of land in the city for new construction, and excessively high densities in much of the city, combined with queues in the surrounding municipalities (which give priority to their residents), would add up to a virtual denial of housing opportunities for city residents.

Development

The muncipalities are responsible for construction of roads, utilities, and schools; to an increasing extent they also are undertaking housing development.

Water and Sewerage. Sweden's problems of adequate water supply and sewerage are similar to those of many other rapidly urbanizing countries. Sweden has been more fortunate than many in having a vast number of lakes which supply fresh water, and a network of swiftly running rivers and extensive seacoast which absorb sewage wastes. However, increasing per capita water consumption, concentration of the population in urban areas and in summerhouse colonies along the seacoast and lake shores, and demands for higher standards of domestic water and sewerage service all have contributed to a growing water supply and waste disposal problem for the municipalities.

As seen in Figure I-6, water consumption grew fourfold in the thirty-year period 1930–62. The larger cities show a higher per capita water use than the towns and rural areas.[66] The largest increase in any type of domestic water use between now and the year 2000 is expected to be for bathing and personal hygiene. Sweden currently ranks tenth in per capita soap consumption (the United States is first), and toilet soap consumption has increased more slowly than the population. With a 1960 population of 7.5 million, toilet soap production was 6 million cakes per year. "The low soap consumption naturally affects adversely the domestic water use in a household."[67] Among industries, the pulp and paper industry is by far the largest water user.

Figure I-6.
Annual Water
Consumption

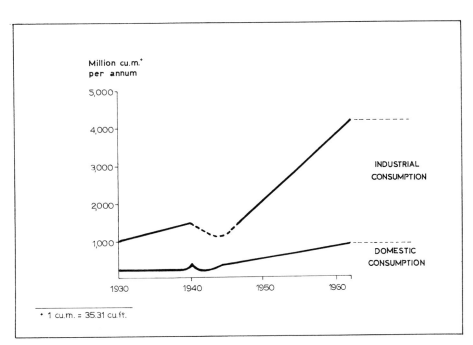

No present or prospective water shortage exists, but there is a problem of distribution. Large urban areas are having to build conduit systems from distant lakes. Usually the municipalities of an urban area cooperate in the planning, financing, and distribution of water. Either the central city will contract to sell water to the surrounding municipalities or, as in the case of the thirteen-municipality Stockholm District Water Supply Association, a group of municipalities will form a water supply organization.

By 1961, 92 percent of the households in communities of at least 200 residents had a public water supply and some form of sewage disposal (up from 66 percent in 1945).[68] Although a majority of rural homes still lack toilets, more than 80 percent of urban homes have them. Urban residents now want water and toilets in their summerhouses, and this is leading to new problems of supply and disposal. Because there is such an abundance of seacoast, lakeshore, and rivers, many Swedish communities for years unconcernedly dumped raw sewage into whatever water was nearby. In the last decade, however, construction of sewage treatment plants has grown rapidly in response to an awareness of the increasing pollution of inland and coastal waters. By 1963, 35 percent of people living in densely settled areas were served by primary treatment plants, 30 percent by secondary treatment plants, and the remaining 35 percent either were not connected to a sewerage system or lived where collected wastes were not treated.[69] Digested sludge is used as fertilizer or is discharged into nearby water. People anxious to preserve amenity and to maintain water recreation areas are concerned about the latter practice.

As in the case of water supply, groups of urban municipalities frequently join together to build sewerage systems. Joint action often is cheaper, and, in addition, treatment at fewer and larger plants results in greater efficiency and fewer discharge points. The largest regional sewage disposal system is that serving the northern suburbs of Stockholm. The Kappala plant on the island of Lidingo serves about half a million people living in eleven municipalities. Tunnels blasted through rock carry the sewage to the treatment plant, which will achieve a 95 percent biochemical oxygen demand reduction before discharging the effluent into the Baltic.

The investment in water supply and sewage disposal systems has risen dramatically since 1950. The state grants funds to the municipalities to aid in construction costs, but the major financial burden is borne locally. Property owners pay a connection charge, payable in up to ten annual installments, for water and sewerage service, plus an annual charge.

Housing. Local governments did not act as housing developers to any appreciable extent before World War II. The continuing postwar housing shortage, local governments' desire to see housing policy implemented, tight money for private enterprise, and favorable loan terms for public agencies all contributed to the rapid rise of the municipality as a housing developer. By 1963 the public sector accounted for 35 percent of all housing production. While technically this includes state, county, and municipal housing development, all but 1 percent of this housing is municipally sponsored. Municipal housing development almost always proceeds under the auspices of SABO, a national organization for non-profit housing development which is owned and operated by the municipalities. The organization, financing, and management of housing are municipal responsibilities but are handled through local branches of SABO. Construction, almost exclusively a private enterprise, is carried out by the low bidder.

The Private Developer

Cooperatives, which prior to World War II were an insignificant factor in housing development, have in recent years accounted for from 25 to 30 percent of housing production. It is the private entrepreneur who has lost as the municipalities, through SABO, and the cooperatives have taken over an increasing share of housing development.

Cooperatives

Housing cooperatives got their start in the 1920s and received further impetus under the act of 1930 which authorized the creation of housing consumer cooperatives, regulated the rights and obligations of their members, and controlled to some extent the operations of their national associations. This legislation left considerable discretion to the cooperatives with respect to the way they would operate, and several types of cooperatives have evolved. By far the largest type are the two national cooperative associations, HSB (The National Association of Tenants' Savings and Building Societies), and SR (Svenska Riksbygger, or Swedish Builders, which is owned in large part by building trade unions). Those cooperatives formed by a group of individuals not affiliated with any national organization constitute the second type. Third are the cooperatives formed by private companies in the building industry, and last is a miscellaneous group not belonging to the first three but including such cooperatives as those formed by employers for the purpose of providing housing for their employees.

HSB was responsible for the construction of 14,000 housing units in 1962, or almost 20 percent of the national total. It is the national organization of some 200 local housing societies devoted to the planning, financing, construction, and operation of cooperative housing. If a person decides he would like to live in cooperative housing, he may join one of the local societies of HSB. The function of the local society is to determine the need for housing in the locality and the feasibility of obtaining financing, acquiring land, and drawing up general building plans. When the decision to build has been made, the local society forms a subsidiary housing cooperative (of which there are now more than 2,200). During the planning and construction phases, the housing cooperative is administered by the local society. Once the building is up, its owner-occupants become members of that housing cooperative and elect representatives who carry on the day-to-day job of operating the project.

HSB administers the National HSB Savings Fund for its members. Fund deposits totaled about $17 million in 1961. They provide an important source of capital, particularly for land acquisition in advance of construction. HSB also provides planning, architectural, and technical services and research facilities for its component organizations, and operates several building material factories and a managerial school for project managers. HSB states as policy that it is completely independent of the state, political parties, and builders.

Prospective cooperative owners must contribute a capital investment equal to the construction cost of their apartment minus the proportion of the co-operative's loan attributable to that apartment.

Private Entrepreneurs

Private entrepreneurs now act as developers for only about 40 percent of the housing built each year—20 percent of the apartments and 90 percent of the single-family houses—but almost all construction is by private enterprise.

The private developer competes for land with the municipalities and co-operatives without either one's sources of capital. A few large developers acquire land, plan its development (in the absence of a municipal plan), secure municipal and provincial planning approval, install utilities, and proceed through development. This requires large capital reserves and is a risky venture because neither acquisition of large tracts nor development goes forward without municipal and provincial approval. A particularly large project might even be referred to the Minister of Communications for approval.[70]

There are a few large commercial builders that operate in different parts of Sweden, many small local firms, and the occasional individual who builds his own home. The work of the large builders is intensively organized and makes use of much prefabrication of structural members and interior units. Although the municipality (through its detail plan) controls such aspects of development as building location, height, and density, the builder for a given site frequently is selected early enough to participate in reaching these decisions.

The Stockholm Region: Planning and Development

The ideas of Mumford, Stein, and Abercrombie are reflected in present-day Stockholm.[71] Satellite communities with greenbelts, neighborhood centers, and local employment have been created on a scale compatible with an urban region of 1.3 million people. First Vällingby, then Farsta, now Skärholmen and Täby, and next Spånga exemplify the evolution of urban planning theory in Sweden.

Stockholm has two unusual planning advantages: enough municipally owned land to accommodate new development, and topography which poses natural impediments to a highway network. Now that the municipal land supply is near exhaustion and a substantial portion of the subway system has been completed, questions common to most other American and European cities arise. How will planning and the availability of land for development be coordinated? Will Stockholm be able to acquire more land for future growth? Will the neighboring municipalities cooperate in development beneficial to the region? Will the people of the Stockholm area use their superior public transit system, or will they demand more and more expressways to carry each worker door to door? The 1970s should tell whether the plans executed during the 1950s and 1960s are sufficiently successful to generate continued application of their basic precepts.

The city of Stockholm was founded on an island at the juncture of Lake Mälaren and the Baltic Sea. Centuries ago, Lake Mälaren was an arm of the Baltic, but a gradual and continuing rise of the land transformed it into a fresh-water lake linked to the sea by an outlet with strong and rapid currents. Stockholm, originally a bastion for the defense of inland areas, became a port for the shifting of cargoes between seagoing vessels and smaller ships that plied the lakes. The city gradually grew north and south of the island which was its original site, and eventually covered other islands and the mainland. Today, northern Stockholm is the commercial and administrative center, while the old island city (Gamla Stan) will be preserved as an architectural and historic monument to Stockholm's earlier days.

Because Gamla Stan is the only land mass closely linking the northern and southern halves of the city, and because Stockholm's planners and City Council wish to preserve its character as well as its buildings, traffic circulation is a problem. Existing roads crossing the island often are clogged, but construction of enough expressway lanes to eliminate congestion would alter Gamla Stan's character and is considered aesthetically undesirable. The subway, being partly underground, causes little spatial or aesthetic dislocation. Two other expressways, crossing islands to the east and west of Gamla Stan, will provide links for the northern and southern halves of the city.

Stockholm's latitude and climate have influenced its development. Stockholm and Helsinki are at about the same latitude as the southern tip of

Greenland and Anchorage, Alaska. While the Baltic Sea has a moderating effect, winter still is long and cold. The average February temperature in Stockholm is 25°F., and the average for July is only 63°F. The city's proximity to the sea results in much cloudy, damp, and rainy weather. (Stockholm has only 1,700 hours of sunshine per year, while New Yorkers enjoy 2,800 hours annually). This, combined with the long, dark winter, causes people to seek the sun whenever it shines and to abandon the city for the outdoors when summer finally comes. Minimum sunshine standards for city apartments, the greater use of public transit in winter when roads are dark and snowy, a demand for balconies in an essentially inhospitable climate, and the widespread ownership of summerhouses all are evidence of the climate's effect on urban design.

Control of summerhouse construction is a real and growing problem. With more than 50,000 summerhouses already built within twenty-five miles of Stockholm, and thousands more being built yearly, the questions of water supply and sewage disposal and of public versus private use and enjoyment of the shorelines are serious ones. Traditional answers are inadequate in the face of burgeoning use.

Plans for the Region

➤ The current master plan for the city of Stockholm was published in 1952. The non-binding regional plan, for the period to 1990, was adopted by the Regional Planning Federation for the Stockholm Area in 1958 and by the national government in 1960. It is a "rolling plan"—that is, it is subject to revision every five years, but it always looks ahead thirty years. The revision which looks ahead to 2000, and to a population of 2.2 million, was published in December, 1966. The master and regional plans envision the location of development in satellite communities of different sizes located along transportation corridors, primarily rail and subway. Half of the labor force would be employed in its home community.

The Regional Planning Federation for the Stockholm Area is composed of forty-five of the fifty-three municipalities in the county, plus the city of Stockholm. The county of Stockholm surrounds but excludes the city of Stockholm. At its greatest extents, the region measures 100 miles (north-south) by 70 miles (east-west); it covers 2,034 square miles of land.

Stockholm is a city of 770,000 people in a metropolitan region of 1,300,000. The 1960 regional plan projects a 1990 regional population of 1,500,000. People are most densely concentrated in central Stockholm; also quite densely settled are corridors running out some sixteen miles from the center city along transit lines. Some of these corridors are separated from one another by the water network, others by low-density farms and forest land which extends in close to the heart of the city. The region's fringes, particularly near the lake and sea shores and in the archipelago, are populated with more summerhouse residents than year-round inhabitants. Many lakes, the convoluted seacoast, and the thousands of islands of the archipelago lend beauty and variety to the landscape. There are a few towns at the edges of the region which are not predominantly oriented toward Stockholm.

Stockholm is, and is expected to continue to be, primarily an administrative, not an industrial, city. Plans for the region and for its satellite communities, both inside and outside the city limits, are based on the desire to reduce residential and office overcrowding of the center city, to provide a convenient and efficient transportation network, and to improve living conditions. In developing the regional plan, it was assumed that the nation's population would continue to increase slowly, while the urban population and Gross National Product continued to grow rapidly; it was also assumed that the service area of the economy would expand considerably. In planning the transportation system, it was predicted that there will be one car for every 2.5 people in 1990.

As the crowded portion of Stockholm thins out and the housing shortage eases, it is anticipated that more families will be able to satisfy their desire for single-family houses. At present, 20 percent of the region's housing is single-family; this is expected to increase to 30 percent by 1990. As car ownership increases and more of the region is urbanized, most summer-house construction will take place beyond the region's boundaries. Office employment is expected to remain concentrated in central Stockholm, which is expected to continue to provide jobs for half the labor force of the city and suburbs. Industrial growth is expected to occur primarily on the fringes of the satellite centers, some twenty to twenty-five miles from central Stockholm. Suburban shopping centers, serving markets of from 50,000 to 150,000 people, will capture an ever greater share of retail trade.

The details provided in the regional plan vary directly with the present urbanization of the portion of the region which the plan effects. In summary, the plan's intent is as follows:

The central part of the Region—Greater Stockholm area—comprises the built-up areas, disposed in radial ribbons along the main arteries of communication converging on the centre of the city. Surrounding the built-up areas and separating the ribbons are continuous green areas. These areas are intended for agricultural and recreational purposes [see Map I-3].

The parts west of the built-up area of Greater Stockholm towards Lake Mälar contain several areas for summer cottages, but otherwise they are mainly rural. An inner coastal and island belt in the east of the Region is dominated by areas for summer habitation, while the green areas beyond are an essential feature of the picture. The whole of the outer band of islands is a continuous natural reserve. The hinterland of the north and south is largely rural.

It is intended that within the areas indicated for summer habitation, any subsequent detailed plan should leave considerable parts for agriculture and recreation, since these residential areas have their raison d'être in close contact with open land and a certain rural character.

Within the areas beyond the built-up area of Greater Stockholm, there are also a limited number of districts for permanent residents, the chief of which are Norrtälje and Nynäshamm. It is assumed that also in the area indicated as rural there will be some small centres of population.[72]

The structure of the metropolitan area has been shaped by past decisions to place development in differentiated nuclei along public transit corridors and close to bodies of water. The regional plan contemplates an extension of these concepts but with some changes. Almost universal car ownership dictates an expanded expressway network and a shift from neighborhood to regional shopping centers. Hopefully, much employment can be created near residential areas, dwelling size will increase, and there will be a wider choice of housing types.

Stockholm Land Policy

The halcyon days of Stockholm municipal land acquisition lasted from 1900 to 1930. The land acquisition program was launched by a conservative municipal government which began buying vast estates well outside the city's boundaries and the developed areas (see Map I-4). As it came on the market, the land was bought by negotiation between the sellers and the city. Most of the land now owned by Stockholm was purchased during these decades, including a large tract to the southwest, outside the city's boundaries, which was purchased to protect the lake that then supplied the city's water. Today,

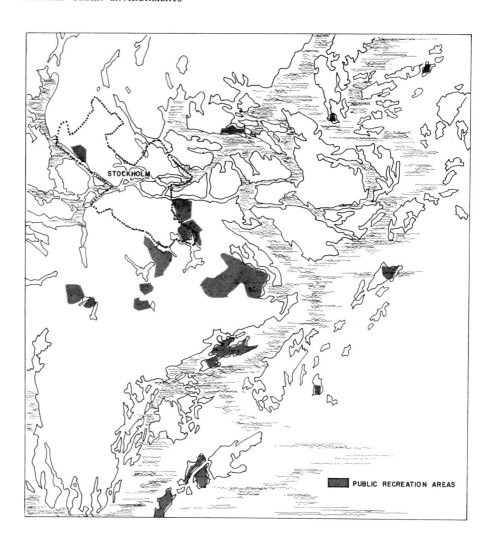

Map I-3.
Public Recreation
Land in the
Stockholm Area

with only 5 percent of the city water supply now being drawn from the lake, there is much demand for development of this tract.

The land acquisition program was re-initiated after World War II, but on a much more limited scale. Most of the recent acquisitions have been for municipal use for parks, hospitals, and other community facilities. An important exception was the city's purchase of enough land at Sätra to house between 20,000 and 30,000 people. Sätra is in the southwest part of the city and will be part of the developing Skärholmen satellite center. Municipal land at Vårby, near Sätra, was annexed to the city in 1962, and also will be part of the Skärholmen development.

No municipally owned land has been sold in the past twenty years; all development land is leased. Stockholm develops land in accordance with its plans rather than as a reflection of the market value of a given site. Land acquisition costs are aggregated so that the rents from a particular site need not return its acquisition cost to the city.

Three-quarters of the housing built since World War II is on municipally owned land. The present satellite communities—Vällingby, Farsta, and Bredäng—were built on city land, as Skärholmen will be, and Bredäng will serve as Skärholmen's first subcenter. The next satellite center, Jârva, will be developed northwest of central Stockholm on land formerly owned by the state and used as a military training area. The land is being divided between Stockholm and four adjoining municipalities. The Jârva area is expected to

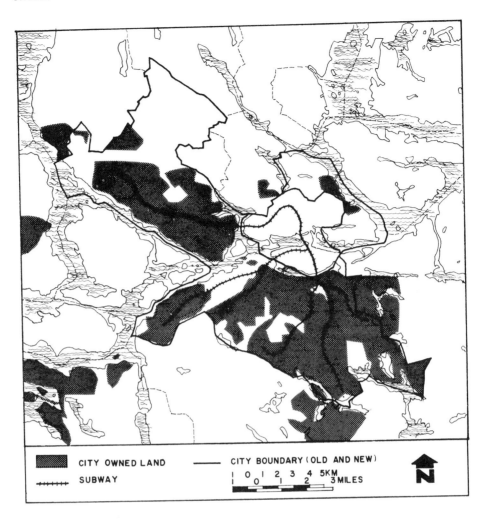

Map I-4.
Stockholm
Municipal Land

CITY OWNED LAND   CITY BOUNDARY (OLD AND NEW)

SUBWAY

accommodate up to 150,000 people, half of them within the city limits. Once Järva is completed, most city land planned for dense uses will have been developed. The city is likely to begin buying additional large quantities of land for future development outside its boundaries. How this land in adjoining municipalities should be developed is presently unclear as to the city's relationship to its neighbors. Thirty years ago neighboring municipalities begged Stockholm to annex them; Stockholm, fearing the high cost of extending municipal services and believing her land reserve to be sufficient for future growth, refused. This has been referred to as one of Stockholm's three major errors.

... The first of these—not to have incorporated sufficient land in good time—does not mean that Stockholm has not carried through any incorporating at all. There were cases of incorporation in 1913, 1916, 1948, and the most recent in 1961, but the mistake is that they haven't been sufficient. The second big mistake is that the city hasn't bought enough land. This doesn't mean that it hasn't bought a great deal of land. Stockholm has, on the contrary, invested unusually large sums in land purchase, but still not enough. The final mistake is that it has been selling land for too long. A municipality should never do this at all. For more than 50 years, Stockholm has carried on new development outside the inner town without selling land. So far as the inner town is concerned, it was not until the 1940's, unfortunately, that the city authorities completely accepted the same kind of land policy.[73]

**Regional
Transportation**

⌄ In Stockholm the transportation network has been not only recognized but relied upon as a principal determinant of urban location and form. A fiscal policy toward the subway which has diverged considerably from that toward municipal land has had an influential role in determining the density and form of Stockholm's satellite communities. ⌄

Stockholm's regional and city plans contemplate the building of two additional subway lines which will traverse central Stockholm, the construction of a circumferential expressway and some radials, and continued reliance on commuter railroads to serve the center city. In 1990, traffic to and from central Stockholm at peak hours (the highways being used to capacity) is expected to be 75 percent public transport, 25 percent private car.[74] It is specifically planned not to construct highways to the center of the city in excess of this capacity so as not to flood the central area with expressways, feeder streets, and parking lots.

⌄ Past transportation planning has reflected a predominant concern with the relation of the center city to its developing satellites; recent planning also shows a concern with the relationship of the satellite centers to one another. Given the hope that residents of the region will work either in the center city or in their immediate communities, radial transportation and circulation within the communities are of primary importance for work trips. Circumferential transportation is important more for shopping, recreation, and visiting, particularly now that people are showing a preference for regional shopping centers rather than for their neighborhood or community centers. No discussion has been noted, however, concerning the desirability or probable fiscal soundness of circumferential transit lines.

The transportation plan adopted by the Stockholm City Council in 1960 sets forth a twenty-year building program. Included in the expressway network are the circumferential, north-south, and east-west arteries through the center city, and radials fanning out from the circumferential lines. Göran Sidenbladh, Stockholm's chief planner, has expressed concern about the effect these expressways will have on city form and appearance.⌄

The difference in scale between the existing city structure and the new traffic arteries has such bad effects that they cannot be overcome only by choosing the best possible form of traffic structure, even if this is an obvious necessity.

In many cases the aesthetics require that the traffic artery shall be sunk or built as a tunnel. In this context one may look at what the railways did to our cities two generations ago. There is little comfort in this prospect. But it must be used to serve as an incitement to a more generous approach to the planning problem.[75]

The T-Bana

⌄ The Stockholm subway, the T-Bana, is the most impressive achievement of the Stockholm Passenger Transportation Company (formerly AB Stockholms Spårvägar, now AB Stor-Stockholms Lokaltrafik). The T-Bana is clean, speedy, comfortable, and heavily used. Its stations are strikingly attractive, convenient, and well designed. The company held design competitions for each of the major stations and awarded cash prizes to the winners. The cost of the art work at the stations is considerably less than 1 percent of the cost of the subway system.[76] Using the subway is a pleasant experience—a feat desired but yet to be emulated in the United States.

⌄ Originally the Passenger Transportation Company was totally owned by the city of Stockholm, but in 1967 it was reorganized and now is owned by a group of municipalities in the Stockholm region, including the city. The company owns all public transportation systems serving local traffic in Greater Stockholm, including the subway, tramways, and buses. Because the public transportation system is publicly owned, operating policies closely reflect city and regional planning decisions. The location of new routes and the time of their construction is closely coordinated with plans for new urban development. ⌐

As of 1965, the company operated more than 150 miles of roads, 25 miles of tramways, and 35 miles of subway track. In 1967, when Sweden switched to driving on the right-hand side of the road, the trams were discontinued. Subway mileage is being increased.

The public transportation system carried 1,000,000 people a day in the winter months of 1965, 650,000 a day in the summer months. Of these people, 525,000 in the winter and 350,000 in the summer used the subway, traveling an average distance of four miles.[77] In 1965, there were 613 subway cars and 58 stations in operation. The cars average 21 mph, excluding time for station stops, and run every two minutes during peak hours and every three to seven minutes in off peak hours.

The system has been subsidized since 1946, at which time the longer distances for suburban travel and the concomitant costs for equipment and personnel caused it to be no longer self-supporting at fares considered reasonable. In 1965, the National Road Board for the first time approved the use of tax revenues from automobiles and gasoline for the construction of subway facilities.

The decision to build the T-Bana was reached in 1941, but construction was delayed by the war. Part of the first line, running from the south side of center city south almost to Farsta (Figure I-7), opened in 1950. Two additional sections of this line were completed in 1951 and 1952, and the major underground link through the center of the city and Gamla Stan was completed in 1957. The second line, from southwest to northeast, was completed in 1967, and, with forty miles of track, gives Stockholm the world's tenth largest subway network, a large system for an urban region of Stockholm's size (see Figure I-8 and Map I-5). Future construction will be in the direction of the northern and northwestern suburbs.

⌐ It has been city policy that each of the subway stations in newly developing areas should be self-supporting. This policy has strongly influenced the design of the satellite centers. From 10,000 to 15,000 people are housed within 3,000 feet of each subway station;[78] this population has been estimated to be large enough for the station to break even financially⌐

Figure I-7.
The T-Bana
at Farsta

Figure I-8.
The T-Bana

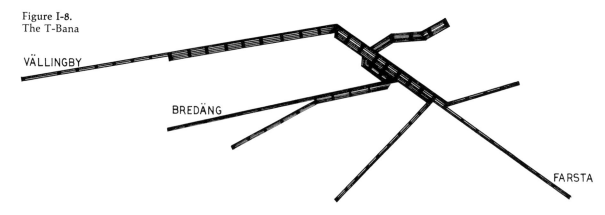

VÄLLINGBY

BREDÄNG

FARSTA

Map I-5.
Urban Stockholm
and the T-Bana

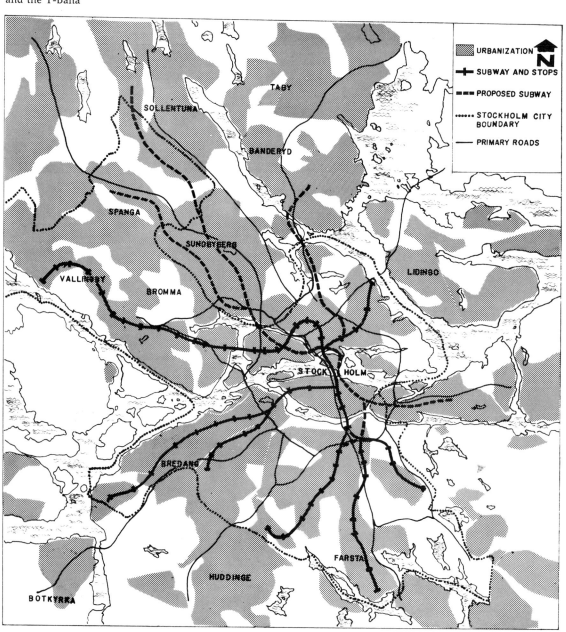

The Satellite Centers

Vällingby, Farsta, Skärholmen, and Järva are the successive physical manifestations of the evolution of planning theory in Stockholm. Täby is a nearby community being developed in accordance with municipal and regional plans. Together, the five satellite centers illustrate the achievements and problems of planning for the Stockholm region.

Plans for a satellite-center pattern of development date back to the mid-forties. Until then, relying on very conservative growth estimates, Stockholm had planned for a high-density center city surrounded by low-density single-family housing. Upon realizing that the population was growing far more rapidly than predicted, new plans were prepared which shifted the concept for the areas to be developed to higher-density concentrations linked to the center city by subway. Each of the satellite centers was to be designed not only to provide easy access to the center city but also to create a sense of place and neighborhood, by providing quick pedestrian access to schools, shops, and community facilities, separating the centers from one another, and by giving each center unique physical characteristics and a readily distinguishable nucleus.

For added convenience, a few stores for daily needs were to be no more than 1,000 feet from all residences.

As many others, we arrived at units with 10,000 inhabitants. By 1961, thirteen such units had been built, varying in population from 8,000 to 16,000. Nearly one-third of the dwellings were built by city corporations, almost one-third by co-operatives and similar non-profit makers, a little less than one-third by private builders and the remaining one-tenth was made up of one-family houses. About 95 percent of all dwellings are financed with public aid and of course there is no upper income level for families admitted to the new buildings.

By 1950 it had been proved that 10,000 people were not enough to support good and complete shopping facilities. For that some 25,000 people were needed. With this goal four units with an average population of 23,000 have been built. They vary between 20,000 to 28,000 inhabitants.[79]

Stockholm's satellite centers have been built as the planners specified, but not all of the planners' goals for them have been met, partly because of the continued intractability of the housing problem and partly because public preferences have shifted with rising real income. A chronological look at each satellite center shows which concepts have remained constant and which experience, combined with public pressures, have modified.

Vällingby

Vällingby, ten miles west-northwest of central Stockholm, was built in the early 1950s on land owned by the city since 1930. The builder, AB Svenska Bostäder (Swedish Housing, Inc.), is a city-owned corporation. Vällingby is a satellite center with a population of 60,000 and serves as a regional center for an additional 40,000 people. As seen in Map I-6, it consists of five subcenters or neighborhoods (Blackeberg, population 9,000; Råcksta, population 5,000; Vällingby, population 18,000; Hässelby Gard, population 14,000; and Hässelby Strand, population 13,000), of which Vällingby is the central and dominant one, being the site of the regional commercial center.

The neighborhoods of Vällingby were built in order of progression out from the city, and subway construction was timed to keep pace with residential development. The subway serves all of the neighborhood centers except Råcksta, and the entire community has convenient access to an arterial highway leading out from Stockholm. The trip from Vällingby to the center city takes twenty-four minutes by subway.

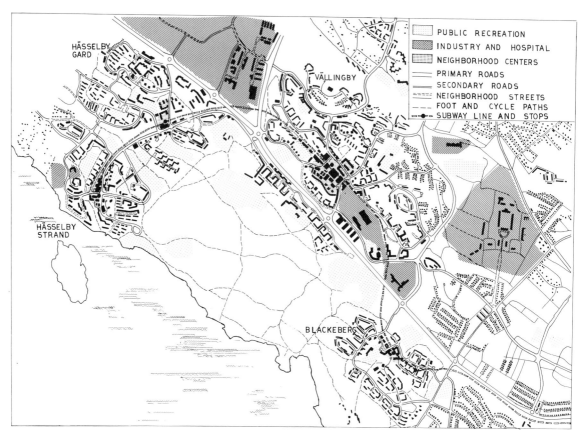

Map I-6.
The Vällingby Plan

Two large and several smaller sites for industry were reserved at Vällingby, but industry has been attracted more slowly than was hoped, partly because of the National Labor Market Board's industrial decentralization policy.

Vällingby is semicircular in shape, with its diameter abutting the shore of Lake Mälaren. The entire center of the half-circle, or approximately one-third of the site, has been left in its natural wooded condition and is intersected only by walking, skiing, and bicycle trails. Additional substantial amounts of open space have been retained in each neighborhood.

Most of the housing at Vällingby is apartments, either nine- to twelve-story "point-block" towers or very long three- to six-story "slab-blocks." A limited amount of single-family row housing is located at the outer fringes of the subcenters. Both to provide visual emphasis to the nuclei of the community and to place many people within walking distance of the subway and a commercial center, tower apartments ring the nuclei. All apartments are within 1,500 feet of a center. The various types of housing at Vällingby are illustrated in Figures I-9 through I-13.

Three sizes of shopping area have been provided: small clusters of convenience shops (Figure I-14) located within walking distance of all homes; neighborhood centers; and the regional center at Vällingby (Figure I-15).

Vällingby has been highly praised for its regional shopping center. According to the Vällingby Center Plan (Figure I-16), a 300-by-100-yard concrete platform, or pedestrian island, covers the subway and service roads for truck deliveries to the stores and offices. The center (Figure I-17) is surrounded by roads, parking areas, bus stops, and taxi stands. Buildings have two underground floors, the lower for truck parking and loading and the upper for storage and servicing the shops. In addition to offices and some seventy stores with 225,000 square feet of selling space, the center has a movie theater,

Figure I-9. Housing at Vällingby

Figure I-10. Housing at Vällingby

Figure I-11. Housing at Vällingby

Figure I-12. Housing at Vällingby

Figure I-13. Housing at Vällingby

Figure I-14. Convenience Shops at Vällingby

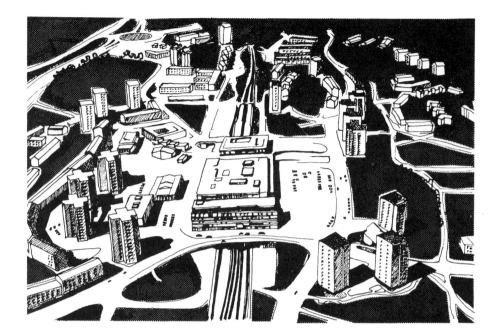

Figure I-15.
Vällingby Center

theater, churches, a community building (Figure I-18), library, post office, and social service facilities.[80] Advertising is controlled at Vällingby Center (Figure I-19), and attractive paving, lighting, fountains, and pedestrian approaches (Figure I-20) add to the pleasure of shopping there.

The original 600 parking spaces for cars proved inadequate, and additional parking, including a parking garage, has been added so that 1,250 cars can be accommodated.

Figure I-16.
Vällingby Center
Plan

1 Department
   store, shops,
   and restaurant
2 Shops and
   post office
3 Subway station,
   shops, and café
4 Offices and
   welfare offices
5 Offices
6 Movie theater
7 Community
   building
8 Hotel and
   police station
9 Library
10 Youth center
11 Church
12 Department
   store and shops
13 Shops
14 Shops
15 Apartments
   and shops
16 Parking garage
17 Bus stop and
   taxi stand

Figure I-17. The Shopping Center, Vällingby

Figure I-18. Vällingby Community Building

Figure I-19. Vällingby: Controlled and Attractive Advertising

Figure I-20. A Pedestrian Approach to the Center, Vällingby

Farsta

Vällingby opened in 1954; the plan for Farsta (Map I-7) was approved in 1957, and the center (Figure I-21) opened in 1960. Therefore, the planners were able to observe how Vällingby worked while they were planning Farsta. The one major change—which makes Farsta Center reminiscent of shopping centers in the United States—was to surround the commercial center with vast asphalted areas for parking more than 2,000 cars. While the additional parking was unquestionably needed, the acres of parking area cut the center off from nearby housing, impairing the sense of urbanity established at the center of Vällingby.

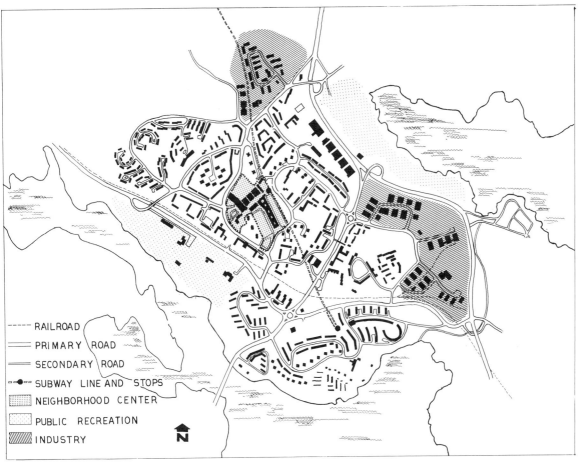

RAILROAD
PRIMARY ROAD
SECONDARY ROAD
SUBWAY LINE AND STOPS
NEIGHBORHOOD CENTER
PUBLIC RECREATION
INDUSTRY

N

Map I-7.
The Farsta Plan

Figure I-21.
Farsta Center and
Office Building

Farsta is six miles south of central Stockholm. Like Vällingby, it is built on city land, is subdivided into several neighborhoods, has substantial wooded lakeshore as natural open space, and is served by the subway. Unlike Vällingby, its shopping center was built privately, by AB Farsta Centrum, a group of five building contractors.

At Farsta, as at Vällingby, it was hoped that half of the residents would find local employment. By 1964, Vällingby could offer jobs equal in number to half its labor force, while Farsta was in about the same position as Vällingby in 1960 (see Table I-9). Today, however, only a minor proportion of the jobs in each satellite center are filled by local residents.

Table I-9.
Local Employment, 1964

	Vällingby	Farsta
Total population	62,100	57,000
Working population	26,700	25,100
Percentage of total population	43	44
Local jobs available	13,000	8,000
Percentage of labor force employed locally	49	32

SOURCE: Giorgio Gentili, "The Satellite Towns of Stockholm," *Urbanistica*, no. 24–25 (1958), reprinted by the Stockholm Department of Planning and Building Control, February, 1960.

Housing at Farsta, much like that at Vällingby, is designed so that the tallest apartment buildings are adjacent to the center (Figure I-22), succeeded first by slab apartments (Figure I-23), then by row houses, and finally by a very limited number of single-family detached houses. The distribution of dwelling types at Farsta is given in Table I-10.

Table I-10.
Farsta: Types of Dwellings

Type	Number of Inhabitants	Percentage of Inhabitants per Type
"Point-blocks," 15 floors	2,620	7.6
"Point-blocks," 10 floors	1,870	5.4
"Slab-houses," 8 floors	6,615	19.0
"Slab-houses," 3 floors	15,400	44.6

Single-family houses,
   including row houses,
   1 or 2 floors
	8,095	23.4

Total	34,600	100.0

SOURCE: Stockholm Chamber of Commerce, *Swedish Shopping Centres* (1965).

Because Vällingby residents found their housing somewhat cramped, the average room size and the average number of rooms were increased at Farsta.

Although the arrangement of the buildings is different, the structure of the Farsta shopping center closely resembles that at Vällingby. In both instances, the architects, Backstrom and Reinius, took advantage of a V-shaped site to provide traffic circulation under a pedestrian platform. At Farsta the subway is nearby rather than beneath the platform, but once again there are two floors below street level and a service road so that storage and shipping are separated from the customer. For plan details, see Figure I-24.

Figure I-22.
Apartments
Adjoining
Farsta Center

Figure I-23.
Slab Apartments
at Farsta

Figure I-24.
Farsta Center Plan

1 Subway
2 Parking
3 Subway station
4 Taxi stand
5 Bus station
6 Pedestrian mall
7 Department
   stores and
   shops
8 Restaurant
9 Movie theater
10 Youth center
11 Offices and
   dental and
   medical center
12 Kindergarten
13 Church

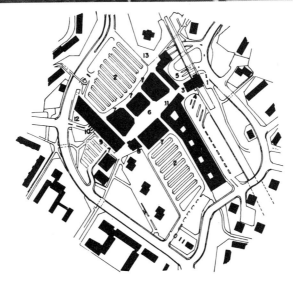

Farsta Center (Figure I-25) is within ten minutes' driving time of 200,000 people, and the parking area already has proved inadequate.[81] The center offers three department stores and forty shops (a total of 302,000 square feet of selling space), a library, restaurant, and church, community rooms, theater, clinics, a movie theater, and a kindergarten—much the same facilities as exist at Vällingby.

The shopping area itself is attractive. The buildings are lively and varied, their composition provides a sense of enclosure, and the fountains and sculpture add pleasing focal points (see Figures I-26 and I-27). The housing, like that at Vällingby, is rather utilitarian and monotonous. The ring of "point" towers provides a sense of density, but it lacks warmth and variety.

Skärholmen

Skärholmen, now under construction, will differ from its predecessors in several important aspects relating to the shopping center. It will be as large as Vällingby and Farsta combined and will serve a potential market of 300,000 people. It is designed to serve people who travel by car as well as those who arrive by subway. It will provide housing for the elderly and educational facilities, including a college and a technical school.

Skärholmen is seven miles southwest of central Stockholm. Like Vällingby and Farsta, it is on a transportation corridor, near water, and will consist of several neighborhoods, including the major centers, of which Bredäng was the first to be built.

The principal highway south from Stockholm adjoins the Bredäng Center and will be linked directly to parking areas in the shopping center (Figure I-28). The parking is ingeniously designed. Each of the four levels will be linked to different access roads. Pedestrians walking from their homes to the shops will have their own separate system, and, as at the other centers, only pedestrians will circulate within the center. One-third of the shopping center area will be devoted to parking, the four levels accommodating 4,000 cars; one-third, or 390,000 square feet, will be for department stores and shops; and the remainder will accommodate a hotel, apartments for the elderly, and educational and recreational facilities. Most of the housing construction at Skärholmen is highly industrialized, as seen in Figure I-29.

Järva

The City Planning Department of Stockholm has presented its plans for Järva, and construction in the southern part began in 1966. Two subcenters, Rinkeby and Tensta, in southern Järva, will house 30,000 people. The site, seven miles northwest of center-city Stockholm, is partly flat and open, partly hilly and wooded. To accentuate the contrast in terrain, the planners propose two- and three-story apartment houses on the flat land and six-story slab buildings in the hilly areas. Although buildings of low and medium height would be used, housing density would be as high as it is in the other satellite centers; buildings would be closer together, and open space would be designed for more intensive use.

To give Järva a more urban feel and to create a unifying element, a central corridor will extend through all three subcenters. The corridor will link the commercial centers and will consist of a pedestrian walkway, streets, community facilities, and a series of "outdoor rooms" or small parks.

It is expected that 4,500 jobs in shops, offices, and schools will be created in the area. This should provide employment equal to 37 percent of the local work force.[82]

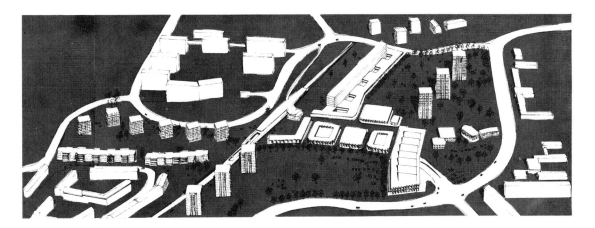

Figure I-25.
Farsta Center

Figure I-26.
Farsta Center

Figure I-27.
Farsta Center

Figure I-28.
Housing, T-Bana,
and Highway
Adjoining
Bredäng Center

Figure I-29.
Prefabricated
Housing under
Construction at
Skärholmen

Täby

Täby is Stockholm's only satellite center now planned and under development which is located outside the city limits. It is being developed by the municipality in which it is located. Although Täby is not a project of the city of Stockholm, its major physical components—excellent access to the center city by public transit, a regional shopping center, high-density housing within walking distance of the center, community facilities at the center, and separation of pedestrian and vehicular traffic (see Figure I-30)—are similar to those of Stockholm's satellite centers. Täby is located about eight miles north of the center of Stockholm and is planned as the principal nucleus for the north-northeast sector of the metropolitan area. It already has a considerable amount of scattered, low-density development, particularly near the seashore.

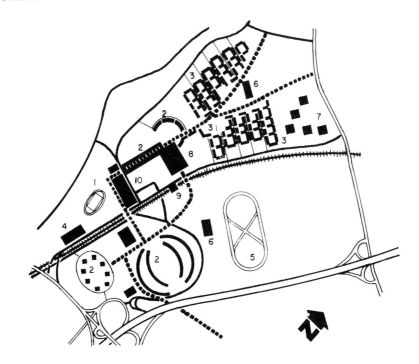

Täby's three private developers, affiliated as the Täby Centre Property Company, plan a shopping center which will serve 100,000 people, high-density housing for 18,000 people within walking distance of the center, and a mix of single-family and apartment housing for some 120,000 more people. Two commuter rail lines serve the town-center site; seventy trains pass through Täby daily in each direction. A radial expressway provides additional convenient transportation between Täby and Stockholm. A feeder bus station will be built near the center, and the subway should reach Täby by 1975.

The shopping center will have 248,000 square feet of selling space and will provide two-level parking for 2,500 cars. Shops and department stores will be located around a covered mall with parking on either side, rail and bus stations at one end, and the terminus of the pedestrian walkway system at the other end. Several large apartment houses will be built immediately adjacent to the shopping area, and schools, sports facilities, and community buildings will be nearby.[83]

Part of the proposed high-density housing near Täby Center already has been completed. The HSB (National Association of Tenants' Savings and Building Societies) of Täby has built Grindtorp and Näsbydal and intends to continue building 500 dwelling units per year.

Grindtorp and Näsbydal are two vast, architecturally distinctive apartment-house complexes, each served by the expressway and linked to the shopping center by walkways. Grindtorp houses 5,000 people in four curved buildings known to some as "moonhouses," while adjacent Näsbydal is a circle of eight identical square towers for 3,000 people (see Figure I-30). Two of the Grindtorp "moonhouses" have eleven stories; two have four stories (see Figures I-31 and I-32). They are arranged in two concentric ovals, one inside the other. Garden and play areas cover the space between each pair of buildings; parking and streets are restricted to the center and exterior of the complex. The apartments range from 654 square feet for a two-room apartment with kitchen to 1,083 square feet for a three-and-one-half-room apartment with kitchen (see Figure I-33). All apartments have balconies; the larger ones have two balconies, with exposures on opposite façades of the buildings.

Figure I-31.
Täby "Moonhouse"

Figure I-32.
Täby "Moonhouses"

Figure I-33.
Grindtorp
Apartment
Floor Plans

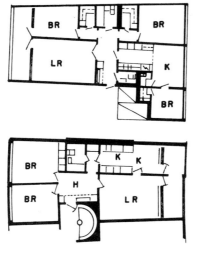
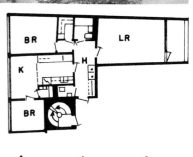

While the design of Grindtorp and Näsbydal is striking, the access by foot or by car is convenient, and the larger apartments are among the more spacious being built, the scale and arrangement of Grindtorp in particular rather dwarf the human occupants.

The satellite centers in the Stockholm region demonstrate that, given control of land use, an opportunity to plan for the related development of transportation, housing, and commerce, and public control of development financing, plans can be executed as and when intended. So far, only limited integration of planning for industrial location with other development planning has been achieved, but it seems that much greater coordination will be achieved here.

Despite its great achievements, however, the Stockholm region faces several difficult, unsolved problems: (1) the present shortage of public funds for local government land purchase programs; (2) the disparity between funds allocated for housing construction and the demand for better housing; (3) the incompatibility of the large, unmet demand for single-family housing and the preference of planners and municipal governments for high-density housing concentrated near shopping centers; (4) the development of a political structure for effectuating regional plans;[84] and (5) the incorporation of means of determining and reflecting people's preferences into the planning process. Because Stockholm has provided outstanding planning leadership to other metropolitan areas of the world, it is to be hoped that it will develop effective, innovative means of meeting these remaining problems.

Notes

1. International Union for Conservation of Nature and Natural Resources, "Sweden: Checklist of Conservation Organizations and Information," mimeographed (n.p., 1961).

2. Åke Smith, "National Report from Sweden" (Report to the Town Planning and Land Development Section of the Eleventh International Congress of Surveyors, Rome, 1965). In Sweden, settlements of 500 or more people are defined as urban.

3. In the United States there are 80,000 units of local government. In 1966 the Committee on Economic Development recommended a consolidation to no more than 16,000.

4. Including Hawaii and Alaska. Compare these with the figure for the Netherlands, 910 people per square mile.

5. Bror Soderman, "Growing Space Needs in the Urbanized Region" (Paper presented at the University of Pennsylvania New Towns Seminar, Tapiola, August, 1965).

6. Smith, "National Report from Sweden."

7. *Christian Science Monitor*, December 7, 1966; this is compared with one car for every five persons in France, Great Britain, and West Germany.

8. This represents a Gross National Product of $2,500 per capita. The per capita GNP remained constant in 1965 and was the highest of any nation in Europe. It compared with $1,600 per capita in Finland, $1,920 in France, $1,810 in Great Britain, and close to $3,000 per capita in the United States (figures from the Organization for Economic Cooperation and Development).

9. The Swedish Institute, *Facts About Sweden* (Stockholm, 1964).

10. Sten Källenius, "The Financing of Swedish House Building," *Byggnadsindustrin*, July, 1965.

11. Ernst Michanek, *Housing Standards and Housing Construction in Sweden*, prepared for The Swedish Institute (Stockholm, 1965).

12. This distribution was almost identical with that in Finland. See Table II-4 for a comparison of Scandinavian housing construction by dwelling type.

13. Just Gustavsson, "The Organizational Structure of Swedish Housing Administration, Financing of Housing and the Role of Physical Planning in Housing Programmes in Sweden," mimeographed (Report prepared for the National Housing Board, Stockholm, 1964).

14. Denmark, National Housing Board, *Housing in the Northern Countries: Sweden* (Copenhagen, 1960).

15. The Swedish Institute, *Old Age in Sweden* (Stockholm, 1963).

16. Defined as more than two persons per room, not including the kitchen. Average room size was 195 square feet.

17. Gustavsson, "The Organizational Structure of Swedish Housing Administration."

18. See Table II-4.

19. Erik Wannfors, "Planning in Sweden," mimeographed (Lecture given at the Reed College Conference on Urban Development, Portland, Oregon, May 3, 1963).

20. *Ibid.*, p. 8.

21. Four hours for apartments with windows on opposite sides.

22. Simon Jensfelt, *Modern Swedish Housing*, prepared for The Swedish Institute (Stockholm, 1962). See *Good Dwelling, 1960* (publication no. 24), and *Live in Small Houses* (publication no. 25), Swedish National Housing Board, for detailed standards.

23. Michanek, *Housing Standards and Housing Construction in Sweden*.

24. Sweden, *Building Statutes for Swedish Towns*, 1874.

25. Conversation with Mrs. Ella Ödmann of the National Board of Building and Planning, Stockholm, July, 1964.

26. Ten thousand summerhouses are built each year.

27. Lars-Erik Esping, "Preserving a Pleasing Landscape," mimeographed (Paper presented at the Fifth World Forestry Congress, Stockholm, 1960), p. 5.

28. Ivar Jonsson and Ella Ödmann, "Memorandum Relating to Standards and General Guidelines Which Are Applied in Swedish Planning of Different Kinds of Development," mimeographed (Report prepared for the National Board of Building and Planning, Stockholm, February 22, 1964).

29. Eva Hamrin and Erik Wirén, *Town and Country Planning in Sweden Today*, prepared for The Swedish Institute (Stockholm, 1964).

30. Göran Sidenbladh, "Urban Planning in the Nordic Countries" (Address to IFHP Conference, Orebro, Sweden, June 29, 1965), printed in *IFHP Bulletin* (The Hague), 1965–66.

31. Conversation with Mr. Harry Bernhard, deputy director-general, National Housing Board, Stockholm, July, 1964.

32. Esping, "Preserving a Pleasing Landscape."

33. Conversation with Mr. Lars-Erik Esping of the Swedish Society for Conservation of Nature, Stockholm, July, 1964.

34. Similar rights are enjoyed by the people of Finland and Norway; see Esping, "Preserving a Pleasing Landscape."

35. Hamrin and Wirén, *Town and Country Planning in Sweden Today*, p. 15.

36. In Sweden the public pays the landowner the costs of hiring expert witnesses to testify as to value.

37. Källenius, "The Financing of Swedish House Building."

38. Conversation with Mr. Harry Bernhard, July, 1964.

39. "Extracts from the Directions of the Government and the National Housing Board Concerning the Housing Loan," mimeographed (n.p., n.d.).

40. Harry Bernhard, *Swedish Housing Policy*, prepared for the National Housing Board (Stockholm, 1965).

41. Källenius, "The Financing of Swedish House Building."

42. In 1942, rent controls were placed on all housing, old and new. Year by year, as housing shortages have declined in less populous areas, rent controls have been lifted, but they are still in effect in all medium- and large-sized cities.

43. Conversation with Mr. Harry Bernhard and Mr. Just Gustavsson, July, 1964.

44. Bernhard, *Swedish Housing Policy*.

45. Hamrin and Wirén, *Town and Country Planning in Sweden Today*.

46. Conversation with Mr. Harry Bernhard, July, 1964.

47. Conversation with Mrs. Ella Ödmann, July, 1964.

48. *Ibid.*

49. Conversations with Mr. Lars-Erik Esping, and with Judge Lars Landh of the Ministry of Justice, Stockholm, July, 1964.

50. There are three classes of municipality: the rural commune (*landskommuner*), borough (*kopingar*), and town (*stader*).

51. Wannfors, "Planning in Sweden."

52. Conversation with Mrs. Ella Ödmann, July, 1964.

53. *Ibid.*

54. The elastic town plan is quite similar to a planned development district provision in a U.S. zoning ordinance; see, for example, the PUD ordinance of New Castle County, Del.

55. Jonsson and Ödmann's "Memorandum Relating to Standards and General Guidelines Applied in Swedish Planning" sets forth many of these standards in some detail, including those for parking, road safety, schools, children's centers, shopping centers, public buildings, gas stations, playgrounds, and noise and air pollution.

56. See p. 85 for a fuller description.

57. Conversation with Mr. Harry Bernhard, July, 1964.

58. Sweden, Acquisition of Land Act of 1949; National Board of Building and Planning, "On the Possibilities for a Commune to Acquire by Force Ground for Dense Development," mimeographed (Stockholm, 1956).

59. Provided for under Sweden's Expropriation Act of May 12, 1917, the Building Act of June 30, 1947, and the Acquisition of Land Act of 1949.

60. H. Pontin, "The Right of the Municipality to Use Private Ground," mimeographed (Stockholm, 1963).

61. H. Pontin, "Private Land-Owners' Contribution to the Exploitation Costs in Sweden," mimeographed (Stockholm, 1963).

62. Section 1, point 16, Expropriation Act of May 12, 1917, as amended by the Acquisition of Land Act of 1949.

63. Ö. Hernbäck, "Memorandum Relating to the Allocation of Land and the Con-

trol of Land Prices for Housing in Sweden" (HOU/114, Annex III), mimeographed, prepared for the National Housing Board (Stockholm, September 25, 1963).

64. National Board of Building and Planning, "On the Possibilities for a Commune to Acquire by Force Ground for Dense Development," citing sec. 46 and 47 of the Building Act of June 30, 1947.

65. Conversation with Judge Lars Landh, July, 1964.

66. A study in the United States by Walter Langbein, "Municipal Water Use in the United States," showed a sharp increase in water consumption as municipal size increased to a population of 5,000. For populations of from 5,000 to 100,000 the demand per capita remained constant. Langbein's article is cited by Gulam M. Quraishi in "Municipal Water Demand in Sweden," *Stadsbyggnad*, no. 3, June, 1964.

67. Quraishi, "Municipal Water Demand in Sweden." One wonders whether Sweden could not be a soap importer.

68. Hamrin and Wirén, *Town and Country Planning in Sweden Today*.

69. Sweden, National Road Board, *The Question of Pure Water in Sweden*, Water and Sewerage Series, Pu 8.3 (Stockholm, 1964).

70. Conversation with Mr. Torsten Josephson, a Stockholm provincial architect, July, 1964.

71. In 1961 Stockholm received the Abercrombie prize from the International Union of Architects for providing "... an example to all other cities because they show foresight in land policy and intelligent coordination of the many problems confronting the modern city."

72. Stockholm Planning Commission, *Stockholm Regional and City Planning* (1964), p. 49.

73. Joakim Garpe (Stockholm's commissioner for city planning), "Stockholm at the Opening of the 1960's," *ibid.*, p. 31.

74. C. F. Ahlberg, "The Regional Plan for the Stockholm Area," *ibid.*, p. 37.

75. Göran Sidenbladh, "Planning Problems in Stockholm," *ibid.*, p. 64.

76. Gunther M. Gottfeld, "The Stockholm Underground Railway," *Stadsbyggnad*, no. 3, June, 1964.

77. These figures are taken from AB Stockholms Spårvägar, *SS Facts and Figures, 1965* (Stockholm, 1965).

78. *Ibid.*

79. Sidenbladh, "Planning Problems in Stockholm," p. 58.

80. Stockholm Chamber of Commerce, *Swedish Shopping Centres* (1965).

81. *Ibid.*

82. I. Dergalin and J. M. Stäck, "General Plan for Rinkeby, Spånga, Kyrka, och Tensta," *Santryck ur Arkitektur*, no. 5, 1964.

83. Allan Westerman, *Swedish Planning of Town Centres*, prepared for The Swedish Institute, Stockholm; Stockholm Chamber of Commerce, *Swedish Shopping Centres*.

84. The Greater Stockholm County Council, which will begin functioning on January 1, 1971, should be a significant step forward.

II | Finland

Tapiola:
A
Suburban
Garden
City

Tapiola Town Center

Contents

The National Setting

While Finland shares many of the urban development problems common to the other European countries included in this study—migration from rural areas to the fringes of the largest cities, only occasional success in persuading industry to locate in smaller urban areas, and the failure even to begin to meet the consumer demand for single-family housing—she has had additional problems comparable only to those of Israel.

As a consequence of World War II, Finland not only suffered substantial physical damage and economic loss but also was stripped of 12 percent of her territory, lost 78,000 men, was faced with 400,000 refugees to house and employ, and was given six years to pay $500 million in reparations to the Soviet Union. The war reduced Finland's capacity to invest in urban development and necessarily resulted in concentration on the most pressing needs— housing for those deprived of it by the war, and industrial production to meet the reparations schedule. Postwar resettlement of refugees in rural areas delayed urbanization, but this now is occurring at a rapid rate.

Comparatively, Finland has a small population and low density. The country is rich only in forests and in the grit and determination of its people. Against this background of relative austerity, the building of Tapiola as a private enterprise new town is all the more remarkable. Appreciation for the natural environment, attention to the quality of living experience provided, and care for detail in site design and landscaping are the town's dominant characteristics.

Historical Background

To understand present-day urban development in Finland, it is important to be familiar with a little of Finland's recent history—her antecedents, her obligations, and some of the influences that have come to bear on her.

Like Israel, ethnically her people are ancient, but as a nation she is young. Finland has been independent only since 1917. From 1154 to 1809 she was part of Sweden, with the city of Turku the provincial capital. (During these hundreds of years, Finns were pawns in Sweden's continuing wars.) Following the Russian victory over the Swedes in 1809, Finland became a grand duchy of Russia. She had her own constitution, and the czar of Russia served as constitutional ruler. Czar Alexander I moved the Finnish capital from Turku to Helsinki in 1812, to locate it farther from Stockholm and nearer Saint Petersburg (Leningrad), then the Russian capital. Throughout these periods of Swedish and Russian dominance the Finns retained their ethnic cohesion and their language, and, in 1917, following the Russian Revolution, managed to establish their independence.

Finland's situation during World War II was incredible; that she managed to survive as an independent nation is a tribute to the unending courage and stubbornness of the people and to the brilliant and resourceful leadership of General Mannerheim. Already in 1938, the Russians began making demands for bases, which the Finns spurned. In 1939 Molotov signed a non-aggression pact with Germany granting the Soviet Union a free hand in Finland. After Finland rejected increased Russian demands, the Russians took up positions along the 800-mile common border and, in November, 1939, sent in tanks after staging an incident as a pretext. The Russians launched twenty-six divisions at six points of attack. The Finns had but one-tenth the Russians' manpower and almost no tanks, planes, or ammunition. Yet they held back the Russians and, through the −40°F. and −50°F. winter, even gained signal victories. The Russians committed more men—one million—and lost 200,000 of them. By March, 1940, however, Finland's manpower and matériel were exhausted, and Russian settlement terms had to be accepted. These terms were far harsher than the demands of the preceding fall. Ten percent of the land was ceded permanently, including Karelia with its port city Viipuri. Twelve percent of the people were forced to flee westward.

This was not all. Finland fought against Russia again between 1941 and 1944, as a reluctant ally of the Germans, back through Karelia to Russia, then in retreat back home again. By September, 1944, the Finns had recognized a new defeat and had negotiated an armistice with the Russians which ceded more land, including Finland's only port on the Arctic Ocean, agreed that the Finns would drive out all 200,000 German soldiers from Finland in two and one-half months, and promised to pay $300 million (later increased to $500 million) in reparations. Knowing that loss of independence would be the price of failure, the Finns, by further acts of courage and self-abnegation, met the Russian demands. Sixty percent of the reparations were to be paid in ships, machines, wire cables, instruments, and other metal products. By the war's end Finland had no capacity to produce such goods. Industries were built or rebuilt, raw materials bought on loan, and a labor force was trained. For years the Finns did without—without adequate shelter, food, or social programs. Little wonder that they have trailed richer countries such as Sweden and Denmark, which had no such wartime history of loss and debt.

Natural Environment

Of Finland's 130,000 square miles, one-third lies above the Arctic Circle. The far north is tundra; the center and south are forested and dotted with shallow, marshy lakes, much like Minnesota. Forests extend over 65 percent of the country, and fields cover 8 percent of the land. At one time central and southern Finland were mountainous, but erosion has left a flat, low plain. Map II-1 provides an over-all view of the country's topography.

Alaska and Finland are at the same latitude—between the 60th and 70th parallels—but Finland is warmer because of the Gulf Stream. Snow blankets southern and central Finland from the end of November through April, and northern Finland from late October to mid-May. The mean annual temperature is 42°F. in the south and 31°F. in the north. However, mild summers in the southern and central portions of the country make extensive agriculture possible. Rainfall is moderate and diminishes toward the north. A more favorable climate in the south and west has contributed to the population migration in these directions. This migration is in opposition to government policy, which encourages decentralization and expanded settlement of the north and east.

Finland's principal natural resources are forests and water with hydro-electric potential. Most of the forests are in central Finland, while streams useful for generating electricity lie to the north. Intensive prospecting for

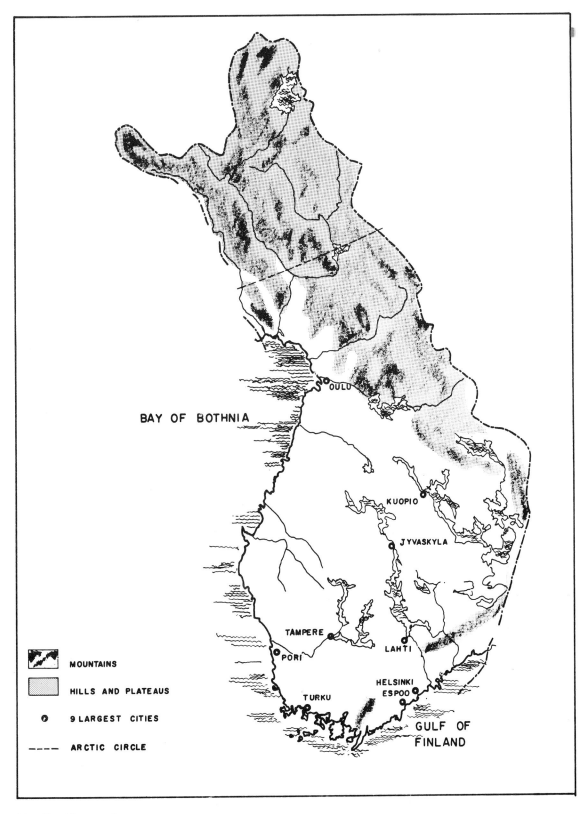

BAY OF BOTHNIA

OULU

KUOPIO

JYVASKYLA

TAMPERE

PORI

LAHTI

TURKU

HELSINKI
ESPOO

GULF OF
FINLAND

MOUNTAINS

HILLS AND PLATEAUS

⊙   9 LARGEST CITIES

---- ARCTIC CIRCLE

Map II-1. Topography

ores in recent years has led to the discovery of deposits of lead, nickel, copper, magnetite, sulphur, uranium, and chrome. These ores are found in central, eastern, and southern Finland. It is hoped that the discovery of minerals, combined with the development of power stations and wood-processing industries, will stimulate growth in central Finland and slow the immigration to the south and west.

The People   *Distribution*

There are 4.6 million Finns. In 1965, 44 percent were living in cities and towns, 56 percent in rural municipalities. Many residents of the latter lived in densely populated areas.[1] However, only 1.6 percent of the land area of Finland is urbanized. The population density is thirty-eight persons per square mile.[2] Finnish is the principal language of most (92.4 percent) of the people, although a small minority (7.4 percent) is Swedish-speaking, and a very few (0.2 percent) speak Lapp or some other tongue.

The Helsinki region, comprising 1 percent of Finland's land area, accommodates 15 percent of her people; by the year 2000 it is predicted that 19 percent of all Finns will live there.[3] Most of the region's growth is the result of immigration from other parts of the country. Of the 686,000 people there, somewhat in excess of two-thirds live in Helsinki proper and the rest in the neighboring suburbs. The old central city's population already is declining, while the population of the area annexed in 1946 and of the suburbs is rising rapidly.

Finland's next largest cities are Tampere (144,000) and Turku (140,000); six other municipalities have a population in excess of 50,000.[4] The rest of the urban population is scattered among small cities and small and medium-sized towns. The still substantial rural population is one by-product of the war. To resettle and feed the 400,000 Karelia refugees, Finland instituted a program of farmland expropriation and redistribution. Partly as a result of this, farm holdings remain small and farm employment is high. In the past decade, however, many young people have been leaving the farms and migrating to urban areas, particularly to Helsinki, or abroad, usually to Sweden.

It is the opinion of the National Planning Office that the present population density of sixty-five persons per square mile in southern and southwestern Finland is about right and that some means should be found to direct further growth to the north in order to develop the resources there.

Employment

Finland's principal industries are construction, wood-processing, and engineering products. The Russian demand for reparations in the form of machinery, appliances, and electric cables, as well as ships, stimulated the growth of these industries, and the country now seeks orders to use the productive capacity it has created.

Table II-1 compares the distribution of the work force with Finland's Net National Income,[5] as derived from each class of employment in 1960, and projects the work force distribution for 1970.

Unemployment, principally of people no longer needed in forestry and agriculture, became a problem in 1968, when 4 percent of the work force was unemployed. The situation improved in 1969, partly because of increased economic activity and partly as a result of the government's retraining programs.

About half of the Helsinki region's labor force works in the city, 23 per-

Table II-1.
Occupations, by Percentage of Work Force and of Net National Income Derived

Occupation	Percentage of Work Force, 1960	Percentage of Work Force, 1970, Projected	Percentage of Net National Income Derived, 1960
Farming	30	23	11
Forestry and Fishing			10
Building Industry	37	39	10
Other Industry			31
Trade and Transport	7	8	8
Commerce	11	13	12
Services	15	17	18
	100	100	100

SOURCE: Work force data from the Central Bureau of Statistics, Helsinki; net national income data for 1960 from the Ministry of Housing, Copenhagen, the National Housing Board, Helsinki, the Housing Directorate, Oslo, and the National Housing Board, Stockholm, *Housing in the Northern Countries* (Copenhagen, 1960).

cent in commerce, 40 percent in transportation and services, 31 percent in industry, and the rest in construction and agriculture. The percentage of workers in industrial employment in the city is expected to decline as decentralization to the suburbs increases. About half of the region's commercial employment is in retail trade, the rest being in banking, insurance, and wholesale trade, for which Helsinki serves as the national center. Employment in services is increasing rapidly and is expected to continue to rise.

Finns work a forty-hour week. All workers have three weeks of paid vacation and, depending on their employer, are entitled to four weeks after ten years of employment. Unemployment compensation is paid jointly by the state and the employer, while the cost of disability and retirement benefits is carried by the state, municipality, employer, and employee.

Finland's 1964 Gross Domestic Product was about $7.3 billion, or $1,600 per capita. Exports have been running around 20 percent of this—too little in the opinion of a number of Finnish economists. Finland's most important trading partners, for both imports and exports, are the Soviet Union, the United Kingdom, and West Germany. In the simplest terms, ships and machine goods go east, wood products go west. Table II-2 shows 1964 foreign trade by type of goods and value.

Finland joined EFTA (European Free Trade Association) in 1961, and also is a party to bilateral trade agreements with communist nations in Eastern Europe. Imports and exports in 1966 were, by area:

	Exports	Imports
EFTA	35%	36%
EEC	28	28
Eastern Bloc	19	19
Others	18	17

Trade with the United States accounted for 6 percent of exports, or $103 million, by 1968, and it has been growing more rapidly than Finland's total foreign trade. Imports from the United States totaled $52 million. Finland is succeeding in its efforts to increase diversification in exports. In 1960, 84 percent of exports to the United States were wood products, primarily newsprint. By 1968, wood products were down to 67 percent, and mink skins, textiles, and metal goods each had gained a niche of 8–10 percent of exports to the

Table II-2.
Foreign Trade, 1964

	Millions of Dollars	Percent
Imports		
Raw materials and equipment for industry	619	41
Other raw materials and equipment	40	3
Fuels and lubricants	159	10
Consumer goods	250	17
Finished investment goods	436	29
Total Imports	1,504	100
Exports		
Agricultural products	72	5
Timber and wood products	308	24
Pulp, paper, and board	631	49
Metal products	191	15
Others	89	7
Total Exports	1,291	100

SOURCE: *Suomi—Certain Facts about Finland* (Helsinki: Kansallis-Osake-Pankki, 1965).

United States. Finnish design in fabrics, furniture, glass, and pottery is becoming increasingly well known and sought after.

Housing

During the war, 110,000 dwelling units—one-eighth of Finland's entire housing stock—were lost through the cession of land to Russia. An additional 9,000 urban dwellings were destroyed or damaged by bombing or burning. By 1950 the housing shortage was estimated to be about 100,000 dwelling units, with more than two-thirds of the shortage in urban areas. By 1960, after the postwar construction of 590,000 new dwellings and an average annual investment of 7 percent of the national income in housing, the estimated shortage had increased to 104,000 dwelling units—79,600 in urban areas and 24,400 in rural areas.[6] Population increase and new family formation absorbed most of the new construction. In addition to an actual shortage of housing, there was a large unmet demand for housing meeting higher standards than either the old housing or postwar rural housing could offer. To meet part of this demand, current housing production is divided about equally between rural and urban areas.

The current rate of construction is 40,000 dwelling units per year, a rate of 8.5 per 1,000 population. The average size per dwelling unit is 650 square feet. These new units just about equal the demand of newly married couples for separate housing and so are not reducing the remaining housing shortage. The large number of young people born after the war are starting to marry, and they will increase the need for housing.

While housing is well maintained, dwelling units often are small, crowded, and lack adequate bathroom facilities. As of the 1960 census, 14 percent of all dwellings were more than fifty years old.

In 1901, although more than half of the population owned their own homes, the average density was 2.4 persons per room. Twenty-eight percent of the population lived in one-room dwelling units; 27 percent lived in two-room units. A kitchen is defined as a room; in a one-room dwelling unit the kitchen facilities are included in the single room.

By 1960, occupancy density had fallen to 1.3 persons per room and to 1.17 in Helsinki.[7] However, much of the population still was housed in one- or two-room dwelling units. Six percent of Finland's rural inhabitants lived in one-room dwelling units and 28 percent in two rooms. Of the urban residents, 13 percent were in one room and 33 percent in two rooms.

Forty-nine percent of the country's housing stock consists of one- and two-room dwelling units, while 60 percent of the individual households are composed of three or more people. The 1960 census showed that, of all dwelling units in the country, 15 percent had one room, 33 percent had two rooms, 29 percent had three rooms, 13 percent had four rooms, and 10 percent had five rooms or more (see Figure II-1). Table II-3 gives more recent figures.

Again as of 1960, only a small portion of all dwellings had both heat and bathrooms. Forty-seven percent had water, 37 percent had toilets, 16 percent had bathrooms, and 31 percent had central heat. Of course, water, toilets, and

Table II-3.
Housing Construction by Number of Rooms, 1964

| Location | Number of Rooms | | | | | | | |
	1	2	3	4	5	6	7 or more	Total
Helsinki	811	1,237	1,513	1,614	467	239	107	5,988
Other cities and villages	2,790	2,501	5,500	4,381	2,276	668	193	18,309
Rural areas	904	1,231	3,197	3,210	1,831	525	186	11,084
Total	4,505	4,969	10,210	9,205	4,574	1,432	486	35,381
Percentage of construction	13	14	29	26	13	4	1	100

SOURCE: Finland, Bureau of Social Research, *Sosiaalinen aikakauskirja, 7–8/1965* (Helsinki, 1965).
NOTE: Minimum room size is 76 sq. ft.; the kitchen is counted as a room, although most one- and two-room dwelling units have a kitchenette, which is not so counted.

Figure II-1.
Housing Production
by Number of
Rooms

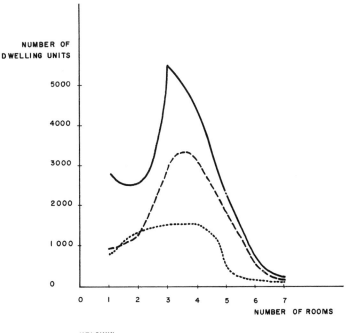

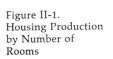
······· HELSINKI
——— OTHER CITIES
– – – RURAL AREAS

central heating are included in virtually all new construction. Of housing built in 1964, 98 percent had water, 94 percent had toilets, 71 percent had bathrooms, and 94 percent had central heat. The sauna is commonly found in all types of housing, although usually it is a shared facility in multi-family dwellings.

Not surprisingly, 83 percent of all single-family houses built in 1964 are of timber construction. Single-family or twin housing predominates in the towns, suburbs, and rural areas, although multi-story housing, mostly of brick construction, is becoming more common. The 1960 census revealed that 26 percent of all *city* dwellings were one-story houses, 36 percent were two-story houses, 8 percent were three-story houses, and 29 percent were structures of more than three stories. Figures for 1964 housing construction show a shift to multi-story dwellings: 30 percent of the dwellings constructed were one- and two-family houses, 5 percent were row houses, 62 percent were multi-story housing, and the remainder were part of structures also used for other purposes. Figure II-2 illustrates contrasting housing types found in present-day Finland. Comparative housing construction figures for 1963 show a close parallel between Finland and Sweden, both of which contrast sharply with the type of housing constructed in Denmark and Norway (see Table II-4). Square-foot construction costs for multi-story and row or single-family housing are about equal.[8]

Table II-4.
Scandinavian Housing by Dwelling Type, 1963

Country	Type of Dwelling Unit		
	Apartment	House	Other
Denmark	36%	62%	2%
Finland	66	31	3
Norway	20	71	9
Sweden	65	29	6

SOURCE: Bror Soderman, "Growing Space Needs in the Urbanized Region" (Paper presented at the University of Pennsylvania New Towns Seminar, Tapiola, August, 1965).

A 1956 study showed that Finns paid an average of 12.6 percent of their income for housing, including taxes, and an additional 3.7 percent for heat and electricity. At that time, most housing was subject to rent controls. These were not abolished in Helsinki until 1962. In 1961, in Helsinki, all housing-related costs averaged 19.7 percent of income. The figure has risen since then.

In speaking of housing types and standards, one must remember that urban Finns, like the Swedes, often have a second home, a simple and secluded summerhouse where they spend summer vacations and weekends.[9] "People like to live downtown as close to the market and as close to each other as possible in the winter time. Then, for the three summer months, they scatter among the islands with families moving out for the entire period as soon as school is out. They may remain within commuting distance of the city, perhaps up to fifty miles away, or there may be summer widows whose husbands commute only for the weekends."[10]

Another Finnish planner suspects that the affinity for summerhouses is linked to inadequate urban housing conditions: "It may, of course, be pointed out, with reason, that if we build our towns and the apartments in them so that they serve their purpose in a functional and aesthetic manner, we no longer need our summerhouses, our villas. It may be that the quality of a town here in Finland may be measured by finding out how large a proportion of the town population have their own summerhouses. The more summerhouses, the worse the town."[11]

Figure II-2. The Contrast in Present-day Housing: A Single-Family Wooden
Structure, Walk-up Apartments, and Modern High-rise Construction

Government Programs and Policies for Urban Development

The national government is potentially the most powerful public or private agent for influencing urban development. To date, however, the dominance of rural interests in Parliament and the retention of power by local governments have restrained the national government from taking a forceful lead in shaping urban development policies. Urban planning and development controls are relatively weak in comparison with the controls employed in other European countries. Insofar as they are exercised, it is the national government which takes the lead. Provincial government, largely an arm of the national government, is employed occasionally to implement national policy.

National Government

Political Structure

The constitution of 1919 established a republican form of government and provided for a president of the republic, elected to a six-year term by a college of 300 chosen by the people, and for a unicameral parliament of 200 members, elected to four-year terms by direct vote of the electorate. Following the 1970 elections, the composition of Parliament is as follows: Social Democrats, 52; National Coalition party (Conservatives), 37; Center party (former Agrarians), 36; People's Democratic League (Communists), 36; Finnish Rural party, 18; Swedish National party, 12; Liberals, 8; Christians, 1. The president, Dr. Urho Kekkonen, is now serving his third term. There is a cabinet of from eleven to fifteen members which is headed by the prime minister. The cabinet is selected by the president with the concurrence of the dominant party or coalition of parties in Parliament. It is anticipated that the newly elected Parliament and newly appointed cabinet will be more urban oriented than previous governments.

It is the responsibility of the president of the republic to reclassify municipalities—for instance, from rural municipalities to cities and towns. He does not have the power to establish new towns. The cabinet is authorized to establish new rural municipalities and to permit a municipality to annex territory from another unit of local government, even when such an action is contrary to the wishes of the inhabitants of the annexed area.

Two administrative arms of the national government exercise particular influence on the course of urban development: the Ministry of the Interior, including ARAVA, the National Housing Board; and the National Planning Office, under the prime minister. Additional national agencies with a role in development include the Ministry of Agriculture's Colonization Board, which is responsible only for housing finance for rural areas; the Housing Bureau in the Ministry of Social Affairs; the Social Research Bureau, also in the Ministry of Social Affairs, which is responsible for housing statistics; and the Central Bureau of Statistics of the Ministry of Finance which conducts the decennial housing census.

Planning

The Ministry of the Interior is the national agency charged with final responsibility for planning and building decisions at the national, regional, and local levels. The National Planning Office may recommend and advise, but the ministry makes policy decisions.

National Planning began in 1951. Since then, emphasis has been on improving agriculture and forestry in the sparsely populated areas of the country, expanding wood-processing industries, particularly in the north and east, developing other industries, and encouraging ore prospecting. The national planning policy for decentralization from Helsinki has been implemented through the establishment of a new university at Oulu in west-central Finland and the relocation of the Institute of Social Sciences from Helsinki to Tampere. Parliament recently passed legislation providing for state loans and tax exemption to industries and other enterprises which would agree to locate in development areas, namely, non-southwestern Finland.

Since 1959 the Ministry of the Interior has been empowered to establish regional boundaries and to require regional planning. Voluntary regional planning has been underway since the early 1940s,[12] and now virtually all parts of the country are included in either voluntary or government-mandated regional planning areas. The ministry's present aim is to establish regional planning on an official basis nationwide, using the twelve provinces as the basic unit. The content and complexity required of the plan depend on the stage of development of the region. The state, through the Ministry of the Interior, provides financial aid to voluntary regional planning agencies and pays half of the cost of compulsory regional planning, with the local governments in the region contributing the remainder. All regional plans must be submitted to the ministry for approval. To date, while many plans are underway, none have been approved.

The approval of municipal plans, including town plans and master plans, and of municipal building regulations also is the responsibility of the Ministry of the Interior.

The National Planning Office was established in 1956 to carry out research. Administratively it is under the jurisdiction of the prime minister and receives additional direction from the National Planning Council, whose members include representatives of ministries and state boards related in some way to national planning. The findings and recommendations of the National Planning Office are transmitted to the Ministry of the Interior and other appropriate ministries for government action. As envisaged by the National Planning Office, the broad role for national planners is to advise on the location of production, the development of existing population centers, and the establishment of new centers. To a lesser extent, administrative organization and the role of cultural institutions are included in national planning. In sum, "The goal to strive for was to be the direction of development, as far as possible, in such a way that the resources of all the parts of the country could effectively be mobilized and the increasing population settled in areas where there is sufficient space and the natural conditions are favorable for expansion."[13]

Development Financing

The National Housing Board, ARAVA, is the chief source of government financial aid to private urban development. A reorganization of government agencies responsible for the planning, financing, and supervision of housing production took effect on January 1, 1967. The reorganized National Housing Board now is located in the Ministry of the Interior. It was established in 1949 to encourage housing production in urban areas by granting government loans in the form of second mortgages. ARAVA now is used to promote the government's policies of relieving the housing shortage, ameliorating housing conditions, and providing wintertime employment.

Loans for the construction of apartments for veterans have been administered by ASO (the Colonization Department of the Ministry of Agriculture). Through the mid-1950s many more homes received ASO than ARAVA support. In recent years, however, the ASO veterans' housing program has declined considerably in importance as a source of housing construction subsidies (see Table II-5).

Table II-5.
Housing Construction Subsidized by the Government and Privately Financed, 1949–64

| Year | Number of Dwelling Units Completed | | | | | Percentage of Dwelling Units Completed | |
	ASO Subsidized	ARAVA Subsidized	Total Subsidized	Non-subsidized	Total	Subsidized	Non-subsidized
1949	14,499	1,124	15,623	13,577	29,200	54	46
1950	12,508	5,401	17,909	8,291	26,200	68	32
1951	11,872	7,420	19,292	9,408	28,700	67	33
1952	14,945	8,603	23,548	8,252	31,800	74	26
1953	14,392	7,797	22,189	7,411	29,600	75	25
1954	14,437	8,966	23,403	8,797	32,200	73	27
1955	12,329	11,324	23,653	9,547	33,200	71	29
1956	10,047	9,648	19,695	10,805	30,500	65	35
1957	9,789	9,681	19,470	13,230	32,700	60	40
1958	9,594	9,532	19,126	10,874	30,000	64	36
1959	5,159	9,923	15,082	14,868	29,950	50	50
1960	4,352	8,539	12,891	18,634	31,525	41	59
1961	4,859	8,311	13,170	24,129	37,299	35	65
1962	3,883	6,490	10,373	27,076	37,449	28	72
1963	3,660	7,532	11,192	32,941	44,133	25	75
1964	2,429	9,263	11,692	23,689	35,381	33	67
Total	148,754	129,554	278,308	241,529	519,837		
Percentage of Total	29	25	54	46	100		

SOURCE: Haaken Bjorkenheim, "ARAVA—The State Housing Board" (Helsinki, May 22, 1963).

ARAVA may loan up to 40 percent of total land and construction costs for owner-occupied housing, and up to 60 percent for renter-occupied housing. Actually, in recent years loans for owner-occupied dwellings have run from 32 to 37 percent of total costs, and those for renter-occupied dwellings from 40 to 50 percent. The purchaser makes a 10 percent down payment and secures the remaining 50 percent of the purchase cost as a first mortgage from a bank. ARAVA's interest rate is 1–3 percent, as compared with the commercial bank rate of 7 or 8 percent. The amortization period is thirty-three years for single-family and wooden houses and forty-five years for non-wooden row houses, apartments, and brick structures, as compared with an amortization period of from ten to twenty-two years from commercial lenders.

About 25 percent of current urban housing construction—some 8,000 dwellings per year—is supported by ARAVA loans. In 1965 the national government allocated $39 million to ARAVA for housing loans. If ARAVA decides that land costs are too high, loans may be refused; however, no one figure has been established above which land will be classed as too expensive, because land costs vary considerably throughout the country. In Helsinki most ARAVA-supported housing is built on land owned or leased by the city. Of all ARAVA housing built so far, about two-thirds consists of apartments and one-third of houses. In 1965, 69 percent of the dwellings constructed with ARAVA aid were owner-occupied. All houses are owner-occupied, although houses with two dwelling units will have one owner occupant and one tenant. An increasing number of apartments are renter-occupied. See Table II-6.

When ARAVA loans are used to subsidize the building of rental housing, ARAVA controls the rents charged, permitting the owner a return of 6.5 percent on his investment. In addition, ARAVA oversees tenant selection to assure that preference is given to those in greatest need of housing. If the owner of multi-story housing backed by ARAVA financing wishes to sell such housing, non-profit housing companies and local authorities have the right to purchase it at a regulated price, thus impeding opportunities for inflationary sales.

ARAVA loans are available to all categories of builders. About 25 percent of ARAVA-financed dwelling units in multi-story buildings are built by local authorities, 25 percent by cooperatives and other non-profit groups, 20 percent by commercial builders, and the rest by private groups or individuals.

With ARAVA financing goes ARAVA control over housing standards. Adequate space and amenity standards are required, but luxury housing is not allowed. The floor area of a dwelling unit may not exceed 100 square meters (1,076 square feet). Multi-story housing must have central heat, hot and cold water, bathrooms, and, usually, a sauna for joint use by the tenants. Requirements for owner-occupied houses are more flexible, depending on what is possible in the locality where the houses are to be built. The ARAVA manual sets forth requirements for equipment, materials, and finishing; it also details minimum space standards. Up to 25 percent of the floor area of an ARAVA-financed building may be used for commercial purposes, such as small shops for the residents.

Much ARAVA financing is granted contingent upon the builder carrying out construction during the winter months. Unemployment among construction workers rises in Finland between October and May, and so ARAVA funds are used to combat this seasonal pattern.

Taxation

An appropriate prelude to a discussion of Finnish tax laws as they affect urban development is the comment of a prominent Finnish planner, who will remain anonymous: "The tax system is so separated from all other planning that it can't really be considered as part of planning. Everyone sees the tax collector as our common enemy." How often similar remarks are made about the relationship between taxation and planning in the United States, as well as in other European countries.

National tax policy is the responsibility of the Ministry of Finance. Real property taxes are levied by the national and local governments and by the Lutheran church, which is the national church. Real property is valued yearly and on the urban fringe reflects the assessor's judgment of its future development potential. It is said that the assessor looks further ahead than the planner, attributing value before plans show that land is open for urban development. High assessments contribute to high land prices on the urban fringe.

Table II-6.
ARAVA-financed Construction by Type of Housing, 1949–65

| | Number of Dwelling Units | | | | | | | | |
| | Apartments | | | Houses | | | Total | | |
Year	Individual Owner	Renter	Total	Individual Owner	Renter	Total	Individual Owner	Renter	Total
1949	2,535	1,498	4,033	1,306	634	1,940	3,841	2,132	5,973
1950	3,717	2,103	5,820	1,901	808	2,709	5,618	2,911	8,529
1951	2,639	1,822	4,461	1,616	694	2,310	4,255	2,516	6,771
1952	3,011	1,105	4,116	1,824	753	2,577	4,835	1,858	6,693
1953	4,269	1,447	5,716	1,966	875	2,841	6,235	2,322	8,557
1954	5,157	1,776	6,933	2,464	1,205	3,669	7,621	2,981	10,602
1955	5,576	1,527	7,103	2,946	1,341	4,287	8,522	2,868	11,390
1956	4,400	1,735	6,135	2,504	1,046	3,550	6,904	2,781	9,685
1957	5,132	1,490	6,622	2,203	838	3,041	7,335	2,328	9,663
1958	4,874	1,811	6,685	1,761	603	2,364	6,635	2,414	9,049
1959	5,670	1,349	7,019	1,770	431	2,201	7,440	1,780	9,220
1960	4,027	2,132	6,159	2,398	461	2,859	6,425	2,593	9,018
1961	3,001	3,102	6,103	2,164	346	2,510	5,165	3,448	8,613
1962	2,786	3,433	6,219	2,361	297	2,658	5,147	3,730	8,877
1963	2,927	2,732	5,659	2,221	97	2,318	5,148	2,829	7,977
1964	3,030	2,854	5,884	2,315	54	2,369	5,345	2,908	8,253
1965	4,792	3,603	8,395	2,455	33	2,488	7,247	3,636	10,883
Total	67,543	35,519	103,062	36,175	10,516	46,691	103,718	46,035	149,753
Percentage of Total	45	24	69	24	7	31	69	31	100

SOURCE: Haaken Bjorkenheim, "ARAVA—The State Housing Board" (Helsinki, May 22, 1963).

Housing size is influenced by a nationwide real property tax exemption available to owner-occupants. All dwellings measuring less than 120 square meters (1,296 square feet) are exempted from all real property taxes for ten years after construction. The sauna and bathroom usually are excluded in computing the 120 square meters. Housing size is further influenced by government repayment of half of the sales tax paid for building materials for up to 100 square meters (1,076 square feet) of a dwelling. This refund is substantial, equalling 2.5–3.5 percent of total building costs.

Municipal land acquisition is abetted by two tax provisions that reduce acquisition costs. Municipalities are exempted from the real property transfer tax, which runs from 3 to 12 percent of the purchase price. In addition, sales by persons in the real estate business are not subject to a capital gain tax when the sale is to a municipality.

Profits from the sale of real estate are taxed as income if the property was acquired by purchase or exchange within the ten years preceding the sale. The August, 1965, report of the Government Committee on Land Supply and Land Prices recommends imposition of a progressive tax on income derived from the sale or exchange of real estate. Most of the revenue generated by this tax would flow to the municipalities, although the national government would garner some of it through the national income tax. This is another tax designed to encourage sales to municipalities by granting sellers a partial tax exemption for such sales. The report also proposes that land designated in a town plan as a building area should be subject to a special municipal tax whose rate would rise periodically, starting with the designation. This tax would be another inducement to bring land into development.

The major source of municipal revenue is the income tax. It is levied on residents, on owners of real property located in the municipality, and on persons or companies engaged in trade in the municipality. The amount of the tax usually runs between 10 and 12 percent of the taxable income for individuals and 45 percent of the net profit for companies. The portion of municipal income derived from the income tax varies with the class of municipality; cities and towns receive 50–60 percent of their income from this source, rural municipalities 40–50 percent. The national government's subsidy to municipalities also varies with the class of municipality, running on the average at 7 percent for cities, 12 percent for towns, and 30 percent for rural municipalities.

Tax relief, in conjunction with road building and the decentralization of government offices, is used to implement the national planning policy of encouraging settlement of northern and eastern Finland. Industries locating in these areas are eligible for a three-year exemption from real property and income taxes. While industry is moving from the city of Helsinki to nearby sites, thus far comparatively few industries have responded to government incentives to move to the less-developed parts of the country.

Provincial Government

There are twelve provinces in Finland, and these, for administrative purposes, are subdivided into counties consisting of one or more municipalities. Various national functions are carried out through districts whose limits may or may not correspond with provincial boundaries.

For regional planning, the provincial administration acts in a supervisory role subordinate to the Ministry of the Interior and subject to advice and coordination from the National Planning Office. Until a regional master plan has been approved, all large-scale development proposals must be submitted to the regional planning office, first for comments and then for approval. Currently, regional and provincial boundaries are not the same; ten regions designated by the Ministry of the Interior have been directed to engage in regional planning, an additional eight are doing so on a voluntary basis, and fifteen other regions are carrying out some form of research and planning work.[14] As previously mentioned, however, the national government is proposing a legislative change which would make regions coterminous with the provinces.

Town plans and building regulations for rural municipalities are prepared and approved by the municipalities. They then are submitted to the provincial administration for approval.

Local Government

There are three types of municipality in Finland: the city, the town, and the rural municipality. As of 1965 there were 46 cities, 24 towns, and 476 rural municipalities. Almost half of the rural municipalities have fewer than 4,000 inhabitants. At present, the national government plays a far more active role in rural municipalities than in cities and towns, both through direct administration of programs and through loans and subsidies. This difference between types of municipalities already is decreasing and is expected to be affected further by the national policy of encouraging stronger local government in the rural municipalities.[15]

Each municipality is governed by a council elected for a four-year term. The council numbers from thirteen to seventy-seven, depending on the population of the municipality. It elects a central board, whose members need not be members of the council. This board handles the day-to-day affairs of the municipality. By law, cities and towns are administered by appointed managers who also sit ex officio as chairmen of the central boards. In large cities the city manager is aided by assistant city managers, who are civil servants and central board members as well, and each of whom is responsible for a branch of city administration. All central boards must have a majority of elected members. Helsinki, for instance, has a seventy-seven-member council, nine elected board members, and six non-elected board members, including the city manager and five assistant city managers.

Planning

Planning at the municipal level, as provided for in the Building Law of 1958, takes three forms: the building plan, the town plan, and the master plan. The building plan is for rural areas only and, as previously stated, is prepared by the rural municipality and approved by the provinical government.

Town plans are detailed plans for densely populated areas—cities, towns, and the built-up portions of rural municipalities. Town plans for rural municipalities are approved by the provincial government, while town plans for cities and towns must be approved by the Ministry of the Interior to be legally effective. If the ministry disapproves the plan, a written explanation of reasons for disapproval must be given the local government. If the local government wishes to have its plan approved, generally it must accede to the ministry's recommendations. Ministry review time averages two months and never exceeds four or five months. Approved town plans, like regional plans, are advisory in nature rather than binding on the community. Permits for multi-story housing or dense development construction may be granted only in areas covered by town plans.

Master plans are outline schemes looking to the future development of cities and towns. Shown thereon are the proposed locations of streets and of water and sewerage systems. Public open space may be shown. Master plans may include restrictions on building for periods not to exceed five years.

Master plans are not mandatory, but, if prepared, they must be approved by the Ministry of the Interior to be legally effective.

Because these planning requirements became effective only in 1959, few plans have been completed and approved, although many are in process.

Land Acquisition

Laws fixing public powers of land acquisition influence the location and form of urban development. Existing laws—or their implementation—have not proved adequate to the task of restraining the price of land in the path of development or of securing development in accordance with plans. Recognizing this, the national government created a committee to study legal reforms. Comments here on proposed changes are taken from the report of this committee.[16]

Finland's practices of municipal land acquisition in advance of development and municipal land ownership originated when Finland was part of Sweden. When the king of Sweden decided to found a city, he would issue a royal charter expropriating all land needed for the city, donating it to the newly formed city corporation, and stipulating that the city could never sell any of the land except to raise funds to buy more land. Under this system, city development in Sweden and Finland occurred on municipally owned land. Usually persons developing city land were granted one-hundred-year leases, although sometimes a city sold land.

Some years ago the law requiring reinvestment in land of all proceeds from the sale of municipally owned land was abrogated. Municipalities still are barred from using capital income for current expenses, however, and many continue to use at least part of their income from land sales and leases for further land acquisition. Today, on the average, cities own about 30 percent of their undeveloped land, although there is considerable variation from city to city. The government has proposed that municipalities buy land for future housing development ten years in advance of need. The government further recommends that this land be leased rather than sold for development.

While endorsing the policy of land acquisition in advance of development, many municipalities are limited in their action by lack of funds. Although a loan program has been recommended, at present the national government provides no loans or grants for this purpose and, compared with many other countries, contributes little to the municipal budget. Therefore, while many cities and towns have active land-buying programs, the extent of their purchases is limited. As the chairman of the Helsinki Regional Planning Agency said when endorsing greater public land acquisition: "If the cities and the counties have bought enough land to offer to builders before the need for the land arises, and have had the chance to provide the land with pipes and streets, lights and schools, so there is ample opportunity for private persons who wish to build one-family houses or for contractors who would like to build 1,000 one-family houses or apartments, then land values are kept at a much healthier level."[17]

The standard price of land in areas of Helsinki planned for multi-story housing is from five to ten dollars per square foot of permitted floor area. Even though the city makes some of its land available for housing at prices well below this, its price levels have not influenced the free market. The city of Turku sells land for low-cost housing at its acquisition cost plus the cost of building roads and utility lines; land for industry is sometimes sold below cost to encourage industry to locate there.

The Planning and Building Act gives cities and towns some powers to expropriate land, but these are seldom exercised, because of municipal fears of high condemnation awards and slow judicial process. By law, the owner of land covered by a town plan may be directed to develop his land in accordance with the plan. If, after seven years, he has failed to do so, he may be expropriated. There are additional instances in which the municipality may expropriate to promote specified building activity. On expropriation the municipality is liable for the current market value of the land taken, but it is not yet clear whether the compensation includes the value added to the land by virtue of the use designated in the plan. The amount of compensation due is determined by a board of three: one person appointed by the condemnor, one appointed by the condemnee, and a neutral person. The board's award may be appealed to a court.

Municipalities are responsible for the construction of roads, utility lines, and community facilities such as schools, municipal offices, water and sewage treatment plants, and recreation areas. In addition, most hospitals are municipally owned. To acquire land for such facilities, municipalities may expropriate within the area of the town plan, paying current market value. For streets, up to 20 percent of an owner's land may be taken without compensation. Somewhere between 25 and 50 percent of the cost of street and sewerage construction is recovered from landowners served by these facilities, the exact amount being fixed by the municipal government. In some large developments such as Tapiola, the developer rather than the municipality has provided the infrastructure.

Local governments are legally authorized to engage directly in housing construction or to grant loans therefor, but with the exception of some of the larger cities they do not usually do so.

The recent report of the Government Committee on Land Supply and Land Prices advocates amendment of the Planning and Building Act to authorize cities and towns to prohibit construction until a transportation and utility network has been built; the power already exists in rural municipalities. Property owners would not be entitled to compensation for denial of permission to build prior to construction of the infrastructure.

The Role of the Private Entrepreneur

Despite Finland's history of municipal landownership, much current urban development is occurring on privately owned land. Most construction, whether on public or private land, is carried out by private entrepreneurs.

The Private Landowner

Historically, Finnish landowners, both urban and rural, were accustomed to public restrictions on their use of the land. In the period after World War I, however, they began to exercise greater dominion over when and how they would build. Today, there is a reaction against arbitrary private land-use decisions, and public agencies from the national to the municipal level are seeking means to assure implementation of their plans. As one planner commented: "Private land ownership is one of the greatest problems in the planning field. The building law hasn't given enough means to deal with a private landowner who is unwilling to go along with the plans."[18] And as another said: "The old, traditional, tight controls of the government or the crown were a very good thing for the most part, particularly as they affected city building. To protect the rights of all property owners, you must have tight regulation; otherwise one speculator, by bad development, can steal his neighbor's rights. If I misuse my car, not much harm is done, but if I misuse my farm the harm can last for many centuries."[19]

Land on the urban fringe usually changes hands two or three years prior to development, with the farmer selling to the developer. Then, if as is often the case there is no completed, applicable plan, the developer will prepare his own plan and present it to the muncipality and to the regional planning commission (if any) for approval. Here the crucial factor is whether the public officials will choose to exert their power in critical review of the plan; if they do, the plan may be rejected, modified, or delayed in execution, depending on which decision seems proper from the over-all planning perspective.

If a completed plan is in force, the landowner may act in accord with it or seek changes. Should the plan deny the landowner a reasonable return from his land, he can demand that the government expropriate him. It is not yet clear, however, whether agricultural use yields a "reasonable return" for urban fringe land or whether compensation will be based on agricultural or development value.

The Private Developer

Although some municipalities act as developers, the bulk of development is carried out by private enterprise, a substantial segment of which is non-profit. Industries often plan and develop housing for their workers, particularly when an industry locates in a small or medium-sized community where an inadequate stock of housing exists.

Whether the developer is an industry or a commercial builder, a profit or non-profit enterprise, and national or local in scope, it is likely to be organized as a joint-stock company or a cooperative.

Cooperatives are common throughout Finland and serve many functions. Frequently a national cooperative organization includes housing as one of its activities. The central office of the cooperative has a staff able to advise local affiliates on housing development schemes, but the local organizations are autonomous and locally initiated. Membership in housing cooperatives may include the central cooperative, the local offshoot, the municipality, and local industry.[20]

The joint-stock company issues shares entitling purchasers to a house or apartment in a development. The shares are sold before, during, or after construction, depending on whether a commercial builder or the shareholders themselves are sponsoring the housing. Shareholders may rent or sell their housing freely, but when the dwelling is offered for sale the joint-stock company has the right to purchase it at the offering price.

Planning in the Helsinki Region

A short description of planning in the Helsinki region, as carried out by the city of Helsinki and by the Helsinki Regional Planning Agency, will provide the setting for a detailed exposition of the development of Tapiola as a new, satellite community within the region.

City Planning

The city of Helsinki was founded by a Swedish king in the sixteenth century. It is built on a peninsula, with water to the west, south, and east serving as a natural divider of urban and suburban development. Causeways link the peninsula to land to the west and east, as seen in Map II-2.

The first city plan dates from the early 1800s and was occasioned by the need to rebuild the city following a disastrous fire. Since Finland was then under Russian control, it was the czar who chose the planner and the architect, J. A. Ehrenstrom and Carl Ludwig Engel. Engel, a German architect, also was engaged by the czar to design buildings for Turku and for central Leningrad. Ehrenstrom and Engel's design for Helsinki was that of a neoclassic town and included a broad esplanade and a forum with administrative buildings dominated by a Lutheran cathedral. Construction was of brick and wood, painted white and pastel shades. These light colors gave rise to the description of Helsinki as the White City of the North. Today this neoclassic core is occupied in large part by national ministries; see Figure II-3.

Plans for the western part of Helsinki were developed in the late nineteenth century, then augmented early in the twentieth cenutry. The 1911 plan included the broad park area which now extends from Töölo Bay north to the city limits. As early as 1915 and 1918, Eliel Saarinen's plans proposed development of independent suburban communities, separated from each other and from the city by open space. Birger Brunila's plan, drawn up after World War II, followed this concept. Much of the planning for the suburbs became planning for Helsinki proper when in 1946 the city annexed land, extending its area from 7,300 acres to almost forty thousand acres (see Map II-3). More than half of the annexed land already belonged to the city, and some preliminary planning had taken place prior to annexation.

The current general plan for Helsinki, dated 1960 and designed for a population of 700,000 stresses proposals for the newly annexed areas. This plan may be modified to reduce the target population for the city to 600,000. In 1968 an unofficial agreement to this effect was reached by the Helsinki City Planning Commission and the Helsinki Regional Planning Agency. A plan for the center city was made in 1954 and is being restudied by Alvar Aalto (see Figure II-4). Under this plan, the Ehrenstrom-Engel center would be retained as a historic monument, but the city's center would be shifted to the site of Parliament and the railroad station.

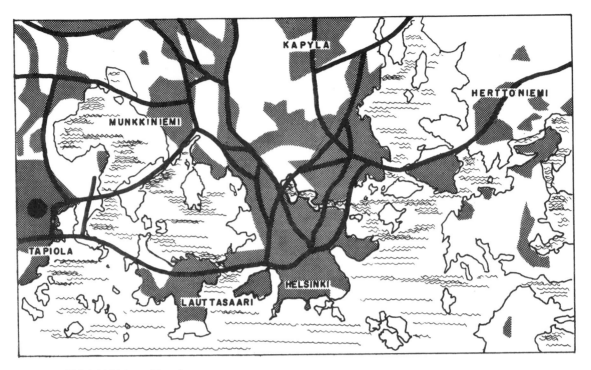

Map II-2. Helsinki Metropolitan Area

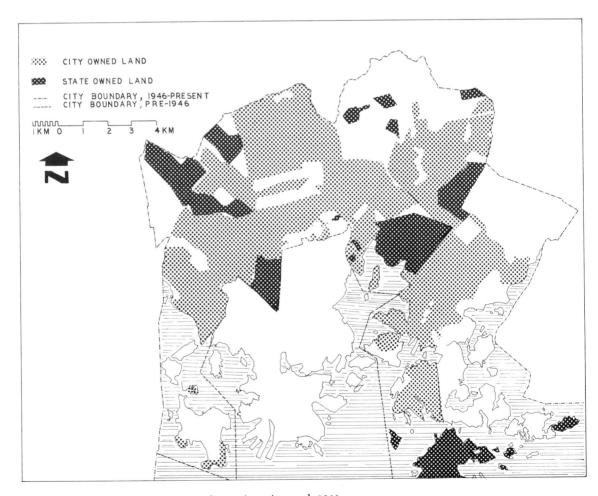

Map II-3. Helsinki: Public Landownership in Area Annexed, 1946

Figure II-3. Senate Square, Helsinki

Under the general plan, approximately 41 percent of the city would be used for residential, commercial, and public structures, 41 percent for open space, 9 percent for industry and the harbor, and 9 percent for all other uses (see Map II-4).

Transportation within the city and region would be by a system of circumferential and radial highways and by subway. Subway stations would be spaced so that pedestrians would not need to walk more than 1,500 feet to reach their homes. Each station would serve 12,500 people. As in Stockholm, the highest-density residential development would be clustered around transit stops; the land within 0.3 miles of the station would have a density of 60 persons per acre. Most of these people would live in multi-story housing. Densities in some older areas of the city would be as high as 360 persons per acre. Stores to meet daily needs would be within 800 feet of all residents of high-density areas, and local centers would be adjacent to all transit stops. All industrial expansion would be in the outlying portions of the city.

There would be 1,050 square feet of open space per city resident, of which 650 square feet per person would be available for active public use. A network of ski trails would lead through the greenbelts and parks to the open country.

Water must be brought from increasingly distant sources. Sewerage systems now serve only 200,000 people; eight treatment plants are planned to provide service city-wide.

Regional Planning

In Finland the need for regional planning is particularly urgent. Like other European countries and the United States, Finland is undergoing a shift from

Figure II-4.
Alvar Aalto's Plan
for a New Center
in Helsinki

HELSINGIN KESKUSTA

HELSINKI,   18.11.1964
ALVAR AALTO, ARKKITEHTI.

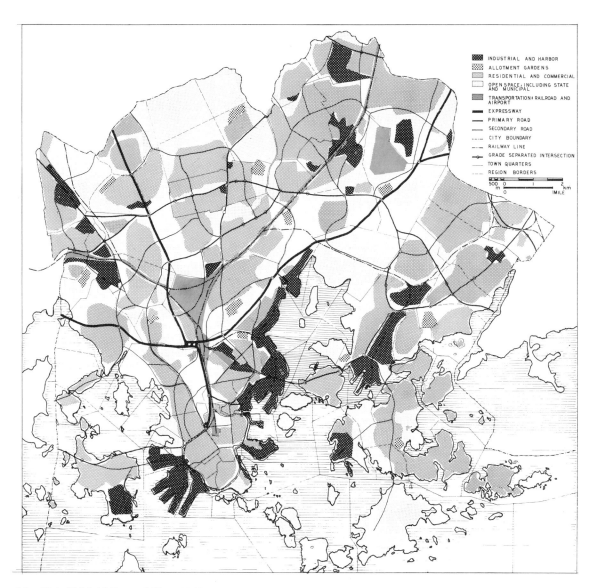

Map II-4. Helsinki General Plan, 1960

agricultural to industrial and service employment, a rapid urbanization of the population, and a rise in income levels. These changes were delayed in Finland by postwar resettlement and reparations problems; now, for the country's economic health, they must be encompassed more rapidly than elsewhere. To date, the dominance of rural interests in Parliament has resulted in a lack of emphasis on urbanization problems. Regional plans, built on decisions as to the form and location of future urbanization, must be developed for areas of population out-migration and for those of in-migration. Heikki von Hertzen sums up the 1980 national planning problem as follows: "In the next fifteen years, a nation of 5 million will have to be able to build dwellings for 900,000 people and provide them with work, schools and cultural centres and all this will have to be placed in urban communities."[21]

For Uusimaa, the forty-six-muncipality province which includes Helsinki, the problems are the most acute of any area in Finland. Already, 20 percent of the Finnish people live in Uusimaa; in 1964 this was 686,000 people. Projections indicate that 75 percent of the population growth between 1960 and 1990 will occur in Uusimaa, and that by 1990 90 percent of the region's people will be urbanized. In 1961 the Ministry of the Interior directed that the voluntary planning agency for eleven municipalities of the province (including Helsinki) be supplanted by an official planning agency. It is anticipated that a plan for the region will be completed in 1970; portions of the plan already have been finished.

The Emerging Plan

Concepts for density, industrial location, transportation, utilities, and open space have been formulated.

The planned over-all residential density for the portions of the region which remain to be developed is thirty persons per acre. Pressure for densities two or three times this high is being exerted by large developers who have invested in open land. To date, however, this pressure is being resisted.

In theory, no more industrial expansion is to occur in the already developed areas of Helsinki. To divert current industrial demand from these areas, firms buying sites for industrial expansion are required to provide housing for at least 25 percent of the additional manpower they will employ. Some industrial developers have sought permission to fill parts of the harbor and build there, but the Helsinki City Council firmly has resisted their pressure, asserting that not an inch of the bay is to be filled. This attitude is characteristic of the respect for the natural environment shown by planners and government officials in the city and region of Helsinki. Given a beautiful site for a metropolis, care is taken to preserve the water, the rocks, the trees, as well as to assure the people of easy access to them.

Transportation planning has come to be recognized as an increasingly important need. At present there is only one car for every nine or ten people, but car ownership is expected to double in the next five years. Thus far, most of the region's population has settled along the two major rail lines, but postwar highway construction of a ring-radial pattern is contributing to a more diffuse distribution. A circumferential about ten miles from the center city is under construction, and planners hope that it will attract industry to nearby locations. Construction of a subway for the region is expected to begin sometime in the next ten years.

Some of the transportation planning principles that are being incorporated in the regional plan are as follows: (1) To avoid street traffic and promote safe play in residential areas, cul-de-sac and loop streets should be used. (2) Housing often can be designed to concentrate parking in lots, and to locate all residents within 1,000 feet of the lots. (3) Neighborhoods of 6,000–10,000 people should be served by ring roads and by internal pedestrian paths which link homes to schools and shops. (4) Homes also should be within 1,000 feet of a transit system, either a system internal to the community with a link to an external system, or an external system with stops in the community. (5) While ample space should be provided for expressways, road networks, and parking, design emphasis in planning should be on short pedestrian distances and on easy access to public transportation, be it bus or train.[22]

Assurance of an adequate domestic water supply for the future poses a problem. Despite the profusion of lakes in Finland, most in the vicinity of Helsinki are too shallow to draw upon and there is little ground water. The current supply, for the region as well as the city, comes from the nearby but small Vantaa River; since 1965, water from Lake Hiidenvesi, thirty-five miles from Helsinki, has been used to augment the supply. By 1975, water will have to be piped from central Finland to the Helsinki region.

Sewage disposal is another growing problem. By law, sewage must be treated, but in fact less than half of the region's effluent now is treated.

Single-family houses are not required to connect to a sewerage system unless they are part of dense development. As previously noted, there is no consistent definition of dense development,[23] so it is difficult to generalize as to when sewerage will be required. However, whatever the minimum connection requirements, the region needs and is planning for construction of further treatment plants.

Open space, both public and private, is valued highly. A completed portion of the regional plan—that for part of the municipality of Espoo—indicated that a substantial area would be kept open. Much of the land would remain in private ownership, subject to taxation, with the owner denied development permission. This land also would be subject to some public use because, by law, the public may go on private land to picnic, fish, and ride horseback. Public purchase would be needed for beaches; existing public beaches are crowded and private beaches are being developed rapidly. Planners for the Uusimaa region state the belief that it will be politically feasible to deny permission to develop to owners of land that has considerable development value and to require public recreational access to the land for a steadily growing population, all without compensation. One wonders whether the comparatively slow pace of urbanization in the past may not have given a false impression of the pressures for development which will be exerted in the future and the consequent strength of land-use controls which will be required to counter these pressures.

The Urban Location Question

While it generally is accepted that, national decentralization policy notwithstanding, Uusimaa will attract most of the projected population increase between now and 1990, there is a division of opinion as to where the newcomers should live. Location, size, and composition of the future urban community all are at issue. Among the possibilities under discussion are continued expansion of the Helsinki suburbs, expansion of selected existing towns other than Helsinki, construction of new towns, or a combination of these approaches.

There does seem to be general accord that the city of Helsinki should not grow further, that, given the population and size of Finland, the principal city already is large enough. This evaluation of Helsinki's size in relation to the remainder of Finland contrasts with the approach in Sweden; there the economists and planners are looking to Sweden's inter-European role. From this viewpoint, they want Stockholm to continue growing so that it will be, and will remain, competitive with other major cities of Northern Europe, including Copenhagen (and the future Copenhagen-Malmö complex) and Hamburg.

Some consideration has been given to a proposal to reduce pressure on Helsinki by transferring the national capital to central Finland. Such action seems highly unlikely. Instead, the government probably will intensify its efforts to attract people to areas other than Uusimaa by concentrating new public facilities in several cities already large enough to have the potential to act as urban magnets.

Within Uusimaa it is inevitable that there will be further growth in the Helsinki suburbs. The major questions to be resolved, however, are whether government resources are to be directed to the stimulation of growth of existing towns, to the establishment of new towns, or to both; how many such urban centers the population and economy dictate; and what measure of government resources should be committed to the development of these urban centers. It is accepted that the possibility of creating a strong economic base is a major criterion either for expanding existing towns or for building new towns. Employment, as well as housing, must be provided. Residents may go to Helsinki for special events or to sightsee in the national capital, but their home communities are to be self-sufficient for their daily lives. To date, officials of the national government have indicated an interest in expanding existing towns. The Helsinki Regional Planning Agency proposes that existing low-density development be provided with greatly improved public services so that the density can be increased while, at the same time, the remaining open space near existing urbanized land can be preserved. Many rural segments of the Uusimaa population, particularly those who are Swedish-speaking, oppose any regional planning because it imports recommendations for development of their areas. Yet ". . . conditions of urbanization make it utterly impossible to defer to parochial local interests if there is to be economic development, which means urban development."[24]

Mr. Heikki von Hertzen is the author of the Seven Towns' Plan (Map II-5). This plan calls for forceful government measures to limit the growth of the Helsinki area and to direct population growth largely to the Uusimaa coast. All of the seven towns except Tapiola would be independent communities, offering their residents jobs, homes, recreation, and cultural activities. Two would be new towns; the rest would be built as extensions to existing towns. According to the plan, if existing town centers were too small to accommodate the proposed target populations, twin towns with large centers might be built adjoining the existing towns. The population of each would range from 50,000 to 200,000. Open space would surround each of the towns and would constitute 90 percent of Uusimaa's land area. This open space ". . . should be placed under the protection of the law and kept as agricultural, forestry and recreational areas. The most beautiful, and culturally and historically most valuable places, could still be saved. These extensive green belts would have well-kept forests, cultivated land and miniature communities where old peasant, village and mill traditions could still be fostered."[25]

Land for the new towns at Espoo Bay and Porkkala already has been acquired by the Housing Foundation (Asuntosäätiö) and planning is well underway. The Swedish-speaking minority is powerful in this coastal area of Uusimaa, and opposition to the new towns has been voiced by those who fear that their inhabitants will be largely Finnish-speaking, thus altering the current political structure. While debate continues, industries are buying land at Porkkala and residential development has begun (see Figure II-5). The government still has the choice of fostering these new towns, directing its resources to other towns, or, through diffused decision-making, permitting development to occur in response to various private market pressures.

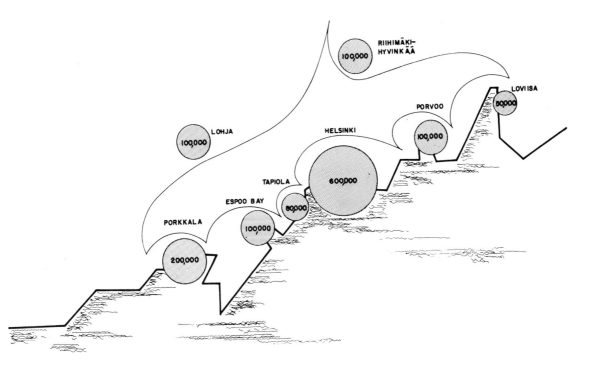

Map II-5. Seven Towns' Plan

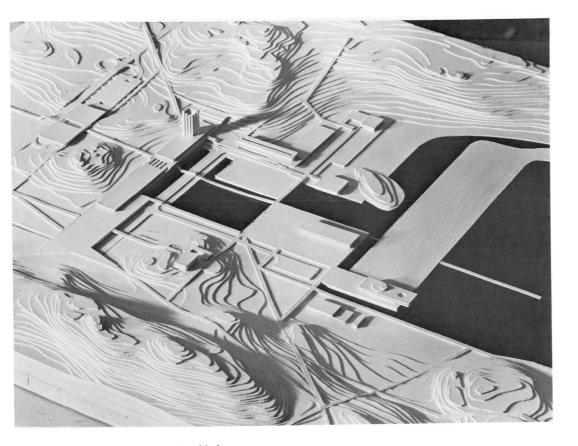

Figure II-5. The Proposed Port of Porkkala

Tapiola

Of all new towns and new communities, Tapiola is thought by many to be the most beautiful and most humane. Located in the Helsinki urban area, six miles west of the center city, Tapiola stands apart as a distinct, unique community which fosters a harmonious relationship between urban man and the natural environment (see Figure II-6).

Efforts have been made to plan Tapiola on a human scale, starting from man's individuality and need of contact with nature. The aesthetic values of nature, trees, and the original contours of the landscape have been retained wherever possible. In contrast to an urban milieu, in Tapiola nature predominates. Architecturally, buildings are a secondary factor. Streets have been kept to a minimum, and have to conform rigorously with the contours. The residents are to be provided with opportunities of outdoor life and work, gardening and exercise.[26]

Designed to provide homes for 17,000 people and jobs for half of the resident labor force, Tapiola, by size, location, and employment opportunities, is not independent of Helsinki and so is more accurately categorized as a satellite new community than as a new town. In addition to respect for the natural environment, Tapiola is notable for the juxtaposition of housing of all types and prices, for the socioeconomic range of its population, for the high percentage of home ownership, and for having been created by non-profit private enterprise.

The Developer

The Family Welfare League acquired the site for Tapiola and then in 1951 brought together five additional welfare and trade organizations[27] to form the Housing Foundation. The foundation's goal is to contribute to relieving the housing shortage by planning and building modern communities that offer high standards of housing and amenities. From the start, Mr. Heikki von Hertzen, the Housing Foundation's managing director, has been its guiding force. Tapiola is the Housing Foundation's first community; it also has completed projects at Jyväskylä in central Finland and at Rovaniemi, the capital of Lapland. Other projects are underway at Oulu in northern Finland and at Porkkala and Espoo Bay in the Uusimaa region.

The Housing Foundation established a council to manage development at Tapiola. The council consists of one nominee of each of the Housing Foundation's six member organizations and nine technical specialists, including architects, engineers, sociologists, and bankers. It elects a board of seven, which meets weekly, and also chooses three directors, who head the operating departments at Tapiola. The managing director of the Housing Foundation

Figure II-6. Aerial View of Tapiola

is, in addition, chairman of the board and director of the Planning Department; this department is responsible for planning everything from the town design to individual buildings to landscaping to outdoor lighting fixtures. Another director heads the Technical Department, which sees to the implementation of the plans either through carrying out or through supervising construction. The third director is responsible for the Administrative Department.[28]

The Planning Department has relied heavily on private architects, who usually have been selected by competition. Initially there was a competition for the town center and northern neighborhood, then for residential clusters with mixed housing types, for separate buildings such as schools, day nurseries, and churches, and for single types of dwellings. More than twenty architects or architectural firms are represented at Tapiola. While the work of several architects is found in the same neighborhood, it is customary for buildings facing each other across a street to be designed by one architect; see, for example, Figures II-7 and II-8.

To assure the realization of its plans, the Housing Foundation prefers to design and construct buildings, then sell them. For about 80 percent of the construction this has been the method used. Alternatively, the Housing Foundation either sells a site and a site design or sells a site contingent upon the buyer's acceptance of design control.

Figure II-7. The Eastern Neighborhood: Chain Houses (Aulis Blomstedt, architect)

Figure II-8. The Eastern Neighborhood: Apartments (Aulis Blomstedt, architect)

The Concept

Espoo was chosen as the location for Tapiola because Housing Foundation officials judged that they would have greater planning freedom there than in Helsinki. In 1951 Espoo was a rural municipality, little urbanized, with few restrictive ordinances or regulations. Had a site in Helsinki been selected, it was anticipated that the novelty of much that was envisioned for Tapiola would have conflicted with the plans and implementing codes for the city. The Espoo officials "... were not very enthusiastic when we came over here. We told them that we would build a modern community here and would need streets, roads, and water. They did not oppose us, but they were not really interested. They gave us the freedom to do it ourselves, and we did. We built a modern community with streets, roads, water pipes, sewer lines and treatment plant, parks, flowers and even kindergartens."[29]

Site assembly was not a problem, because the 670-acre site had previously been held in only two tracts.

The principal aim of Tapiola's planners was to create a community for the enhancement of man. With this objective before them, the planners faced questions of density, community structure, housing type and mix, transportation, open space, community facilities, and employment possibilities.

A maximum density of thirty persons per acre was fixed; as built, the actual density at Tapiola is twenty-six persons per acre. As seen in Figure II-9, 56 percent of the site was retained in open space, 24 percent was allocated for housing, and 9 percent for roads, parking, and squares; the remaining 11 percent was designated for industry, commerce, and institutions. In form the community was divided into five parts: the town center to serve 30,000 people, including the 17,000 Tapiola residents and their neighbors from nearby suburban developments; the industrial zone, near the town center and buffered by open space from residences; and three neighborhoods, two of 5,000 people each and one of 7,000 people. Each neighborhood includes shops for weekly needs, a primary school, kindergarten, and youth center, and grocery stores within 250 yards of each dwelling (see Figure II-10). There is one excellent nursery school (Figure II-11), and more are needed.

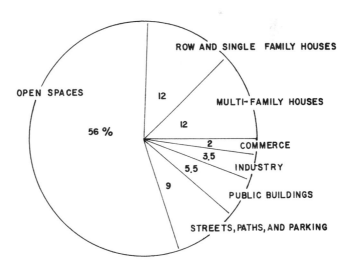

Figure II-9.
Tapiola Land
Distribution

All housing types, from high-rise towers to single-family houses, are mingled throughout the community, as seen in Figures II-12 and II-13. The mix of housing types provides variety, as well as high enough localized densities to support neighborhood shops, services, and central heating (see Figures II-14 and II-15). Units in the towers are small, in the expectation that single people, couples without children, and the elderly will live there. Fami-

Figure II-10. Western Neighborhood Center

Figure II-11. Nursery School (Aarne Ervi, architect)

lies with children live in walk-up apartments and in row or single-family houses, all with easy access to the outdoors. While the planners recognized that Finns prefer single-family houses, economic considerations precluded this for most of the housing. Had the housing been substantially single-family, the goal of creating a community in which people of all income levels can afford to live could not have been realized.

Another of the leading principles in the planning of Tapiola has been the consistent placing of multi-story buildings alternately with low buildings. As far as I know, this is to some extent rather a revolutionary solution. We all know the general opinion held almost all over the world is that one-family housing estates and higher multi-story buildings must be kept in separate areas. This old rule has been broken in Tapiola. The purpose of this type of planning is quite clear: with the help of low buildings and private gardens a certain spaciousness is achieved as well as variety between multi-story buildings. As a counter service it has been possible to equip one-family houses, terrace houses, and row houses with the same facilities and servicing as multi-story buildings, which were the only privileged ones before. Thus, these two different ways of building benefit each other and make it possible to create an urban milieu, an urban environment with humanity, variety, and beauty.[30]

A radial expressway leading out from Helsinki has an interchange near Tapiola and thus provides easy access to the town center and to the neighborhoods. Within Tapiola, arterial roads connect the neighborhoods and the

Figure II-12. The Eastern Neighborhood: Single-Family and Row Houses, Walk-up and High-rise Apartments (Alvar Aalto, architect of high-rise apartments)

Figure II-13. The Western Neighborhood: Row Houses and Walk-up and High-rise Apartments

Figure II-14. Modest Income Apartments with Convenience Store

Figure II-15. Nearby Luxury Housing (Kaija and Heikki Siren, architects)

Figure II-16. The Secondary School, Pedestrian and Bicycle Paths

Figure II-17. Pedestrian Walkway Linking the Town Center to the Western
Neighborhood

Figure II-18. Apartments at Home with Nature (Viljo Revell, architect)

town center, passing around rather than through the center. Neighborhood roads are designed as loops or dead-end streets to minimize through traffic. Pedestrian and cycle paths, located apart from the roads, link all portions of the community and often are the most direct routes from point to point (see Figures II-16 and II-17).

Open space accounts for 56 percent of Tapiola's land area. Ski trails, walks, gardens, playfields, and children's play areas abound. Wherever possible, the natural topography, the rocks, birches, and evergreens have been left untouched, as seen in Figure II-18.

Among the community facilities provided by the Housing Foundation are laundries, saunas, recreation centers, day nurseries, and large, heated garages. There is but one smokestack in Tapiola—that of the power plant, which provides heat, hot water, and electricity for the entire community. The plant is located in the industrial area, which was planned for and accommodates clean, quiet industry. These details are noted on Map II-6.

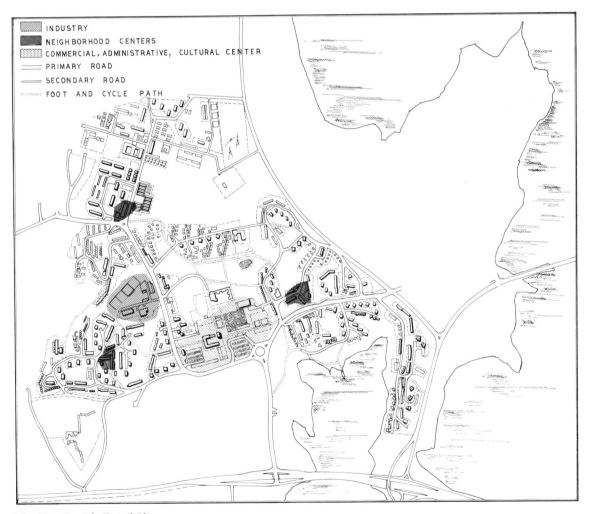

Map II-6. Tapiola Detail Plan

Tapiola Today

As of March, 1965, residential construction at Tapiola was almost complete; 4,380 of a planned 4,575 dwellings had been finished. Industrial and commercial construction was not so far advanced; firms employed only 2,300 persons, as compared to a future anticipated employment of 5,650 persons. Recreational, educational, and cultural facilities were well along.

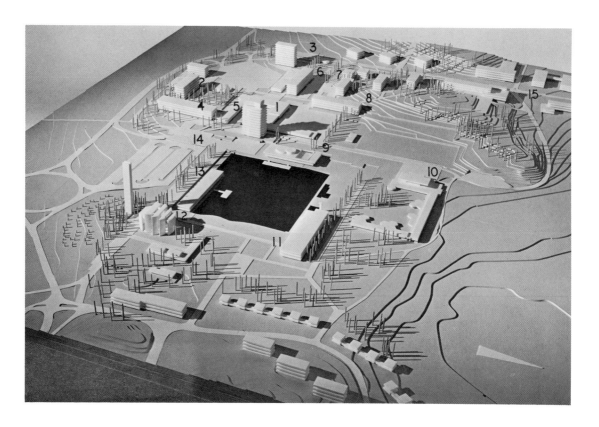

Figure II-19.
Model of the Town
Center (Aarne Ervi,
planner)

1–3 Offices
 4 Administration
    building
 5 Shops
 6 Department
    store
 7 Health clinic
 8 Gymnasium
 9 Theater,
    concert hall,
    and library
10 High school
11 Swimming pool
12 Church
13 Hotel
14 Information
    center
15 Vocational
    school

The Town Center

Aarne Ervi won the 1953 competition for the town center by submitting a plan to convert an existing gravel pit into a two-and-one-half-acre pool, and to make this pool the focal point for the public and commercial buildings of the center (see Figure II-19). Already completed at the town center are a shopping area and a thirteen-story office building, on the top floors of which are a terrace café and a first-class restaurant (see Figures II-20 through II-22). The restaurant serves excellent food, and in the evenings an orchestra provides music for dancing.

A building housing a magnificent indoor swimming pool (Figure II-23), plus a sauna and snack bar, is owned by the town of Espoo and is open to all Espoo residents. The site for the building was donated by the Housing Foundation. The secondary school, which accommodates 900 students, is nearby. A church, youth center, and ice skating rink also are part of the town center. A second office building has been completed, and a hotel, library, theater, concert hall, and public health center will follow.

Housing

The Housing Foundation has built dwellings which are as spacious as possible. For the 80 percent of the housing which is ARAVA financed, however, this has meant building up to ARAVA maximums but no larger. Under the ARAVA program, single-family houses run 1,075 square feet, semi-detached houses 935 square feet. The three- and four-story walk-up apartments commonly have 935 square feet for four rooms, kitchen, and bath; 625–775 square feet for three rooms, kitchen, and bath; and 500–600 square feet for two rooms, kitchen, and bath. The efficiency and two-room tower apartments range from 260 to 365 square feet. The rest of the housing is both larger and more expensive.

Figure II-20. The Town Center: Shops and Office Tower

Figure II-21. In the Town Center

Figure II-22. The Office Tower by Night

Figure II-23. The Swimming Pool

Visually, Tapiola seems a community of many row and detached houses, and there are, in fact, more such structures than apartment buildings (see Figures II-24 through II-27). However, in 1962, 87.1 percent of the dwelling units were apartments (see Table II-7). Two rooms plus kitchen is the most prevalent dwelling size; in 1962, 79 percent of the dwellings had three rooms or less, plus kitchen or kitchenette (see Table II-8).

Table II-7.
Distribution of Housing Types in Tapiola, 1962

Housing Type	No.	Sq. Ft.	Dwelling Units	Percentage of Dwelling Units
High-rise tower	14	1,426,000	698	24.0
Walk-up tower	41	1,696,000	757	26.8
Walk-up multi-story	37	2,884,000	1,021	36.3
Semi-detached	33	961,000	228	8.1
Single-family or two-family	107	486,000	108	3.8
Total	232	7,453,000	2,812	99.0

SOURCE: Jorma Aaltonen, comp., *Tapiola 62* (Tapiola, 1963).

Table II-8.
Rooms per Dwelling, Tapiola, 1962

Dwelling Type	Number	Percent
1 room and kitchen or kitchenette	643	22.9
2 rooms and kitchen or kitchenette	993	35.3
3 rooms and kitchen or kitchenette	582	20.7
4 rooms and kitchen or kitchenette	397	14.1
5 rooms and kitchen or kitchenette	173	6.1
6 rooms and kitchen or larger	24	0.9
Total	2,812	100.0

SOURCE: Jorma Aaltonen, comp., *Tapiola 62* (Tapiola, 1963).

The People

Tapiola is a young town, with a higher percentage of children than either center-city or suburban Helsinki. For a comparison of populations by age, see Table II-9.

Table II-9.
Age Distribution in the Helsinki Area

Age (years)	Helsinki, 1955		Tapiola, 1959
	Center City	Suburbs	
Birth–6	9%	14%	20%
7–14	13	14	17
15–29	19	24	20
30–40	23	25	32
45–64	28	18	10
65 and over	8	5	1
	100	100	100

SOURCE: Jorma Aaltonen, comp., *Tapiola 62* (Tapiola, 1963).

Figure II-24. High-rise Apartments in the Eastern Neighborhood Center, with Floor Plan

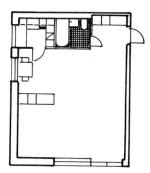

Completion date	1954
Housing type	1 room, kitchenette
Sq. ft.	486
Avg. purchase price	$7,568
Avg. down payment	$1,700
Avg. rent, 1965	$45
Architect	Aarne Ervi

Figure II-25. Walk-up Apartments for Small Families, with Floor Plan

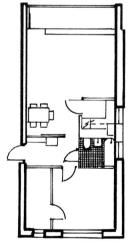

Completion date	1954
Housing type	2 rooms, kitchenette
Sq. ft.	605
Avg. purchase price	$9,177
Avg. down payment	$2,512
Avg. rent, 1965	$55
Architect	Markus Tavio

Figure II-26. Single-Family Chain House, with Floor Plan

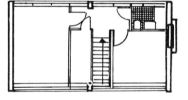

Completion date   1954
Housing type   5 rooms, kitchen,
                       and sauna
Sq. ft.   1,048
Avg. purchase price $16,871
Avg. down payment $6,141
Avg. rent, 1965 $104
Architect   Aulis Blomstedt

(Room at far right belongs to next house)

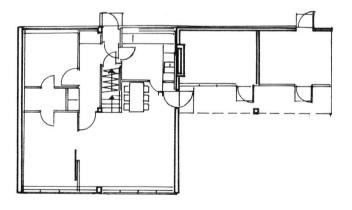

Figure II-27. Single-Family Row Houses, with Floor Plan

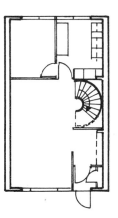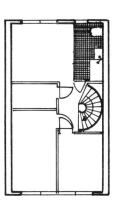

Completion date	1955
Housing type	5 rooms, kitchen
Sq. ft.	929
Avg. purchase price	$10,236
Avg. down payment	$2,779
Avg. rent, 1965	$58
Architects	Kaija and Heikki Siren

The town has succeeded in attracting a mixture of socioeconomic groups, although the more highly paid and more highly educated groups are represented in greater numbers at Tapiola than in the Finnish population as a whole. In 1959 the distribution was as follows:

Social Group I (36 percent): Persons with a university degree; most of the people practicing a free trade; persons in leading positions, etc.

Social Group II (26 percent): Persons carrying on a technical profession; foremen; independent small-scale enterprisers; artisans; office staff doing independent work, etc.

Social Groups III and IV (38 percent): III, other office staff, craftsmen with less than two years' training, shop assistants, tram collectors, waiters, etc.; IV, Craftsmen's assistants, auxiliary workers, common laborers, charwomen, housemaids, etc.

Today about 55 percent of the residents are white-collar workers and 45 percent are blue-collar workers.

A cross-section of apartment owners in two ARAVA-financed buildings in the northern neighborhood of Tapiola shows the range of incomes and occupations typical in these apartments (see Table II-10).[31] It also indicates that many Finnish women hold full-time jobs. As Mr. von Hertzen has said:

We have succeeded in getting a university professor to live side by side with skilled workers without any problems at all. When you put people who have different standards of living together, there are three possibilities: the environment you create can be that of the higher standard people or the lower or something in between. We immediately tried to make the environment for all people, even in the low income groups, the same as for the highest, and we succeeded. It was an amazing and inspiring thing to observe how soon the lowest groups accepted the highest standards.[32]

Table II-10.
Cross-Section of Apartment Owners by Occupation and Income, Tapiola, 1964

Occupation of Head of House	Monthly Salary		Apartment Type	Square Feet
	Husband	Wife		
Telephone fitter	$208	$161	3 rooms and kitchen	691
Painter	264	109	2 rooms and kitchen	540
Telegraph clerk	169	169	3 rooms and kitchen	664
Slag roaster	205	109	2 rooms and kitchen	540
Pipe fitter	310	—	4 rooms and kitchen	815
Businessman	496	—	4 rooms and kitchen	815
Ex–lieutenant colonel	409	—	3 rooms and kitchen	734
Railway official	211	234	1 room and kitchen	356
Office assistant	131	—	1 room and kitchen	356
Mechanic	186	93	2 rooms and kitchen	562

Employment

Employment opportunities have developed more slowly than housing, but now all sites for industry have been sold or leased, new office construction is underway, and further institutional building soon will occur; many new jobs will be created. Of Tapiola's 17,000 target population, it is expected that 7,500, or 47 percent, will be employed. The Housing Foundation estimates that 6,100 jobs will be available in Tapiola; theoretically this means that there would be jobs for 81 percent of the resident job-seekers. However, because Tapiola is part of the Helsinki urban area, it is reasonable to anticipate that many Tapiola residents will work elsewhere and that many Tapiola jobs will be filled by non-residents. The figures in Table II-11 indicate recent and projected job distribution at Tapiola.

Table II-11.
Job Distribution at Tapiola

Type of Employment	As of 3/15/65	When Tapiola is Completed
Office	580	1,800
Industry	520	2,000
Stores	340	650
Other (schools, social institutions, hotels, restaurants, etc.)	860	1,200
Total	2,300	5,650

SOURCE: Heikki von Hertzen, "Planning, Design and Management of Tapiola."

Financing Development

The Housing Foundation began its program of land acquisition, planning, and development in Tapiola with no national or local government support.

Espoo, then a rural municipality, had done little planning and could not afford to provide the services usually furnished by a municipality to new urban development. While this situation enabled the Housing Foundation to plan Tapiola as desired, it also imposed on the Housing Foundation the added burden of financing such services as roads, streets, water and sewerage systems, and electricity. These costs had to be recovered from the sale and rental of land and buildings.

The Housing Foundation had almost no capital when it launched Tapiola. Yet $625,000 was needed at once for acquisition of the 670-acre site. ". . . Not a single bank wanted to help us. The plan was too utopian and the price which we were going to pay for the land exhorbitantly high. None of the bankers was willing to take part in an action like this. But we wanted to get over the difficulties, and we wanted to break through. Ultimately we succeeded in getting the necessary purchase money from a private source—at first for two months only."[33]

In the beginning only short-term commercial bank loans (2 months at 7.5 percent interest) could be obtained. After about a year and a half ordinary bank loans were granted. During the first two years, before any income was received from the sale of building sites, it was necessary to build roads and utility lines, pay staff, and pay interest on the loans. After three or four years the state made a thirteen-year loan at 3 percent interest. This loan was the first of its type made by the government and was granted only after cabinet approval.

The total cost of building Tapiola has not been calculated. It is estimated to be in the range of $62 million, of which land totaled 1 percent, utility and street costs 7 percent, and the town center about 7 percent.[34]

Income is derived from the sale of building sites. The maximum price for land on which ARAVA-financed housing is to be built is set by ARAVA. Eighty percent of the housing at Tapiola has been constructed with the support of ARAVA, and this has established maximum price limits on much of the land available for sale.

Building costs for houses in Tapiola have been lower than the national average for ARAVA-supported housing, even though the cost of the infrastructure and the community buildings is included at Tapiola.

Financing Home Ownership

More than 90 percent of Tapiola residents own their houses or apartments. Demand for all types of housing is great; currently there are twenty times as many applicants for rental housing as there are units available. Recently, 500 units of ARAVA-aided housing were offered for sale; they were snapped up in two hours' time.

The housing companies at Tapiola which have relied on ARAVA financing usually have received 40 percent of their land acquisition and construction funds from ARAVA, 40 percent from a commercial lender, and 20 percent from the prospective owners as a down payment. The Housing Foundation, in cooperation with the banks which are financing housing production at Tapiola, offers a special savings program to enable people to accumulate funds for a down payment. Twice yearly the Housing Foundation advertises that the banks will accept applications for a given number of savers and states that houses or apartments will be available for the savers at the termination of the savings period, which runs for three or four years. Applicants agree to save a specified amount monthly in an interest-bearing account. Until recent years Finland has had virtually full employment, and it has been within the earning power of most people to save the necessary down payment.

The Housing Foundation Board decides whose application to buy or rent at Tapiola shall be accepted. The applicant's need for housing and the Housing Foundation's aim of achieving a broad socioeconomic distribution are the principal criteria in making this decision. ARAVA has a voice in the selection of occupants for housing which it helps to finance. The Housing Foundation must submit to ARAVA a list of applicants, including under each name such items as family size, age, income, and need for housing. ARAVA then will specify space standards per family and permitted income ranges.

Administration   Services at Tapiola are provided both by the town of Espoo and by three internal organizations called supply companies. Espoo furnishes to Tapiola residents the same services it provides to all other residents of the town. These include firemen, police, schools, and a contribution for roads. The additional services offered at Tapiola—such as central heat, gardens, a nursery school, and street lights—are financed by separate taxes paid to the supply companies.

The supply companies were established by the Housing Foundation and initially were under its control. As its dwellings are completed, each of the housing companies becomes a shareholder in the supply companies. Gradually, full control of the supply companies is transferred from the Housing Foundation to the housing company shareholders so that, when Tapiola is finished, the Housing Foundation will have no further management responsibilities. Owners of single-family houses enjoy the services provided by the supply companies but are not shareholders.

The supply companies own the heating plants, the "Children's House," the central garages, and some business properties. They supply all buildings with heat, hot water, and electricity; maintain the open space, play areas, flowers, shrubs, and lawns; collect trash and garbage; maintain the sewerage system and the roads; plow snow; cover the cost of welfare services to children and young people; underwrite rentals for clubs and hobby rooms; and act as financial agents for the housing companies.

There are three major sources of revenue for the supply companies. For services provided, all home owners and all owners of rental units pay a general tax, calculated at a fixed rate, on the size of their dwelling and a heating charge based on the amount of heat consumed. In 1965 the general tax rate was ninety cents per square yard per month. The housing companies pay the supply companies for handling their finances, which include bookkeeping, rent collection, and payment of bills. A further source of income is the rents paid to the supply companies for lease of the commercial properties they own.

Conclusion

Tapiola may be the most successful new community yet built. What are the elements of this success, and what is the background against which it was achieved?

Tapiola's success has been people's response to it. People want to live there; they enjoy it. No group in Finnish society is foreclosed from the possibility of living in Tapiola, and all groups pursue the possibility. Tapiola offers them humanity and convenience, modernity and comfort, urbanity and nature, people and tranquillity, taste and modest cost, variety and cohesion. It is a setting for the enhancement of man's spirit. Yet, as its principal creator, Heikki von Hertzen, recognizes, Tapiola's success does not indicate that it should be a prototype for all future urban development. It is one model of a desirable urban environment for man. Many other models are needed to provide sufficient choice for all men.

Tapiola's achievements are all the more remarkable in the context of the financial austerity, governmental indifference, and national rigors which existed at its inception. Finland was just emerging from the crushing postwar burdens of resettlement and reparations. Money was tight, planning was rudimentary, and urbanization was a minor concern of the rural-dominated Parliament. Tapiola seemed an impossible vision and possibly not even a desirable one.

In addition to the intangibles of unwavering determination and of moral support from the Housing Foundation's six-member organizations, Tapiola initially was the product of short-term, high-interest commercial loans, the government's ARAVA second-mortgage program, imaginative planning aided by freedom from local land-use restrictions, and competitions from which to choose the work of Finland's best architects. Could it also have been built by a profit-making enterprise or by the government? The essential elements are vision and will power. Given these, the greater the need for profit, the less the opportunity (under stringent circumstances such as existed at Tapiola) of providing a community which all sectors of the population can afford. Government as the entrepreneur would have had less flexibility, but it might have counterbalanced this with the ability to buy land more cheaply and to establish less costly financing terms.

What is the likelihood in Finland for reproductions of Tapiola or for the construction of new and different forms of urban communities? The national government's awareness of the problems of urbanization and of the need for legislative and planning reforms has grown rapidly, and far greater support for creative urban solutions can be expected. Evidence of this is the current government proposal for public land acquisition ten years in advance of need, coupled with interim lease-back. Except in already urbanized areas, local governments have been less responsive to the need to plan for development. Either this attitude must shift, or the national government will be forced to take a more active role in stimulating urban development. With full employment, rising incomes, and satisfaction of the most acute housing shortages, the desire of people for more dwelling space and for single-family housing will affect the character of future urban growth.

The Helsinki area will grow rapidly in the near future. Already there is general agreement between government leaders and planners that the city proper should not grow beyond a population of 700,000 and that future growth should be concentrated in large urban settlements. Still to be decided are the number, location, and size of these communities and whether they should be new towns or expansions of existing towns. It is likely that these questions will be resolved and that the national government will provide more help to private enterprise than it has in the past in order to create these large urban areas.

Notes

1. Densely populated areas are defined in Finland as settlements of 200 or more people, all living at a maximum distance of 200 meters (650 feet) from their nearest neighbor.

2. By comparison, the United Kingdom has 564 persons per square mile.

3. In Sweden, it is projected that 20 percent of the population will live in the Stockholm region by 1990.

4. Lahti, 80,000; Oulu, 80,000; Espoo, 75,000; Pori, 60,000; Jyväskylä, 51,000; and Kuopio, 51,000.

5. Net national income is Gross National Product less deduction on the capital.

6. Finland, National Housing Board, *Official Statistics of Finland: General Census of Population 1960* (Helsinki, 1961), pts. 1 and 10; Finland, Bureau of Social Research, *Sosiaalinen aikakauskirja, 7–8/1965* (Helsinki, 1965).

7. In 1951 the density for Glasgow was 1.27 persons per room. In 1961 the density of the greater Stockholm area was 0.87 persons per room.

8. Remarks by Mr. Heikki von Hertzen at the University of Pennsylvania New Towns Seminar, Tapiola, August, 1965.

9. One in five Finnish families, one in eight Swedish families, and one in twenty Danish families have a summerhouse.

10. Conversation with Mr. Pekka Sivula, city planner for Turku, July, 1964.

11. Lassi Iharvaara, "Principles and Policies of Regional Planning" (Paper presented at the University of Pennsylvania New Towns Seminar, Tapiola, August, 1965), p. 13.

12. Alvar Aalto's regional plan for the Kokemäenjoki Valley, prepared in 1942, was the first to be finished.

13. Väinö Paavilainen, *National Planning in Finland*, National Planning Office Series A:14.3 (Helsinki, 1963), p. 11.

14. Iharvaara, "Principles and Policies of Regional Planning."

15. Arno Hannus, "Government Organization, Land Use Controls, Financing and Taxation as Related to New Town Development" (Paper presented at the University of Pennsylvania New Towns Seminar, Tapiola, August, 1965).

16. Finland, Ministry of the Interior, *Condensed Proposals and Opinions of the Finnish Government Committee on Land Supply and Land Prices*, prepared by Arno Hannus, chairman of the committee (Helsinki, 1965).

17. Conversation with Mr. af Heurlin, July, 1964.

18. Conversation with Mr. Pekka Sivula, July, 1964.

19. Conversation with Mr. af Heurlin, July, 1964.

20. See R. W. G. Bryant, "Finland: Organization of the Environment" (Paper presented at the Institut d'Urbanisme, Université de Montréal, 1965), for further details about the operation of the cooperatives.

21. Heikki von Hertzen, "Planning Problems in the Province of Uusimaa: Seven Towns' Plan and its Underlying Principles" (Paper presented at the University of Pennsylvania New Towns Seminar, Tapiola, August, 1965), p. 2.

22. P. V. Rytila, "New Town or Satellite Community Planning and Transportation" (Paper presented at the University of Pennsylvania New Towns Seminar, Tapiola, August, 1965).

23. In Espoo, a town within the region, dense development is one dwelling per 107,600 square feet, but elsewhere it is defined as one dwelling per 53,800 square feet or per 37,660 square feet.

24. Comment by Dr. William L. C. Wheaton at the University of Pennsylvania New Towns Seminar, Tapiola, August, 1965.

25. Von Hertzen, "Planning Problems in the Province of Uusimaa."

26. Jorma Aaltonen, comp. *Tapiola 62* (Tapiola, 1963).

27. The Mannerheim League, the Confederation of Finnish Trade Unions (SAK), the Society of Civil Servants, the Central Association of Tenants, and the Finnish Association of Disabled Civilians and Servicemen.

28. Heikki von Hertzen, "Planning, Design and Management of Tapiola" (Paper presented at the University of Pennsylvania New Towns Seminar, Tapiola, August, 1965).

29. Conversation with Mr. Heikki von Hertzen, July, 1964.

30. Von Hertzen, "Planning, Design and Management of Tapiola," p. 3.

31. Drawn from "Two Extracts from the Residents' Lists for Owner-Occupied Buildings in the Tapiola Northern Residential Group—1964," mimeographed (from Heikki von Hertzen's personal files).

32. Conversation with Mr. Heikki von Hertzen, July, 1964.

33. Heikki von Hertzen, "Practical Problems of New Town Development" (Paper presented at the University of Pennsylvania New Towns Seminar, Tapiola, August, 1965), p. 1.

34. Von Hertzen, "Planning, Design and Management of Tapiola."

III Israel

Caesarea

Contents

The National Setting

Present-day Israel is a fascinating experiment in urbanization. Its new citizens, mostly destitute immigrants from extremely divergent cultural and economic backgrounds, have created a cohesive nation with a comfortable standard of living. This has been achieved within two decades under the most arduous conditions.

Israel has been a planner's laboratory. Detailed national and regional plans have guided the allocation of human and economic resources. While Israel's problems are distinguished by their very immensity, nonetheless, many of these problems also are common to Europe and the United States. Rapid urbanization, competition for scarce land resources, water shortages, and a lag in the shift from agrarian political power to urban all are familiar problems. In addition, Israel has a unique congeries of problems. The nature of the nation's birth, its growth in a hostile environment, and its participation in prolonged conflict have shaped the character of its citizens, strained the economy, and influenced urban development decisions. As is typical of real-life planning experiments, however, it has been impossible for the planners to foresee all of the changing forces which have and will affect the implementation of plans. Politics, people, natural resources, and money are the principal ingredients of Israel's experiment in urban growth. Of these, only the natural resources have been susceptible to planned management.

War has been a constant, varying in scale from open conflict to individual acts of terrorism. Urban development policy has directly reflected Israel's need to protect her borders from invasion and infiltration. Small urban settlements have been established near the borders so that there will be people ready to discourage and oppose Arab intrusions. Defense has been a dominant consideration in determining the location of these communities. Often they do not fit the detailed national and regional planning design for a hierarchy of urban settlements linked physically, economically, and culturally. Failure to reach peace with Lebanon, Syria, Jordan, and Egypt has, in addition to constituting a direct drain for defense expenditures, handicapped Israel's physical development by diverting some growth to areas less able to sustain it economically and less socially appealing.

Israel's population policy has two objectives: to provide a haven for all Jews, and to build up a population large enough to discourage attack. The nation's explicit guarantee to receive any Jew whenever he wishes to immigrate meant, in the early years, that the country was called upon to absorb a precipitous migration of hundreds of thousands of people and to provide food, homes, and jobs where none had existed before. First, from the concentration camps and ghettos of Eastern Europe, came the survivors of World War II; then came the North African and Middle Eastern Jews, fleeing persecution by the Arabs; and then came second waves of Jews from both East European and Arab countries. The people came in reverse order to the nation's capacity to absorb them. As the early hardships eased and people were needed to settle and build the remainder of the country into a further bulwark against attack, the flood of immigrants tapered off. Now there is a new, unresolved refugee problem—that of the Arabs who wish to return to land captured by Israel during the June, 1967, war.

Development planners have had the extraordinary advantage of being able to settle many of the new immigrants where the country needs them, but they have been unable to predict the rate or volume or character of immigration. Thus, while the direction of growth can be predetermined, the timing cannot.

The policy of rapid, continuing growth is dictated by Israel's defense needs but is not supported by her natural resource base. The land is largely desert and mountain. The water supply is inadequate and unevenly distributed. The National Water Project, already well on the way to completion, will make maximum economic use of the available water supply. Until desalination becomes economically feasible, however, there will not be enough water.

Much of the fertile land that receives adequate rainfall lies on the coastal plain, where urbanization has occurred and spread despite government sanctions and pressures. The government has succeeded in diverting some urban development from good farmland to the mountains, dunes, and desert, but much growth continues on the coastal plain. Mineral resources are found in the inhospitable desert. New towns have been built there to provide a local labor force for mineral extraction, and roads and railroads have been built to carry the raw materials to factories or ports.

The desert blooms, yields mineral wealth, and supports people. A respectable industrial plant and remarkable housing stock has been created. The price in capital investment and labor has been high. So far, the economy has been sustained by German reparations, foreign capital contributions and investments, and immigrants' investments. Now the reparations have almost been paid off, other unilateral transfers have declined, and foreign loans are the major source of new capital. At a time of economic stress, when the country was attempting to reduce consumption and expand exports to achieve a balance of payments, the Arab-Israeli war exacted a heavy toll. New capital has been received, but the direct costs of the war, plus the new burdens of additional lands and a population suddenly increased by one million Arabs, are placing severe strains on an already precarious economy.

Whether the defense-dictated policy of continued rapid growth through Jewish immigration makes economic sense is questionable. Nevertheless, within the confines set by circumstance, Israel has made remarkable progress in the settling and development of a modern, urban nation.

Israel has enjoyed the unusual advantages of a new start—largely unsettled land, a new population, and a new government—plus heavy infusions of capital and talent. The very diversity of her people's heritage has made it possible to develop a legal, political, and economic structure which draws on the relevant experience of other nations but which also has created something new and uniquely suited to Israel. Planners have had enormous scope. Their schemes for the development of towns and resources and for the distribution of people were vital to the nation's growth, and it has been possible to shape laws, administrative practices, and the allocation of public resources to secure implementation of the plans. Counterweighting this unusual power to execute plans is the fact that planners have been handicapped by inadequate interministerial coordination, a high degree of uncertainty as to how fast the population would grow, how the Arab-Israeli conflict would develop, and at what rate foreign financial aid would continue to be received.

**The
Government**

Prelude to Independence

At the time of her independence, Israel had many antecedents: wars, betrayals, race hatreds, conflicting nationalisms, genocide, terrorism, vacillation, and selfish national policies. With such a heritage, it is remarkable that the nation came into being and even more remarkable that it has survived and flourished. These undoubted triumphs must be credited to the resolve and single-mindedness of the Jewish settlers, born of desperation and opportunity, and also to the worldwide financial support of other Jews.

Independence was proclaimed on May 14, 1948. Major milestones on the road to independence were the first 'alīyāh,[1] which began in 1882; the founding of world Zionism in 1897; the British occupation of Palestine and the Balfour Declaration of 1917; the 1922 mandate of the League of Nations; the Peel Commission's 1937 recommendation for partition; and the 1947 U.N. resolution for the partition of Palestine.

Zionism kindled desires to create a Jewish state in Palestine and sparked immigration. The Balfour Declaration at least partially committed Britain, and then the League of Nations, to aid in the realization of these desires. Arab claims to Palestine were alternately acknowledged and ignored by the British between 1915 and 1947. The desperation of the plight of Jews elsewhere was a good barometer of the British position. The rise of Nazism in the 1930s drove many Jews from Germany. Israel was the destination for several hundred thousand of these refugees. The next refugees were the destitute, homeless Jewish survivors of World War II. Through its partition resolution, the United Nations acknowledged the world's obligation to provide a home for Jews, but Arab claims to the whole of Palestine never were answered satisfactorily. This unresolved issue underlies the continuing warfare.

In the last quarter of the nineteenth century there occurred a sudden revival of interest among Jews in a return to the Holy Land and a revival of Hebrew culture. The Russian pogroms provided a quite different incentive for immigration. Many small communities of Jews had been settled in Palestine for several generations. To these were added first small, then larger, groups of pioneers who went to Palestine to build towns and reclaim the soil (see Figure III-1). In 1897, under the leadership of Theodore Herzl, the World Zionist Organisation was founded, and it gave added impetus to the return to Palestine. The Turks, then the rulers of Palestine, accepted this migration. By 1914 there were 85,000 Jews in Palestine.[2] The Arabs, who constituted 90 percent of Palestine's population, became alarmed that they would be engulfed by Jewish refugees. The Zionists, with the motto "A land without people for a people without land," largely ignored the Arabs.

World War I began, and the Turks joined the Germans. In 1915 the British induced the Arabs to revolt against the Turks and to join the Allies by promising them an independent Arab nation in the Middle East. An unspecified strip of coast was omitted from this offer, and the British later claimed that this included Palestine.[3] In 1917 the British captured Palestine and occupied it. On November 2, 1917, the British government issued the Balfour Declaration. On behalf of the cabinet, Arthur Balfour, then British foreign secretary, pledged Britain's help to the Jews in the establishment of a national home in Palestine: "His Majesty's Government view with favor the establishment in Palestine of a National Home for the Jewish people, and will use their best endeavors to facilitate the achievement of this object, it being clearly understood that nothing shall be done which may prejudice the civil and religious rights of existing non-Jewish communities in Palestine."[4]

With the termination of World War I and the expectation of renewed Jewish immigration, the Zionists sought to reach an amicable understanding

Figure III-1. Degania, the First Kibbutz, on the Sea of Galilee

with the Arabs. Prince Feisal, leader of the Arab revolt against the Turks, accepted the prospect of Jewish immigration so long as it did not lead to a Jewish state. "We are demanding Arab freedom and we would show ourselves unworthy of it if we did not now, as I do, say to the Jews, 'Welcome back home.' "[5]

Regrettably, Feisal did not speak for the other Arab leaders, who repudiated his agreement and sought to limit Jewish immigration. The British had made several conflicting promises: one to the Arabs guaranteeing them sovereignty in the Middle East, one to the French to split the Middle East, and the Balfour Declaration on behalf of the Jews. The British kept their bargain with the French. In the British portion of the Middle East, they established and controlled Iraq, Transjordan, Palestine, and Egypt until each was strong enough to wrest its freedom. The Balfour Declaration, which was in the form of a letter to Lord Rothschild, president of the World Zionist Organisation, was interpreted by the Jews as a guarantee to assist in establishing a nation. It is considered the legal basis for the Zionist claim to the right to settle Palestine. The British interpreted it as an assurance of the right to immigrate.

In 1922 the League of Nations adopted the mandate for Palestine, granting the British the task of administering Palestine, incorporating the Balfour Declaration in the mandate, and defining as one purpose of the mandate the creation of a Jewish national home. Once again terms were vague and gave rise to the question of whether national home meant independent nation. The mandate recognized the World Zionist Organisation as an appropriate

Jewish agency to cooperate with the British in developing the country.[6] The Zionists persuaded the British high commissioner for Palestine, Sir Herbert Samuel, to open the land registry so that land could be bought and sold. They then bought large estates and villages from Arab landowners to make room for incoming Jews. The Arab peasants received nothing; their leases were terminated by their former landlords, and they found themselves without land to farm. As immigration increased, so did Arab anger and resentment. Samuel set an annual quota of 16,500 on Jewish immigration, but this did not assuage the Arabs. Next the British government stated that, because the land could not support it, no more immigration to Palestine would be allowed. Jewish outrage forced the rescission of this policy and a return to the prior, limited rate of immigration.

Riots and terrorism in Palestine increased, as did immigration pressures when Hitler came to power. Immigration rose to 62,000 in 1933.[7] By 1937 the Peel Commission on Palestine had recommended partition into Jewish and Arab states. The commission stated that the Jewish Agency, an outgrowth of the World Zionist Organisation, "... amounts, in fact, to a Government existing side by side with the Mandatory Government." The Zionists accepted; the Arabs refused. Arab revolts increased. The British vacillated again, abandoning the partition policy for restricted immigration and limited independence for Palestine in the future. This was unacceptable to the Zionists.

Later, as World War II waned, terrorist acts against both the British and the Arabs increased in frequency and intensity. By then there were 650,000 Jews in Palestine; 100,000 more, survivors of the Nazi slaughter of six million Jews, were struggling to reach Palestine. The United States urged Britain to permit them to enter, but declined to offer military aid to maintain order between Jews and Arabs. The British, despairing of their ability to reach a solution, turned to the United Nations in the spring of 1947. The General Assembly resolution of November 29, 1947, recommended the partition of Palestine into an Arab and a Jewish state. The United States and Russia voted for partition; Britain abstained. A Palestine Partition Committee was established by the United Nations to implement the resolution. The Jewish Agency accepted the resolution; the Arab nations denounced it and stepped up attacks on Jews then in Palestine. The Jews retaliated. War broke out.

On May 14, 1948, the state of Israel was born. On May 15, the British withdrew, immigrants began to pour in, and the armies of Egypt, Jordan, Syria, Lebanon, Iraq, and Saudi Arabia invaded the new nation. Simultaneously, a government had to be formed, a war fought, immigrants welcomed, and everyone—sabra, refugee, and new immigrant—fed, housed, and armed. The Israelis were hard pressed until the United Nations arranged a truce. They then bought more arms, organized more efficiently, and attacked. Within seven months the war was over, and armistice agreements were signed with the four Arab nations contiguous to Israel. The 7,000 square miles which would have been Israel under the U.N. partition plan had become 8,000 square miles. Israel had gained the Galilee, the Jerusalem corridor, and part of the city of Jerusalem, which would have been internationalized under the U.N. plan. No permanent boundaries ever were established.

... The area that was under Jordanian occupation, and the Gaza region, which the Egyptians ruled, were held by them not by right but by force, as the result of military aggression and occupation. This occupation was recognized, it is true, in the armistice agreements, but these agreements have been nullified by military provocation and aggression on their part. Moreover, it was agreed between the parties in

1949 that the armistice lines had been determined only by military considerations and did not have the character of frontiers.[8]

No peace treaties ever have been signed, and twice—in 1956 and again in June, 1967—the war has flared up. The land captured in June, 1967, has more than doubled the area under Israeli control. In the absence of open warfare, there have been continuing raids, border incidents, and verbal incitements between Israel and the Arab states.

Keeping the country on a wartime footing has handicapped planning for urban development. Defense costs are a heavy drain on the budget. Then there is the unquantifiable but ceaseless stress of knowing that the enemy's unchanging intent is to obliterate the nation. The war status is more directly reflected in plans for the location and priority of urbanization. Were Israel assured of peace, more development would occur on the hilly central spine and less in inhospitable areas near the borders. Whether land acquired in the June, 1967, war will be retained and how it will affect development policy remains at issue. Former Premier Eshkol has suggested that Israel will insist on a redefinition of the borders at the Gaza Strip and the Jordan River's west bank. He also has stated that prior conditions on the Syrian border, in the Sinai Peninsula, and in the Gulf of Aqaba cannot be permitted to recur. The former Jordanian sector of Jerusalem already has been consolidated into Israel.

Government Today

Israel is a parliamentary democracy whose laws and government most closely resemble those of Britain. Its Declaration of Independence sets forth the principles and guarantees of the state:

... The State of Israel will be open to Jewish immigration and the ingathering of exiles. It will devote itself to developing the land for the good of all its inhabitants. It will rest upon foundations of liberty, justice, and peace as envisioned by the Prophets of Israel. It will maintain complete equality of social and political rights for all its citizens, without distinction of creed, race, or sex. It will guarantee freedom of religion and conscience, of language, education, and culture.[9]

The national government consists of the Knesset—the unicameral legislative body—and of the president, prime minister, cabinet, and judiciary. The 120 members of the Knesset are elected every four years under a proportional representation system. All citizens aged eighteen or over are eligible to vote. This includes Arabs. Arabs may be elected to the Knesset. The Sixth Knesset includes six Arabs (three Muslim, three Christian) and one Druze. There are a dozen political parties which offer lists of candidates to the electorate nationwide. To date, no party has obtained a majority, and therefore all governments have been coalitions. In 1969 the Labor and Mapam parties, together constituting the alignment faction, held a small majority in the Knesset.

Laws are passed by majority vote of those present, except for certain fundamental laws—affecting the Knesset, the president, and the government—which must be passed by a majority of the Knesset as a whole. These laws are intended to serve as the nucleus of a future constitution. Because the judiciary has ruled that it does not have the power to hold legislation invalid because it conflicts with the fundamental laws,[10] the laws passed by the Knesset are the law of the land. This is consistent with Israel's heritage of British law and the division of power between legislature and judiciary.

The Knesset elects the president, who serves a five-year term and may be re-elected once. The president's office is largely ceremonial. He is not the chief executive.

The party or parties in power in the Knesset choose the prime minister and the cabinet ministers. Today the Labor Party (Ha Avodah) is the dominant party, but, because it does not have a majority in the Knesset, the cabinet positions are shared with the Mapam. Ministers usually are Knesset members, but need not be. The cabinet serves until it resigns or until there is a Knesset vote of no confidence. Most legislation is proposed by cabinet members to the Knesset, although Knesset members also may introduce bills. The government ministries of Jerusalem appear in Figure III-2.

The judiciary consist of magistrates' courts and municipal courts, both courts of first instance; district courts and the Supreme Court, both appellate courts and courts of initial jurisdiction; and religious courts. Each major religion has its own court, which has jurisdiction over personal matters. See Figure III-3 for the architectural style of one Tel Aviv court house.

Figure III-2. Government Ministries, Jerusalem

Figure III-3.
District Court
House, Tel Aviv

There are only two levels of government: national and local. However, the national government has divided the country into six administrative districts, each of which has a central office operated by the Ministry of the Interior for the administration and coordination of national programs. The districts, and the cities in which their offices are located, are as follows: Jerusalem (Jerusalem); Northern (Nazareth); Haifa (Haifa); Central (Ramla); Tel Aviv (Tel Aviv); and Southern (Beersheba).

Municipal government is locally elected, but municipal administration is supervised by the Ministry of the Interior. There are 185 local governments, including 26 municipalities (two Arab), 112 local councils (38 Arab and Druze), and 47 regional councils composed of 670 villages.[11] The city hall of one municipality appears in Figure III-4.

Figure III-4.
City Hall, Holon

The laws governing Israel are almost as much of a potpourri as are the people of Israel. There is an Ottoman legal base modified by French civil law; this is overlaid with British common law and statutes; and now part of the system has been supplanted by portions of Israel's basic laws and ordinances. The constitution will be developed chapter by chapter from the basic laws. Among the chapters already enacted by the Knesset is "The Basic Law: Israel Lands," passed in July, 1960. Among its provisions is one that public land may not be sold, except in unusual, specified situations.

The People

The population goal set by Israel in 1948 was to welcome, locate, and provide equal accommodation for all Jews who wished to come. It was "to bring the maximum number of Jews from the lands of their dispersion back to the country of their biblical origin, and to integrate the newcomers into the framework of the new State. A further basic aim was to develop, populate and provide employment in the entire territory of the State in order to achieve, in course of time, a fairly equal standard of living in all parts of the country."[12] Immigration also is essential to Israel's survival. Surrounded by 60 million Arabs dedicated to her destruction, Israel necessarily has sought immigrants to provide a counterforce. At first, too many came; then, because of better conditions elsewhere and a recession in Israel, too few came. There has been an upsurge in immigration since the 1967 six-day war, with more than 30,000 people arriving, largely from Western countries.

On November 8, 1948, Israel's population was 870,000, of which 82 percent was Jewish.[13] Seventy percent of the Jewish population lived in the urban areas of Tel Aviv, Haifa, and Jerusalem; 80 percent lived in the central coastal area, which includes Tel Aviv and Haifa. The non-urban Jews, many of whom had been attracted to Israel by the 'alīyāh, which dated from 1882, and by the Zionist movement, were scattered among the cooperative (moshav) and collective (kibbutz) farm villages and in a few towns, areas chosen for settlement because they had been the sites of biblical towns. The non-Jewish population was principally Arab, both Muslim and Christian. It also included about 20,000 Bedouins living in the Negev and 20,000 Druzes.[14]

After independence, the British policy of restricted Jewish immigration was at once reversed, and immigrants, particularly the survivors of the concentration camps, flooded in. For several years immigration averaged 200,000 people per year. In March of 1949, 1,000 immigrants arrived daily. Most immigrants in the early years came from Eastern Europe and from Arab countries. The first immigrants included 60,000 people from camps for displaced persons in Germany and 15,000 from Austria, all survivors of the Nazi slaughter of the Jews. Thirty-three thousand came from Turkey, 20,000 per year were permitted to leave Czechoslavakia, 36,000 came from Bulgaria, 7,000 from Yugoslavia, 30,000 from Libya, 5,000 from China, 45,000 from Yemen, and 88,000 from Rumania. For fourteen months Poland permitted Jews to leave; during this time 28,000 reached Israel. In 1950 Iraq passed a law authorizing Jews to emigrate during a one-year period; 100,000 were airlifted to Israel during that time. Between independence and the close of 1951, 684,000 immigrants reached Israel. Most were penniless and without possessions; neither they nor Israel could control their arrival to coincide with the availability of housing, jobs, and food. They spoke a welter of tongues; few spoke Hebrew, the language of Israel. Many were ill or too old or too young to work. About one-quarter could neither work nor care for themselves.[15] Nevertheless, by May, 1951, two-thirds of the immigrants had been placed in more or less permanent housing. All were fed, and all who were able were working.

In 1952, immigration declined drastically. The displaced person camps were almost empty, and most countries of Eastern Europe no longer permitted emigration. Conditions in North Africa were tolerable enough to discourage many from assuming the hardships of life in a pioneer country.

By 1955 the economic and political balance had begun to shift, and more North African Jews, particularly from Tunisia and Morocco, decided to go to Israel. Because the lives of these people were not in jeopardy, Israel insisted that each family that would be dependent on the Israeli government for travel and living expenses include one wage-earner under the age of forty-five and that the entire family meet certain standards of physical and mental health. In 1956, following the resumption of the Egyptian-Israeli war, 12,000 Egyptian Jews immigrated to Israel. In 1957 about 40,000 Jews were allowed to leave Eastern Europe.

In recent years immigration has not matched government hopes or anticipation. New people, the basic ingredient for development, growth, and security, have been in short supply. Better conditions elsewhere, some diminution of the early pioneer spirit, and increasing economic problems in Israel all have had their effect. For an over-all view of immigration during the first eighteen years of Israeli independence, see Figure III-5.

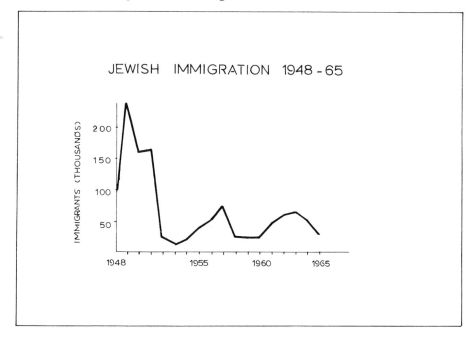

Figure III-5.
Immigration,
1948–65

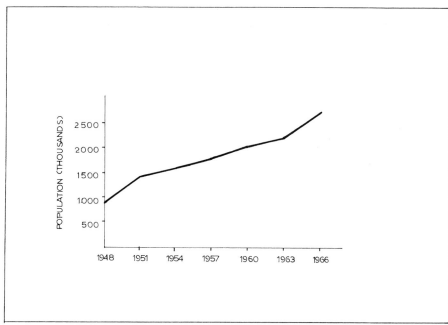

Figure III-6.
Population Growth,
1948–66

Immigration also has fluctuated with economic and political conditions in other countries, with the willingness of East European countries to permit emigration, and with Israel's economic situation. A lack of promising opportunities has caused Israel to lose many young doctors, engineers, and other professionally trained people. Poverty and unemployment among many of the newest immigrants settled in the new communities has further discouraged others from immigrating. The spirit of 'alīyāh alone has proved an insufficient incentive. Particularly, it has failed to attract immigrants from the West, who are wanted by the government to balance the infusion from the Middle East and Africa. Israel hopes to retain some of the young, Western volunteers who came during the June, 1967, war and is providing housing and tax incentives to encourage them to remain. Attracting and retaining Western Jews is difficult because they possess the education and skills already overabundant among young Israelis. Yet the government wants them to provide more of a cultural balance between Western and so-called oriental Jews from Africa and the Middle East.

By September, 1966, the population had reached 2,643,000,[16] of which nearly 90 percent was Jewish. About two-thirds of the population growth from 1948 to 1966 was the result of immigration (see Figure III-6); of the indigenous population, natural increase was much greater among the Arabs than among the Jews (forty-two per 1,000 per year as compared to seventeen per 1,000 per year). The Arab population almost doubled during this fifteen-year period. Now there are approximately one million additional Arabs in the territory controlled by Israel. Israel's stand on the return of some of the territory captured in 1967 surely will be shaped by her judgment of her capacity to assimilate this new Arab population.

Natural Resources

Israel offers a Mediterranean climate, strikingly varied topography, some very rich soils, and limited mineral reserves. Half of the land is the arid wilderness of the Negev. The country's major shortage is water. Even when all available water is used and re-used most efficiently, only 40 percent of the arable land can be irrigated, and irrigation is essential to successful agriculture. Economical desalination is the key to further agricultural expansion.

Israel is located on the southeastern shore of the Mediterranean and is bordered by Lebanon on the north, Syria and Jordan on the east, and Egypt on the southwest. Prior to June, 1967, Israel's area was 8,000 square miles, or slightly larger than the state of New Jersey. The country stretches 260 miles from the Lebanese border south to the Gulf of Aqaba; its width varies from three miles at Eilat to seventy miles at Beersheba.

Topography was a major determinant of the borders of Palestine; in 1948, war altered these borders so that much of the topographic rationale was destroyed. Now, following the 1967 war, geography may at least be a factor in realigning the borders.

As seen in Map III-1, Israel is divided into three longitudinally parallel strips: the coastal plain, the mountain spine, and the Jordan Rift. The coastal plain averages ten miles in width and breaches the mountain range only in the valley of Jezreël, near Haifa. The mountains rise to a maximum height of 3,600 feet in Upper Galilee (Figure III-7) and 3,000 feet in the Negev. Their seaward slopes are moderate, while the slopes facing east to the Jordan Rift are steep and rugged. The mountains of the Negev are windswept, eroded, and cratered, reminiscent of the lunar landscape. The Jordan Rift runs from the headwaters of the Jordan south through the Gulf of Aqaba. The Jordan River rises in Upper Galilee, 635 feet below sea level, and flows down to the Dead Sea, the lowest place on earth, 1,292 feet below sea level.[17] The Jordan Rift then forms the Arava Valley of the Negev, and continues south to Eilat, and then underlies the Gulf of Aqaba. Although the rift forms a logical geographic boundary, most of the Judean and Samarian hills (Figure III-8) and much of the valley west of the Jordan River were held by Jordan prior to the recent war.

The coastal plain has a long, hot, and humid summer, a moderate and rainy winter. Summer discomfort is relieved by sea breezes. The mountains of Samaria, Judea, and Galilee are somewhat less hot and much drier. The Jordan Valley is extremely hot in summer and temperate in winter. The mountains and the Arava Valley of the Negev are extremely hot in summer,

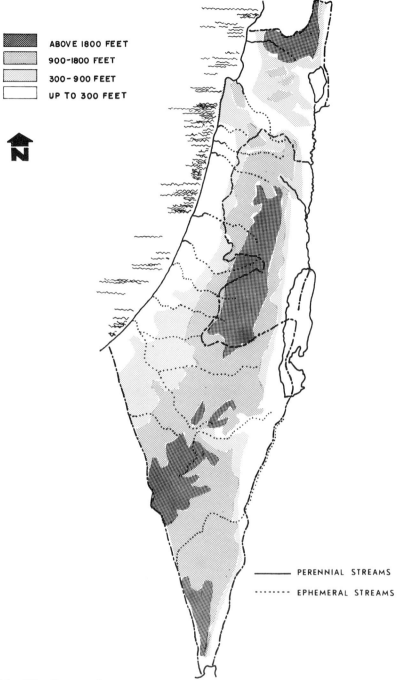

ABOVE 1800 FEET

900-1800 FEET

300-900 FEET

UP TO 300 FEET

N

PERENNIAL STREAMS

EPHEMERAL STREAMS

Map III-1. Topography

warm in winter, and continually dry, except for sudden and brief storms. At Eilat the minimum and maximum average daily temperatures in August are 78°F. and 105°F.[18]

Starting with a land of desert, mountain, dune, and swamp, the Israelis have achieved extraordinary results in restoring productivity by altering the distribution of the available water supply and through land conservation practices. Still, only 20 percent of the land is suitable for cultivation, and much of this also is under pressure for urban development. An additional 16 percent of the land can be afforested.[19] The sand dunes along the Mediterranean are one area where a conflict over potential uses does not exist; the dunes are

Figure III-7. Mountains of Upper Galilee

Figure III-8. The Desert of Judea

unsuitable for cultivation but are proving very desirable for urban development. The coastal plain inland from the dunes has sandy red soil ideal for citrus culture; here there is real competition between developers and farmers. The eastern edge of the coastal plain, marked by heavy, black soil and former swamps (Figure III-9), was drained by early Jewish settlers at a great cost in disease and death from malaria. This soil is excellent for vegetables and non-citrus fruits, but it requires drainage to maintain the necessary low water table. The red loam of the mountains is of very good quality for fruit trees, grapes, olives, tobacco, and grain, but much of the mountain area is badly eroded and the Negev portion is too dry. Only by terracing can further erosion be avoided. Eastern Galilee has dark soil similar in character to the mountain soils. The loess soil of the northern Negev is quite fertile but forms a heavy crust under winter rains, then gullies. In the summer it

Figure III-9.
The Huleh Swamps

crumbles to dust and is easily blown away. The rest of the Negev has very limited agricultural potential.[20] Throughout the country, contour plowing is required by law in order to minimize further erosion.

The suitability of land for agriculture really cannot be evaluated without also considering the availability of water. Rainfall varies from one inch per year at Eilat to forty inches at Tirat Ya'el in the far north. It does not exceed four inches in the Negev, which is insufficient for unirrigated farming. The rainy season is short and does not coincide with the growing season. Drought years are frequent. Except for the Jordan, the only perennial flow in streams extends a few miles inland from the northern half of the coastal plain.

The estimated annual available water supply is 1,700 million cubic meters. Of this, 55 percent comes from springs and streams, 40 percent from underground reserves, and 5 percent from storm runoff. In the future, Israel plans to augment this supply by 126 million cubic meters per year through the reuse of sewage and irrigation water.[21] At present, 90 percent of all available water is used,[22] one-quarter for domestic and industrial purposes, three-quarters for irrigation.

National water management principles are: (1) the maximum amount of water should be made available for use; (2) reservoirs should be designed to hold rainy season runoff and to store water for drought years; (3) water should be piped to the places where it can best be used.

National water planning includes projects for local collection and storage of water, as well as the National Water Project, the pipeline system for carrying waters of the Jordan and Yarkon rivers to the Negev (see Figures III-10 and III-11). Also under way is the creation of one national system linking the regional projects which will balance surpluses and shortages.

In some parts of the Negev the entire annual rainfall occurs within a few days. Here, small dams in the wadies are planned to capture and hold the runoff from the rare but intense storms. This is the manner in which Nabataeans managed to retain water to grow grains, fruits, and vegetables in the Negev.[23]

Along the Mediterranean coast, Israel is beginning to intercept and capture ground water before it reaches the sea. A chain of boreholes is expected to make possible the recovery of an additional five million cubic meters of ground water each year.

The north has a water surplus, and the coastal plain is adequately supplied. The major area of need is the towns and agricultural land of the Negev. The main pipeline of the National Water Conduit runs from the Sea of Galilee south almost to Beersheba, and supplemental pipelines reach out to settled areas, even to Eilat. None of the towns of the Negev and few crops could survive without the waters collected and distributed by the National Water Project. Even where there is sufficient total rainfall, many of the crops to which the soil is best suited require irrigation. The yield from irrigated land averages five times the yield from unirrigated land. When the present water projects are completed, there will be sufficient water to irrigate 40 percent of the cultivable land (see Figure III-12). Future efforts will go toward the desalination of sea water and of underground supplies of brackish water.

Most of Israel's mineral resources are found in the Negev. Their discovery in amounts warranting exploitation has been an unexpected and fortuitous one, for the British had rejected most of the Negev as wasteland—noncultivable, unproductive, and basically uninhabitable. The mining of copper at Timna dates back to King Solomon's time, when copper was exported to Africa and the Orient from Eilat. The reserves will meet all of Israel's needs and provide a surplus for export. Recovery of potash from the Dead Sea began under the British. In addition to potash, the Dead Sea now yields

Figure III-10.
Tel-Or Power
Station, Jordan
Valley

Figure III-11.
Laying the
Negev Pipeline

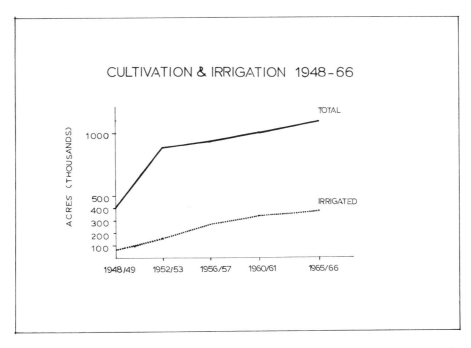

CULTIVATION & IRRIGATION 1948–66

Figure III-12.
Cultivation and
Irrigation, 1948–66

magnesium chloride, common salt, potassium chloride, magnesium bromide, and calcium chloride in almost limitless amounts. After extensive Israeli geologic exploration, deposits of phosphates, manganese, feldspar, glass sand, ball clay, kaolin, chrome, sulphur, bituminous shale, marble, gypsum, petroleum, gas, and iron were found. The phosphates and potash supply all of Israel's fertilizer demands and provide a surplus for export. There is sufficient glass sand, clay, gypsum, and marble to meet internal demands. The amount of oil and gas so far discovered is limited—two million tons of oil and, in gas, the equivalent of 1.6 million tons of oil. Prospecting continues, while the present supply of gas and oil provides 14 percent of Israel's fuel needs.[24]

The Economy

Israel's economic situation has been perilous since birth, and it remains so today. The financial demands of war, of accommodating one million immigrants, and of creating an agricultural and industrial economy virtually from nothing continually have been in excess of available funds—this despite very substantial foreign investments totaling some $7 billion since 1948.

Without the contributions of the Jewish Agency for Israel, German reparations, and the United States government, Israel hardly could have survived. This investment, combined with the growth and productivity of the labor force, enabled the Israeli Gross National Product to grow at an average rate of 10 percent per year[25] from 1950 through 1969. Growth was 12 percent in 1968. As a result of this investment, exports have been rising, self-sufficiency is increasing, and the gap in the balance of payments declined until the 1967 war. In 1966 the import surplus was $460 million, and 47 percent of the development budget came from foreign investments.[26] Starting in 1965, attempts were made to move in the direction of eliminating this imbalance, and by 1967 had lowered the deficit to $212 million. These efforts, however, also stopped growth and brought recession and unemployment. The recession ended with the Arab-Israeli war, but so did the improved trade balance. The gap in 1968 was up to $600 million. Since the June, 1967, war, the next steps for the economy have remained unclear. The government has not raised taxes and has kept wages constant in an effort to combat possible inflation. Price rises have been kept to two percent during the past two years. There has been a new flow of $350 million in capital contributions from abroad, but there are also new burdensome defense and refugee resettlement obligations.

The Gross National Product was $240 million in 1952 and $3.4 billion in 1967. Of each year's 10 percent growth, 3.5 percent has been attributed to increased capital investment, 2.5 percent to more manpower, and 4 percent to more efficient use of labor and capital.[27] Because the population has grown so rapidly, the rise in Gross National Product per capita has not kept pace with the total rise in GNP. However, Gross National Product per capita has risen from $500 in 1954 to $1,500 in 1966,[28] a rate of 6 percent per year. Income per capita was $1,000 in 1966.[29]

Capital Investment

Some of the foreign capital invested in Israel has no strings attached; it is an outright investment of funds which involves no obligation for later repayment outside Israel. These unilateral transfers have included German reparations to the Israeli government, German restitution to individuals, investments made by immigrants, and grants from the Jewish Agency, United States government, and other sources. West German reparations totaled $864 million, while Jewish Agency contributions—three-quarters of them from the United States—equaled $1.5 billion.[30] Other foreign investments, in the form of loans, bonds, and private funds, must be repaid when mature, through the export of capital. For a comparative summary of Israel's capital inflow during 1959 and 1964, see Table III-1.

Table III-1.
Capital Inflow, 1959 and 1964

(millions of U.S. dollars)

Capital	1959	1964
Total Unilateral Transfers	251	335
Personal restitution from Germany	71	134
Immigrants' and other private transfers	30	96
By Jewish Agency and other institutions	74	80
German reparations	66	17
U.S. grants-in-aid	10	8
Total Capital Investments	108	230
Private investments	13	133
U.S. government loans	45	32
Independence and development bonds	35	24
Other	15	41
Total Inflow of Capital	359	565

SOURCE: Avner Hovne, *The Economy*, Israel Today no. 23 (Jerusalem: Israel Digest, 1965).

With decreased immigration, the termination of German reparation payments, and a decline in outright grants, Israel can no longer look to unilateral transfers as a major source of capital funds. Further foreign capital investment is needed; yet, while soliciting it, the government is cognizant that it is not yet in a position to repay.

For a decade, Israel consistently allocated annually more than 25 percent of all foreign and domestic resources available to capital investment. This high, sustained rate of investment is Israel's route to self-sufficiency; it has enabled industrial and agricultural productivity to rise dramatically, thus making possible larger exports and more goods for domestic consumption. In 1966 private consumption rose and investment declined. In that year Israel's resources and their allocation were as listed in Table III-2.

Table III-2.
Sources and Uses of Israel's Resources, 1966

Sources		%	Uses	%
Gross National Product		90	Private Consumption	61
Import Surplus		10	Public Consumption	20
Imports	20		Gross Investment	19
Exports	10			
		100		100

SOURCE: Israel, Ministry of Foreign Affairs, *Facts About Israel, 1967* (Jerusalem: Jerusalem Post Press, 1967).

Capital investment has been shifting from housing and agriculture to industry. Between 1950 and 1963, investment in housing dropped from 45 to 31 percent of all investment, and in agriculture from 20 to 12 percent, while investment in industry rose from 14 to 34 percent.[31]

The Labor Force

The shift in type of employment has followed the shift in capital investment. As industry has expanded, as agriculture has become more efficient, as basic housing needs have been met, and as services have become more important in the economy, there has been a shift in employment away from the farms to the towns and cities and away from agriculture and construction to industry and services. Seventy percent of the immigrants have changed jobs since coming to Israel.

The farm labor force rose between 1948 and 1961, then began to decline, and was down to 13 percent of all employment in 1965. Arabs and immigrants from Asia and Africa are most concentrated in agriculture, although Arabs also are in construction in numbers disproportionate to their distribution in the population. Thirty-five percent of the labor force now is in industry, while services account for most of the remainder. Health and education services alone employ 15 percent of the labor force, a level which is typical of a wealthy, developed country rather than of a newly developing one. Two of Israel's outstanding universities are Technion, in Haifa (Figure III-13), and Hebrew University, in Jerusalem (Figure III-14).

Given the size of Israel's population, her labor force has been comparatively small. About one-third of the population is under the age of fourteen, many young people over fourteen are in school, a large segment of the population is retired on pension, and a number of immigrants arrived in Israel disabled, ill and/or unskilled. Nonetheless, the labor force has been growing at an annual rate of 4 percent, and the number of people employed has increased by 4.5 percent annually. Unemployment has been a serious problem twice: during the 1953 recession, when the accumulated burden of massive immigration led to a currency devaluation and sharp curtailment in government spending for housing and public works, and during the 1966 recession.

Figure III-13. Technion, Haifa

Figure III-14. Hebrew University, Jerusalem

Imports and Exports

The importation of goods, as well as of capital, has been vital to the building of Israel's physical plant. Imports for personal consumption have been restricted; currently, only 11 percent of imported goods goes directly to the consumer. Imports from 1964 through 1966 were stable, while exports increased. While exports totaled only 11 percent of imports in 1949, they had risen steadily to 58 percent by 1966. Despite a substantial increase in exports during 1968 and 1969, imports rose even more rapidly, further widening the balance of payments gap. Obviously, exports must increase much more before the country can begin to achieve economic stability. The quality and price of export products must become more competitive on the world market so that export revenues will balance import costs. At present, Western Europe and the United States are the sources of 69 percent of Israel's imports, while they purchase 59 percent of her exports.

Israel is self-supporting in most foodstuffs, some minerals, and many manufactured goods. It must import most of its grains, fats, and fuels. There is no domestic water power or coal, and little oil for fuel.

The Net Domestic Product in 1966 was derived from the following sources: mining and manufacturing, 25 percent; private trade and services, 19 percent; government services, 20 percent; agriculture, forestry, and fishing, 8 percent; communications, 8 percent; ownership of dwellings, 7 percent; construction, 6 percent; finance, insurance, and real estate, 5 percent; and miscellaneous, 4 percent.[32]

Leading industrial output, in order of value of finished goods, is in foods and beverages, textiles, metals and machinery, chemicals and petroleum products, diamonds, and wood and wood products. Industrial production tripled in value between 1955 and 1966, when it reached $2.3 billion.

Agriculture is one of Israel's outstanding achievements. With the support of sound technical advice and a national commitment to provide water, the unlikely combination of city-bred immigrants and dry, unkempt land has resulted in sound land management. Newly productive acres feed Israel and provide substantial surpluses for export. Domestic agricultural production accounts for three-quarters of internal consumption and one-third of Israel's

Figure III-15. Orange Groves along the Yarkon River

exports. Citrus fruits top the list (see Figure III-15), but wine, olive oil, fruits, poultry and eggs, and flowers also are important. Only grain, fats, and oils are in short supply, because their production is least compatible with the soil, water, and topographic conditions.

Services, particularly tourism, shipping, and aviation, account for 40 percent of all exports. Principal export goods are cut diamonds (38 percent of goods exported, with export sales of $200 million in 1968) and citrus (15 percent). All industrial products together account for 81 percent of goods exported, and the remaining 19 percent consists of agricultural products.[33] The government looks to services as the area in which exports can most easily be expanded, and the promotion of tourism is an important government activity. In 1968 the income from tourism was 82 percent higher than the figure for 1967 and 30 percent above that for 1966.

To improve sales of export goods, Israel needs more efficient industries and better marketing ties with Europe and the United States. Failure to obtain full membership in the Common Market has been a considerable handicap. Foreign talent has been sought and accepted for physical planning; more is needed for industrial development. In part, foreign companies have avoided investment in Israel because of fear of Arab economic reprisals. Coca Cola did enter the Israeli market and promptly lost its substantial market in some Arab countries.

In 1965 the government decided that the time had come to begin the effort to balance payments. Investment was shifted away from construction and consumer goods to export products. Not unexpectedly, this brought on a recession. Internal expansion slowed sharply, but foreign purchases did not pick up the slack. Citrus and diamonds sold well on the world market, but clothing, chemicals, and scientific instruments fared less satisfactorily.

The recession of 1966 brought unemployment, particularly among the young, the women, and the recently arrived, less educated immigrants. Out of a work force of 900,000, estimates of unemployment in the early part of 1967 ran as high as 120,000, or 13 percent.[34] This was up from a 3.3 percent unemployment rate in 1964. By 1968 the rate was down to 6 percent, and at the start of 1969 it had declined to 5 percent. The government committed more funds to public works and attempted to stimulate foreign and domestic investment to get the economy moving again and to reduce unemployment. Israel followed Britain's lead in devaluing its currency, in the hope that this would provide an added, necessary impetus for foreign purchases and would counteract the effects of the increased public works program. The June, 1967, war solved Israel's recession problems in part, but it brought added financial burdens.

Planning Structure and Planning Powers

National, district, and local planning are provided for by the Planning and Building Law, which became effective February 12, 1966.[35] This law replaced the Mandatory Town Planning Ordinance of 1936, drawn up by the British and amended by five British and four Israeli laws. Thus the planning and plan implementation which took place between 1948 and 1966 were carried out in accordance with the prior, amended law, while that taking place currently is covered by provisions of the 1966 law.

The new law, prepared after many years' experience in administering the 1936 law, includes many more provisions that enable government to secure the implementation of plans. Therefore, when reviewing some of the shortcomings of earlier plan implementation, it is necessary to remember that the applicable enabling laws have now changed.

National, District, and Local Planning Organization

Because national plans take precedence over district plans, and the latter, in turn, take precedence over local plans, it is preferable to outline Israel's planning structure from the top level down (see Table III-3).[36]

National Planning

National planning is the charge of the National Planning Council. The twenty-two-member council consists of eight representatives from national ministries; six representatives of local government, including the mayors of Tel Aviv, Haifa, and Jerusalem, one other mayor, one local council president, and one regional council president, all chosen by the minister of the interior; and eight representatives of specified professional or public groups, including a planner, a conservationist, a sociologist, an architect or engineer, and a representative from the appropriate group of women's organizations, most of whom also are chosen by the minister of the interior. The council is chaired by the minister of the interior.[37] The Planning and Building Law authorized the council to prepare a National Master Plan (sometimes referred to as the National Outline Plan), to amend and update this plan, to coordinate and approve district plans, to hear appeals from district commissions concerning local planning,[38] and to advise the government on all questions of planning and building.

Under the former law, the Ministry of the Interior prepared physical plans at the national and regional levels, but they were advisory plans only. The first of these was the Regions of Priority for Directed Development Plan. Completed in 1955, and subsequently adopted by the government, this plan established six classes of priority for development assistance. All land in Israel was placed in one of these classes according to its comparative need for government aid to encourage development. The Negev, the areas south

Table III-3.
Israeli Planning Organization

Plan	Prepared by	Approved by	Appealed to
National master plan	National Planning Council	The government	
District master plan	District commission	National Planning Council	
Local master plan	Local commission	District commission (after notice to minister of the interior)	National Planning Council (1) by local commission or member of National Planning Council after rejection; (2) by member of district commission after approval
Local detailed plan	Local commission, landowner, or district commission	District commission	National Planning Council (1) by local commission or member of National Planning Council after rejection; (2) by objector; under statute after approval
New town master plan	Special commission	Minister of the interior (with recommendation of minister of housing)	
New town detailed plan	Special commission	Special commission	

SOURCE: Adapted from M. D. Gouldman, *Legal Aspects of Town Planning in Israel* (Jerusalem: Hebrew University of Jerusalem, 1966), p. 49.

and east of Dimona, and the northernmost sector of the country were placed in the highest priority class, while the coastal areas of greater Haifa, Tel Aviv, and Netanya were ranked in the lowest priority class. The plan did not specify the amount or type of government assistance to be provided to areas in each priority class, but instead left these decisions to the implementing ministries. Implementation, in fact, has taken the form of allocation of public investment for roads, schools, hospitals, immigrant housing, and local government aid in relation to the plan's priority rankings. In addition, lower land prices and lower taxes prevail in the top-priority areas. It is expected that priorities for development will shift over time and that areas therefore may be reclassified.

Similarly, the Plan for Population Distribution is an evolving plan which projects anticipated population over a 20-year period and indicates the government's preference for the distribution of this population.

Other national plans developed by the Ministry of the Interior prior to the 1966 law include the Plan for the National Communication Network (Map III-2), including roads, railroads, airports, and seaports; the Plan for the Economic and Social Functions of Towns; the Plan for Location of Industry; and the Plan for Parks and Nature Reserves.[39] Under the last plan, 10 percent of the state will be maintained as national parks and nature reserves. These plans now are being revised and updated.

Other ministries, including those of Housing and Labor, also have engaged in various aspects of national planning and plan implementation, and this has led to some confusion and conflict among objectives and in implementation. It is hoped that the new structure for national planning will resolve these problems of overlapping authority and interagency conflict and competition. Under the 1966 law the National Planning Council is directed to submit its plan, accompanied by the comments of the district commissions, to the government for approval. As is true for district and local plans, national plans must incorporate timetables and stages for their implementation. Once approved, a national plan takes precedence over all other plans.

One role of the national plan is to provide for the location of different types of land use. Among the possible uses of land, special emphasis has been given to the preservation of agricultural land. A National Planning Council committee, the Committee for the Protection of Agricultural Land, has been established to make recommendations pertaining to agricultural land preservation. The law specifically provides that, once the committee has declared that any given area is to be agricultural, no development of such land shall occur and no plan affecting the land may be confirmed without specific approval of this committee.

The Planning and Building Law also specifies that the national plan should provide for the location of industrial areas; for transportation and communication routes, from airlines to power lines; for water systems; and for conservation areas to serve natural resource preservation, recreation, historic, and religious objectives. In regard to population distribution, the law states that the plan may provide: "a forecast of the changes in the distribution of the population within the state, the stages in the development of such distribution and their proper timing, the estimated size of settlements, the siting and size of new settlements, and the location, classification, and size of settlements."[40]

As previously noted, much national planning for these objectives occurred under the 1936 law. However, the government has not adopted a single national master plan which expresses the combined judgment of the concerned ministries or is in any way binding on either national or local development. It is expected that national planning, as constituted by the new law, will be a much more effective mechanism for developing and effectuating national policies.

District Planning

Regional planning under the 1966 law is the charge of six district planning and building commissions. Membership on these commissions consists of eight government officials, each representing a national ministry; five members recommended by local authorities; and two members with planning and building training or from experienced professional organizations. Members from the last two groups are appointed by the minister of the interior.[41] The district commissioner or another representative of the Ministry of the Interior serves as commission chairman.

By 1971 the district commissions must have completed district master plans and submitted them to the National Planning Council for approval. At the

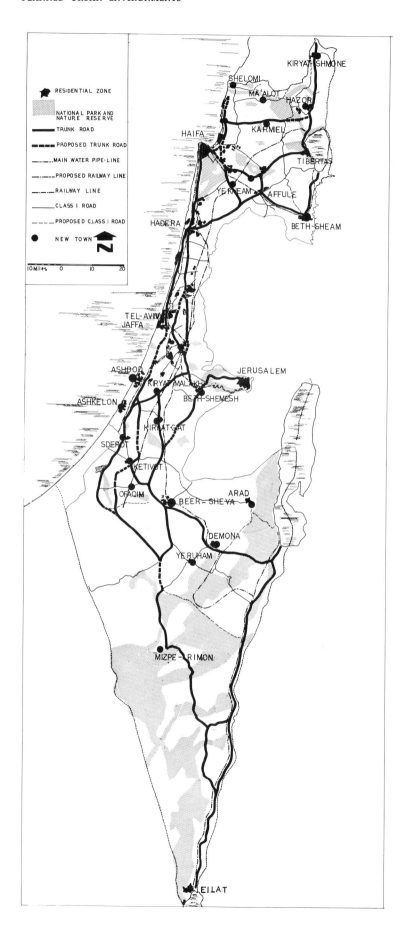

Map III-2.
National
Communication
Network

request of the National Planning Council, the Planning Department of the Ministry of the Interior has developed outlines and work programs to assist the district commissions in preparation of the plans. The primary function of each district master plan is to state in greater detail the means by which the National Master Plan is to be implemented in that district. Specifically, the plan may establish boundaries between urban and rural areas, locations for industry by type of industry, an intermediate-level road network, sites for afforestation, rules for the preservation of seacoasts, antiquities, or other unique areas, and rules for exceptions to the plan's requirements. The district commissions also are responsible for reviewing and approving local master plans and local detailed plans.[42]

Physical development plans had been completed for each district prior to the passage of the 1966 law. Because the six districts—Northern, Haifa, Central, Tel Aviv, Jerusalem, and Southern—were established for administrative purposes, their boundaries do not always coincide with geographic divisions within the country. For this reason, regional plans have been prepared for areas comprising a physiographic unit, particularly those areas faced with special development problems. These plans sometimes cover land in more than one district.

Local Planning

There are two administrative structures for local planning: the local commissions in the sixty-six designated town planning areas and the special commissions in the new towns. Each is responsible for the preparation of two types of plan: the master plan and the detailed plan. The master plan takes precedence over the detailed plan, unless the master plan provides otherwise. This is a significant and desirable change from the 1936 law, under which there was no statement of precedence between the two plans. Before 1966 it was possible to gain approval of a detailed plan for a limited area, such as a small neighborhood, before any master plan had been prepared for the entire town planning area.

One serious shortcoming of the Planning and Building Law is its inadequate fulfillment, through the organizational and administrative provisions of the law, of the intent to create a dominant position for national planning in relation to local planning.

... Thus the continued identity between planning and local government bodies and the fact that the representatives of the Ministers concerned with planning and building are not full members of the Local Commissions leave planning at the local level largely in the hands of laymen and subject to the short-term considerations of local government politics. Moreover, the need of the State to apply to the Local Commissions for permission to build is likely to result in undesirable clashes of interest between central and local government.[43]

The local council or authority usually also constitutes the membership of the local commission. The council, by law, appoints a subcommittee for planning and building which carries out most of the detailed planning work, meeting regularly with appointed representatives of the national ministries most directly connected with local planning. The representatives of these ministries —Interior, Housing, and Health—meet with the commission and the subcommittee in an advisory capacity. The national representatives' only direct authority is to require that a matter be referred to the district commission for decision, and all three representatives must concur for such a demand to be effected.

The local council subcommittee passes judgment on applications for building permits under the detailed plan and enforces regulations enacted under the plan. The local commission is responsible for amendments to the master plan and for expropriation decisions. Authorizing the subcommittee to act on building permit applications should reduce the delays experienced under the former law, when such decisions could be made only by the commission.

In some instances the area designated for local planning is larger than the area served by one local authority. In these cases the local commission consists of representatives from the local authorities, from the three national ministries, and from the district commission. This structure is preferable to that of the local commission (consisting exclusively of local council members) because commission members are less committed to the promotion of short-run local concerns at the expense of the national interest.[44]

The 1966 law directs that local master plans be completed within three years. Of course, many communities already have completed master plans and face only the task of revising and updating them. Others must start from scratch. The national government has provided grant funds which will enable the local governments to hire planning staffs, but more funds are needed. The finished plans go to the district commission for approval or, if an appeal is taken from the district commission's decision, to the National Planning Council.

Each special commission established to plan a new town consists of eleven members. Nine are representatives of seven national ministries, and two are representatives of the local government where the new town is to be located, if a local government already exists.[45] One of the two representatives of the Ministry of the Interior acts as chairman. The completed plans of the special commissions must be approved by the minister of the interior.

Government Policies and Programs for Population Distribution and Land Use

In Israel the national government determines policies for the distribution of population and the use of land. Government at the district level is but an arm of the national government and so reflects national policy. Municipal government, which shares responsibility for the implementation of national policies, has evolved under the aegis of the national government. While municipal government is responsive to national policies, in the past there has been some slippage between intent and results in municipal implementation of plans. Tel Aviv, Haifa, and Jerusalem, the three large cities which existed prior to independence, exert pressures that counter national policy, but these pressures are largely involuntary and are the result of economic and social attraction rather than of political opposition to national policy. Recalling that Israel is no larger than New Jersey, and being mindful of its military and economic exigencies, the strength of the national government relative to local government is hardly surprising.

Lack of a strong tradition of home rule, settlement by an immigrant population without a network of local ties, and the existence of common and undoubted perils have combined to create a consensus for strong central government control. Control of population distribution and land use has been but one aspect of this central authority. Israel's experience in implementing national planning is of particular interest to countries (including the United States) whose planning and land-use powers are more fragmented and whose local governments are the most powerful and well-entrenched forces for controlling land use.

Israel has clearly articulated national population distribution and land-use and development policies which are clearer and more precise than those of any country in Western Europe. There is nothing comparable to them at the national level in the United States. Israel also has an administrative framework more conducive than most to the implementation of these national policies. What Israel has not had—and it is this which hampers a judgment of the success of the government in implementing its policies—is any degree of predictability concerning future events. The number and qualifications of immigrants, defense needs, and the amount of foreign investments all have been variable and uncertain.

It is the policy of the government to welcome all Jews; to settle them in heterogeneous communities, mixed as to culture, level of education, place of origin, and native tongue; and to locate them as economic and defense needs dictate. When compatible with these needs, towns have been located on the sites of biblical towns. Rural, village, and town settlement has been designed as a hierarchy of linked units to assure rural residents of access to urban services and contact with urban life. Additional locations chosen for town and city development have been border areas requiring a ready defense force, coasts suited to port and/or resort use, and sites in the Negev near mineral reserves. Economic policy has dictated that the fertile coastal plain should remain in agricultural use and thus has limited the space available there for further urban development. A good transportation network and a strong system of public education and community services have been recognized as necessary to foster a sense of equality between city and rural residents and to blend differing cultural heritages into a compatible mix.

These policies have been translated into action programs, some highly successful, some less so. The national government has been faced continuously with the problem of adequate resources for policy implementation. While achievements are enormous, government officials readily admit that much remains to be done and that implementation measures often have been chosen on the basis of cost and so have not always yielded the results desired. Methods of implementation have included direct government investment in development and services; government incentives to private enterprise, both foreign and domestic, to participate in development; government location incentives and penalties for individuals and entrepreneurs; and government landownership.

First among Israel's many successes in the implementation of planning policy is the fact that a place has been found for every immigrant. Decent shelter, public education, food, and job training have been provided for all in need of them. Employment has been found for most. Given the erratic immigration flow and the destitution of most immigrants, this is Israel's most remarkable achievement.

An extensive system of new cities, towns, villages, and rural settlements has been established and developed in accordance with national plans.

The country's economic base is growing, although Israel is far from self-sufficient. Agricultural productivity has greatly increased because several aspects of development plans have been implemented successfully: major portions of the water distribution and irrigation system have been completed; immigrants have been induced to settle on the land and to learn modern farming methods; and ample supplies of fertilizer have been manufactured from the rich mineral resources of the Dead Sea and the Negev. Mineral exploration and mining development have led to greatly increased yields.

Common schooling and military service have given the young people a sense of identity with their country and its language.

There also are disappointments, delays, and partial failures. The socioeconomic dichotomy between country and city has not been erased; if anything, it seems to be growing. The immigrants from Asia and Africa, who are poorer and more poorly educated than European immigrants, are disproportionately concentrated in the rural areas and small towns where assimilation into the prevailing culture is more difficult. Conversely, the European immigrants are concentrated in urban areas. They and the sabras and pre–World War II immigrants dominate the national government; the urban, European voice is over-represented in national affairs. The Arab population has not been fully assimilated (see Figure III-16) and, given the increasing terrorist activities of the surrounding Arab nations since June, 1967, now occupies an even more ambivalent position.

Immigration has tapered off disappointingly, and this has made it impossible to proceed as rapidly as desired with new town settlement. Of the people who have come, too many have settled in the coastal plain, despite the government's programs of incentives and penalties. The desire for an urban life and the cultural and economic attractions of the larger urban centers, particularly Tel Aviv and Haifa, have led many immigrants—primarily those

Figure III-16. An Arab Village

Europeans with sufficient funds and job skills to make a choice—to forgo the short-term economic advantages of settling where government financial incentives are greatest. Public ownership of 92 percent of the land has not been sufficient to combat this centripetal drive, because private lands are within and adjoin urban areas.

Population Distribution

It is not possible to consider Israel's population distribution policies and programs without an awareness of land-use policies and programs, and the converse is equally true. Both are a reflection of the unique combination of social, economic, and military factors which has shaped the country since 1948.

Plan Implementation

While the hierarchy of plan precedence is from the national master plan down to the local detailed plan, heaviest responsibility for plan enforcement rests with the local commissions. Major investment decisions are made at the national level, but it is the careful supervision and stringent enforcement of detailed plans which can assure implementation of the whole structure of plans. If development is allowed to occur in contravention of plans, or if exceptions are loosely granted, the existence of plans is of little relevance. Of course, this is fully as true in the United States as it is in Israel. Israel's advantage is that she has a number of effective means of securing plan implementation which are not now available in the United States. First, when adopted by the appropriate body, the plan is a binding document. Building permits may be issued only if the proposed construction meets the requirements of the plan. Second, much urban fringe land is publicly owned. Third, there are extensive eminent domain powers which may be used in conjunction with the conversion of land to urban uses. Fourth, there is an extant, if not entirely satisfactory, system of compensation and betterment. In addition to these controls which differ from those now used in the United States, there is direct public investment. Its role will be discussed with reference to the realization of specific land-use and population distribution objectives.

Given this wider panoply of public powers and the considerable and increasing coordination of planning among national, district, and local governments, it is significant to observe that Israel still has enjoyed only partial success in persuading the private market to follow where the government leads. Economic uncertainty deters the private entrepreneur and the individual settler from committing themselves to the new towns and rural settlements. For the individual the social and cultural shortcomings of the development areas (when compared to the older urban areas) are another serious deterrent. If one's yardstick for measuring Israel's success in determining the location of development is stated objectives, her achievements definitely fall short of the mark. However, if one compares Israel's achievements with those of other countries stating similar planning objectives, the degree of success in Israel is far greater. To what extent one can credit this comparative success to the methods employed for plan implementation, and to what extent Israel's extraordinary circumstances are responsible, it is impossible to say. There is no question, however, but that her development controls have been of major significance. Because they differ from those used in the United States and provide a greater measure of public control, it is important to see how the major development controls operate.[46]

The Plan as a Binding Document

Under the 1966 Planning and Building Law and its predecessor, development was forbidden if it contravened a properly adopted plan. Under the earlier law, however, many communities did not have master plans, and, even when they did, a detailed plan prepared by a developer for his own land could be approved, despite the fact that it disrupted a master plan. Because the 1966 law requires planning at each level of government and explicitly specifies the order of precedence for plans, development now should proceed more closely in accordance with plans. This requirement does not, of course, provide any assurance that development will occur at all on land planned for development. If the private entrepreneur judges that the use shown on the plan is not economically feasible, he will not develop.

Because 92 percent of Israel's land is publicly owned, concern about control of the development of the remaining 8 percent may seem needless. As seen in Map III-3, however, virtually all of the private land is either in or on the fringes of existing urban areas or along the coastal plain, areas where development pressures and speculation are greatest. Without stringent controls, this land would be developed or redeveloped intensively, thereby frustrating government policies for population distribution and the preservation of agricultural land.

The Planning and Building Law requires that a permit be obtained from the local commission for any construction, including alterations or additions to existing buildings and changes in the existing road network. The local commission may grant permits when the proposed construction meets the requirements of the adopted plans; if a permit for a non-conforming use or a variance is sought, the district commission, as well as the local commission, must assent.[47]

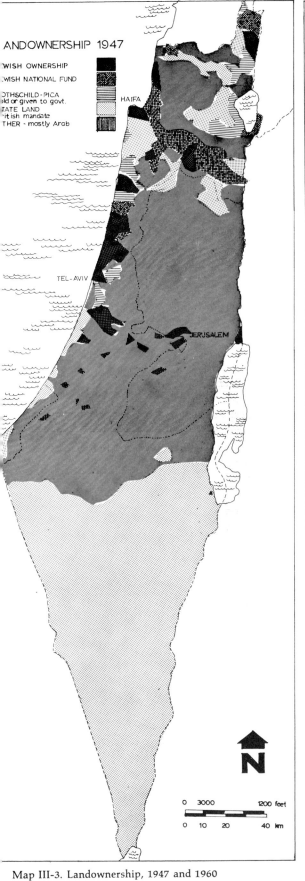

LANDOWNERSHIP 1947

JEWISH OWNERSHIP
JEWISH NATIONAL FUND
ROTHSCHILD-PICA
sold or given to govt.
STATE LAND
British mandate
OTHER - mostly Arab

HAIFA

TEL-AVIV

JERUSALEM

N

0   3000   1200 feet
0   10   20   40 km

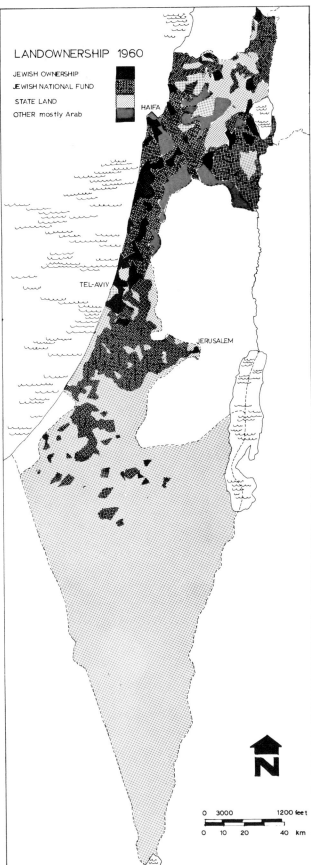

LANDOWNERSHIP 1960

JEWISH OWNERSHIP
JEWISH NATIONAL FUND
STATE LAND
OTHER mostly Arab

HAIFA

TEL-AVIV

JERUSALEM

N

0   3000   1200 feet
0   10   20   40 km

Map III-3. Landownership, 1947 and 1960

These permit requirements place a heavy burden on the local commissions, which often lack professional staff or even sufficient manpower to keep up with the applications. Delays are common. Delay also occurs if the local commission is in the process of altering its plan when an application for a building permit is filed. The permit may not be granted, but on the other hand the local government may not postpone unduly the completion and submission for approval of its revised plan. What would be considered undue delay[48] awaits further court interpretation. Although plan review and revision do occur continually, the 1966 law does not require reviews at fixed intervals. As M. D. Gouldman notes, this is regrettable.

... There are many factors affecting planning (e.g. the rate of immigration) which cannot be accurately forecast. It is true that town planning schemes are constantly being replaced and revised but a statutory obligation to review them would have the effect of keeping the Planning Commission on its toes and compelling it to consider how well its schemes were working. It would have to think ahead instead of waiting until changed circumstances forced it to move—by which time it is often too late for effective action.[49]

As is true in most countries of Western Europe, but not in the United States, a landowner does not have the right to develop his land other than as such right is created by an official plan. For example, a plan may place land in a permanent agricultural district. The fact that the owner could make considerably more money from the land by developing it is simply not relevant to the validity or enforceability of the plan. The law specifically includes preservation of agricultural and scenic lands as a proper objective of the local master plan.

... The objects of a local outline scheme are: (1) to control the development of the land within the local planning area, whilst preserving the agricultural designation of land suitable therefore; (2) to secure proper conditions of health, sanitation, cleanliness, safety, security, transport, and amenity and to prevent nuisances by means of land-use planning, including the demarcation of residential, industrial, and trading zones; (3) to preserve any building or object which is of architectural, historical, archaeological, or similar importance; (4) to preserve and develop places of natural interest or beauty.[50]

Public Landownership

Public landownership has been a vital ingredient of the new towns and of rural land settlement programs in Israel. The national government has been able to choose sites for development in accordance with economic and social goals, unimpeded by private speculation in land. The national network of roads, railroads, water conduits, and pipelines has been built without intervention by private landowners claiming compensable loss in the value of their land. The extension of public services was planned to create values and development incentives in accordance with government plans rather than in response to diverse private pressures. Because public landownership is limited in and around the principal urban areas, however, Israel has been less successful than Sweden in using it as a method of securing plan implementation in these areas.

Israel's public lands are owned by the national government, the Jewish National Fund (Keren Kayemeth Leisrael), and, to a lesser extent, by the local governments. It is government policy, a reflection of religious belief, not to sell public land.[51] The Torah (Lev. 5 : 23) says: "And the land shall not be sold in perpetuity, for the land is mine." Israelis believe that the private individual does not have an unlimited right to use the land as he pleases, but is rather a custodian of the land. Where private use is desired, land is leased for a long term, usually forty-nine years, and provisions are made for renewal and hereditary rights.

Public landownership in Israel dates back to 1901, when the Jewish National Fund was established. The fund's express purpose was to acquire land, in what was then Palestine, for Jewish immigrants. In accordance with the spirit of Zionism, land was acquired for rural settlement by kibbutzim and moshavim. Little land was acquired near existing urban settlements, because it was intended that the immigrants should live in small communities and engage in active farming. The Zionist ethos even prescribed which rural lands should be purchased. Investment in the red coastal soils was rejected because these soils were best suited to orchards and vineyards, both labor-intensive types of farming. Noting that earlier settlers had become entrepreneurs by employing Arab laborers, the fund decided to avoid this pattern by buying land suitable for grain crops. Each immigrant would work on the land, and none would occupy the role of entrepreneur. Given this objective, the small, early land purchases of the fund were concentrated in the dark soils of Lower Galilee, even though there was a dearth of water in that area. Other purchases were made in the Judean Hills and in the Kinneret Valley near Lake Tiberias (the Sea of Galilee). Because of the disastrous experiences of earlier Jewish settlers in the malarial coastal marshes, land there was not sought out at this time.

Later, in the 1920s, when more funds were available for land purchase, tracts large enough for a group of interrelated settlements were bought. At this time, marshland in the Jezreël Valley and elsewhere was bought from Arab landowners, and the expensive, arduous task of drainage began.

Land acquisition in the 1930s was hampered but not halted by the Land Transfer Regulations enacted by the British to slow Jewish immigration and reduce Arab animosity.[52]

As of 1962, one-third of Israel's Jewish population lived on Jewish National Fund land, either on farms or in 640 small settlements.[53]

Since 1948 the fund's principal task has been rural land management. Because the fund's 900,000 acres are largely rural, it has agreed with the government to accept responsibility for soil reclamation, clearing rocks, terracing, afforestation, and drainage of this and all other such land in Israel. As of 1967 more than 255,000 acres had been reclaimed, 90 million trees had been planted,[54] and trees had been planted along 550 miles of highway.[55] The fund also builds roads that will encourage settlement of rural border areas.

State lands are all those lands which were held by the mandatory government at the time of the creation of the state of Israel, as well as ownerless tracts in Israel—namely, those abandoned by Arabs who fled the country at the time of independence. These lands are held directly by the national government or by its subsidiary, the Lands Authority, which administers all national lands. The Lands Authority carries out all types of development, including the construction of buildings, bridges, roads, waterworks, and power lines. Its policies are set by a fifteen-member executive council chaired by the minister of agriculture.

There are exceptions to the prohibition on the sale of public lands.[56] These relate to specified urban development situations, to the restoration of abandoned property to previous owners, or to the fulfillment of obligations that predate the Basic Law. The Lands Authority has been given limited powers to sell or exchange land, including the power to transfer up to 100,000 dönüms (25,000 acres) for urban development.[57] Under certain circumstances, people who fled when Israel was created, or their heirs, may establish claims to public land in exchange for their abandoned land, which had been acquired by the custodian of absentee property. Similar claims may be established by people who did not flee but who were classed as subjects of an enemy state and dispossessed of their land.[58]

Public landownership has made it possible for Israel to locate new towns and rural villages without concern for problems of land acquisition and to build much more cheaply than would have been the case had there been private land speculation. Land speculation is a serious, continuing problem in the cities and coastal belt. In Jerusalem, Haifa, and the suburbs of Tel Aviv, land represents from 25 to 30 percent of the cost of an apartment; in central Tel Aviv, land may exceed 50 percent of the price of an apartment.[59] In these areas, public landownership has been largely irrelevant as a means of plan implementation.

Eminent Domain

Eminent domain, or expropriation as it is commonly called in Israel, is neither a legally nor a financially feasible means of coping with the problem of urban land speculation. Nevertheless, it offers some limited opportunities for land acquisition not common in the United States.

The Planning and Building Law is more limited than was the Town Planning Ordinance in its statement of the purposes for which a local commission may exercise the power of eminent domain. The plan must designate that the land is intended for public purposes—that is, for roads, parks, nature reserves, parking areas, airports, harbors, railroad or bus stations, markets, institutions, and water supply or sewage disposal works. There is no specific provision in the law which authorizes eminent domain for redevelopment or for low-income housing, but the court might interpret these as falling under the non-specific clause of this section, which permits eminent domain for "any other public purpose certified by the minister of the interior."[60]

One interesting section of the law is that which, according to a theory closely akin to betterment, permits eminent domain without compensation. Up to 40 percent of a tract may be taken by eminent domain without compensation if it is to be used in developing roads, parks, playgrounds, or buildings for educational, cultural, religious, or health purposes. However, this partial taking is forbidden, with or without compensation, if the remainder of the tract would decline in value as a result of the taking.[61]

In the United States it is customary to require the construction and dedication of roads in a subdivision. Here, however, when land is taken for arterial highway construction, payment is made to the landowner without consideration of the enormous increase in value which may accrue to the remaining land as the result of the highway construction. Mandatory dedication of land or a money equivalent by a subdivider for park or recreation purposes also is gaining judicial acceptance in the United States. Again, however, the knowledge that the creation of a park or other community facility greatly increases the value of surrounding land has yet to lead to any technique by which the U.S. public can realize this rise in value. Israel's provision for eminent domain without compensation captures part of this gain accruing to land severed from that taken by the public. It is a rough means of balancing the loss in land against the increase in value of the remaining land, but it is a step in the direction of equity. Because it is a form of betterment, the value of land taken may be deducted from the betterment tax, if such a tax is assessed against the property. Frequently, the local commission can forgo the use of eminent domain in conjunction with large-scale private development.

... Generally an agreement is reached with regard to the layout of the estate or development project and the developer readily agrees to surrender 40 percent or even 50 percent of his land to the Local Commission, knowing that his estate cannot exist without roads, parks, schools, and other public amenities and that their provision will enormously enhance the value of his project.[62]

One problem with the new eminent domain provisions is that the law is silent on the question of how much time may elapse between a plan's designation of an area for acquisition by eminent domain and the actual acquisition. Because land planned for future public uses loses its value for development and is difficult, if not impossible, to sell on the private market, the owner is placed in a financially awkward position during the period between the adoption of the plan and public acquisition. From the few cases decided so far, it seems that more than three, but less than twelve, years has been judged a reasonable range within which to fix the time limit between adoption of a plan showing areas to be acquired for public purposes and the actual acquisition of the land.

Taxation

Income, excise, and real property taxes, all levied by the state, are sometimes used as tools to further planning objectives. Foreign investment in Israel, export trade, industrial location, and housing location and development all are influenced by differential taxation. Manipulation of these tax tools through substantive change and through rate changes occurs frequently. Unless otherwise noted, rates cited here were those current in 1969.

Since Israel's independence, the income tax has become a steadily more important source of tax revenue for the government. In 1948–49, only 25.5 percent of tax revenues were derived from the income tax; by 1964–65, 50.2 percent of tax revenues came from this source. Initially, the government found it difficult to collect the income tax because many Israelis had come from nations where this tax was not levied. Thus, initially, it was simpler to obtain revenue from the more aggressive, indirect taxes—sales taxes, luxury taxes, and other taxes on expenditures. In 1948–49, taxes on expenditures accounted for 62.5 percent of tax revenues. By 1964–65 the income tax had been accepted and collection procedures had improved; taxes on expenditures that year accounted for only 40.4 percent of Israel's tax revenues. The real property tax has a rather consistent record; since 1948 it has contributed 4 percent of tax revenues and about 5 percent of taxes on transactions.[63]

The real property tax is levied on owners of both improvements and land, including fee and leasehold interests. Assessments are established on the basis of actual current rental value, or, if a structure is vacant, the rent which could be obtained. Only vacant land is assessed on the basis of market value. In general, rates on improvements are much higher than those on land, although the tax on vacant land held as a speculative investment may be higher than that on developed land. Rates vary according to location, being much higher in large cities than in small cities and rural areas. In 1962, on an assessment rate of 85 percent, rural land or interests in land were taxed at 0.5 percent, city land at up to 1.5 percent. Apartments in Tel Aviv are taxed at 12.6 percent of 85 percent of the rental value. New buildings and additions to existing buildings are exempt from two-thirds of the property tax for five years; if the construction was for the builder's personal use, the exemption period is ten years.

There also is a property tax (the general rate) levied on the occupant of the property. Occupants of residential property pay a fixed tax, the amount of which is determined by the type of housing and its location. Occupants of other buildings pay a tax based on rental value, the rate being determined by the category of building and its location. Users of land without structures pay a fixed tax based on type of use and location; agricultural rates are pegged at one-quarter the rate on other similarly located land used for other purposes.[64]

An assessment committee fixes assessments, which may be appealed to the district court. The municipalities classify properties by rates, and the rates, as so established, must be confirmed by the Ministry of the Interior. A portion of the property tax is distributed to the municipalities.

Currently, industries which export at least 50 percent of their production are entitled to rebates on real property taxes of up to 50 percent. In addition to the real property taxes there is a value-added tax of between 20 and 40 percent on improvements, the rate being determined by the value of the improvements in relation to the acquisition value of the property. Improvements of up to 200 percent of the acquisition value are taxed at 20 percent, those between 200 and 400 percent of the acquisition value are taxed at 30 percent, and those over 400 percent of the acquisition value are taxed at 40 percent.[65]

Capital gain taxes are payable on the sale of the fee or leasehold, the rate varying between 5 and 40 percent of the gain, depending on the amount of the gain and the time which has elapsed between acquisition and sale.

Land transfer taxes are levied by the state and are paid in part to the Treasury, in part to the municipality in which the land is located. The sum collected on behalf of the local government is one-half of that levied by the state. If there is no local government in existence where the land is located, the local government share of the tax is paid to the appropriate district commissioner.[66]

The income tax, like the property tax, sometimes is employed to further government land settlement and development policies. Lower rates in the new towns and lower rates for foreign investors—individuals and corporations— are intended to stimulate, respectively, new town development and foreign capital inflow.

Individuals pay a tax of from 22.5 to 60.0 percent on taxable income. Income earned abroad as well as in Israel is taxable, although some provisions have been made to avoid double taxation. Taxable income is determined much as it is in the United States: exemptions are granted for dependents, and deductions are allowed for health insurance, medical expenses, charitable contributions, and the like. One notable difference is that the amount of the exemption for each child increases up to the fourth child; this reflects the government policy of encouraging women to bear many children. The exemption for one child is 250 £P (about $71); it is 375 £P (about $107) for the fourth child and for each additional child.

Special tax rates cover several situations. Workers receiving bonuses for high productivity are taxed at the rate of 15 percent on those bonuses. Overtime pay, when the overtime work is required by the employer, is taxed at 30 percent. Those living in new towns receive a one-third reduction in their income tax. The poor are exempt.

The individual income tax on dividends is withheld by corporations at the rate of 25 percent. Persons in a higher tax bracket pay the additional tax. Dividends on "approved" investments in foreign currencies are charged only the 25 percent tax.

The rate of sales taxes on domestic consumer goods ranges from 7.5 to 50 percent.

Excise taxes are considerably higher on imported goods; they reflect the government policy of encouraging domestic production and discouraging imports. Take cars, for example. The tax on a car produced in Israel is 36 percent; that on imported cars is 150 percent.

Municipalities impose business taxes, license taxes, and entertainment taxes. "Approved" specialists coming from abroad to work in Israel pay a maximum rate of 25 percent during the first three years of their employment in Israel.

In addition to the regular income tax, there is an 18 percent surtax in the form of a compulsory loan to the government. This loan pays interest at the rate of 4 percent, and 10 percent of the principal balance is repaid annually. Persons with a taxable income of less than approximately $700 pay a compulsory loan surtax at the rate of 12 percent.

Corporations pay a company profits tax of 30 percent on their chargeable income. Then, on the net income, which is chargeable income minus the company profits tax plus dividends, an income tax of 25 percent is payable, plus a surtax of 12 percent of the remaining net income after payment of the first two taxes. Special provisions exist for the rapid depreciation of the investment industries make when locating in development areas. Under the Encouragement of Investments Law, they and other "approved" companies also receive special income tax treatment during the first five years in which the corporation shows a profit, provided that this occurs within ten years of the establishment of the corporation. The company profits tax is payable, but the income tax is not levied. Dividends need not be distributed during this period, but, if paid, are exempt from the individual income tax. In special instances a portion of the company profits tax may also be waived. For instance, "approved" industries locating in Dimona are entitled to a one-third reduction in this tax for the first five profitable years.[67]

Compensation and Betterment

As part of her heritage from British jurisprudence, Israel has struggled with the problem of compensation and betterment. The theory of the British approach—that substantial losses in private land values caused by a plan should be publicly compensated for, while, conversely, the public should recover substantial gains attributable to plans—has been accepted and is reflected in the Israeli law. Few other countries have progressed beyond an acknowledgement of the problem and a recognition of its complexity.

Unlike Britain, where the Town and Country Planning Act of 1947, its predecessors, and successors have been enforced nationwide, Israeli compensation legislation has been employed selectively while the betterment legislation remains largely unenforced. The greater urgency of other development questions and the lack of government financial resources limited enforcement of the law as it existed prior to 1966.

Because it was initially drawn up by the British during the mandate period, the Town Planning Ordinance derived much from British legislation, including the compensation and betterment provisions. The compensation provisions are clearly at variance with the theory that no development rights exist until created by a plan and that, therefore, if a plan does not create such rights, no obligation to pay for this non-allocation of development rights is incurred. This theory supports public creation of imbalances in land values through planning. Provisions for compensation, on the other hand, tend toward equalization of the impact of planning.

The 1966 Planning and Building Law is closely related to the Town Planning Ordinance in its compensation and betterment provisions. Its compensation provisions are similar to those now coming to be employed in the United States under the term "inverse condemnation." The initiative rests with the landowner to claim that the use restrictions placed on his land are so severe as to entitle him to compensation. The government neither wants nor takes fee title to the land, but, if the landowner is successful, is ordered to pay damages and may be held to have condemned a less-than-fee interest. Under Israeli law, landowners have one year from the adoption of a plan to file a claim with the local commission stating that their "land is injuriously affected" by the plan and that they therefore are entitled to compensation. After the claim is filed, the local commission makes a report stating its recommendation and submits it to the district commission for approval. Payment is made by the local commission if it so recommends and the district commission concurs.[68] Rejections of claims may be appealed to the courts.[69] The law enumerates several planning provisions which, by law, are deemed not to affect land injuriously, "provided that the injury does not go beyond what is reasonable in the circumstances of the case and that it is not equitable to pay compensation to the person aggrieved."[70] Included in this list are changes in boundaries of land-use districts; specifications for building set-back, size, density, and design; prohibition of building where it would "be likely to lead to danger of flooding or erosion or to danger to health or life or to the excessive expenditure of public money in the provision of roads or drains or in the supply of water or other public services"; restrictions on building use; and parking and loading requirements. It is too soon to say how the courts will interpret the reasonableness test established here; as Mr. Gouldman suggests, the clause "is calculated to invite litigation. For what landowners will agree that it is equitable not to pay him compensation!"[71]

Compensation, if due the landowner, is payable when the claim is established rather than when an actual loss is suffered, and this creates the difficult problem of calculating the amount payable. Because local governments are charged with paying compensation when it is awarded, and because their limited revenues are severely taxed, they obviously are inclined to deny claims and to discourage landowners from filing them.

Although it provided an opportunity for the government to realize some of the gains from planning permission, the betterment law has been even more neglected than the compensation law. Just as there is a difficult problem of measuring loss due to planning when no sale of property has occurred, so there is the equally difficult problem of measuring gain under similar circumstances. If betterment is to be collected, the government must be in a position to demonstrate the amount of gain. The initiative in compensation law proceedings rests with the private landowner, who feels himself wronged by the strictures of the plan, while it rests with the government in betterment law enforcement; this may explain why the compensation provisions have received relatively more use and more judicial interpretation than the betterment provisions.

The betterment law permits local commissions to levy a betterment tax on increases in private land value attributable to municipal plans. Any time within two years after adoption of the plan, the local commission may demand payment of a sum equal to one-half of the increase in value attributable to the plan. This poses a serious valuation problem—namely, how much of the rise in value has occurred as a result of the plan and how much as a result of other factors? Pending enactment of a better law, the local commissions are dependent on this one to attempt to counterbalance the claims made on them under the compensation law.

The betterment law was part of the Town Planning Ordinance. Given the fact that there was general dissatisfaction with it, several new proposals were placed before the Knesset at the time the Planning and Building Law was adopted. Regrettably, they were not thoroughly considered, and the preexisting provisions were retained in the new law. The law provides a substantial opportunity for the local commissions to share in the gain accruing to private land as a result of the allocation of development rights under a plan. Whether the local commissions, having been denied a new and more workable law, will attempt to resolve the administrative and valuation problems posed by the law in order to touch a needed, additional source of revenue remains to be seen. A few local commissions have enforced the law in the past, to their distinct advantage. Tel Aviv received 2 million £P ($667,000 at the then prevailing rate of exchange) from its betterment tax in 1964–65.[72] This was at a time when private land prices in central Tel Aviv were rising 200 percent per year. On the Tel Aviv urban fringe, where plans permitted conversion from agriculture to urban uses, land prices were rising even more rapidly.[73] In this context the amount realized by the betterment tax is miniscule.

While the struggle to develop a workable method of compensation and betterment is important to the Israeli economy, it is understandably less critical than it would be in a nation whose government did not hold more than 90 percent of the land. Nonetheless, much of the post-1948 profit from land development in Israel has gone to private entrepreneurs. Because the possibility of realizing this profit, and of realizing it on one tract rather than on another, was in large measure a result of a government planning policy, it would be equitable for the government to capture a greater share of the profit. For example, economic considerations alone might have dictated a more urbanized, concentrated form of development, yet this would have been unacceptable militarily and undesirable under the prevailing Zionist ideology. On the other hand, the Zionist ideal of settlement in small rural cooperatives or collective villages was impractical economically and counter to the preferences of most immigrants. Israel today is a mélange of these influences. Fortunately, the development policies are dynamic. Some past programs, appropriate for existing circumstances, are being revised. Others, reflecting accepted policies, never proved satisfactory in implementation. Still other programs proved successful and need further emphasis. The government has indicated that it recognizes the need to temper ideology with pragmatism and to learn from experience.

It seems probable that the rather elaborate structure of a hierarchy of settlements will be abandoned for a simpler system of rural villages linked to major urban centers. The attraction of large urban centers cannot be denied further; to attain the social goal of an integrated population, it will be necessary to make it possible for African and Asian immigrants to exercise their locational preference, as the economically self-sufficient already have done. Farm life, in the old kibbutzim-moshavim pattern, is attractive to an ever smaller segment of the population, and so the rural settlement pattern must change. New town programs will metamorphose to new city programs in order that the goal of an equal standard of living may be realized nationwide. Ashdod is the leading example of the attraction of a new city conceived on a sufficiently large scale. Given the vitality and flexibility exhibited in Israel's first two decades, there is every reason to expect her to shift the direction of development toward an even more successful amalgamation of her people and exploitation of her limited resources.

Actual Distribution, Past and Present

In 1948 the Jewish population of Israel was most heavily concentrated in the metropolitan areas of Tel Aviv and Haifa, in Jerusalem, and along the coastal plain. The Negev, constituting the southern half of the country, was unsettled. Today the metropolitan areas of 1948 have expanded greatly, in area and population (see Figures III-17 and III-18). In addition, however, the countryside of the Galilee and the northern Negev down to Beersheba have been settled with 400 rural communities. Twenty-seven new towns of up to 50,000 people have been created, from Qiryat Shemona in the far north, to Eilat on the Red Sea. It is planned that some of these new towns will continue expanding until they are medium-sized cities. The future population of Ashdod is projected at more than 300,000. Most of the new development away from pre-existing urban centers has occurred counter to the compelling attractions to the individual of an easier life offered by the urban areas—a wider choice of jobs, greater job security, better schools, and more community facilities.

It is not much of an overstatement to say that, to the extent that the immigrant population did not settle in the Tel Aviv, Haifa, and Jerusalem metropolitan areas or on the coastal plain, the government's population distribution policy has succeeded (see Map III-4). While the three principal metropolitan areas have more than doubled, their percentage of the total population has declined. Table III-4 shows the shift in population by region from 1948 to 1961, while Table III-5 lists the population of each of the three major metropolitan areas according to its percentage of the total Jewish population. The most marked changes occurred in Greater Tel Aviv, where the total Jewish population declined 8.7 percent, and in the Southern region, where an actual increase from 19,000 to 167,000 people and a percentage increase of 4.4 percent of the total population took place.

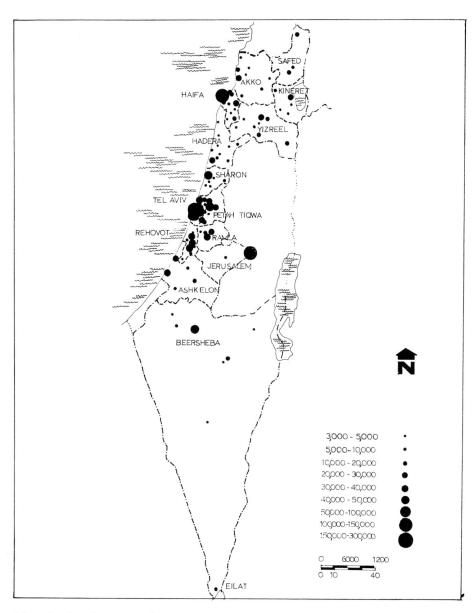

Map III-4. Population Distribution, 1965

Figure III-17. Tel Aviv

Figure III-18. Dizengoff Circle, Tel Aviv

Table III-4.
Population Distribution by Region, 1948 and 1961

Region	1948		1961	
	Number of People (in thousands)	Percentage of Total Population	Number of People (in thousands)	Percentage of Total Population
Northern	147	17.9	337	15.5
Haifa	151	18.5	370	17.0
Central	109	13.3	406	18.9
Tel Aviv	306	37.5	684	31.8
Jerusalem	86	10.5	188	8.8
Southern	19	2.3	167	7.7
Total	818	100.0	2,152	100.0

SOURCE: Jacob Dash and Elisha Efrat, *The Israel Physical Master Plan,* prepared for the Ministry of the Interior (Jerusalem, 1964).

Table III-5.
Population of Major Metropolitan Areas, 1948 and 1961

City or Metropolitan Area	1948		1961	
	Number of People (in thousands)	Percentage of Total Jewish Population	Number of People (in thousands)	Percentage of Total Jewish Population
Greater Tel Aviv	290	41.3	630	32.6
Greater Haifa	100	14.3	211	11.0
Jerusalem	82	11.7	165	8.5
Total	472	67.3	1,006	52.1

SOURCE: Israel, Ministry of the Interior, Planning Department, *National Planning for the Redistribution of Population and the Establishment of New Towns in Israel* (Jerusalem, 1964).

National Plans

So far, six successive national plans for population distribution have been prepared. In each the conflicting forces that affect population distribution have been recognized—the military requirement that border areas be settled, the Zionist ideological preference for small, rural settlements, the shortage of capital investment funds, and the need for sufficient industrial concentration to enable Israel's products to compete in world markets.

The 1964 population distribution plan for 1982 envisages a population of four million. The proportionate distribution would follow the actual past trend, with more of the population urban, but with a smaller percentage located in the three major cities. A few additional new towns would be built, and the existing villages and new towns would become considerably larger. The countryside, except for the coastal plain and the southern Negev, would be more thickly settled than at present. The major conurbations would spread out still further, and their percentage of the total population would rise slightly, although their center city population percentages would decline somewhat. On the coastal plain a greater demarcation between rural and urban land would have developed.[74]

Shifts in national policy can be discerned in successive population distribution plans, as shown in Table III-6. Between the 1951 and 1964 plans, the percentage allocated to rural areas dropped from 22.6 to 13.0. Most of the shift away from the rural areas would be directed to towns and moderate-sized urban communities.

Table III-6.
Population Distribution Plans: Urban-Rural Allocation

Type of Settlement	Proposed Population Distribution		
	1951 Plan	1957 Plan	1964 Plan
Greater Tel Aviv, Haifa, and Jerusalem	35.1%	37.1%	37.9%
Other towns and urban areas	42.3	47.5	49.1
Rural settlements	22.6	15.4	13.0

SOURCE: Jacob Dash and Elisha Efrat, *The Israel Physical Master Plan*, prepared for the Ministry of the Interior (Jerusalem, 1964).

This planned drop in percentage allocation to the rural areas has met with considerable opposition from the older Zionists. Even recognizing that the most efficient use of labor dictates that fewer people will be needed for agricultural production, theoretical adherence to the concept of settlement in small rural collectives and cooperatives leads to opposition to greater urbanization. Nevertheless, the 1964 plan was adopted by the government and is official government policy until replaced by a subsequent plan.

Theoretical Bases

Earlier population distribution plans had a carefully reasoned theoretical basis quite apart from zionism. Whereas Zionist policy prior to independence resulted in settlement assuming a polar pattern, the early planning theorists endorsed a hierarchical pattern. The polar pattern emerged from two divergent directions of immigrant settlement: dispersion across the land in small kibbutzim and moshavim, and concentration in the three major cities. Few small or medium-sized towns were established. Although this pattern developed for ideological reasons, many of Israel's planners recognized it as the pattern also prevalent in technologically advanced, developed countries, where the links between rural areas and major cities are direct. Believing this to be the appropriate future pattern for Israel as a developed country, they thought it unnecessary for the country first to pass through the stage of hierarchical settlement in which rural areas are served by small towns, which in turn are supported by regional centers. However, the viewpoint of the planners who endorsed the hierarchical pattern prevailed. These planners looked to Christaller and his theories of the laws of spatial structure of human settlements. They noted the epitomization of these theories in the development of Central and Western Europe. Although they recognized that the pattern had been established prior to the Industrial Revolution, they still believed that it offered a flexibility better suited than the polar pattern to Israel's projected rapid growth and change.

The attitude of the planners responsible for guiding national planning was, however, different. They evaluated such "polar" pattern as undesirable, and considered it suitable for the primary and pioneering period of development only. They inclined to welcome a gradual evolution from this pattern towards a hierarchy of urban centres approaching the European model. Such a pattern, in their opinion, appeared to be more mature and more adequate, for a country which was to become a densely populated and intensively developed one. This attitude was obviously influenced by a "regionalistic" approach. . . . Theoretical insight, which anticipated the rise of the "tertiary" or service sector in the occupational structure of modern society had a certain influence too. In spatial terms services tend generally to hierarchical patterns, and therefore support or contribute to the crystallization of an hierarchical network of urban centres.[75]

Circumstances favored the hierarchical view. Immigrants had to be settled, and money was scarce. Land in the urban areas was privately owned and relatively expensive, while outlying land was public and therefore free for government development. For defense reasons, people had to be settled near the borders, and because a rural density was insufficient, towns had to be built. Jobs were available far from the urban centers. Road building, construction of the water system and of irrigation works, housing construction, and land reclamation and afforestation work went forward throughout much of the country, thereby creating a need for nearby towns for workers.

The hierarchical pattern adopted by Israel's planners consists of five levels (A through E in Table III-7) of town settlement; three of these levels lie between and augment the rural-village and large-city polar pattern which existed prior to independence. Over time the theoretical populations for these three new types of settlement have been revised upward. B centers most recently have been planned for 2,000 people, D centers for populations of from 40,000 to 60,000.[76]

Table III-7.
Urban Settlement Hierarchy

Type of Settlement	Population	Characteristics
A—village, kibbutz, or moshav	Up to 500	
B—rural center	500–1,000	Economic, social, and cultural center for 4–6 moshavim. Residents to be craftsmen, people providing services.
C—rural-urban center	6,000–12,000	To serve an area with a radius of approximately 10 miles, including 30 villages. To include secondary schools, housing for farm labor, rural-related industry, some administrative services.
D—medium-sized town	15,000–60,000	Regional center for commerce, culture, and administration. Industry locationally independent.
E—large city	100,000 and over	Major central functions of government, education, and commerce.

SOURCE: Eliezer Brutzkus, *Physical Planning in Israel* (Jerusalem, 1964).

Theoretically, new development would have been directed first to the B centers; due to the sudden deluge of immigrants, however, it was decided that it would be cheaper and quicker to focus development in fewer locations. Therefore, the regional centers—the D towns—received the largest investment first. Because later experience has shown that only the larger towns can compete with the major urban areas in attracting and holding both industry and residents, it is fortunate that so much of the early investment was in these towns.

The locations chosen for C and D towns were of several types: pre-existing small towns along the coast, including Hadera, Netanya, and Rehovot, which had housed the orange grove workers; old towns with a historical *raison d'être*, mainly populated by Arabs prior to 1948; and wholly new towns, many located on the sites of and named for biblical towns, such as Hazor, Eilat, and Ashdod.

Implementation

The purpose of the population distribution plans is threefold: (1) to provide a national framework for city and town planning; (2) to offer guidelines for national programs which can influence the location of development; and (3) to guide public agencies in determining the size and location of public services and institutions. The most direct impact on population distribution has occurred through national programs to influence development location, particularly the location of immigrant housing and industry.

The national government uses quotas for immigrant housing construction which accord with population distribution plans. In new or expanding areas, it was assumed that immigrants would be employed for two or three years in housing, road, and infrastructure construction and, to a lesser extent, in nearby agriculture. Therefore, it was not considered vital that industrial development take place simultaneously with town settlement or expansion. Because much of Israel's industry is location-free, it was assumed that industry could be directed to a new or expanded town to provide jobs (in addition to those provided by services and any pre-existing industry) as soon as the work of town construction had been completed. In fact, this has not always proved to be the case, partly because the Ministry of Commerce did not move rapidly to implement the plans, and partly because some industries resisted the combination of penalties and incentives designed to lure them away from the major metropolitan areas. The attractions of cheap and plentiful land, government loans at favorable rates, lower taxes, and the availability of sufficient labor did attract many, however.

Coordination between the Planning Department of the Ministry of the Interior and the Housing Department of the Ministry of Labor has been close. Each year, beginning in 1949, the Housing Department, and then, after the mid-1950s, the Ministry of Housing, set quotas for immigrant housing construction which followed the recommendations of population distribution plans. In accordance with these plans, housing construction for the urban areas of Tel Aviv, Haifa, and Jerusalem was left to private enterprise and thus served a higher income market. Except for the few with private means, immigrants had no choice of housing other than the developing towns. In the early years of massive immigration, these people were housed temporarily in transit camps and then in *ma'abarat*; by the mid-1950s, however, they went directly from their point of arrival to housing and employment in developing towns or in agricultural areas.

The newer areas did not always grow as rapidly as had been planned. If industry did not come, jobs were scarce and some of the immigrants moved to the metropolitan areas in search of employment. Housing standards and community facilities were of a lower quality than those in established urban areas, and the pre-1948 urban population resisted efforts to induce them to move to the new communities.

Recognizing that additional government measures were needed to counter the attraction of the major urban areas and to carry out population distribution plans, an interdepartmental committee of the national government drew up a series of proposals.[77] Among them were the ideas that towns still lacking an economic or cultural basis be consolidated; that towns with a population of a few thousand or less be expanded; that, with two exceptions, no additional new towns be established in the near future; that government loans and grants to enterprises on the coastal plain be reduced, and that similar funds for development areas be expanded; that professional people be subsidized to settle in development areas; and that the building on and lease of public lands along the coastal strip be limited. These proposals are a tacit acknowledgment that the smaller settlements under the hierarchical plan are not viable and that, unless the investment in the development areas is greatly increased, they will not become economically or socially competitive with the established urban areas. The undesirable social implications of a geographically stratified population have been recognized and have caused acute concern among planners.[78] Present government policy is directed toward carrying out the 1964 population distribution policy and, simultaneously, toward achieving a sounder population mix in the development areas.

Land Use

Ideology is now of lesser importance than economics in influencing land-use policy. Today the dominant determinant of land use is Israel's resolve to gain maximum return from the available but limited resources. To the extent that Israel can be made self-sufficient, this is being done. Available water supplies are measured and captured, used and re-used. The national water carrier distributes the supply to support crops, trees, and people in arid areas, sustaining life where it would otherwise be untenable. Mineral exploration and exploitation also receive high priority. Urbanization is encouraged where it can be economically profitable, as at the ports of Ashdod and Eilat, and discouraged where it would destroy the most productive agricultural uses. Although Israel still is far from being self-sufficient, the economic development which has occurred through stringent controls on the allocation of limited resources for land development is phenomenal and is far in excess of what anyone would have predicted in 1948. Once again, it is necessary to examine Israel's success in implementing land-use policies, whether for agriculture, mineral resources, or urban growth, in the context of her particular circumstances.

Agriculture

Agricultural development policy reflects the shift from strict adherence to ideological precepts toward greater economic determinism. Today it is difficult to comprehend the early Zionists' abjuration of rural settlement on the coastal plain because vineyard or citrus cultivation might lead to an entrepreneurial structure of agriculture. Land is studied for its most productive use and the type of rural settlement built is dictated in considerable measure by the pattern of cultivation. Where there is truck farming, or fodder-growing on irrigated land, or similar labor-intensive agriculture, farm houses are spread out, and each farm family is adjacent to its fields. Where there are field crops such as grains, cotton, or groundnuts, or orchards and vineyards, farmers are settled in small villages of from 80 to 250 families. Whichever pattern is employed, the rural settlement at this level generally consists of immigrants from a single country with a common language. The farm holdings may be held in common and the settlement may be a kibbutz; alternatively, the settlement may be a cooperative (*moshav*), or each farmer may lease and operate his holding independently.[79]

As industrial crops, namely those requiring processing after harvesting, have increased, the link between the rural settlement and the C or D center has been strengthened, for many workers in the center are employed in processing farm products, be it spinning cotton or canning vegetables.

Before 1948 there was little planning for the coordination of services and community facilities for rural settlements. The lack of convenient schools, shops, doctors, dentists, and recreational centers often made life on the land both dull and trying. The hierarchical pattern was intended to relieve this condition. Serving from four to six villages, the rural center (B) could lease and repair expensive agricultural machinery, offer services to the farmers, and provide an elementary school and some recreational and cultural opportunities. Here, the children would learn Hebrew at school and the parents would pick it up more gradually in commerce and in social interchange with immigrants from other countries. The B center was to be within one and one-half miles of the farm or farm village, so that people could walk there easily. Because initially many, if not most, immigrants arrived with nothing but the clothes on their backs, they could not afford bicycles or bus fare to travel further for errands or leisure. Now, with a far higher standard of living, the rationale which dictated the development of B centers no longer is relevant. People have scooters or money for public transportation. Car ownership is increasing. Given their greater mobility, the people's preference for larger towns is evident. The rural centers will either grow or wither.

When the immigrants arrived they were destitute and they lacked any agricultural skills. The Jewish Agency for Israel screens immigrants for skills and health and then, except for those few who have a job awaiting them, assigns them to housing. If they are assigned to rural housing, the Jewish National Fund, through its Agricultural Settlement Department, takes the immigrants to the rural area where they are to settle, trains them in the type of agriculture suited to the land, works with them to build rural settlements, provides housing at a nominal rent, supplies farm equipment, and assists the immigrants in the cultural adjustment to Israel. While the initial housing units built were small and modest, the scale of construction surely was not. The Jewish Agency has built 480 rural settlements since 1948, and 210,000 people now live in these villages.[80] Without financial support from Jews throughout the world, none of this would have been possible.

There was some initial conflict between the type of rural development built by the Jewish Agency—following the pattern of early twentieth-century Zionist settlement—and that recommended by the Ministry of the Interior.[81] Gradually the government's recommendations were accepted.

It soon became apparent that the methods in use until then would not be suited to these settlers and would not ensure their absorption. New ways had to be found to harmonize the knowledge and skills with the social structure and mode of life of the Afro-Asian newcomers. A further change took place in the economic conditions. The rise in the general standard of living, the necessity to ensure that these immigrants remain among the agricultural population and the need to raise the volume of exports, led to new agricultural methods based on increase of efficiency and specialization and the maximum exploitation of each region's natural resources and conditions.[82]

The Lachish regional development plan epitomizes the agricultural development proposals of the Ministry of the Interior at the time of massive immigration and development. Development in accordance with the plan was carried out by the Jewish Agency starting in the mid-1950s. The Lachish region covers 175,000 acres, all state owned, and lies north of the Gaza Strip, extending from the Mediterranean Sea east across the coastal plain and up the Judean Hills. As seen in Map III-5, the regional development plan covered the entire area and employed the hierarchical concept. A, B, and C type settlements were envisaged, with clearly specified links between them.

Although the soil of the Lachish region is quite fertile, before independence the land was not cultivated. Instead, it was used by Bedouins for grazing their animals because there was insufficient water for agriculture. Once the Yarkon-Negev pipeline provided a supply of water for irrigation, rural settlement began. The land in the central and western parts of the region was planted with sugar beets, peanuts, and cotton—all crops most efficiently cultivated in large tracts. Because each farm was to be worked by the farm family only, with no hired help, from ten to twelve acres was fixed as the appropriate size for each farm. Farm housing was clustered and thus made it possible to save on the roads and infrastructure serving the houses. In the hills to the

Map III-5.
Lachish
Regional Plan

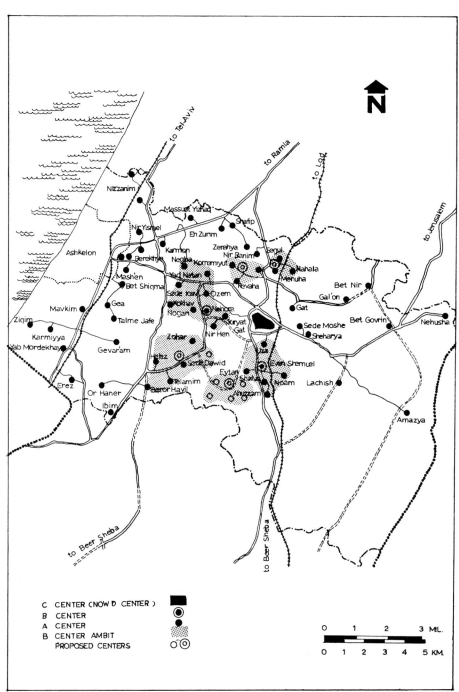

east, water was not available for irrigation, so planting was restricted to grains and orchards and much of the land was maintained for grazing. In this area farm size was set at forty acres. The planners' goal was that a farmer should be able to earn as much money as an industrial worker.[83]

In the A villages, kindergartens, the first grade of elementary school, club rooms, clinics, and synagogues were included. All other frequently needed local services were to be provided by B centers. Each B center was planned to serve from four to six A villages, all located within two and one-half miles of the B center. B centers included an elementary school, farm service shops, a dispensary, a movie theater, cafes, and a cultural center. The C center was to fill the function of a regional cultural and administrative center and was to be the primary processing center for the agricultural produce raised in the region.

The timing of development in the Lachish region proceeded in accordance with the regional development plan. The plan indicated the appropriate locations for the rural settlements, rural B centers, and for Kiryat Gat. Next, engineering work for the irrigation system and road network was completed and the pipes were laid and the roads built. Soil conservation and land cultivation plans were made and the soil was prepared. Then houses were built, immigrants moved in, and planting began. Training in agricultural skills, as well as in adaptation to prevailing Israeli cultural patterns, began. Finally, the settlements became independent, taking over their agricultural equipment and local administration.

Most of the settlers were from Africa and the Middle East. Each A center was settled by only one national group, while the B centers were mixed. For instance, Nehora, a B center settled primarily by sabras, serves Naga, a Kurdistan village; Otzem, settled by Moroccans from the Attas Mountains; Zohar, settled by Tunisians; Nir Chen, an Israeli village; Shahar, settled by immigrants from Tunisia and Tangiers; and Sde David, settled by Moroccans from Casablanca. This policy of settling people with a common place of origin in the same village resulted in a drop in the percentage of families moving away from the village from the 30 to 35 percent found in mixed villages to 15 percent.

By 1966 more than 40 percent of the land in the Lachish region was under cultivation. Much of the rest, lacking sufficient water for irrigation, was used to pasture beef and dairy cattle. Fifty-six rural villages, twenty-seven of which had been built since 1955, had a total population of 17,500.[84] Only two of the six planned rural centers had been built, largely because of the water shortage.[85] Kiryat Gat, begun in 1956 and planned for 7,000, had grown rapidly to a town of more than 20,000 people. It had proved so successful that it had been reclassified as a D center, with a target population of 80,000. It is a principal highway junction for roads linking Ashkelon, Beersheba, Jerusalem, and Ramla. The railroad to Beersheba has a station at Kiryat Gat. Factories have been built for cotton fiber production, dyeing and weaving, for peanut sorting, and for sugar beet refining, as well as for the manufacture of Scotch tape, diamond cuttings, and electronic equipment.

Changed conditions of immigration and agriculture reduce the likelihood that a plan like that for Lachish will be carried out again. Immigration in 1968 exceeded 40,000 because of the 1967 war and the subsequent departure of many of the remaining Jews from North Africa. However, the sustained flow of immigrants is more likely to be on the order of 10,000 per year. What will happen to the Arab refugees remains an open question. In addition to the predicted low rate of immigration, agricultural production is becoming increasingly mechanized, requiring less labor for increased yields. Therefore, until cheap desalinized water is available, thus making increased irrigation financially possible, the agricultural labor force will continue to decline. Those workers who remain on the land will be skilled farm laborers, productive enough to earn good wages and, in turn, to demand a level of services commensurate with those enjoyed by urban dwellers.

Today's rural planning task is to make rural living more appealing by bolstering the quality and variety of services and activities offered in the nearby towns. If this can be achieved, it also will make these towns attractive to more of the non-immigrant population than the 10–15 percent now living in them. In this way the current socioeconomic imbalance between urban and rural areas can be reduced. The task of making the best use of agricultural land within the limits of existing resources has been met; the task of equalizing urban-rural opportunities remains.

Resource Development

Without water, the rural land development program could not have succeeded. Fertilizer, manufactured from the potash of the Dead Sea and the phosphates of the Negev, also has been an essential element. The minerals from the Dead Sea, the reserves of gas and oil, and the metals and minerals of the Negev all must be tapped, mined, or recovered for use inside Israel and to contribute to reducing the export deficit. Because many of these mineral resources exist in the Negev and in the Arava Valley, locations most inhospitable to man, planning communities for the necessary labor force presents special problems. Much of the time the Negev and the Arava are fiercely hot. They also are waterless and barren. The Negev is windswept, while the Arava Valley along the shores of the Dead Sea (Figure III-19) lacks any breezes to dispel the heat.

Although settlement is economically essential, location, design, and services alone cannot make life in the Negev and Arava towns competitive with life on the slopes of Mount Carmel overlooking Haifa Bay. There is enough water for domestic consumption and industry. Additional water to make possible widespread air-conditioning and a generous cover of trees and plants would help considerably, but it is not yet available. Sizable financial inducements are offered to those willing to live in these towns and to work in the mines or Dead Sea factories. As the immigrants now there develop the skills and financial independence to move away to an easier life elsewhere, it is probable that the various forms of government subsidy to residents and private industry will have to be increased.

Most industry in Israel is privately owned, but that connected with mineral development in the Negev is either public or in mixed public and private ownership, because private enterprise was unwilling to assume the financial risk of mineral exploration and exploitation. Some private industry, unrelated to mineral development, is located in Negev towns; at Dimona, for instance, there is a large textile plant.

Since the Negev is one of the two top priority areas for development, the Industrial Development Bank of Israel offers favorable loan terms to industries willing to locate there. The bank varies the percentage of the necessary fixed investment it will lend according to the priority for development in the area. In the two top priority areas, the Negev and Galilee, the bank will lend up to 70 percent of the total investment cost.[86] The Industrial Development Bank's loan funds come from the government, from other banks, and from local and foreign investors. During 1966 the bank loaned 942,000 £P ($33 million), its particular emphasis being on industries planning to locate in the Negev.[87]

The rationale for development of Negev towns, other than to provide communities for those working in mineral extraction or mineral-related in-

Figure III-19. The Dead Sea Shore

dustries, is to establish population nuclei for defense. Residents of the towns are trained to combat infiltrators attempting, for example, to destroy communication lines between Eilat and the northern part of the country.

The gas fields so far discovered are near the Dead Sea. Pipelines have been built to carry the gas to Oron for the phosphate plants, to industries in Dimona, and to residents of Arad.

Arad is one of the new towns built for workers in the mineral industries. It also is a multi-purpose regional center (see Map III-6). After the gas reserves, phosphate deposits, and other minerals were discovered and plants had been established for the extraction of Dead Sea minerals, the government determined to combine the need to provide housing for workers in Dead Sea industries and the gas fields with the need to find a site and develop a D-level town to serve as the regional center for a 200-square-mile area extending from Beersheba to the Dead Sea. Because heat makes living along the Dead Sea insufferable, workers had been commuting three hours daily from Beersheba to their jobs. The new town also was to be the site of a petrochemical complex and industries to process marble, cement, and phosphates. If the town were pleasantly situated, it would serve as a center for tourists visiting the nearby archeological and historic sites (see Figure III-20) and for users of the sulphur springs near the Dead Sea. If location-free industries could be attracted to the town, thereby stimulating its growth, it would be better able to fill a defense role.

The plan to attract tourists reinforced the need to select a scenic and climatically desirable site. The location chosen met all requirements, but it also posed problems common to other Negev new town sites. Arad has a pleasant desert climate. It is located at an altitude of 2,000 feet on the eastern ridge

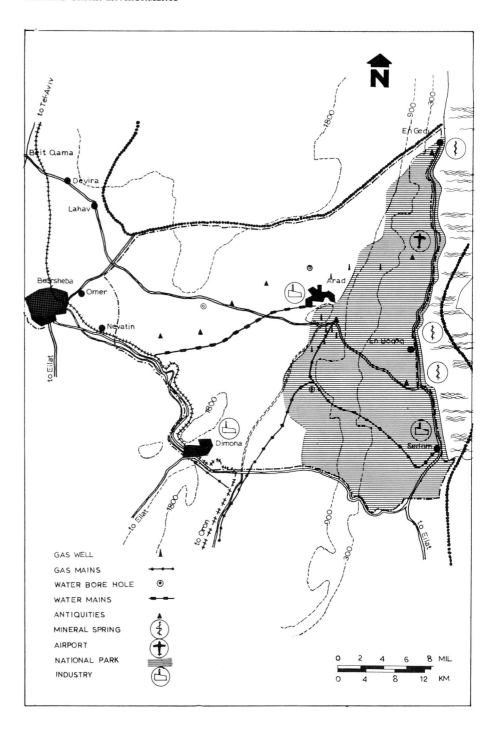

Map III-6.
The Arad Region

of the Negev Plateau and overlooks the Dead Sea almost 4,000 feet below. There are cooling breezes and a splendid view of the Dead Sea and the mountains of Jordan beyond. When the site for the town was chosen, however, there were no roads in the area, only goat paths. Also lacking were a railroad, an airfield, and a water line. The four-inch annual rainfall precludes native vegetation.

By the time Arad was planned, however, the government had had considerable experience in planning and building new towns under difficult conditions. It also was well aware of the past failure to attract native-born Israelis to the new towns. At Arad the government was determined to profit from the lessons of the past. To this end, good communication links were planned and

Figure III-20.
Masada

their construction was scheduled to coincide with town construction; the town was designed on the site; and the initial residents all were native Israelis.

The mountainous terrain makes road building slow and expensive, but one of the best roads in the Negev was completed in 1963 as a link between Arad and Beersheba. Then, in 1964, this road was extended to join the road running along the Dead Sea shore, thus providing the workers easy access to Arad and convenient transportation for the minerals from the Dead Sea works. An additional road south to Dimona and Oron also is to be built, despite difficult topography. Local air service now is available at the nearby Dead Sea town of Masada. The railroad, which is needed to carry minerals and mineral goods for export to the ports of Eilat and Ashdod, was extended in 1965 to Dimona, some fifteen miles away, and now is being continued to Oron. Water has been piped in.

Other new towns were designed from offices in Tel Aviv or Jerusalem, and often this is obvious. The team which designed Arad, however, lived on the site. "However great the difficulties may have been in establishing and running a modern technical office in a remote wilderness, 100 miles from the centres of the country, nevertheless, the spirit of the first months face to face with the desert, and absorbed by a grand and inspiring task, has remained unforgettable for the architects, engineers, draughtsmen and all voluntary helpers coming along."[88]

The town has been planned for 50,000 people on a site of 4,200 acres. Climate, topography, and function all have influenced the design. The plan (Map III-7) consists of a rectangular core and several outlying areas. The core is surrounded by a ring road, bisected by a commercial-administrative axis, and further subdivided into six neighborhoods of 5,000 people each. Each neighborhood has a density of between forty and fifty-five dwelling units per acre and offers residents shops for daily needs, elementary schools, meeting rooms, clinics, and synagogues. The outlying areas include a large site, downwind and somewhat downhill, for industries; sites for larger institutions, including hospitals and secondary schools; several separate residential areas for a total of 20,000 people, each with a neighborhood center; and a hotel and recreation area located to take maximum advantage of the view. The housing was designed to provide shade and protection from the wind and also to lessen construction and infrastructure costs. The British garden city, with its single-family detached housing and winding streets, no longer influenced design.

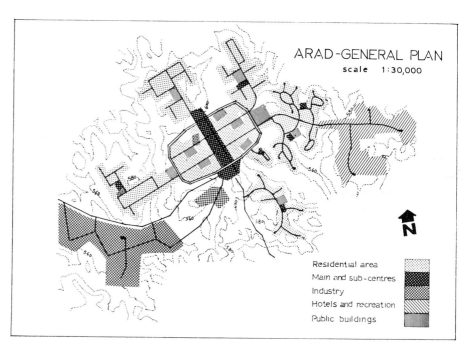

Map III-7.
Arad General Plan

Construction began at Arad in 1962. Young sabras in good health and with some skill suited to life there were recruited through appeals to the pioneer spirit. All were volunteers, but two inducements not always present during the settlement of earlier new towns were offered. Settlers were paid higher than average wages for the work performed, and they were assured that community facilities—movies, concerts, shops, doctors, schools—would be provided from the start. Most unskilled construction work was performed by Bedouins; the new settlers were employed from the start in the mineral industries, in services, or in administrative jobs. Only after the initial social fabric of the new town was created were immigrants brought in to participate with the sabras in the further growth of Arad. When they arrived they found a growing enterprise imbued with the zest and confidence of its young settlers, a town with a future.

More time, more immigrants, and extended development of the Arad region's resources are needed before it can be determined whether this revised approach to new town development has brought about a town that is socially and economically sound.

Urban Areas

Discussion of agricultural and resource development has led, inevitably, to discussion of policies and programs for housing and services to workers in both types of enterprise. Even given the government's past extraordinary power to direct immigrants to settle in the locations and undertake the types of work it preferred, it has long been obvious that people's preferences also must be considered if a productive, dynamic society is to grow. Through experience the Israeli government has learned that its theoretical hierarchy of urban settlements does not conform with the way people wish to live or with job availability. Rural employment will continue to decline, and industry will continue to locate in larger cities. Because the smaller towns in the hierarchy satisfied neither farmers nor industry, the concept has been revised in favor of larger and fewer urban centers. The government also has realized that the new towns must be made attractive to both immigrants and native-born Israelis so that the existing social stratification between the new towns and the older metropolitan areas will be eliminated. Arad and Ashdod are examples of planning revised to reflect lessons learned from the recent past.

Government housing programs have been the principal direct means of implementing policy decisions concerning urban development. Since 1940 the government has fixed quotas for construction of immigrant housing in direct response to national plans for population distribution. The Planning Department of the Ministry of the Interior, the Ministry of Housing, and the Employment Department of the Ministry of Labour have cooperated so that housing, immigrants, and jobs all would be available in accordance with plans. These programs have undergone considerable refinement during the past twenty-three years. Today's immigrant goes directly into good, cheap housing with convenient services; in addition, the housing is located so as to further the government's urban location policy.

From the earliest days of the transit camps and then the *ma'abarot*, through the first permanent housing with an area of 240 square feet for a family of four, to today's minimum size of 480 square feet in towns and 450 square feet on farms and in rural villages, there has been a gigantic advance in housing conditions. While a minimum standard of 450 or 480 square feet for a family of four or less may be inadequate by American standards, this achievement must be judged with reference to pre-existing conditions and the scale of the task undertaken. Between 1939 and independence almost no housing construction occurred; by 1948, much of the existing housing stock had deteriorated and was inadequate by any standard. As of January, 1949, housing density was 2.18 people per room.[89] Starting at independence and a population of 870,000, many of whom were badly housed, and adding 1,210,000 immigrants (317,000 families) by 1964, the fact that no arriving immigrant lacked shelter for a single night is fantastic in itself.

By 1964 the government had built 187,700 permanent urban dwelling units. Another 57,200 rural homes had been built. Public building companies engaged by the government built an additional 89,000 units. The private market accounted for the remainder, or approximately one-third, of the 556,670 permanent dwelling units built in this period. These units, containing 1,185,670 rooms, provided homes for 1,689,000 people. On the average, one room per year was built for every 0.9 new inhabitant.[90] Between 1949 and 1964, $1.67 billion (at current 1964 prices) was invested in housing, with public construction consuming 44 percent of this sum. Because public housing was smaller and cheaper than private, public expenditures paid for 58 percent of the housing built. Of the housing stock that existed in 1964, the average dwelling unit contained 2.6 rooms and 564 square feet, while the average unit built during that year had an area of 710 square feet.[91]

As immigration declined, as building materials became more plentiful, and as financial resources increased, public and private housing standards rose. In the early years, heavy taxes and building permit restrictions severely limited private construction. Today, the taxes are substantial, but, given enough money, people can build whatever housing they wish. Much of the earliest rural and single-family housing has been enlarged and improved. By 1964 the average density per room had fallen to 1.7 persons. Overcrowding still is prevalent, however, particularly among immigrants from Africa and Asia, who have the largest families. For the degree of crowding among Jewish families, see Table III-8.

Table III-8.
Housing Density per Room, 1963

Persons per Room	Percentage of Jewish Families
Less than 1	9.3
1–2	49.0
2–3	25.1
3–4	9.2
More than 4	7.4
	100.0

SOURCE: David Krivine, *Housing*, Israel Today no. 17 (Jerusalem: Israel Digest, 1965).

Of the housing currently built in Israel, walk-up apartments are the prevalent type, although the number of elevator apartment towers is increasing. Because land planned for urban uses is in short supply, particularly in the urban areas of the coastal plain, single-family construction is discouraged. The gross ground area per capita for housing is about 120 square feet. Most apartments have balconies; they provide additional space, and because of the Mediterranean climate are used extensively. Almost all housing is supplied with water, electricity, and bathrooms; for example, 97 percent of the dwelling units have running water and 84 percent have flush toilets.

Design has improved along with better space and equipment standards (see Figures III-21, III-22, and III-23). Speed, the shortage of funds, and a shortage of skilled labor dictated that early construction would follow only a few models. There was not time or knowledge to design with reference to climate, topography, or the varied cultural preferences of residents. Local building materials had not been discovered. Today all this has changed. Housing is designed for Arabs and Bedouins which reflects their different living patterns in site layout, external appearance, and internal arrangement.[92] There is housing to meet the differing climatic conditions and density requirements of various urban areas. Local cement and local stone, including granite and marble, are used, and the building-materials industry provides better quality products for interior finishing.

Housing is built by the government, by public-private and private enterprise for the government, or by private enterprise on its own initiative. The government has complete control over the type, location, and volume of its housing construction and has considerable influence on private construction. The aims of government housing policy are to carry out development plans and to provide adequate housing for every family at a price it can afford.

In the smaller new towns and urban areas that have difficulty attracting private investment, almost all housing is government housing. In the new towns with greater drawing power, such as Ashdod, private enterprise also participates. Construction of government housing is coordinated with all other construction for new urban areas, that is, with roads, utilities, and shops. Price and type of construction are scaled to the expected population distribution. Whatever the initial occupancy terms, eventual purchase by the occupants is encouraged. Home ownership in 1961 was 60 percent.[93]

The least expensive housing, and that which offers the lowest space standards, is immigrant housing. It is built by the government, through the Ministry of Housing, in urban areas and by the Jewish Agency, financed by the government, in rural areas. The floor plan for a rural immigrant house appears in Figure III-24.

In the new towns, 81 percent of the housing has been immigrant housing. Rents are fixed at between 7 and 10 percent of the new immigrant's wages. For those unable to work, rents are nominal—a bit more than $1 per month —and dwelling units are provided on the basis of family size, not income. Rents vary with the priority for development of the region in which the housing is located. Initially, if he is able, or later, as his income rises, the tenant is encouraged to purchase by being offered terms that are far more favorable than those available on the private market. In recent years private mortgage financing has been available for 20 percent of the purchase price; such a mortgage is payable over a ten-to-twelve-year period at 8 percent. By contrast, in immigrant housing the purchaser need pay only 10–20 percent of the apartment's cost as a down payment. More than half of this may be met through rents already paid. The purchaser can obtain a forty-year mortgage at 4.5 percent. In rural areas the terms are 100 percent financing over a period of thirty years at 3 percent. Some 53 percent of the housing built under government programs is immigrant housing.

Inaugurated in 1952, popular housing was another government program for new town development. Under this program any married citizen without a private apartment could buy a 2½ room apartment of 550 square feet for $2,000. Half of the purchase price was covered by a medium-term, low-interest mortgage. In the next few years, larger apartments at higher prices also were offered. The program was exceedingly popular, but circumstances soon forced prices up sharply. Construction costs spiraled, largely because of higher wages. These costs had to be added to apartment prices. In addition, to slow inflation, the government added a building materials tax to popular housing. A shortage of credit forced the mortgage coverage down from one-half to one-quarter of the purchase price. These events led, in 1955, to the Saving for Housing Scheme.

This is a government-initiated system similar to that used so successfully in Finland. The prospective apartment owner deposits savings in a bank on a regular basis, with a minimum required initial and monthly deposit. Initially, when his balance reached 60 percent of the purchase price, he received his apartment with a government mortgage at favorable rates covering from

Figure III-21. Tel Aviv Apartments under Construction

Figure III-22. Beersheba Apartments

Figure III-23. Housing in Eilat

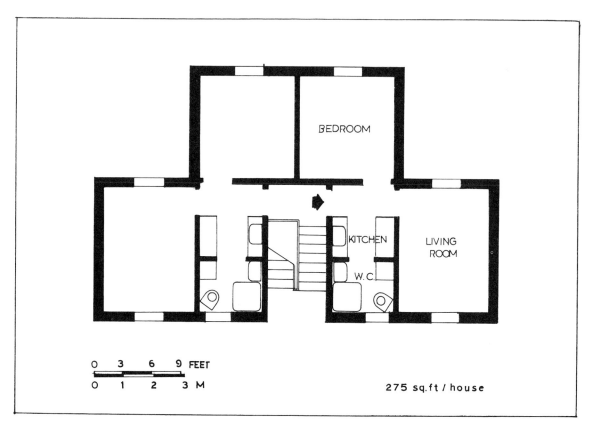

Figure III-24. Floor Plan for a Rural House

20 to 25 percent of the cost and a private bank mortgage at 6 or 7 percent covering the remainder. (As is evident from these figures, neither the government nor the private banks had sufficient capital to cover a higher percentage of the purchase price through mortgages, and the money market became even tighter in later years.) Construction is paid for from savings funds and government loans, with the degree of government participation depending on the priority of an area for development.

Standards for this housing are considerably higher than those for immigrant housing. At first the floor area ranged from 650 to 750 square feet. In 1962, standards were raised, and apartments of up to 850 square feet were built. More recently, units of 1,000 square feet have been built. The Saving for Housing Scheme apartments are much better finished than those under the immigrants' housing program. There is much more closet space, kitchens are tiled, doors and windows are larger, and the toilet is separate from the bath.

With increased quality, however, has come increased cost. Although the 4–6 percent interest paid on the saver's deposit is exempt from income tax, this advantage is outweighed by the fact that the purchaser now must provide 75 percent of the purchase price from his savings and obtain a conventional bank or building company mortgage for the remainder. In 1965, conventional mortgages were for ten years at 8 percent. Therefore, except through the income tax forgone, the government no longer is financing this housing.[94] As of 1964 more than 43,000 Israeli families were participating in the plan, and 14 percent of housing built under government auspices or with government assistance involved the Saving for Housing Scheme.[95]

A program of housing for young couples is used to attract people to the development areas. Built in new towns and other outlying areas where growth is wanted, the units are small, averaging 560 square feet, and include two rooms, bath, and kitchen. Their attraction is that the couple can move in at once and take possession with no down payment. Part of the rent is applied to the purchase price until it is paid in full.[96]

Construction of housing under the various government programs may be by the government directly, by the public-private Israel Housing and Development Company, by public housing companies owned by unions or religious groups, or by private companies. Histadrut (the General Federation of Labor) and RASSCO (Rural and Suburban Settlement Company, Ltd.) are the largest in this group of companies, but their structure and organization are illustrative of the role of some of the smaller companies as well.

The Israel Housing and Development Company is a government company run as a profit-making enterprise financed by government funds and private capital. As a subsidiary of the Ministry of Housing, it is the builder of several standards of housing, including immigrant housing, housing for young couples, popular housing, and housing under the Saving for Housing Scheme. It also builds shopping centers and civic centers. The company provides the site, the plans, and the financing; it then contracts with private companies for construction. The immigrant housing built by the Israel Housing and Development Company is of a higher standard than the government's average immigrant housing. Dwelling-unit size is between 600 and 800 square feet, and most units are sold at once to immigrants with some private means. By allocating units of this type to the new towns and developing areas, the government has been in a better position to attract professionally trained immigrants to these areas.[97]

Histadrut's housing company, Shikun Ovidim, is a public company established during the mandate period primarily to build housing for workers on a cooperative basis. By 1964, 350,000 people, all members of Histadrut, lived in this housing. Housing types include immigrant housing, housing for young couples, housing under the Saving for Housing Scheme, and housing built directly for the private market. Shikun Ovidim has bought land in advance of development and has built on it; it has also built on government land in development areas. Financing for Shikun Ovidim land acquisition and construction has come from a fund set up by U.S. labor unions and, in more recent years, from the Housing Mortgage Bank, established jointly by Shikun Ovidim and the Workers' Bank. Histadrut has 230 member housing cooperative societies, ranging in size from 20 to 5,000 families. Each cooperative is responsible for maintenance of the property owned by its members.[98]

Like Shikun Ovidim, RASSCO dates back to the 1930s. It was established by the World Zionist Organisation to build middle-class rural villages. Since 1948, it has built housing for the Ministry of Housing, housing for the private market, and all other types of construction, including luxury hotels for tourists and part of Hebrew University. RASSCO's 150,000 middle-class immigrant residents own or rent their homes—either apartments or single-family houses—in neighborhoods equipped by RASSCO with shops, schools, clinics, and synagogues (see Figure III-25). Much of RASSCO's non-governmental capital is raised abroad.[99]

Primarily because of the pronounced disparity in land prices, an apartment built by Shikun Ovidim or RASSCO will cost more than twice as much in Tel Aviv as in Beersheba. In 1963, land represented 35 percent of the cost of all housing built on privately owned land but only between 9 and 13 percent of the cost of housing built on publicly owned land.[100]

Amidar (Israel National Housing Corporation for Immigrants Ltd.), 75 percent of which is owned by the government, 25 percent by the Jewish Agency, is the public housing company which acts as manager for the housing built under various government programs. It sells apartments, collects rent and

Figure III-25. RASSCO Shopping Center, Tiberias

mortgage payments, maintains the property inside and out, and organizes community services for the residents. Amidar provides gardens, playgrounds, trash collection, and sewage disposal. It teaches the tenants to care for their apartments, to cultivate gardens, and to participate in local affairs. In 1964 Amidar managed about 230,000 dwelling units housing one million residents. Sixty-five percent of the units were occupied by renters.[101] Because rental terms are so favorable, the government has been dissatisfied with the number of purchases. To stimulate sales, and so to recapture more of its capital investment, the government, through Amidar, has proposed an increase in rents of from 100 to 150 percent and a greater variation in the rent scale based on the size and location of the housing.[102]

Ashdod, A Current New Town

Having reviewed Israeli land development and population distribution policies, the constraints imposed on them by fluctuating immigration, capital shortages, and sporadic warfare, and the responses of the market and the people to these policies, it is possible to discern the current direction of government policies by examining the program for development of one of the most recent new towns. Ashdod is the most appropriate choice for this purpose because it is an entirely new town—it was not launched until the first series of new towns had been in existence long enough for evaluation—and because it does in fact reflect a considerable rethinking of past policies. Ashdod will be far larger and more densely populated than the older new towns. Its site was dictated primarily by national economics, and, in that sense, it is a national town rather than a regional center. Its location, design, facilities, and employment opportunities reflect peoples' preferences, as evidenced by the fact that it has attracted immigrants and established settlers without difficulty. It is a town privately developed on public land.

Ashdod was included in the early plans for new town development as a possible port location to be accompanied by a moderate-sized town, but no final decision was made until 1956. Selection of the site for development of a 300,000-kilowatt power station and accompanying housing began in 1953, and presaged the subsequent decision to build Ashdod. Implementation of the 1956 decision was delayed by a recession until 1960, when major construction began.

Israel's three existing ports—Haifa, Tel Aviv–Jaffa, and Eilat—were inadequate to handle the growing citrus and mineral exports from the southern coastal plain and northern Negev. Haifa, a fine port, was operating almost at capacity,[103] and was too far north for economical shipment. Tel Aviv–Jaffa was not a good port; it was not built for deep-sea shipping and had insufficient shore space for handling goods without first undergoing expensive clearance and redevelopment. Access also was poor. Furthermore, government policy was to shift development away from Tel Aviv and Haifa. Eilat was a new and growing port, but its location on the Red Sea made it suitable only for exports to Africa and the East. Also, the lack of a rail line linking Eilat with the rest of the country was a handicap for transporting goods to the port. All of these factors pointed to the location of a new port near the production centers of export goods.

There was no natural harbor between Tel Aviv and the Gaza Strip at that time, so one site would have been as satisfactory for port development as another. Ashkelon already had been established as a regional center and seashore recreation area and did not need the further stimulus of port development. The area around the Ashdod site was relatively undeveloped for the coastal plain. It was beyond the Tel Aviv metropolitan area, but it was easily accessible from Tel Aviv and was near Kiryat Gat, the citrus lands, and

Dimona and Arad; roads and rail spurs could be extended comparatively inexpensively. The sand dunes were wide enough for a city to be built without impinging on good agricultural land. The Planning Department stated its reasons for choosing Ashdod as follows:

> In spite of the demographical and industrial weight of the Tel Aviv region, the anticipated cargo arising from the Negev mineral deposits—like potash and phosphates—could eventually outweigh the total volume of exports and imports handled in the Tel Aviv region. Therefore the location of a sea outlet more southwards, could be justified on purely economical grounds.
>
> There were additional advantages of location at Ashdod from the point of view of national planning. A site at Ashdod would contribute to the economic development of the South, and at the same time prevent the addition of a powerful stimulus for the further industrial and demographical growth of the Tel Aviv region. This additional growth, of necessity would be at the expense of orange groves and agricultural soil. Construction of a deep-sea harbour at Tel Aviv would involve the demolition of existing town quarters, indemnities for the expropriation of very expensive urban land, and overcoming considerable traffic difficulties.
>
> On the contrary, siting the harbour at Ashdod on uninhabited and extensive sand dune areas owned by the state would not only evade the above technical difficulties, but would offer a chance to create a big new town on "tabula rasa" without impairing any agricultural areas. Such a decision was in the line with the general aims of the planning policy, when intended to transfer urban development from fertile agricultural areas to regions unfit for cultivation.[104]

By 1953 no decision had been made as to whether or not Ashdod would be developed as a new port. Many interests in Tel Aviv were resisting a plan which would result in the elimination of the Tel Aviv–Jaffa port. At this time, however, it was necessary to choose a site for a power plant to serve the developing south-central part of the country. The Planning Department of the Ministry of the Interior and the Ministry of Development insisted on Ashdod as the site, despite the opposition of the Israel Electric Corporation. Some immigrant housing was built for power plant employees, and access roads were built. In 1956 the government committed itself to building a deep-water port and major town at Ashdod and projected for it a population of 150,000. However, having made the decision, the government found itself financially incapable of undertaking the substantial investment required. It therefore embarked on a previously untried course for new town development: it granted a concession to a private corporation for planning and developing the town. The fact that a private company was ready to invest heavily in Ashdod's future is evidence that the location and the policies for its development were valid on economic grounds alone, a statement which could not be made about many, or perhaps most, of the preceding new towns.

The Ashdod Development Company was granted the right to buy the 10,000-acre new town site, subject to the obligation to develop according to a timetable agreed upon by the government and the company.[105] Because the initial agreement later proved to be more profitable to the company than had been intended, it was revised to raise the amount of payments for the land and to give the government a 50 percent interest in the company.

The master plan prepared by the company envisages a future population of 350,000, more than double the government's initial projection. The average density would be eighty people per acre. The port would be capable of handling four million tons per year, or more than 60 percent of projected imports and exports.[106] The site is all sand dunes, a strip seven miles along the coast extending from one to two and a half miles inland. The direction of prevailing winds dictated that the port and major industrial area would be located at the northern end of the site. A smaller industrial site was located where the existing coast road and railroad abut the town site. The town center is adjacent to the shore, centrally located for the surrounding residential areas, and accessible by arterial roads from the port and industrial area as well as from the coast road.

A design competition was held in 1965 to select a detailed plan for Ashdod's development; the winning plan appears here as Map III-8. Sixteen residential areas will vary in density from fourteen to twenty-four dwelling units per gross acre, giving them a total population of between 12,000 and 20,000 people each. These areas, each with its neighborhood center and each separated from its neighbors by an arterial road, are grouped about the town center in two semicircles. The lower-density areas are those in the outer semicircle. The southern section of the site is to be temporarily afforested and held for future residential expansion. The entire coast, except for the port itself, is to be held in open space for recreational use. Greenbelts will adjoin some of the arterial roads and, on a smaller scale, will link residential and commercial areas within each neighborhood.

Housing planned for the denser residential sections is mostly three- to five-story apartment buildings, while in the lower-density sections one- and two-story detached and row housing prevails. See Map III-9 and Figure III-26.

The government plans to improve access to Ashdod by building better and more direct roads to Tel Aviv, Jerusalem, and Beersheba, by linking the coast

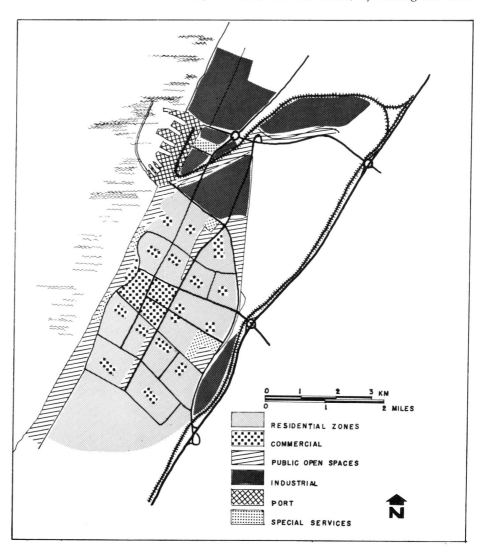

Map III-8.
Plan for Ashdod

railroad with the Tel Aviv–Beersheba line, and by building a local airport midway between Ashdod and Ashkelon.

Implementation of the Ashdod plan began with the port and the residential areas nearest the port. Because construction of the town center is not scheduled to begin until after a number of residential sections have been completed, many administrative and commercial activities which eventually will take place in the town center are temporarily located in the neighborhood centers.

... Central functions concerning the whole town have to be sited provisionally in the various neighborhood centres, the town administration here, the port authority there, the labour exchange and the health insurance office in yet another centre. In these circumstances, too, it takes many years before the town at least physically reaches its central area, a period in which it also remains without focus and core. The advance of capital and the subsidizing of central institutions, even if they remain under-used and under-occupied for some time to come, theoretically the best solution, can hardly be realized in a developing country with tremendous shortage of capital and strong inflationary tendencies.[107]

Financing construction on such an extensive scale—$120 million for the port alone—has been achieved because the Ashdod Development Company turned to sources outside as well as within Israel. Foreign investors were given considerable tax incentives: higher depreciation allowances, initial exemption from property taxes, reduced income tax rates, and the right to take profits abroad in the currency of the initial investment. The International Bank for Reconstruction and Development has loaned money for the port. Some residential sections are being wholly developed (roads and commercial buildings as well as housing) by private companies, whose work is subject to all specifications of the master plan. Most housing construction still is being carried out under the various government housing programs, but housing standards for all types of residences are higher than they have been in other new towns. Most immigrant housing is at least 600 square feet in area, while private housing is as large as 1,100 square feet. Standard apartments have two bedrooms and two balconies (see Figures III-27 and III-28).

The first phase of port development, including construction of a massive 1.4-mile breakwater, was completed in 1966, and the port already is handling more than one million tons of cargo annually.

The response to Ashdod by individuals and industry has far exceeded government expectations. Growth has been rapid: from 219 people in 1956 to 20,000 in 1965, with 100,000 anticipated by 1975. In 1965 more housing was under construction at Ashdod than at any other new town in Israel. Many of the early settlers at Ashdod were recent immigrants from North Africa and the Middle East, as has been true at all of the new towns. In addition, as the Tel Aviv port closed down and the Ashdod port came into operation, many of the Tel Aviv port workers moved to Ashdod. Each worker who moved received a $2,500 grant for expenses incurred in moving and acquiring new housing, plus special housing loans.[108] As numerous industries have settled in Ashdod, there has been a constant demand for skilled labor, and people have been attracted from all parts of the country. The largest employers, other than the port itself, are textile plants and a motor vehicle assembly plant. Already government investment has been reduced; loans for new industry are only 30 percent of total capital investment. Land prices tripled between 1962 and 1965, when they reached $1.65 per square foot.

Ashdod's first local council was elected in 1963, and on February 1, 1968, the minister of the interior constituted Ashdod a municipality. With schools, sports facilities, parks (see Figure III-29), a movie theater, clubs, and synagogues, Ashdod is gradually taking social form. So far, it has been absorbed

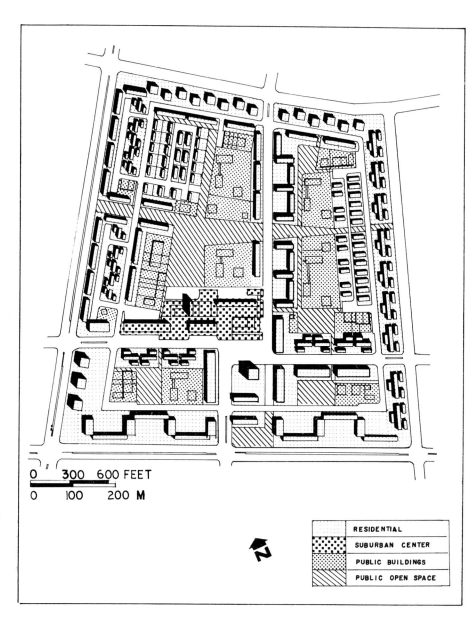

0   300   600 FEET
0   100   200 M

	RESIDENTIAL
	SUBURBAN CENTER
	PUBLIC BUILDINGS
	PUBLIC OPEN SPACE

(right)
Map III-9.
Ashdod Residential
Quarter

(far right)
Figure III-26.
Ashdod Quarter
No. 1, Aerial View

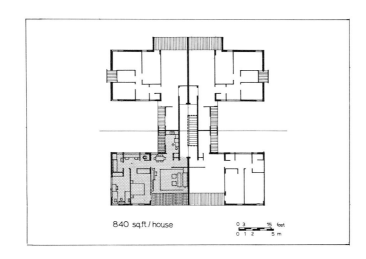

840 sq.ft./house

(left)
Figure III-27.
Ashdod
Apartments,
Quarter No. 1

(right)
Figure III-28.
Floor Plan for
Ashdod
Apartments

Figure III-29. Street Scene, Ashdod Quarter No. 1

Figure III-30. Shopping Center, Ashdod Quarter No. 2

Figure III-31. Neighborhood Shops, Apartments, and Single-Family Homes,
Ashdod Quarter No. 2

Figure III-32. Ashdod Seashore Park

in its own boom and is characterized by hard work, good pay, and rapid change. It has developed few links, other than economic ones, with the surrounding region, and its people have scarcely had time to form the social ties with one another which will make Ashdod a community. Absorption with development so far has obscured whether or not the social cleavages between old and new, European and non-European—cleavages that have caused dissatisfaction in the other new towns—will be avoided at Ashdod. Because it is attracting all types of settlers, and because its economic opportunities are excellent, the prospect is that Ashdod will be Israel's most successful new town.

Given the struggles and successes of the past twenty-three years, one can but wish that Israel's aspirations for an economically self-sustaining, culturally rich, and socially satisfying urban nation will be realized. The unresolved problem of bitter Arab enmity, the present inability to achieve integration of the internal Arab population, the likelihood of continued low rates of immigration, and the decreased prospect of foreign investment all present obstacles which might seem insurmountable except for the knowledge of what Israel already has achieved. If the country's vitality and sense of purpose can be sustained, if the vision and leadership of the new generation can match that of the old Zionists, one must believe, on faith, not evidence, that Israel's goals can be met.

Notes

1. Hebrew term for the return of Jews to Palestine.

2. Israel, Ministry of Foreign Affairs, Information Division, *Facts About Israel, 1967* (Jerusalem: Jerusalem Post Press, 1967).

3. *Life*, October 20, 1967.

4. *New York Times*, November 3, 1967. It has been suggested that one of Lord Balfour's motives was to relieve himself of the charge of being anti-Jewish. He was responsible for the British Aliens Act, designed largely to prevent Jewish immigration to Britain. He may have seen the declaration as a gesture which would relieve him politically and also help solve the Jew's historic problem of homelessness.

5. Prince Feisal to Lord Rothschild, as quoted in *Life*, October 20, 1967.

6. *The Jewish Agency for Israel*, Israel Today no. 16 (Jerusalem: Israel Digest, 1962).

7. *Life*, October 20, 1967.

8. Prime Minister Levi Eshkol, quoted in the *New York Times*, October 31, 1967.

9. Excerpt from the Israel Declaration of Independence, dated May 14, 1948.

10. Doris Lankin, *The Legal System*, Israel Today no. 19 (Jerusalem: Israel Digest, 1964).

11. Ministry of Foreign Affairs, *Facts About Israel, 1967*.

12. Israel, Ministry of the Interior, Planning Department, *National Planning for the Redistribution of Population and the Establishment of New Towns in Israel* (Jerusalem, 1964), p. 1.

13. Israel, Ministry of Housing, Planning Department, *Housing Policy in Regions of Rapid Population Growth in Israel* (Jerusalem, 1964).

14. Jacob Dash and Elisha Efrat, *The Israel Physical Master Plan*, prepared for the Ministry of the Interior (Jerusalem, 1964).

15. Arthur S. Super, *Absorption of Immigrants*, Israel Today no. 18 (Jerusalem: Israel Digest, 1963).

16. *Ibid.*

17. *Ibid.*

18. *Ibid.*

19. *Ibid.*

20. Efraim Orni, *Reclamation of the Soil*, Israel Today no. 26 (Jerusalem: Israel Digest, 1963).

21. Dash and Efrat, *The Israel Physical Master Plan*.

22. Ministry of Foreign Affairs, *Facts About Israel, 1967*.

23. Orni, *Reclamation of the Soil*.

24. Ministry of Foreign Affairs, *Facts About Israel, 1967*, "The Negev."

25. *Ibid.* In comparison, Gross National Product rose an average per year of 7.5 percent in West Germany, 4.5 percent in the Netherlands, and 3.3 percent in the United States during this same period.

26. *Ibid.*

27. Avner Hovne, *The Economy*, Israel Today no. 23 (Jerusalem: Israel Digest, 1965). The Gross National Product rose 12 percent in 1968.

28. Ministry of Foreign Affairs, *Facts About Israel, 1967*.

29. Per capita income in the Netherlands, Austria, and Italy was about equal to that in Israel.

30. *New York Times*, May 2, 1968.

31. Hovne, *The Economy*.

32. *Ibid.*

33. Ministry of Foreign Affairs, *Facts About Israel, 1967*.

34. Eli Ginzberg, "The Manpower Problem," *The Reporter*, November 16, 1967.

35. 467 *Book of Laws*, no. 5725, p. 307.

36. The source of much of the ensuing discussion of the new planning law is Jacob Dash, "National Physical Planning in Israel" (Paper presented at First World Congress of Engineers and Architects, Israel, 1967).

37. Planning and Building Law, sec. 2(b).

38. Under the prior law, no administrative appeal could be taken from the district commission to the National Planning Council. However, M. D. Gouldman, writing in Dash and Efrat, *The Israel Physical Master Plan*, notes that, under the Courts of Law of 1967 (*Laws of the State of Israel*, vol. 11, p. 157), appeals to the Supreme

Court may be and frequently have been taken from administrative planning decisions on the ground that administrative powers were unfairly and unreasonably exercised.

39. See Dash and Efrat, *The Israel Physical Master Plan*, for details concerning each of these plans.

40. Planning and Building Law, sec. 49 (7).

41. *Ibid.*, sec. 7(a).

42. In Municipality of Bat Yam v. Tel Aviv District Planning and Building Commission, HCJ 152167, 21 (2) Piskei Din 485 (1967), the Supreme Court ruled on the role of the district commission in deciding appeals. Bat Yam is a seaside residential town adjoining Tel Aviv. A large regional cemetery is located there. The cemetery entrepreneurs presented an expansion plan to the local commission, which rejected it. On appeal by the entrepreneurs, the district commission ordered that the plan be accepted. The local commission appealed this decision, alleging that the cemetery was to serve residents of Greater Tel Aviv and therefore could only be part of a district master plan, not of a local detailed plan. Interpreting sec. 57(6), 63, and 64 of the Planning and Building Law, the Supreme Court upheld the district commission, stating that it had the duty to consider the general public welfare as well as the interests of the local people most immediately affected.

43. M. D. Gouldman, *Legal Aspects of Town Planning in Israel* (Jerusalem: Hebrew University, 1966), p. 111.

44. See *ibid.* for a discussion of the original proposals and Knesset modifications of the applicable sections of the 1966 law.

45. Planning and Building Law, sec. 34.

46. The principal source for this discussion is Gouldman's excellent study, *Legal Aspects of Town Planning*. See this book for further information, including reports of leading judicial decisions in the land-use field and the full text of the 1966 Planning and Building Law.

47. Planning and Building Law, sec. 145, 146.

48. The Interpretation Ordinance, sec. 6, says that when no time is specified in the law the "thing shall be done with all convenient speed" (*Laws of the State of Israel* [new version], vol. 1, no. 5714, p. 2).

49. Gouldman, *Legal Aspects of Town Planning*, p. 46.

50. Planning and Building Law, sec. 61. In 1966 a roadside advertising control law was passed, under which billboards and advertising signs have been removed from highways (The Roads [Sign Advertising] Law, 1966).

51. "The ownership of the state lands, i.e., lands within Israel belonging to the state, the Development Authority, or the Jewish National Fund shall not be transferred, either by sale or by any other method" (translated from "Basic Law: Israel Lands," *Laws of the State of Israel*, vol. 14, p. 48, sec. 1).

52. Orni, *Reclamation of the Soil*.

53. *The Jewish Agency for Israel*.

54. Avraham Harman, *Agricultural Settlement*, Israel Today no. 2 (Jerusalem: Israel Digest, 1965).

55. Ministry of Foreign Affairs, *Facts About Israel, 1967*.

56. Israel Lands Law, *Laws of the State of Israel*, no. 5720 (1960).

57. Yehoshua Freudenheim, *Government in Israel* (Dobbs Ferry, N.Y.: Oceana Publications, 1967).

58. Absentee Property Law, *Laws of the State of Israel*, no. 5710 (1950).

59. Eliezer Brutzkus, *Physical Planning in Israel* (Jerusalem, 1964).

60. Planning and Building Law, sec. 188.

61. *Ibid.*, sec. 190(a) (1).

62. Gouldman, *Legal Aspects of Town Planning*, p. 66.

63. Nadav Halevi and Ruth Klinov-Malul, *The Economic Development of Israel* (New York: Praeger, 1968).

64. See Municipal Corporations (Amendment) Law, 5712 (1952), and Local Councils (B) Amendment (no. 3) Order, 5722 (1962), for details on the property rate and the general rate.

65. Walter H. Diamond, *Foreign Tax and Trade Briefs* (New York: Matthew Bender, 1969).

66. Freudenheim, *Government in Israel.*

67. Diamond, *Foreign Tax and Trade Briefs.*

68. Planning and Building Law, sec. 197, 198.

69. *Ibid.,* sec. 256.

70. *Ibid.,* sec. 200.

71. Gouldman, *Legal Aspects of Town Planning,* p. 74.

72. *Ibid.,* p. 80.

73. H. Darin-Drabkin, *The Nature of the Urban Land Market and Methods of Compensation,* prepared for the Ministry of Housing (Jerusalem, 1965).

74. Dash and Efrat, *The Israel Physical Master Plan.*

75. Brutzkus, *Physical Planning in Israel,* p. 17. Brutzkus has been the leading proponent of the hierarchical pattern from before independence to the present.

76. Erika Spiegel, *New Towns in Israel* (New York: Praeger, 1967).

77. See Ministry of the Interior, *National Planning for the Redistribution of Population,* for further details.

78. Israel, Ministry of Housing, *Abstracts of Seven Sociological Studies on Housing and Urban Settlements* (Jerusalem, 1967).

79. Jewish Agency for Israel and Ministry of Housing, *Rural Planning in Israel* (Jerusalem, 1964).

80. Ministry of Foreign Affairs, *Facts About Israel, 1967.*

81. Brutzkus, *Physical Planning in Israel.*

82. Jewish Agency for Israel and Ministry of Housing, *Rural Planning in Israel.*

83. Avshalom Rokach, *Regional Rural Development,* Israel Today no. 32 (Jerusalem: Israel Digest, 1964).

84. Ministry of Foreign Affairs, *Facts About Israel, 1967.*

85. Brutzkus, *Physical Planning in Israel.*

86. *Ibid.*

87. Ministry of Foreign Affairs, *Facts About Israel, 1967.*

88. Spiegel, *New Towns in Israel;* see pp. 168–73 for a more extensive discussion of the planning of Arad.

89. This and subsequent figures are from David Krivine, *Housing,* Israel Today no. 17 (Jerusalem: Israel Digest, 1965).

90. Israel's rate of construction consistently has been higher than that of any country in Europe or that of the United States. In 1962, for instance, it was 16.2 dwellings per 1,000 population, compared with 7.9 in the United States, 6.6 in France, 6.7 in the Netherlands, 8.0 in Finland, and 9.8 in Sweden.

91. Israel, Ministry of Housing, *Housing and Integration of Immigrants* (Jerusalem, 1964).

92. Detailed site plans and photographs are included in Israel, Ministry of Housing, *For Better Living* (Jerusalem, 1964).

93. Spiegel, *New Towns in Israel.*

94. *Ibid.*

95. Krivine, *Housing.*

96. Ministry of Housing, *Housing and Integration of Immigrants.*

97. *Housing and Development for Israel Ltd.* (undated government pamphlet).

98. *Ibid.*

99. Shikun Ovidim Ltd., *Histadruth Cooperative Housing* (Tel Aviv, 1964).

100. The RASSCO Organization, *RASSCO* (Tel Aviv, n.d.).

101. Darin-Drabkin, *The Nature of the Urban Land Market.*

102. Ministry of Housing, *Housing and Integration of Immigrants.*

103. Krivine, *Housing.*

104. By 1964 it was handling 3.3 million tons per year; see Spiegel, *New Towns in Israel.*

105. Brutzkus, *Physical Planning in Israel.*

106. Much of the data in the ensuing discussion of Ashdod are from Spiegel's very detailed and thorough *New Towns in Israel.*

107. *Ibid.*

108. *New York Times,* October 29, 1966.

IV | The Netherlands

Too Many People, Too Little Space

Alexanderstad, a Rotterdam Satellite

Contents

The National Setting

The dominant problem facing the Netherlands today is overcrowding. The Dutch have been attacking the problem with characteristic vigor and thoroughness, but within the constraints of too little space and too many people. The Netherlands is the most densely populated country in the world, except for Monaco and Hong Kong. Of course, this fact must be viewed in relation to the country's small size. It is but one part of the densely settled region of Northwestern Europe. The space shortage is aggravated because the Dutch, like people worldwide, are attracted by better job opportunities to the urban areas, which threaten to run together rather than retain their current clear separation. The Dutch preference for low-density housing, combined with the rise in car ownership, increases the danger of urban sprawl.

Building on a successful heritage of land reclamation which dates back to the thirteenth century, today's Dutch are carrying out ever more ambitious projects to hold back the sea and thereby create new land and new freshwater lakes. A popular aphorism is: God made the world, but the Dutch made Holland. Another favorite is: The Dutch can be saved only by being dammed. The scope of the Dutch effort in hydraulic engineering and land reclamation is matched in the present day only by the Israelis. However, the exceptional skill of both nations in managing their environment has yet to be matched by a comparable skill in population management. Both wish to limit expansion of their principal urban centers by encouraging settlement in less favored portions of their countries in a pattern of concentrated deconcentration, but both have found that the incentives so far offered and the development restrictions imposed have been insufficient to achieve fully the goals sought. The established principal urban areas remain the magnets around which development spreads. The Netherlands seeks to spur emigration, Israel encourages immigration; each has had some success but has not met its goals.

In the Netherlands, amenity is the national government's basic reason for wishing to limit metropolitan growth. In this the nation differs from and is in advance of the rest of Europe and the United States. Most nations, including Sweden, Finland, France, and Israel, are concerned primarily with the economic implications of concentrated urban growth. Stockholm, and to a certain extent the Swedish government, welcomes greater growth for metropolitan Stockholm so as to place it in a more competitive position with other major North European cities. France and Finland fear that further concentration in Paris and Helsinki will contribute to the weakening of their other urban centers. In Finland, this fear has a strong social as well as economic basis. Israel's economic concern extends to protection of arable land from urbanization and to promotion of mineral resource development. Israel's policy of deflecting growth from its principal metropolitan areas also reflects two special concerns: defense needs and ideology. In determining national development policies, only in the Netherlands is the development argument weighted so heavily in the direction of a widely shared concern for the character of man's daily life. No other national government demonstrates the same concern for the impact of urban living on man. This concern encompasses the preservation of a choice among living environments, housing density, ease of access to job and countryside, sense of place, healthfulness and beauty of the living environment, and protection of individuality. This concern underlies the conviction that the Randstad cities—the ring of cities which includes Rotterdam, The Hague, and Amsterdam—should not grow together. The central farmland at the core of the Randstad is of greatest value because it separates the circumferential cities, permits quick travel between them, and is an easily accessible natural environment offering recreation opportunities to urban residents. Of course, amenity has an economic value, and the government recognizes this. Rotterdam already finds its crowded housing and its inadequate recreation opportunities something of a handicap in attracting workers for its booming industries. Yet Rotterdam takes a view contrary to that of the national government, seeking growth in the belief that this is necessary in order to remain economically competitive on the European scale.

Many people concur with the government's development policies as national objectives but do not see them as personal or business restraints. The growth rate of the Randstad has declined substantially, but settlement of the north and southwest lag behind it. In a very egalitarian society the government has offered only weak financial incentives to carry out its land-use policies. Retention of the Randstad's green core and city separators is a major national goal. So, too, is balanced development of the polders and other areas outside the Randstad. To realize these goals, firmer planning implementation measures will be called for. National ownership of the polders and municipal land acquisition programs have been the most critical elements of the successes so far enjoyed. To them should be added a stronger role in implementation for regional and national planning, greater financial incentives for settlement in development areas, and revisions in the tax distribution system. Beyond the national arena, the government has endorsed the necessity of international planning for the region of which the Netherlands forms a central part.

In the post–World War II years the Netherlands has been engaged in a remarkably successful water management program, including polder creation, the Delta Works, and pollution control. The country has enjoyed an economic boom characterized by overemployment in the Randstad, rapid industrialization, and vast—though still insufficient—housing construction. During this period central Rotterdam has been totally rebuilt, and its port has become the world's largest in tonnage. With much that the war's destruction made most urgent now completed, it is significant that the principal national goal is a good life, and that this is defined in environmental as well as economic terms. Surely full employment and a rising standard of living are sought, but so too is a healthy environment for urban man. The resolution of the conflict between the traditional Dutch respect for individual freedom and the need to regulate this freedom to achieve nationally agreed upon objectives may yield a system of planning controls which is effective and compatible with both Dutch and American ideals of individual autonomy.

**The Natural
Environment**

In describing the setting for planning, in the Netherlands it is fitting to look first to the natural environment, for the Netherlands "natural" environment, both land and water, is mostly man-made. More than half of the land would be subject to intermittent flooding were it not for dikes and dams. Almost 20 percent of the land has been created from the sea. Water constitutes 16 percent of the Netherland's total area,[1] and much of the water network is man-made. First the Zuyder Zee and now the Rhine-Meuse Delta area are being converted from salt-water bays or estuaries to fresh-water lakes. There are enough drainage canals to encircle the earth six times. Amsterdam's shipping channel, linking the Rhine to the sea, is artificial. A national water management program shapes the natural environment of the future by holding back the sea, draining the land, maintaining an adequate fresh-water supply, and creating new land.

Before man, water shaped the Netherlands. Such uplands and slopes as there are, rising to a maximum height of 1,000 feet above sea level, are located in the east and southeast. This land is glacial moraine, deposited during the Pleistocene, then cut and crisscrossed by the Rhine and Meuse rivers. To the west of this higher ground, alluvium was deposited, and peat bogs developed in lagoons sheltered by sandbars from the open sea. Over time, parts of these peat bogs in the north and west were washed away and became lakes and river estuaries, while the central peat bogs were overlaid with sea clay.

For man to inhabit the lowlands, it was necessary to erect defenses against the sea and rivers. Much of the land had settled so that it was below mean sea level, protected only by the coastal dunes. To avoid loss of life, destruction of property, and salinization of the soil during storms, this land had to be shielded from salt-water incursions. Miles of dikes were built along the estuaries and river banks. Because the land was below sea level, artificial drainage by pumping excess rainfall and by infiltration to a network of diked canals was necessary (see Figure IV-1).

Protecting existing land was not enough; more land was needed. And so the creation of polders by erecting further barriers to the sea began. From 1200 until today, 2,800 polders have been created. Each of these incorporates a separate and independent water management system of dikes, pumps, and drainage canals, yet all are linked to form one system. More than 1.5 million acres of land have been reclaimed from the sea by dredging, diking, and pumping. This land constitutes nearly 20 percent of the Netherlands' total land area of some 13,000 square miles. Today the Netherlands is half as big as Pennsylvania and still growing. When completed, the Yssel Lake polders now being created in the former Zuyder Zee will increase the land area by 7 percent.

With the polders and bogs combined, more than half of the land lies below mean sea or river level (as seen in Map IV-1). Without the dikes, much of this land would be permanently under water and the rest would be subject to flooding twice daily. The land level varies, with the lowest polders lying 21'8" below sea level (see Figure IV-2). Because of this variation, not only dikes and drainage canals but also a complex system of some 7,000 locks are required to achieve adequate drainage as well as to permit navigation throughout the country.

Urban development on the lowlands is expensive and difficult because of soil conditions and the high water table; yet this is where most of it has occurred, largely because of port growth on the estuaries. The peat of the lowlands is from sixty to seventy feet deep, so that construction of roads and buildings requires fill and pilings. Pilings must be sunk through the peat to solid ground, and the height of buildings is restricted. The cost of roads

Figure IV-1. Open-Ditch Drainage System in Central Randstad

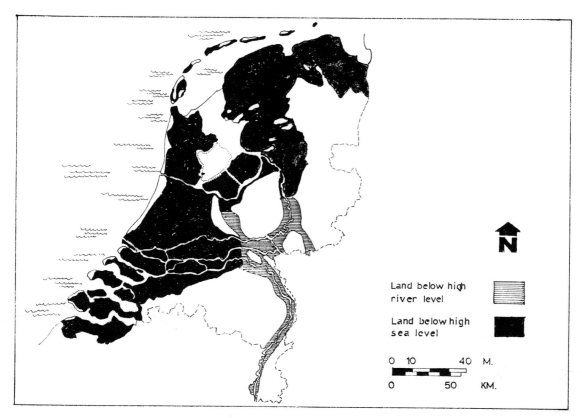

Map IV-1. Land below Sea Level

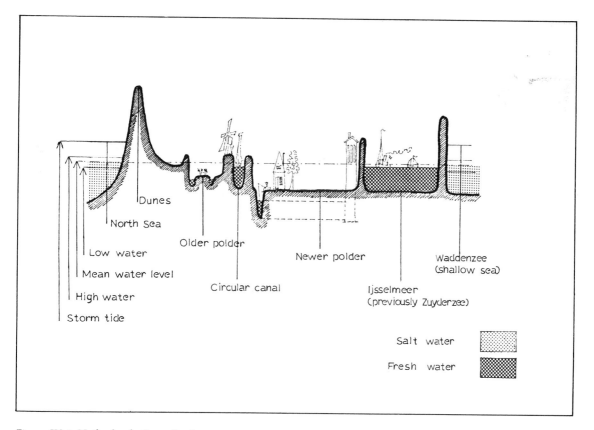

Figure IV-2. Netherlands Cross-Section

and the cost of public utilities are up to three times greater than those in the south and east of the country, where the ground is stable. The old inner section of Rotterdam was built on pilings but was not filled, while newer areas have been filled to raise them above mean sea level and to provide a more solid foundation for building. When the subway was built, it was cheaper to open trenches, let them fill with water, and then sink sections of the subway tunnel rather than to attempt to keep the excavations pumped dry. In Amsterdam the land is filled some six feet, which leaves it below mean sea level but high enough to be removed from the polder management system. The Hague was built on the edge of the coastal dune where accumulated sand provided a higher and more solid foundation.

Land reclamation by diking alone had two major disadvantages. Being so extensive, the dikes were difficult and expensive to maintain. In addition, as the demand for fresh water grew and the ground-water supply in dune areas was tapped increasingly, saline-water intrusion became a mounting problem, affecting both the water supply and the soil. To conquer both problems simultaneously, the Dutch began replacing the dikes with dams across the mouths of the bays and estuaries. While enormously expensive to build, these dams are cheaper and easier to maintain than the miles of dikes. They prevent the sea from sweeping across the land during severe storms, and they convert the salt-water bays and estuaries into fresh-water lakes which recharge the ground water, thus combatting the saline-water intrusion problem. Map IV-2 shows the land reclaimed between 1200 and 1968 and the sites proposed for future reclamation.

Floods precipitated the major estuary damming projects of this century. The Zuyder Zee project, given impetus by the flood of 1916, was the first major bridging of an estuary mouth with a barrier dam. Completion of a twenty-mile dam shortened the coastline by 186 miles and began the conversion of the saline estuary into the present fresh-water Yssel Lake. The lake is fed by 10 percent of the Rhine's flow. When the Delta Works are completed, this flow will be increased to provide a greater supply of fresh water to combat saline-water intrusion and to provide a fresh-water supply which can be drawn upon during the annual period in which consumption exceeds precipitation and river flow. The creation of Yssel Lake made possible the subsequent and continuing reclamation of the Yssel polders.

Further serious and costly flood damage led to the adoption of the Delta Plan. During World War II, 890 square miles of estuary land was flooded. Then, during the devastating flood of 1953, 620 square miles of land were flooded, more than 300 miles of dikes were destroyed or damaged, and some 2,000 lives were lost. Under the Delta Plan (see Map IV-3), all but two of the Rhine and Meuse estuaries will be closed to the sea. The New Waterway, a canal which serves the port of Rotterdam as well as general Rhine traffic, will be one open link between the rivers and the sea. The Western Scheldt estuary of the Scheldt River, which provides access to Antwerp, also will not be dammed. The Delta Plan will shorten the Netherlands' 1,120-mile coast by 435 miles[2] and will create large fresh-water lakes for recreation and ground-water recharge.

Flow in the entire delta system will be measured and regulated by a single computer system. Normally, the principal flow of the Rhine will be directed through the New Waterway and thus will provide a sufficient volume of fresh water to combat the increased salinity caused by the deepened channel. In high flow periods, water will be diverted to the fresh-water lakes created by the dams. In flood periods, excess water will pass through the Haringvliet locks (Figures IV-3 and IV-4) at a maximum rate of 21,000 cubic meters per second.

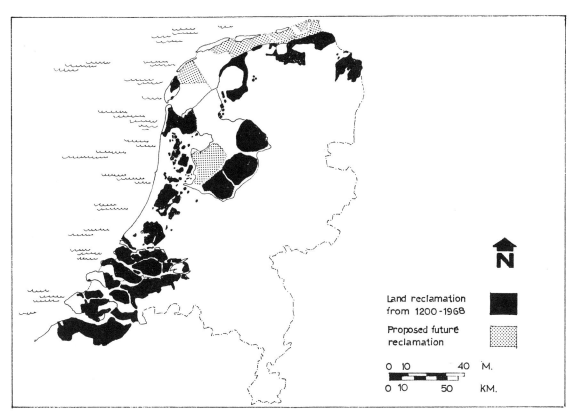

Map IV-2. Land Reclamation

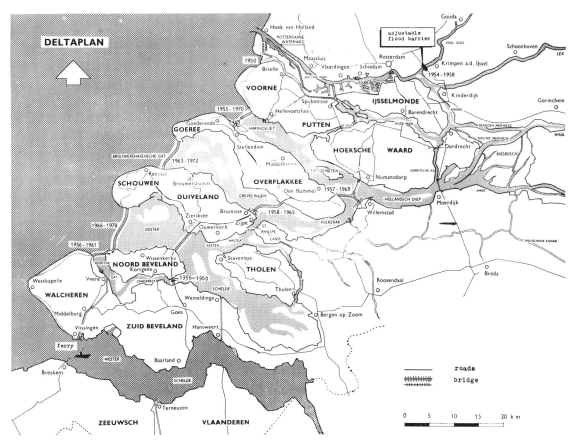

Map IV-3. The Delta Plan

Figure IV-3. Haringvliet Enclosure Looking North

Figure IV-4. Haringvliet Enclosure Looking South

The nineteen sluices will be built by dropping fill from cable cars. Pilings for the cables already are in place.

Figure IV-5. Volkerak Dam under Construction. When all caissons have been sunk, their valves will be closed and they will form the backbone of an earth dam.

The design and construction of the Zuyder Zee and Delta Works are stupendous feats of hydraulic engineering. Dams such as the Volkerak (Figure IV-5) are designed to protect the country against floods whose frequency is estimated to be once in 10,000 years. It has been necessary to design so that construction can proceed despite high tide flows—of up to one billion cubic meters in the East Scheldt, for example.[3] The largest discharge lock in the world has been built as part of the Haringvliet Dam. It will be opened when it becomes necessary to discharge excess flow from the river. It has been designed to permit fish migrations and the passage of eels.

The closing off of these estuaries has caused one resource loss—shellfish. Salt-water fish are replaced by fresh-water species, but there is no fresh-water replacement for the oysters and shrimps which flourished before. In the Wadden Sea, however, there has been some success with a fresh-water counterpart to the mussel.

Some thought is being given to a plan to link the Wadden Islands, which parallel the northwest coast of the Netherlands, through a series of dams. This would create additional fresh water and provide the opportunity for reclaiming more land, but it also would result in the destruction of an important migratory bird sanctuary. Such areas already have been lost through the Delta Works and through construction of a deep harbor for tankers at Europort. The future of the Wadden Islands area is an issue of international concern.

Water in recent years has presented another mounting problem: pollution. Sixty-five percent of the country's fresh-water supply comes from the Rhine and its tributaries.[4] Yet, when they reach the Netherlands, the Rhine, Meuse, and Scheldt carry a heavy load of organic and inorganic pollutants discharged by cities and industries in Germany, France, and Belgium. Salts from the potassium mines, coal fields, and chemical industries constitute the major inorganic waste problem. It has been calculated that, to have satisfactory chloride-ion levels in the water used for irrigating farmlands, the maximum chlorine content in the Rhine should average not more than 200 parts per million. This maximum has been exceeded regularly, and the chlorine content of the Rhine still is rising. At times it has reached 300 parts per million, making the water unsuitable for cattle, domestic consumption, and many types of crops.[5] The Netherlands is seeking an international agreement with France and Germany which would set the maximum salt content of the rivers at 200 parts per million.

With 30 million people living in the Rhine drainage area, organic pollution also is great. Inorganic and organic pollution are responsible for the disappearance of salmon from the Rhine. From an annual catch of more than 100,000 in 1875, the industry has declined to zero today. In terms of color, oxygen content, ammonia content, smell, and taste, the water of the Rhine is classed as "unsuitable as an element for the manufacture of drinking water."[6] Yet the supply of ground water is inadequate. Although the Netherlands is doing an increasingly effective job of managing its own wastes, it cannot control the quality of water entering from across its borders (see Map IV-4). For this, international agreement and enforcement are the only answers. West Germany now has an extensive program for controlling industrial pollution of the Rhine. It is hoped that a Rhine Basin Authority will be formed to establish and enforce a pollution control program.

Valuable resources of the Netherlands are the bog and polder soils. They are rich and fertile, well suited to the production of fruits, vegetables, and flowers and to the provision of lush pasturage.

The Netherlands' moderate, moist climate is an important contributor to her productive agriculture and active foreign trade. Because it is neither hot

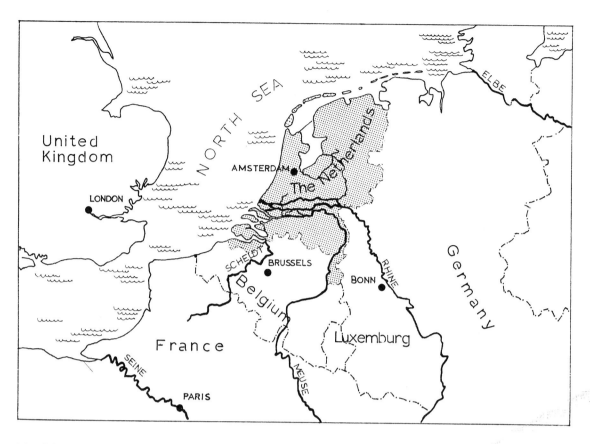

in summer nor cold in winter, the growing season is long. In addition, the weather is damp, windy, and cloudy almost all year. Rain falls on 200 days of the year, and average daily sunshine is but a few hours. Because the seaports are ice-free throughout the winter, they are open to ocean-going vessels all year long.

The only major resources of the Netherlands not created or manipulated by man are her minerals—coal, oil, and gas. Substantial deposits of coal exist in the southern part of the country, but mining no longer is profitable. The postwar discovery of oil and gas in the southwest, northeast, and along the shore of the North Sea was of great economic significance. At Slochteren, in the northeast, for example, it is estimated that natural gas deposits exceed 400 billion cubic meters. Annual gas consumption now runs at one billion cubic meters.[7] Domestic oil meets 25 percent of the Netherlands' annual domestic needs, its production having expanded more than twenty times since World War II.

The People

Although the Netherlands is underendowed with natural resources, it has attracted and held an overabundant population. Whereas Israel, Australia, and New Zealand are hunting for immigrants, the Netherlands has sought to spur emigration.

Comparisons of population densities in the Netherlands and the United States at a national scale are misleading because there is such an enormous disparity in the size of the two nations. It is more meaningful to compare populations and densities in Northern Europe and the Northeastern United States and Canada, or in the Netherlands and the U.S. East Coast Megalopolis. First, look at Northern Europe. If one starts at The Hague and draws a circle 380 miles in radius, it will include parts of England, Germany, and

France, and all of Belgium, Luxemburg, and the Netherlands. Within the circle live 160 million people, or about 80 percent of the population of the United States. An area of similar size in the Northeastern United States (extended to include Montreal, Canada) has 60 million people.[8] Within this crowded area of Northern Europe, the Netherlands is the most densely populated country, with 990 people per square mile and a total population of nearly 13 million. In Megalopolis, crowded though it is, there are but 700 people per square mile. Just as in Megalopolis, the over-all population density of the Netherlands is not evenly distributed (see Figure IV-6). Close to 50 percent of the people live on 22 percent of the land. Most existing development is concentrated in the Randstad, although there are a number of thriving, rapidly growing cities outside the Randstad, including Eindhoven, Geleen/Sittard, Emmen, Apeldoorn, and Nijmegen.

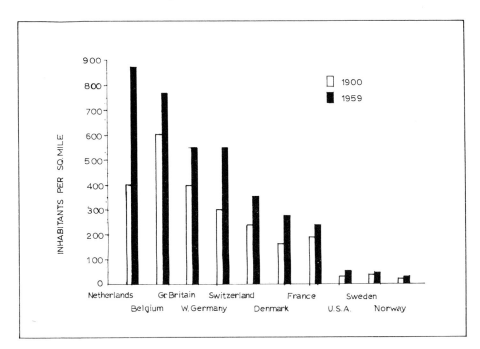

Figure IV-6.
Population
Densities,
1900 and 1959

Figure IV-7.
Population Growth,
1829–1960

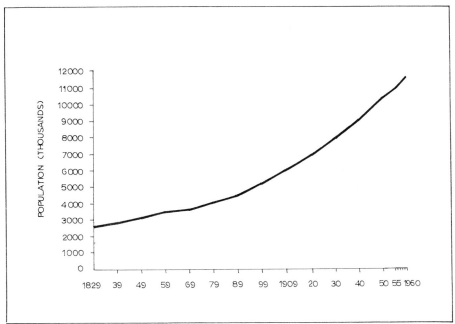

Not only have the Dutch sought to export people to limit internal growth, but they also have struggled to limit growth in the Randstad and the western portion of the country. In both efforts they have enjoyed limited success, although not as much as desired. In some years there has been a small annual net emigration, but in most years since 1961 immigration has exceeded emigration. In 1968, for example, net immigration was about 6,000 people. Internal migration to the west and north has reversed, so that the east and south are gaining, but the west continues to grow through natural increase.

The Dutch population has grown by at least 1 percent per year since 1870 (see Figure IV-7), and currently is growing at the rate of 1.3 percent per year. With low infant mortality, a low death rate, and a relatively high birth rate compared to the rest of Europe, its growth is faster than that of most other European countries. Between 1962 and 1967 its rate of growth per 1,000 people overtook that of the United States.

Today the proportion of elderly is smaller in the Netherlands than in most European countries. With an increased life expectancy and low death rate, however, the Netherlands will have an increasing percentage of elderly people.

Sixty percent of the population is classified as urban—that is, lives in towns of more than 20,000 population.[9] As more and more of the labor force is employed in industry and the tertiary sector, it is predicted that by 1975 the urban share of the population will rise to 70 percent. By 2000 it is estimated that it will be more than 90 percent.

In the three western provinces of North Holland, South Holland, and Utrecht, in which the Randstad is located, the density already is 2,250 people per square mile. In the Randstad itself, the density is 6,650 per square mile. Of the nation's nearly 13 million people, 4.5 million live in the Randstad—more than one-third of the people on 5 percent of the land.[10] By contrast, there are about 3,700 villages in the Netherlands, of which more than half have fewer than 500 inhabitants. Rural densities vary from 80 to 100 people per square mile in the new polders to as low as 40 people per square mile in the large recreation areas. Table IV-1 gives a percentage breakdown of the population by size of municipality.

Table IV-1.
Population Distribution by Size of Municipality, 1968

	Percentage of Population by Size of Municipality		
Region	Under 5,000	5,000–100,000	100,000 or more
The West (North and South Holland, Utrecht)	8.9	45.5	45.6
The Rest of the Netherlands	14.3	68.7	17.0
Total	11.8	57.9	30.3

SOURCE: The Netherlands, Ministry of Housing and Physical Planning, The Hague.

The people are where the jobs are, and, in the past, most of the non-agricultural jobs have been concentrated in the Randstad. Traditionally, Rotterdam has been the port and industrial city, The Hague the administrative city, and Amsterdam the commercial and cultural city. They are the three largest cities of the Netherlands, with 1968 populations, respectively, of 699,000, 564,000, and 848,000; their rates of growth can be compared in Figure IV-8. In 1966 their respective urban area populations were 1,044,000,

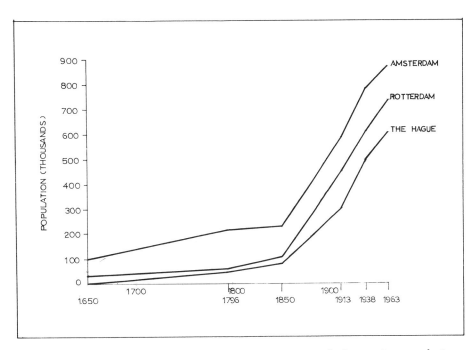

Figure IV-8.
Population Growth
in Amsterdam,
Rotterdam, and
The Hague,
1650–1963

745,000, and 1,043,000. While the center cities are declining in population, the urban areas continue to grow.

In recent years, cities outside the Randstad have been gaining population rapidly (see Map IV-5). Cities in the southern provinces of North Brabant and Limburg have prospered and grown. The Philips Company, with its vast electric and electronic products industry, and later DAF, the automobile company, have been primarily responsible for the booming growth of Eindhoven, now the fifth largest city. Eindhoven has seen a sevenfold increase in population, while the rest of the Netherlands' population has doubled. By 1968, Eindhoven's population was 187,000, that of its urban area around 300,000. The city's people and buildings are young; almost half of the population is under twenty-five.

In the north, employment in the natural gas and salt-related industries has contributed to the growth of Delfzijl.

Thus far the polder areas of Yssel Lake and the delta area of the southwest in the Province of Zeeland have not participated in the urban expansion of the country, but outmigration from these areas has been stemmed. Completion of the Delta Works, including highways across the dams, will provide much easier and quicker access to and through the delta and doubtless will stimulate growth there. The government is attempting to stimulate growth in the area of Yssel Lake and already has begun construction of a regional new town, Lelystad.

Although substantial amounts of new agricultural land are being created, the increasing industrialization of agriculture and the merging of tracts into larger landholdings mean that fewer and fewer workers will be employed in agriculture. These workers will go to the cities, but, if government incentives succeed, this no longer will mean that they will leave their region. In the 1950s the Randstad gained heavily in population, primarily at the expense of the north, including the provinces of Groningen, Friesland, and Drenthe. In the 1960s, thanks principally to government programs, net migration to the Randstad decreased, and outmigration from the north was markedly reduced. The gains in the east (the provinces of Gelderland and Overyssel) increased. A comparison of net internal migration in the Netherlands as a whole during these two decades can be made by referring to Table IV-2. However, because

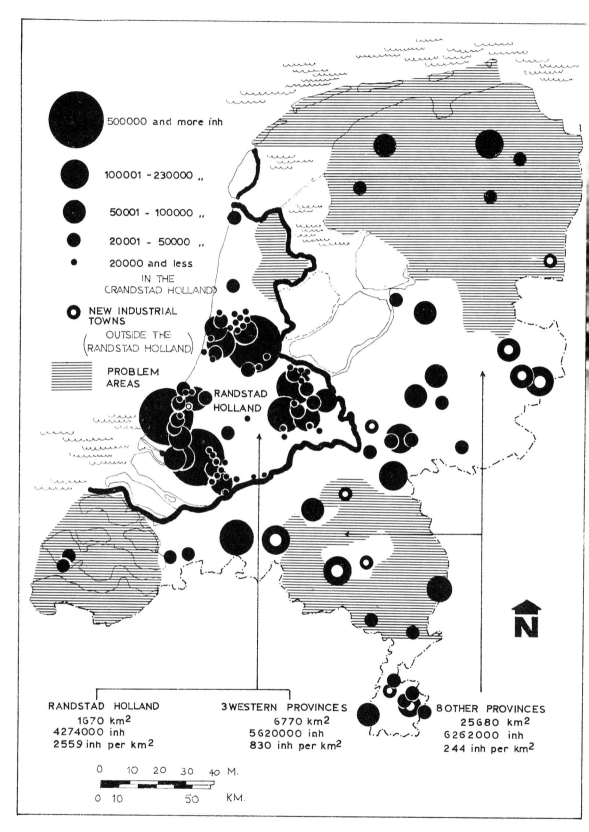

Map IV-5. Population Distribution and Regional Development

these figures refer only to internal migration, they should not be interpreted to mean that the Randstad, for example, is declining in total population. The annual natural increase in the existing population in the Randstad is approximately 25,000, or roughly five times the annual outmigration. Outmigration from the western provinces must triple its present rate to achieve by 1980 what the government views as a successful population distribution.[11] Table IV-3 shows changes in the percentage growth by region from 1951 through 1969. While the west's rate of growth has been considerably stemmed, it still remains the fastest growing region in absolute numbers.

Table IV-2.
Net Internal Migration, 1950–59 and 1960–68

	Area				
Period	North	East	West	South	Southwest
1950–59[a]	−81,000	26,000	75,000	22,000	−16,000
1960–68	−14,000	48,000	−46,000	23,000	−6,000

SOURCE: Theo Quené, "Planning Ideas and Ideals in a Small European Country" (Speech delivered to the Citizen's Council on City Planning, Philadelphia, Pa., July 2, 1968).
[a] Including 26,000 from the Central Register of population.

Table IV-3.
Regional Growth, 1951–69

Region	Percentage of Total Population 1/1/51	Percentage of Growth					Percentage of Total Population 1/1/69
		1951–55	1955–59	1959–63	1963–67	1967–69	
North	12.0	3.5	3.8	7.0	10.1	10.5	10.9
New Polders	0.1	2.2	1.6	0.6	1.3	2.0	0.3
East	17.5	20.3	20.9	22.2	22.4	24.3	18.4
West	48.0	44.6	43.9	40.9	37.3	36.7	46.6
South	19.7	28.7	28.5	29.0	27.4	24.0	21.4
Southwest	2.7	0.7	1.3	0.3	1.5	2.5	2.4
Total	100.0	100.0	100.0	100.0	100.0	100.0	100.0

SOURCES: "Physical Planning as a Means of Balanced Development in the Netherlands" (Paper presented by the Netherlands to the Economic Commission for Europe, February, 1964); the Netherlands, Ministry of Housing and Physical Planning, The Hague.

Since World War II, emigration has been endorsed by the government as a partial answer to population growth. To implement this policy, the government has agreed to pay up to 30,000 people per year the cost of traveling from the Netherlands to their destination countries.[12] One reason for encouraging emigration is that, although the Netherlands has been in an era of overemployment, the government is concerned that there are not enough skilled jobs to match the qualifications of the Dutch labor force and that this problem will be aggravated by further growth. In addition:

... The emigrant is not merely a compatriot to be subtracted from the population total. He is also a kind of ambassador for his country. It is of primary significance for a small, densely populated country to become known and to continue to become known abroad, and to acquire a good reputation as a result of the labours of its sons and daughters. Business relations spring up; export increases. Holland, with its dense population confined to a small territory, is largely dependent on forging trade relations. Emigration is an indirect means of causing these to flourish.[13]

The government's annual goal of 30,000 emigrants was exceeded in the years 1951–54, but it has not since been reached. Currently, emigration is around 10,000 people per year. In the favored destination countries—Australia, Canada, and New Zealand—the Dutch now constitute 1 percent of the population. In the earlier years of the program, emigration was counterbalanced by Dutch people coming to the Netherlands following the independence of Indonesia. In recent years, Dutch emigration has been counterbalanced by the importation of unskilled labor from Southern Europe, although these workers are unlikely to become Dutch citizens. Recently, job opportunities for skilled workers have been plentiful in the Netherlands and thus have decreased the incentive to depart.

The Economy   The Netherlands is a highly developed, technologically advanced nation. The standard of living is high, though not as high as that of several other European countries. Income is quite evenly distributed: there is little poverty or great wealth. Agricultural and mineral resources are managed soundly and contribute significantly to national income, but it is the growing industrial complex, with its highly refined products, the massive Europort, and skilled technicians, which produces much of the wealth of the Netherlands. Although the country's economic strength lies in a very competitive field, its combination of technical expertise, good management, and fortunate location seem destined to lead to continued growth and national prosperity.

The completion of docking facilities for tankers drawing sixty-two feet of water and weighing up to 250,000 tons characterizes the ability of the Netherlands to anticipate and meet the needs of the future (see Figure IV-9). A major concern of Dutch economic planners is the potential role of the Netherlands in the highly competitive economy of Western Europe. Another critical issue is the future role of the government in national growth.

The Netherlands suffered heavy damage during World War II. Much of the land was flooded and had to be drained and reconditioned at considerable expense. Ports, roads, bridges, and railroads were destroyed, as were many houses, factories, and office buildings. The heart of Rotterdam, as well as the oil storage and refining works nearby, was completely destroyed by bombing. Structures which survived deteriorated from lack of maintenance. Despite their losses, the Dutch set out to rebuild, to expand their industrial base, and to capture a larger share of foreign trade than had been theirs prior to the war. In this they exceeded their own expectations.

Notwithstanding the many almost insurmountable difficulties which the Minister of Economic Affairs still sees, he feels it is incumbent on him to express his satisfaction with regard to the development of the industrialization of the country. Not because he is convinced that the realisation of the programme is making such rapid progress that its success appears to be assured. The most difficult part of the road to be traversed is still before us. The impression, however, that the whole Netherlands people, every man in his place, has put its shoulders to the wheel is a source of great satisfaction and gratitude.[14]

It can be stated with satisfaction that the industrial development in the years 1952–1957 has proceeded in a gratifying way. The fear that after the rapid expansion of industry at first thought impossible in the period 1948–1952 further industrialisation would go at a slower rate has seemingly proved unfounded.[15]

Comparative Income Levels

While the postwar recovery, the maintenance of full employment during the shift of many workers from agriculture to industry and services, and the increase in purchasing power per capita all have been significant achieve-

Figure IV-9. Two-Hundred-Thousand-Ton Tanker Leaving Main Europort Canal

ments, the situation in the Netherlands cannot be isolated from that in Europe generally, particularly that in the other nations of the European Economic Community. Here the results are less satisfying. Even given the low postwar starting point, income in the Netherlands has remained comparatively low (see Table IV-4). In 1960, of the EEC countries, only Italy had a lower per capita income. In 1963, income per capita in the Netherlands was $700, still one of the lowest in Western Europe.[16] By 1966 the position of the Netherlands had improved, although, of the EEC countries, France and West Germany still were well ahead in terms of purchasing power per capita (see Table IV-5).

In addition, productivity per worker and per capita are rising about 0.5 percent per year more slowly in the Netherlands than in the EEC as a whole. The annual rise in Gross National Product during the 1960s was estimated in 1967 to be 4.8 percent. During this period, output per worker was estimated to have risen 3.4 percent per annum, largely as a result of increased capital investment. For production in the Netherlands to be competitive with that of the EEC nations as a whole, capital investment in business must continue to rise. It is estimated that, in real terms, capital investment in the sixties was slightly less in relation to Gross National Product than the EEC average. The government recognizes that increased capital investment is essential. It has been recent government policy to place one-quarter of the national income in capital investments. In 1965, public investments were 4.6 percent of the Gross National Product; for 1970 they are estimated at 5.8 percent, as compared with 3.9 percent for the EEC as a whole.[17] To a large extent this invest-

Table IV-4.
Increase in Income, 1950–60

| Country | Percentage Increase per Year | | |
	Real National Income	Population	Real National Income per Capita
West Germany	7.3	1.1	6.2
The Netherlands	4.8	1.3	3.5
France	4.0	0.9	3.1
The United States	3.3	1.7	2.6
Sweden	3.3	1.7	1.6
The United Kingdom	2.0	0.4	1.6

SOURCE: J. E. Andriessen, "Economic Development in the Netherlands," *Planning and Development in the Netherlands*, 1, no. 1 (1962).

Table IV-5.
Comparison of Income Levels in EEC Countries, 1966

| Country | Income Level per Worker on Basis of | | Income Level per Capita on Basis of | |
	Rate of Exchange	Purchasing Power	Rate of Exchange	Purchasing Power
Belgium	120	96	127	101
France	115	96	134	111
Italy	57	62	67	72
The Netherlands	100	100	100	100
West Germany	97	83	130	112

SOURCE: The Netherlands, Ministry of Economic Affairs, "A Summary of the Memorandum on the Growth and Structure of the Dutch Economy" (no. S24 564001), mimeographed (1967).

ment has been directed to the underdeveloped portions of the country—the areas of lower incomes, lower service levels, and higher outmigration.

These differences in income levels and services are noticeable but diminishing, largely as a result of government efforts to encourage the location of new industrial facilities in the north and southwest. Predictably, income and the level of services enjoyed are highest in the Randstad. In 1950, for example, income in the Randstad province of North Holland was 116 in relation to a national index of 100, while in the northeastern province of Drenthe it was 79. In 1960, income was 25 percent higher in the west than in the rest of the country. In 1960 there was one doctor per 663 people in the west, compared with one per 1,236 in the south. More than twice as many university students come from families living in the west than from the rest of the country, and three of the four state universities are located there. However, several private universities, two state technological institutes, and the state agricultural institute are located in other parts of the country.

In 1962 there were seventy-one cars per 1,000 people in the west and fifty-one per 1,000 in the south.[18] Car ownership is increasing rapidly throughout the country, but bicycles and motor bikes still are used widely. Distances are small from farm to town or from home to work, and the terrain is flat, so cars are less of a necessary than they would be elsewhere. There is one bicycle per 2.5 people.

In the Netherlands today, there are few very rich people and few who are very poor.

... Our distribution of national income has been changed very much. When I was a young boy, there were very rich people and also there were very poor people. Now there is not much difference. One could say that the highest officials earn about four times as much as the people working in modest jobs. Our tax system is such that if you own[ed] much property and much money the taxes cut into it so much that many people just left the country. Many owners of large property went to the United States where the taxes are much milder for them.[19]

Employment

The Netherlands' skilled and stable labor force has cooperated with management and government to increase production and restrain inflation. Between 1959 and 1967 the rise in the cost of living was held to 30.0 percent. In 1968, however, wages rose 6.5 percent, while productivity rose only 5.0 or 6.0 percent.[20] Then, early in 1969, the steel industry granted a wage increase of 6.5 percent. Because the steel industry sets the pattern for wage contracts, and because its increase exceeded the government's projection of 4.0 percent, this action gave rise to an inflation scare.

The country's employment level has been consistently high: 98.5 percent of the labor force from 1956 to 1960, and 99.2 percent from 1961 to 1967. With a constantly growing, skilled labor force and limited raw materials, the only course open to the Netherlands in order to provide an increasing number of well-paid jobs in industry has been to import additional raw materials and process them into finished goods for export. Despite the creation of additional agricultural land, jobs in agriculture have been declining and will decline further as a result of modernized farming methods and the reallocation of farmland. Agriculture's share of the labor force declined from 31 percent in 1900 to 20 percent in 1947 to 8 percent in 1969.[21] In actual numbers, there are more people working in agriculture today than in 1900, but even this will no longer be true by 1980.

Of the 8 percent of the labor force employed in agriculture, those working in the labor-intensive horticultural and bulb industries are better paid than those employed in dairy and crop agriculture.

The percentage of employment in industry and services has been increasing about equally at the expense of agriculture (see Table IV-6). In the future, industry's share of employment is expected to taper off as increased automation reduces manpower requirements.

Table IV-6.
Distribution of the Work Force, 1950, 1960, and 1980

Sector	1950	1960	1980[a]
Agriculture	14.1%	10.4%	5.0%
Industry	40.5	41.4	40.7
Services	45.4	48.2	54.3
Total	100.0	100.0	100.0

SOURCE: The Netherlands, Government Physical Planning Service, *Second Report on Physical Planning in the Netherlands* (The Hague: Netherlands Printing Office, 1966).
[a] Projected figures.

Employment in industry is concentrated in metals—iron and steel manufacture, metallurgy, machine and tool production, electronics, electrotechnical and vehicle manufacture. Of industrial jobs, 35 percent are in metals, 14 percent in foods and luxury industries, 11 percent in textiles, and the remaining 40 percent in all other industries.[22] Industry is the sphere of employment which relies most heavily on the importation of unskilled labor from those areas of Southern Europe where serious unemployment exists. In some metal and textile industries, foreign labor constitutes 10 percent of the work force.

Production

Industry is the major contributor to the present-day Dutch economy. It is estimated that, in 1970, 54.9 percent of all production came from industry, 37.9 percent from services, and only 7.2 percent from agriculture (see Table IV-7). The metal industry is expected to remain the most important in terms of value of production, while the chemical industry will grow the most rapidly. For instance, given an index of 100 for the year 1963, production in chemicals and petroleum had risen to 177 by 1967; in the same period the index for metals rose only to 121, while that for textiles dropped to 96.[23] Much of the production in the metal and chemical industries is by large companies with efficient production and marketing systems. It has been recognized that increased concentration in other industries will be necessary if the Netherlands is to compete effectively in world markets.

Table IV-7.
Level and Movement of Gross Value Added per Sector, 1960-70[a]

Sector	Absolute Level, 1960		Average Annual Rise in Percentage		Absolute Level, 1970[c]	
	Billions of Guldens	Percentage of Total	1961-65	1966-70[b]	Billions of Guldens	Percentage of Total
Agriculture	4.70	10.5	0.2	2.5	5.34	7.2
Industry, including building	21.80	48.7	6.2	6.8	40.82	54.9
Services, excluding house property	18.20	40.8	4.9	4.1	28.22	37.9
Total	44.70	100.0	5.1	5.3	74.38	100.0

SOURCE. The Netherlands, Ministry of Economic Affairs, "A Summary of the Memorandum on the Growth and Structure of the Dutch Economy" (no. S24 564001), mimeographed, (1967).
[a] Based on 1965 prices. [b] Estimated for 1970. [c] Projected figures.

The fortuitous discovery of oil and gas in the Netherlands has provided the nation with an important new resource, stimulated the growth of an already powerful petrochemical industry, and provided an additional, much-needed export. In addition, the location of the deposits is a lever in the government's industrial decentralization policy. However, because oil and gas are capital rather than labor-intensive industries, they do not in themselves attract much new development.

The refining of imported and domestic oil, as well as related petrochemical production, occurs on the New Waterway at Europort. The Shell refinery there is Europe's largest, and Rotterdam is the world's largest port in tonnage. In 1968 the port handled 155 million tons, 10 percent more than in 1967. The volume of oil, ores, and general cargo handled by the port all increased substantially in that year, with ores showing the greatest percentage rise.[24] When Europort's facilities for servicing super tankers are completed, further growth of the petrochemical industry is anticipated. The port and petrochemical activities of Europort are stimulating the growth of related industries and of service jobs in this area of the Randstad.

Iron and steel manufacture is concentrated at the sea terminus of the North Sea Canal, near Amsterdam, using iron ore imported from Sweden and Spain.

Agriculture is the problem area, particularly field-crop and dairy farming. Subsidies are needed, and international competition is severe.

... At the moment the problem is that our agriculture as a whole can only survive by rather big subsidies, mostly indirect, by the state. Horticulture is profitable and in fact is a booming business—bulbs, trees, tomatoes, cucumbers, grapes, flowers. ... But it is absolutely impossible to use all the cultivated land for horticulture. We have about one million acres of cultivated land and approximately five hundred thousand acres of horticultural land, so it would be a large proposition to transfer all our agricultural land into horticulture. Instead we have to modernize our agriculture by increasing the size of holdings, by better water control, and by reallocation of land. An area of about 10,000 to 12,000 acres would be just large enough to be kept as a pasture area. We would hope that, after this modernization, agriculture could operate without subsidy.[25]

The horticultural industry is located mainly in the west (see Figure IV-10). It is labor intensive and has been highly profitable, but competition within the Common Market now is reducing its profitability. Much of Europe's fresh produce comes from the vast areas of "glass-houses" interspersed between cities of the Randstad, particularly between The Hague and Rotterdam. The "glass-house" district adjacent to The Hague covers an area larger than that city. Cut flowers for Europe and the East Coast of the United States are grown south of Amsterdam near the airport. The soil, climate, and convenience to sea, air, and rail transport make this location ideal. The bulb industry is centered near the west coast. Although these forms of agriculture are labor intensive, nonetheless, they account for only 6.5 percent of the employment in the western provinces.[26]

The remaining forms of agriculture—dairying, field crops, pasturage—are located in the north, east, and southwest. They pose economic and social problems. Many landholdings are too small for efficient farming and currently require subsidies. Many young people no longer wish to continue farming as a way of life. The government's program for modernizing agriculture is particularly important in the north and southwest, where more than 50 percent of the labor force still is engaged in farming.[27] Even with improved conditions, however, the demands of farm life drive many farmers' sons to the cities. "Don't forget this: we haven't many farmers anymore. The farmers say, 'My wife said we have to go out on the weekend and she doesn't want to live with me anymore when I am always sitting on the couch.' We can join each other a little bit and split up the work so that the farmers take turns on weekends. They now are speaking about the cow hotels where a farmer can bring his cows for a weekend."[28]

Land Use

Although a decreasing percentage of the population is engaged in agriculture, land does not lie fallow. Particularly in the north, in the polders where grains are grown, land is being assembled into larger and more efficient parcels. More than three-quarters of the country's land is cultivated, nearly 10 percent is urbanized, 7 percent is forested, and only 6 percent is classed as wasteland (see Figure IV-11).[29] This represents an increase during the twentieth century of urbanized and horticultural land and a decrease of wasteland. The term wasteland actually is a misnomer and might better be described as open land. The acreage classified as wasteland consists of dunes and other

Figure IV-10. Ilpendam, a Horticultural Village in North Holland

recreation areas and of biologically or botanically important sites. Because the demand for recreation land is increasing rapidly, there is little opportunity for further conversion of this land either to urban uses or to intensive agriculture. In addition, the preservation of its natural character is considered necessary for the protection of the biosphere. Only through further reclamation will additional land be provided for agricultural uses.

Figure IV-11.
Netherlands Land
Use, 1900 and 1950

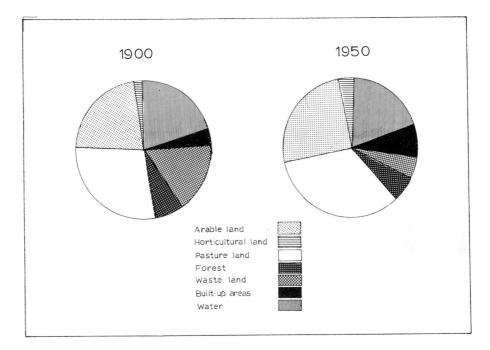

The Netherlands in the World Market

Because of the Netherlands' size, location, and limited natural resources, foreign trade is a key factor in the nation's internal economic vitality. "We depend so very, very much on the international exchange of goods and services. We are based largely on our port function between Europe and the outside world."[30] Fully recognizing this, the government consistently has followed a policy of international economic cooperation. Successively, the Netherlands helped to form, then joined, Benelux, OECD (the Organization for Economic Cooperation and Development), the European Coal and Steel Community, and the EEC (European Economic Community). Benelux, with its common market for goods and its joint customs for foreign goods, served as a model for EEC.

Trade is primarily with Europe, particularly the EEC countries, and secondarily with North America and Asia. Major countries or areas from which imports originate are: Belgium, Luxemburg, West Germany, the United Kingdom, Asia, and the United States. With the exception of the United States, these also are the principal countries to which the Netherlands exports her goods. More than 25 percent of the exports are to West Germany alone, while 40 percent of imports and exports alike involve non-EEC countries. Gas is exported to Belgium, France, and Germany, and, largely as a result of gas sales abroad, mining now accounts for 7 percent of industrial exports.

The economic growth of the Netherlands is largely attributable to increased exports. During the 1950s they rose 250 percent; by 1960 they were responsible for 43 percent of the nation's income. In 1967 the Netherlands led Europe and the United States in terms of exports as a percentage of Gross National Product (see Figure IV-12). Exports for 1968 exceeded the 1967 figure by 15 percent, but they have not yet compensated for the country's import appetite. Between 1955 and 1967 the export-import value ratio ranged from 76 to 92 percent. Nevertheless, from 1958 through 1966 the Netherlands enjoyed a favorable balance of payments on the total account for all years except 1959 and 1962.

Figure IV-12. Exports as a Percentage of the Gross National Product, 1967

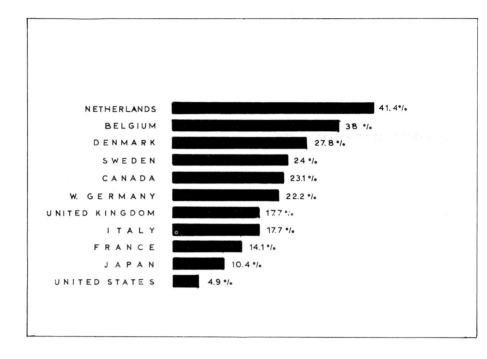

The Government

The Netherlands is an old nation. An ancestor of the reigning House of Orange led the fight to secure independence from Philip II of Spain, and the autonomous republic of seven sovereign provinces came into being in 1579. During the brief period of French domination from 1795 to 1813, the government became more centralized. A monarchy was constitutionally established after the French were repulsed in 1813, and the country took the name "Kingdom of the Netherlands."

The first constitution limited the autonomy of the seven provinces, and of the four provinces later established, by creating the power of royal assent and by making the provinces dependent on national funding. This early recognition of the power of the purse served as a precedent for the subsequent national control of municipal funds.

The Netherlands has a three-tier system of government—national, provincial, and municipal. There are 11 provinces and 935 municipalities. The municipalities range in population from 300 to Amsterdam's 848,000. The need to reduce the number of municipalities is widely recognized, but no program to achieve this has been enacted. Also under consideration is the possibility of reducing the number of provinces to correspond with the regions defined by nature and economics.

There is a long tradition of municipal dominance over development decisions in the Netherlands, although certain questions—especially that of water—have been recognized as the province of national planning and management. There also is cooperation at the municipal and national levels with corresponding levels of government in neighboring countries, particularly in regard to water resource management.

National Government

The national government consists of the crown, the ministers, the Council of State, and the bicameral States General (Parliament). The crown and ministers constitute the executive branch of government. The constitution specifies that the crown (the king or queen) "is inviolable, the ministers ... responsible." In other words, the king can do no wrong, but his ministers must answer to Parliament for the government's policy. Most legislation is initiated by the government through the submission of draft bills to Parliament. The minister president, however, differs from his British counterpart in that he has no authority to direct the decisions of the other cabinet ministers.

... The Ministers are equal ranking and each of them is responsible in his own domain. This is, in a way, a drawback for the framing of a homogeneous and consistent policy in matters which are of interest to various ministries, such as national planning. Besides, the political situation in our country makes it virtually impossible to have a homogeneous cabinet. Nearly all our cabinets are coalition cabinets, based on a compromise on the main political issues, but leaving room for diverging opinions on other points.[31]

The ministers are appointed by the crown, but they must resign if their policy conflicts with that of Parliament. Each department of the executive branch of government is headed by a minister, some of whom are seconded by one or more secretaries of state. Together the ministers form the cabinet, which is headed by the minister president. Currently, the cabinet is a coalition of the Christian and Liberal parties. The Socialists are the major opposition party.

The Council of State is an advisory body to the crown. It has a maximum membership of sixteen and is presided over by the vice president or, on rare occasion, by the reigning sovereign. The council reviews bills prior to their submission to the legislature, advises in instances in which royal assent is required, and considers administrative issues in dispute. Among the matters which come before it are appeals concerning the approval of local development plans. In addition, the council exercises the functions of the crown during interregnums.

The legislature, or States General, consists of the First Chamber (Senate) and the Second Chamber (Chamber of Deputies). There are 75 senators, elected to staggered six-year terms by the provincial councils. The 150 members of the Chamber of Deputies are elected directly every four years by a system of proportional representation. Bills initiate with the crown or, under the "right of initiative," with the Chamber of Deputies. This right of the Second Chamber to initiate legislation is rarely used, however. Amendments to bills can be made only by the Chamber of Deputies, which must approve all bills before they are voted on by the Senate. Both chambers have the right of interpellation—the right to put questions to the executive branch of the government.

Dutch political parties are based on political and/or religious affiliations. They include: the Roman Catholic People's party, Party of Labor (Socialist), People's Party for Freedom and Democracy (Liberal), Farmers' parties, Anti-Revolutionary party, Democrats '66, Christian Historical Union, Political Reformed party, Communist party, and Pacifist Socialist party. The first three parties dominate by capturing close to 75 percent of the vote.

Once enacted, legislation is binding unless subsequently revoked or altered by Parliament. It is not subject to scrutiny by the judiciary for its relation to provisions of the constitution.

Of particular significance in Dutch government organization is the tax structure. In essence, most taxes are collected at the national level, and some of these are then distributed to the municipalities in accordance with various formulas. Some 90 percent of municipal revenues are received from the national government. Table IV-8, which shows national, provincial, and municipal budgets for 1963, and municipal budgets for 1970, indicates clearly the financial dependence of the municipalities on the national government and the relatively weak position of the provinces.

Table IV-8.
Government Budget, 1963 and 1970

(millions of guldens)

	1963	1970
National Income[a]	46,320	100,000
Net National Budget (exclusive of contribution to municipalities)	9,590	28,965
Budget of the Provinces	190	691
Budget of the Municipalities:		
Allocated from the municipal fund	1,816	3,724
Allocated from real estate tax	—	202
National contributions	1,634	3,367
Municipal tax yield	200	500
Profits from municipal land and enterprises	40	80
Total income	3,690	7,873
Capital expenditure	2,200	5,885[b]
Total municipal budget	5,890	13,758

SOURCES: "Physical Planning as a Means of Balanced Development in the Netherlands" (Paper presented by the Netherlands to the Economic Commission for Europe, February, 1964); "Kommunale Finanzstruktur und Raumordnung" (n.p., n.d.); and a personal communiqué from Mr. Jasper Vink.
[a] Approximates Net National Product, as the term is applied in the United States.
[b] Figure for 1968.

National government expenditures in 1962 were distributed as shown in Table IV-9. Expenditures for physical development as a percentage of all state expenditures increased from 15.6 in 1964 to 18.1 in 1969; as a percentage of national income these expenditures rose from 4.5 in 1964 to 6.0 in 1969. State expenditures for physical development other than housing have risen more rapidly than those for housing.

Expenditures for some purposes, such as housing and education, are made in part through payments to the provincial or municipal governments for capital expenditures and ordinary operating expenses. Some of the payments from the national government to the municipalities are block grants from the Municipal Fund; these are available for any use chosen by the municipality. Other payments are earmarked for specific purposes.

The national government finances municipal government by distributing tax revenues from the Municipal Fund and through direct grants from the national Exchequer. The Municipal Fund is the principal source of municipal income. The national government levies and collects the land tax (levied on the landowner), the house tax (levied on the occupant of the house), the income tax, the wage tax, the corporate tax, the import and excise taxes, and, since 1969, the value-added tax. The Municipal Fund consists of part of the yield from 13 separate taxes. Its total is approximately one-eighth of all taxes collected by the national government. All land and house taxes are returned

Table IV-9.
National Expenditures for 1962 and 1970

Expenditure	1962	Estimated for 1970[a]
Education, Culture, Recreation, and Sciences	20%	29%
Military	16	14
National Debt	11	7
Social Programs, including pensions	10	10
Housing	9	9
Communications, Transportation, and Waterways	8	10
General Public Administration	7	4
Agriculture and Fisheries	6	4
Foreign Relations	4	4
Judiciary and Police	4	5
Trade and Industry	2	2
War Damage	1	—
National Health	1	1
Miscellaneous	1	1
Surinam and Netherlands Antilles	—	—
Total	100	100

SOURCE: Developed from figures cited in G. W. Toebes, "Centralization and Decentralization in the Field of Public Finance in the Netherlands," mimeographed (1963), and from information given to the author by Mr. Jasper Vink.
[a] In billions of guldens, a total expenditure of 28.9 ($8 billion).

to the municipalities from which they were collected. It is now proposed that the land tax be locally assessed, but it is likely to remain a comparatively unimportant tax. In 1963, 13 percent of the total of the remaining taxes also was distributed to the municipalities. While the state administers the Municipal Fund, on matters of policy it must consult with the Council for Municipal Finance, whose members are elected by the Union of Dutch Municipalities, to which all municipalities belong.[32]

The Municipal Fund is distributed in several payments, each calculated on a different basis. The general payment is calculated in relation to population, surface area, the density of developed areas, and the cost of social welfare services. The allocation can be varied according to legislatively specified criteria or when it is determined that particular conditions in a municipality justify a temporary increase in funds. The complementary payment supplements the yield from land and house taxes if this revenue for a municipality falls below the national average per capita. (Such a provision would be of great significance in the United States, for it would remove the real property tax yield as a prime determinant of municipal land-use and zoning policy.) A third payment covers the cost of elementary and technical education in the municipality.

Direct payments from the state Exchequer are made on the basis of actual costs incurred by the municipalities to cover education (including college education), police and a portion of social welfare, low-income housing, and industrial development. Additional grants for infrastructure and industrial development are available to municipalities designated in national plans as development locations.

Provincial Government

The weakest level of the Dutch government always has been the province, but the pattern now shows signs of changing. Recognition of the importance of regional planning, and of a regional role in development, has resulted in a relative increase in strength at this level. Provincial supervision of municipalities (Map IV-6) and water boards is assuming greater importance.

Provincial government is unusual in that it is a composite of provincial autonomy and national control. The provincial government has extensive power to enact legislation. Yet it also may be called on to implement national policy, either through legislation or by executive action.

The provinces are governed by provincial councils (Provincial States) consisting of popularly elected members and a chairman, or royal commissioner, appointed by the crown. The size of the provincial councils varies from thirty-nine to eighty-three members, depending on the size of the provincial population. Council members are elected every four years in the same manner as members of the Second Chamber. The royal commissioner serves for an indefinite period and is paid by the national government. He and six members of the council, elected by their fellow council members, serve as the College of the Provincial Executive (Deputed States). The provincial council is authorized to enact any legislation concerning provincial affairs as long as the legislation does not conflict with the national constitution or national legislation. In addition, any provincial legislative actions which relate to the water system are subject to royal assent, as are some actions relating to provincial finance. The provincial council may levy specified taxes—namely, additional percentages on the ground tax and the tax on residential rental value.

Map IV-6.
Provinces and
Major Cities

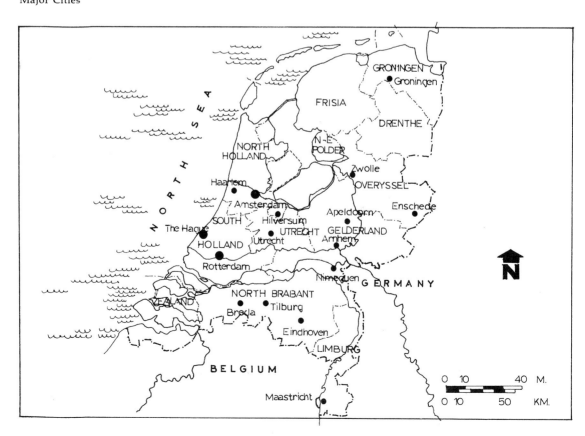

The executive functions of the provincial council, which are carried out through the Deputed States, include partial management (under the direction of the national government) of the water system—dikes, canals, bridges, locks, roads, and pumps; provincial planning, housing, and utility systems; partial supervision of municipal government; and administrative review of municipal actions in a quasi-judicial capacity.

New polders initially are owned and controlled by the national government; then, as settlement progresses,[33] they have been incorporated into existing provinces, as new municipalities are created. The future political status of the new polders in Yssel Lake is as yet undecided.

The *waterschappen* (water boards) are administrative districts organized for local water management under the provincial executive and provincial council and are subject to the policies of the Ministry of Water Control and Transportation. The districts' boundaries do not correspond to municipal boundaries. The *waterschappen* are elected by the landowners of the several polders within their jurisdiction. The number of votes accorded the landowners is determined by the acreage of their holdings. The local regulations of the water boards may even carry penal sanctions, provided that these are approved by the provincial executive.

Municipal Government

The powers and duties of municipalities are set forth in the Municipal Act of 1851, as amended. There are no classes of municipalities; all have the same powers, with the sole legal difference being the size of the municipal council and the municipal executive. The council varies from seven members, for municipalities with populations of less than 3,000, to 45 members, for municipalities with populations of 200,000 or more. See Table IV-10 for the distribution of municipalities by size. The executive varies from three to seven members, including the burgomaster.

Municipal government organization parallels that of the province: there is a municipal council, a burgomaster, and a College of Burgomaster and Aldermen. As is true of the Second Chamber and of the provincial council, the municipal council is elected to a four-year term through a system of pro-

Table IV-10.
Number of Municipalities by Size

Number of Municipalities	Population, 1/1/69
13	under 500
36	500–1,000
113	1,000–2,000
278	2,000–5,000
224	5,000–10,000
155	10,000–20,000
77	20,000–50,000
24	50,000–100,000
11	100,000–200,000
4	200,000 or more
935	

SOURCE: Conversation with Mr. Jasper Vink, 1970.

portional representation. The burgomaster is appointed by the crown on the recommendation of the provincial royal commissioner; his term is six years, but customarily he is reappointed or, if he wishes, is appointed burgomaster of another municipality. He is less closely tied to the national government than the royal commissioner, and his salary is paid by the municipality. The burgomaster is chairman of the municipal council and of the College of Burgomaster and Aldermen. The aldermen, ranging in number from two to six depending on the municipal population, are chosen by and from the municipal council members. They are salaried.

The powers and duties of the municipality also parallel those of the province: the municipal council may legislate on matters pertaining to the municipality, as long as these ordinances do not conflict with the constitution or with national or provincial legislation; the municipal council administers the municipality; in addition, the council is one implementing agency of the national and provincial governments. The aldermen and burgomaster act, as does the Deputed States, to carry out the day-to-day administrative chores. Municipal legislation is subject to scrutiny by the national and provincial governments, which have powers to approve and to annul. All municipal legislation concerning taxes must be approved by the crown. Much other municipal legislation must be approved by the provincial executive; a denial of approval may be appealed to the crown. In addition, any municipal legislation found by the crown to be contrary to existing law or to the general interest may be annulled. In considering such questions, the crown must review the issues with the provincial executive and the Council of State.

Intermunicipal cooperation on a voluntary or mandatory basis is provided for by national legislation. The grounds for mandatory cooperation are quite limited, but voluntary cooperation occurs frequently. International municipal cooperation also occurs. Recently, five Dutch and seven Belgian border municipalities established a program for voluntary cooperation on such common problems as water, fire, public transit, education, and refuse collection. Two other border municipalities have planned together for several years and now are creating an industrial site and an indoor pool.

Application of the various formulas for revenue distribution to the municipalities results in some variance for each municipality from the average figure of 90 percent of municipal income derived from the national government. In addition to the funds received from the national government, municipalities have several sources of local income—namely, taxes, utility revenues, and revenues from municipally owned land. The principal municipal taxes are surtaxes on national land and house taxes, the road tax, the betterment tax, and the entertainment tax. When the land tax becomes a local tax, the surtax will be discontinued. Municipal tax rates are subject to crown approval.

Municipal investment in land, infrastructure, housing, and schools is equal to state investment and accounts for 20 percent of all national investments, including those that are private. Municipal investment is subject to approval by the provincial executive, and terms for municipal borrowing are regulated by the national government.

Municipalities have the right (subject to state supervision and regulation) to borrow for capital expenses. Quite frequently, the state has restricted this right; it provides capital loan or grant funds for housing and school construction, but for most other capital expenses municipal governments must depend on their borrowing power. The Rotterdam subway, for instance, is municipally financed by a loan based on anticipated revenues. "[T]he same applies to the tunnel in Amsterdam. The central government said to the city you may not use your money for that, because the central government wanted to make another connection. They hampered the city, but the city is executing it now."[34] During the last several years the state has undertaken a grant program to the municipalities to improve traffic movement and public transportation.

The Netherlands' central cities have difficulty financing major facilities to serve their metropolitan areas. Because the largest cities are losing population, in common with major cities worldwide, their share of the general payment from the Municipal Fund is declining. "The financial relation between the central municipality and the neighboring municipalities is a problem in itself. We think that the Home Ministry should promote fresh legislation or regulations to enable the central municipalities to run their affairs according to their central functions in spite of getting less money from the Municipal Fund."[35] Although centralization of revenue collection and distribution for municipal expenditures has enabled the national government to even out local disparities, some difficulties still remain. Nonetheless, this approach can be credited with a reduction in competition among municipalities for revenue-producing land uses and with the willingness of municipalities to consider metropolitan rather than strictly local needs.

Housing

With the exception of a brief period following World War I, the Netherlands met the interwar demand for housing. World War II, however, brought large-scale destruction of housing through bombing and burning, and little renovation or new construction was attempted. As a result, by the end of the war there was a considerable housing shortage. Despite the continued large volume of construction since the war, a high marriage rate and an increased demand for private dwellings by elderly people now able to afford separate housing have prevented the increasing supply from meeting the demand. The 1960 housing deficit for the nation stood at about 215,000 units. The government has recognized the need for increased housing construction and, between 1956 and 1968, annually has invested from 4 to 6 percent of the nation's income in new housing. At last, production is beginning to cut into the deficit.

Supply and Demand

During World War II, almost one-third of the nation's housing stock was damaged or destroyed. Dwelling units destroyed numbered 90,000, 55,000 were badly damaged, and 515,000 sustained some damage.[36] In addition to the war destruction and damage, much housing deteriorated through lack of maintenance.

For two years after the war, the government carried out a centralized emergency program of repairs and temporary housing. Almost no new construction occurred. Between 1947 and 1954, major reconstruction projects were undertaken by the government. Since 1954, construction increasingly has been initiated by private enterprise and assisted by the government.

By 1960, new construction and repairs still had not returned the Netherlands to its prewar position of having an adequate housing supply (see Table IV-11). Higher incomes, more working women, better retirement provisions, and a lower death rate all led to a rise in the demand for housing.

By 1964, conditions had improved considerably, but the over-all shortage remained high. The housing stock had passed the three million mark, and the average number of persons per dwelling unit had fallen below four. Nevertheless, it was estimated that annual production would have to exceed 90,000 dwelling units even to begin to eliminate the deficit of approximately 200,000 units. The first 90,000 units would be consumed by the annual increase in demand of about 75,000 units and by replacement of about 15,000 existing substandard dwellings. While 90,000 was a minimum target figure, actual production in the immediately preceding years had been only about 80,000 dwelling units (see Figure IV-13). The 1962 construction rate of 6.7 per 1,000 population was, however, the fifth highest in Europe; Sweden was third, with 9.9 per 1,000 population. In an attempt to reduce the deficit, a program was established with a considerably higher target of 125,000 units per year. By 1967 the target had been reached.

Table IV-11.
Housing Supply and Demand

Population and Housing Stock	1899	1930	1960
Population	5,104,137	7,935,565	11,461,964
Number of dwelling units	—	1,935,442	2,823,685
Occupied dwelling units	1,088,763	1,885,567	2,800,478
Vacant dwelling units	sufficient	49,875	23,207
Housing deficit	none	none	−216,900
Number of inhabited boats and trailers	10,669	18,827	23,841
Desired number of dwelling units[a]	1,111,500	1,923,000	3,077,700
Inhabitants per dwelling unit	—	4.10	4.06
Inhabitants per desired number of dwelling units	4.59	4.13	3.72

SOURCE: The Netherlands, Ministry of Housing and Building, *Housing in the Netherlands* (The Hague, 1964).
[a] This assumes a 2 percent vacancy rate.

Figure IV-13.
Postwar Housing
Construction,
1945–65

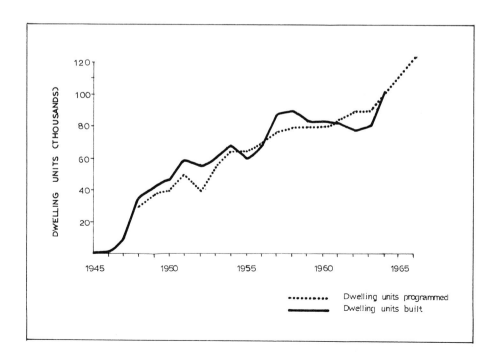

As of the end of 1968, about 1.7 million dwelling units had been built since the war, and the age distribution of the housing stock reflects this: 47 percent of all housing has been built since the war; 18 or 19 percent was built before 1906.[37] Much of the older housing stock should be demolished and replaced, while many other units are in need of renovation to meet today's higher standards.

Housing Types and Standards

Far more than many European countries, including Finland and Sweden, the Netherlands has responded to people's acknowledged preference for single-family housing. Before World War II, almost all housing except that near the center of the larger cities was single-family housing. Since the war, preferences have remained about as before, but the impending shortage of land near the major urban areas, the need for rapid construction, and the necessity of building many small dwelling units to stretch housing construction funds all led to the building of many apartments.

. . . The demand is for the one-family house. . . . Housing problems are one of the greatest political problems, and the general effort of everybody, including my ministry, is to build more and more houses. On the other hand, we have to limit the housing cost because the majority of housing is still being subsidized by the state. Apartment houses can be built in larger numbers and at cheaper costs than one-family houses. I am afraid that, when we have overcome the housing shortage, people will dislike to live in what we are building now. They will want to build a house outside of town.[38]

Since the war, apartments have constituted slightly less than half of all subsidized housing built. Because about 85 percent of all housing construction has been subsidized, this represents the distribution of housing type for most construction. Of course, a higher percentage of non-subsidized housing is single-family construction. In 1963, for example, it was 68 percent, and in 1968 about 86 percent.[39] "I think nearly everyone would like to have a one-family house with a garden, but this is not possible. Our new development areas are mostly a mixture of row houses, one-floor houses for the old . . . people, and apartments of six to eleven floors or even higher. Most of our housing is subsidized, but we never can get a subsidy—or more than a very small one—for a detached house."[40] Already, urban families not in need of housing subsidies are beginning to settle in single-family houses in the suburbs. Good new highways, as well as good rail connections, make it possible for them to commute to the cities.

Increasingly, high-rise buildings rather than walk-up or low-rise buildings are being used for apartments. In 1968, 15 percent of all apartments were in four-story walk-up buildings, while 13 percent were in two- and three-story buildings, 24 percent in five- to seven-story buildings, and 48 percent in buildings of eight or more stories.[41]

Housing densities vary, of course, from rural villages to the cities. Gross density in the villages averages four dwelling units per acre, from twelve to sixteen dwelling units per acre is customary in medium-sized towns, and from fourteen to eighteen units per acre is the prevailing figure in the cities.[42]

Housing standards are rising. Occupancy density is falling, while space and equipment standards are improving. The average number of rooms per dwelling unit for postwar subsidized housing—5.2 including kitchen—is the highest in Europe. In 1968 the average floor area for new construction was 700 square feet for subsidized housing and 880 square feet for non-subsidized housing. Single-family houses were larger than apartments, on the average by one more room and an additional 100 square feet. The minimum space required, inclusive of kitchen and exclusive of storage space, runs from 285 square feet for a family of two elderly people to 904 square feet for a family of thirteen or more. The minimum space for a family of four is 420 square feet.[43] Additional, subsidiary minima are set for the living room, kitchen, and bedroom(s). Balconies are customary on apartment buildings, and elevators are usual for buildings of more than four stories. In 1968, central heating was supplied in 99 percent of the new apartments, but in only 57 percent of single-family houses.

Who Builds

Several factors contributed to the inadequate rate of postwar construction. Until factories could be rebuilt, there was a shortage of building materials. Then there was a shortage of funds, and more recently there has been a shortage of labor in the construction trades. Workers have been imported from Southern Europe, but this alone has not relieved construction problems. In 1963 the minister of housing and physical planning recommended to Parliament a program to improve the status of workers in the building trades, to use the government's financial incentives to improve production capacity, and to restrain building costs.

Four hundred thousand people, or about 10 percent of the labor force, are engaged in the building industry. Of these workers, about 20 percent are employed in housing construction. Given the constant unmet demand for construction, unemployment in the building trades is minimal. Industrialized housing is taking over an increasing share of the market, particularly in the larger cities. In 1961, 11 percent of all dwelling units built were classified as "systems" housing; in Amsterdam, Rotterdam, and The Hague, the figure was 40 percent. By 1968, comparable figures were 23 percent for the nation and 55 percent for Amsterdam, Rotterdam, and The Hague. While industrialized housing results in a savings in man-hours of from 40 to 75 percent for the skills in shortest supply, it has yet to produce cheaper housing.[44]

Of the 1,681,537 dwelling units built between 1945 and 1968, 1 percent were built by the national government or its subsidiaries, 45 percent by private enterprise, 27 percent by municipalities, and 27 percent by non-profit housing associations. The private enterprise share had been mounting steadily; in 1963 it reached 56 percent. Then, with the new government program for increased production, it dropped to 45 percent. In the near future, the private enterprise share is expected to rise to about 55 percent.

Subsidies

Government housing subsidy programs have been responsible in large measure for the Netherlands' postwar housing achievements. Housing location has been influenced by the national government's annual allocation of funds to underwrite a specified number of dwelling units in each of the provinces and, by municipality, within each province. These allocations are part of the annual building program of the Ministry of Housing and Physical Planning. Until July, 1967, this program also permitted the government to control the volume and location of non-subsidized housing, for state and municipal building permits were granted only for construction which met the specifications of the building program. Housing size has been affected by maximum as well as minimum floor-area standards for eligibility for government assistance.

The government's participation in housing dates back to the enactment of the Housing Act of 1901. Under this act, all municipalities were required to enact building regulations and to enforce them. Municipalities of more than 10,000 population were required to prepare a development plan. All municipalities were authorized to condemn land for housing sites, and provision was made for municipal and national grants to assist in the development of low-income housing. The act, considerably amended, remained in force until a few years ago, when it was superseded by the Housing Act of 1962 and the Physical Planning Act of that year. The new Housing Act retains the format and much of the content of its predecessor.

The first period of substantial government assistance to housing occurred between 1919 and 1925. The second such era began with construction following World War II. High building costs, controlled rents, and capital shortages made government participation essential to a high rate of construction. For a brief period the government participated directly in most housing construction. Where it did not participate directly, subsidies usually were available. Altogether, since 1945 about 85 percent of all housing has received some form of subsidy. Only since 1961 have a substantial number of units been built without government subsidy.

Until 1968 there were two major subsidy programs. The first, for "Housing Act dwellings," provided national subsidies to municipalities or non-profit housing associations to stimulate construction of rental housing for families of low or modest income. There were two forms of assistance for Housing Act units: one was a loan to cover land acquisition and construction costs, the other an annual contribution to operating costs. The loan terms were 75 years for the land and 50 years for the buildings, each at 4 percent interest. The amount of the annual contribution depended on several factors, including the number of people who could be housed in the unit, the type of municipality, and the housing type. In the mid-1960s the annual contribution averaged $50. A rent subsidy was granted for a limited number of standardized, low-cost dwelling units for people of lowest income.[45]

The second national government subsidy program applied to privately built dwelling units only. There was an annual subsidy for rental housing if rents were kept within specified limits. The subsidy for sale housing took the form of a grant, the amount of which varied with the municipality where the housing was to be built and the price of the housing, which could not exceed specified limits.

In 1968 the two systems were merged into a housing subsidy program which would be available to any category of builder. The subsidy takes the form of an annual grant, its amount being determined by the cost of the dwelling unit. For owner-occupied units the amount of the annual grant is reduced by one-tenth yearly so that after ten years the owner is paying the full cost of the unit. An annual increase of 6 percent is allowed for rental units, and the annual subsidy grant is reduced in a manner similar to that for owner-occupied units.

In addition to this uniform system, the loan program continues, limited as before to non-profit housing associations and municipalities. The loans now are made at the market rate, and the annual subsidy covers the rise in the interest rate over the former, controlled rate of 4 percent.[46]

Private ownership is encouraged through municipal mortgage guarantees which cover up to 90 percent of the purchase price. The national government, in turn, will guarantee half of the municipality's guarantee.

Additional rent subsidies are provided by the national and municipal governments for construction of housing for the elderly. There also are government assistance programs for slum clearance and rehabilitation.

Through the Ministry of Housing and Physical Planning, the government has repeatedly revised the rents of prewar and postwar housing, its goal being equal treatment. Before long it hopes to abolish rent controls and to reduce the state subsidy except as it applies to low-income housing. Under the Netherlands' housing subsidy system, it is the unit, rather than the individual, which is subsidized. Of course, income determines an individual's eligibility for Housing Act units.

Income in the Netherlands is comparatively low, but so are housing costs. In 1961, housing absorbed an average of 8.1 percent of family income.[47]

The question of a government guarantee of adequate housing for all was considered and rejected prior to passage of the Housing Act of 1901. "The government considered such a provision to be quite inappropriate. It regarded the provision of a proper dwelling for those who could not pay the rent to be a matter concerning poor relief. No benefits, however, could be derived from poor relief in those days."[48] The 1962 act contains a recognition of the government's responsibility to assure adequate housing for all. The act requires the Minister of Housing and Physical Planning to submit annually to Parliament a report on current housing needs and the government's program to meet them.

Planning Organization and Planning Powers

The Netherlands has engaged in physical planning for centuries, ever since it began reclaiming land from the sea. While the term "physical planning" (*ruimtelijke ordening*) still is used to describe the government's programs, it it understood to take into consideration the economic and social components of planning as well. "In an official Memorandum to Parliament, the Netherlands government has characterized it [physical planning] as the government activity whereby guidance is given to the physical development of the country in its constant interaction with the economic growth and the social, cultural and spiritual evolution of society."[49]

Planning has been largely a national and municipal activity, with the provinces acting as an intermediate review arm of the state. The role of the provinces has grown, however, as the need for regional planning has manifested itself. For, despite provincial review and coordination, planning by hundreds of small, egocentric municipalities has resulted in a disparity of planning goals. While this type of planning is appropriate on a detailed scale, it is unsuited to the development of unified plans for a metropolitan area or an economic region. Municipal annexation,[50] consolidation, and cooperative agreements do occur, but not with sufficient frequency to obviate the need for regional planning. "The legislation provides . . . the possibility for a combination of municipalities to draw up a cooperative plan. This has not proved to be popular, however. . . . The government has tried several arrangements for obtaining a suitable solution on the super-municipality [district] level, but up till now without satisfactory results."[51]

Hopefully, the changes wrought by current planning laws will meet the need for regional planning. The legislative framework for planning at all three levels of government was set by the Physical Planning Act of 1962. The predecessors of this act were the 1901 Housing Act, which established municipal planning procedures and requirements; the temporary regulations promulgated after World War II; and the temporary Act on National and Regional Planning of 1950. In addition, there are many acts which govern particular aspects of planning, including water management, land consolidation, nature protection, and transportation. Planning for water is subject to strict national controls and proceeds separately from, but coordinated with, other physical planning.

Figure IV-14 outlines the organization for physical planning under the 1962 act. At the national and provincial levels, agencies with a diverse range of concerns participate in the planning process through permanent membership on committees and on the Council for Physical Planning, which consists of the ministers of housing and physical planning; transport and *waterstaat*; agriculture and fisheries; economic affairs; cultural affairs, recreation, and

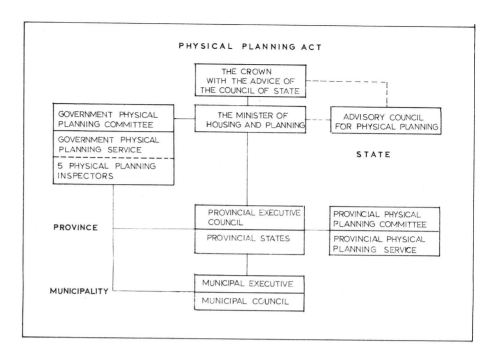

Figure IV-14.
Physical Planning
Act—Government
Organization

social work; finance; home affairs; and defense. The council is chaired by the minister president. Any minister not a member of the council may attend its meetings.

Under the 1962 act, only municipalities adopt binding plans. The plans of the regions and nation take the form of dynamic policies, planning directives issued by the provincial executive and the minister respectively, and specific programs enacted to carry out the policies. Flexibility and responsiveness to change are the objectives for the national and provincial levels of government.

National Planning

Principal responsibility for national physical planning is vested in the Ministry of Housing and Physical Planning. Economic planning is directed by the Ministry of Economic Affairs. Social planning is the charge of the Ministry of Cultural Affairs, Recreation, and Social Work. The Council of State exercises the plan review function, but the appropriate minister is responsible for the decision of the crown.

Physical Planning

The minister of housing and physical planning is advised in national planning matters by the State Physical Planning Service, the staff agency created to carry out national planning, and by a standing committee of members of all ministries concerned with the various facets of national planning.

The minister of housing and physical planning's responsibilities extend over all national physical planning. He issues planning directives, which are binding on regional and municipal plans. He is responsible to the crown for deciding appeals concerning municipal plans. On questions of national physical planning policy, he must present his recommendations to his colleagues on the interministerial Council for Physical Planning. He cannot issue policy directives without their approval, and, because the other members are his co-equals, he cannot demand approval. The minister president, who chairs the council, also lacks any power to demand decisions by other ministers. When questions of national policy are presented to the council, the other ministers are charged with raising, through their staff representatives on the standing committee, all proposals within their ministries which have a bearing on the policy questions presented. When disagreement on a national planning question cannot be resolved at the standing committee level, the issue is taken to the Council for Physical Planning. The council is required to reach an agreement on policy questions brought before it.

This structure for democratic decision-making on planning questions is one reflection of the strongly held national view that the government's role in planning is to lead and advise, but not to force. It is accepted that the government—state, provincial, and local—should implement planning policies through direct expenditures, such as for polder development, seaport development, drainage, roads, and urban infrastructure. Indirect state programs, such as those offering tax incentives, also are accepted. Direct state controls on private development, either negative or positive, are abhorrent to the Dutch, but nonetheless are relied on to a limited extent. "The whole of this forms the 'challenge' from the side of the government to the private forces in society. Then all depends on the 'response' from the private side. If society does not respond sufficiently—if, for instance, in spite of all efforts private industry would not like to locate factories in a desired area—then the government could not force them to come; at best it could press up the incentives."[52]

This reluctance to coerce private enterprise to follow national policies is not applicable to the relationship of the national government to the provinces and municipalities. Once national planning policies have been approved by the Council for Physical Planning, the minister of housing and physical planning can issue directives to the provincial governments, which, in turn, must pass them on to the municipal governments. Although stated as requests, these directives are mandatory. "The Minister can say, for instance, to the municipality of Rotterdam: 'Will you please allocate land in this or that part of your municipality for port development, or for housing development, or for any other matter which is important enough to belong to national planning policy.' "[53]

If a municipality is directed to act to further national planning policy, it can request the national government to reimburse it for costs incurred in excess of those related to strictly municipal benefits. Alternatively, the municipality can appeal the directive to the crown. The advice of the Council of State is sought on such requests.

There is a national physical plan for the year 2000; it was presented to Parliament as a statement of government policy in 1966.[54] The plan states clearly the intention of the government that the plan be indicative, not binding, in nature. The goals of the plan have been described elsewhere; restated in brief, they are to encourage concentrated urban development in the currently underdeveloped portions of the country, to direct and contain in towns the overspill from the Randstad, to protect the health of the environment, to provide an efficient transportation system, and to maintain adequate open space for recreation and for buffers between urban areas.

The 1966 policy statement also recommended that planning proceed across national boundaries and relate to the principal development prospects of Northwestern Europe. Among the actions requested was that of carrying out comparable data collection from Great Britain to West Germany. Cooperation now exists on data collection, and several efforts to coordinate policies are being made, through Benelux, German-Dutch planning committees, and through personal contacts. Also, there is a private Conference for Physical Planning in Northwest Europe, on whose board the principal planning officials of the participating nations sit as individuals.[55] By law, the annual report of the minister of housing and planning to the States General must document current government policy for physical development in relation to this long-term policy of international planning.

Economic Planning

The Central Planning Bureau, established by national legislation in 1947, is the national agency responsible for economic planning. The bureau is part of the Ministry of Economic Affairs. The enabling law states that the bureau shall prepare an annual, advisory "central economic plan" which provides "a balanced system of estimates and directives with regard to the Netherlands economy." Included are data yielding estimates on future production, price levels, and national income. The Central Planning Bureau is moving toward a national capital program, as well as toward regionalization of its "central economic planning."

While there is growing cooperation between the Central Planning Bureau and the Government Physical Planning Service, "there is not always an obvious and direct relation between the macro-economic and quantitative terms in which the Central Planning Bureau mostly expresses its views, and the concrete physical development on which our work is focussed."[56]

Plan Review

The Council of State has an important appellate function. When approved or disapproved local plans are appealed, they are heard by the Council of State. Appellants may be either private citizens who filed objections to the plan at the initial hearing or municipalities whose plans were disapproved at the provincial level. The Council of State must hold a public hearing on the issues raised and then advise the crown, which issues the decision. The minister of housing and physical planning is responsible for preparing the crown's decision. This decision may be contrary to the advice of the Council of State. If it is, the council must be given an opportunity to review the draft decision and to alter its advice. If the Council of State stands by its initial advice, the minister must publish the advice with his decision in the royal gazette. When a plan has been rejected by the crown, a new plan, which takes into account the objections raised, must be submitted for approval within one year.

Provincial Planning

The planning organization at the provincial level closely parallels that at the national level. Its standing committee, called the provincial physical planning committee, includes representatives from the various substantive areas concerned with physical planning. However, the provincial administration is autonomous and is not hierarchically related to the national planning administration.

The provincial government's roles in planning are to oversee municipal planning and to undertake regional planning. In the first, its major responsibility is to oversee the development of municipal plans and to review and approve them. Development plans are mandatory by law and must be approved by the provincial executive. Once a municipal development plan has been adopted, it is submitted to the provincial government, which must receive objections filed with the municipality, review the plan, and, within one year, approve the plan, in whole or in part, or reject it. In its capacity as overseer, the provincial government transmits national planning directives to the municipalities and checks on their enforcement.

The second planning role of the provinces is regional planning. Under the 1962 Physical Planning Act, regional plans, like national plans, are advisory only. Nevertheless, regional plans also can serve as the basis for provincial directives to the municipalities with respect to municipal development plans.

A regional plan can be developed for an area coterminous with provincial boundaries, but generally areas delineated as regions are smaller than the provinces. For instance, as of January 1, 1969, eighteen regional plans had been adopted within the three Randstad provinces. Nationwide, thirty-four regional plans had been adopted and twenty-five more were in preparation.[57] Regional plans are developed in consultation with the affected municipalities and are adopted by the provincial council. The affected municipalities and private citizens have an opportunity to file objections to proposed regional plans, which must be available for public inspection for a period of two months. The provincial Physical Planning Service must answer these objections before the provincial council acts on a proposed plan.

Ysselmonde

The regional plan for Ysselmonde, adopted in 1961 by the Province of South Holland, is illustrative of the procedural and substantive issues which arise in the regional planning process.[58] Parts of the island of Ysselmonde are included in urban Rotterdam and Dordrecht (see Map IV-7); the rest of the island is subject to the considerable pressures of urban growth. Despite the fact that a regional plan had been adopted in 1938, and the creation of a new regional government was anticipated (the Rijnmond [Mouth of the Rhine] Council was established by Parliament in 1965 for Rotterdam and twenty-six other municipalities), the growth pressures on Ysselmonde were so great in the late 1950s that the Province of South Holland undertook to develop and enact a new regional plan.[59]

Map IV-7.
Ysselmonde

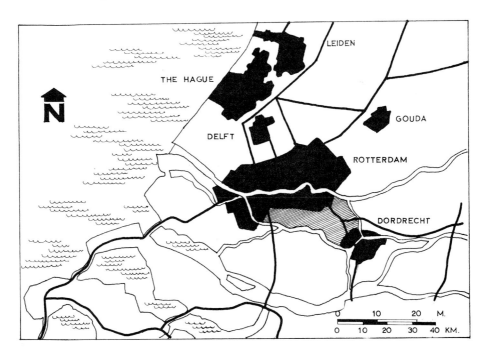

Ysselmonde land is valuable for several competing uses: as greenbelt, and for recreation and intensive agriculture; for industry and urban residential development. The direction of change under the separate municipal plans had been toward residential and industrial growth at the expense of open space. The new regional plan proposed permitting some further growth out from Rotterdam and Dordrecht but no further expansion of the rural villages

Rhoon and Poortugaal. It also proposed that a greenbelt be maintained between Rotterdam and Dordrecht, that industrial growth along the right bank of the Old Maas River be restricted in favor of recreation uses, and that much land be maintained in agricultural use, some of it for horticulture in "glass-houses," some for pasture and field crops.

During the two months in 1961 when the plan was open for public inspection, thirty-nine complaints were filed with the Permanent Commission of the Planning Board of the Province. The complaints were from municipalities, other public and semipublic groups, and private individuals and companies. Excerpts from the complaints and responses illustrate the nature of the objections and of the commission's considerations.

Complainant: Municipality of Barendrecht

Complaint: The plan does not allow sufficient future residential expansion of Barendrecht.

Answer: As of 12/31/61, the population of Barendrecht was 8,930. The plan allows residential growth to 12,000, which is considered sufficient for the next 10 years. One of the basic goals of the plan is to prevent the island from developing into one continuous urban area. The plan is an attempt to balance unavoidable urban growth, improvement of living conditions by an "open area" policy, and agricultural and rural interests.

Complaint: The city objects to the zoning of all land along the Waal River for recreation uses and suggests that part be zoned for "city and village" use.

Answer: The Waal River has more than a municipal function, particularly for recreation. This, however, does not affect existing developments.

Complainant: Municipality of Hendrik-Ido-Ambacht

Complaint: The regional plan differs from the present approved expansion plan in that a projected residential area is smaller.

Answer: The regional plan is an attempt to separate two metropolitan areas, Rotterdam and Dordrecht. Every reduction of the present open area should be avoided. The plan allows for future growth of Hendrik-Ido-Ambacht from 9,000 to 15,000. The requested additional expansion possibility, therefore, does not seem to be necessary.

Complainant: Municipality of Zwijndrecht

Complaint: The city proposes to zone a different area for unrestricted agriculture and to zone the Walburg area for residential use.

Answer: Soil conditions of the other area are not as good as Walburg and, therefore, it would be an inadequate substitute.

Complaint: The city gravely objects to the proposed railroad yard.

Answer: This is unavoidable, since it is the best available location near Rotterdam.

Complainant: Chamber of Commerce, Rotterdam

Complaint: The Chamber disagrees with the agricultural policy, especially around Ridderkirk and Barendrecht. The plan should have allowed for more industrial expansion opportunities.

Answer: Industry is not the only factor which shaped the plan. Agricultural interests are equally important. The soil conditions of the area mentioned are perfect for intensive agriculture. Areas of restricted agriculture also have an urban meaning as open green space.

Complainant: Board of Agriculture of South Holland
(The Board stated its appreciation of the consideration given to agricultural interests.)

Complaint: The plan distinguishes between restricted and unrestricted agricultural use. (In the latter areas, "glass-houses" are allowed.)

Answer: The imposed restrictions are based on landscaping and spatial considerations. The open area policy is considered to be necessary in order to improve living conditions of the surrounding urban agglomerations.[60]

After receipt of all complaints, some minor revisions were made to the proposed regional plan, and it then was presented to the South Holland Council for approval. Following approval, an ordinance was enacted to carry out the plan. Under the 1962 Physical Planning Act, the plan would be advisory only, if adopted, but the South Holland Council could issue directives to the municipalities to make their plans conform to the regional plan.

Municipal Planning

Today, under the 1962 act, it is the municipalities which are given the responsibility of assuring that development proceeds in accordance with municipal plans and with regional and national policies made explicit by provincial and national directives. Municipal plans consist of the voluntary, non-binding master plan (*structuur* plan) and the mandatory development plan (*bestemmings* plan), which covers all undeveloped areas and may cover built-up areas planned for redevelopment. Building permits are not granted unless the proposed development accords with the mandatory development plan.

The master plan covers an entire municipality, or, if two or more municipalities cooperate, may be intermunicipal. It establishes general policies and a timetable for future development. The development plan for undeveloped areas covers land and water and specifies future road locations, sites for future public facilities, and types of future use in some detail. More specificity customarily is provided for areas soon to be developed than for those where development appears more remote. For areas where development is imminent, the type of use and the boundaries for each use must be indicated. Where housing is to be built, plans must state the density, building type, and number of stories. Further detail is provided in building regulations.

The development plan is enacted by the municipal council. Prior to approval, public notice of the availability of the plan for public inspection must be posted. During the four-week public inspection period, complaints may be filed. The administrative appeals procedure already has been described. The law provides some flexibility by specifying that the municipal council may permit the burgomaster and aldermen to amend the plan within specified limits or to develop it in greater detail.

Development plans for the entire built-up area of a municipality are not required. The more usual practice is for a development plan to be prepared for each specific area planned for redevelopment, in advance of the redevelopment.

Much municipal planning is carried out by private consultants, although the larger municipalities have professional planning staffs.

Expropriation and Compensation

The law permits a municipality to expropriate land to implement its development plans in order to acquire land for public facilities, to acquire land for development when the owner refuses to develop in accordance with the plan, or to maintain existing uses such as for the preservation of natural areas. Expropriation proceedings can be brought only after the owner has refused to sell voluntarily. Compensation is paid when land is expropriated, and it also may be claimed if the municipal development plan unreasonably restricts the owner in the use of his land.

Expropriation occurs under the Expropriation Act of 1851, as amended. The municipal council, with the approval of the crown, undertakes the expropriation proceedings either on its own behalf or for another public corporation or housing association. An opportunity is provided for the submission of objections.

The crown must approve the expropriation, the procedural route being a request to the province for approval. After the province passes on the municipal expropriation decree, the Council of State must give its advice. This is a lengthy process: four months at the provincial level and nine months, at most, at the national level. Following approval of the expropriation decree, the municipality must again try to reach a voluntary sale agreement. Failing this, the district court sets the compensation.[61] The amount of compensation is the fair market value of the property at the time of expropriation plus other losses incurred as a direct result of expropriation. The specific planned future use of the land is not considered an element of value. Because expropriation is so cumbersome, and because the landowner cannot gain financially from a court-fixed price, the municipalities and the landowners prefer to reach a voluntary agreement.

The Physical Planning Act of 1962 provides, for the first time, a nationwide framework which regulates compensation for damages suffered as a result of municipal planning decisions. The 1962 law authorizes landowners to apply for compensation when they believe that, as a result of the municipal development plan, they have incurred unreasonable and uncompensated losses in the value of their property. The municipal council hears and approves or rejects the application. The owner, or other interested party, may appeal the decision to the crown.

Prior to passage of the 1962 law, each municipality had the option of enacting a compensation ordinance. Many of the largest cities, except The Hague, had refrained from enacting compensation ordinances because they feared being inundated with claims.[62] Hundreds of small municipalities, however, had local ordinances; these established procedures under which landowners could request municipal compensation for damages incurred as a result of municipal planning. While these ordinances varied considerably in their provisions, generally the landowner would file a petition with the municipal council, alleging compensable loss. If it was determined by the commission appointed by the council to hear the case that the landowner's situation was covered by the ordinance, damages would be assessed. The landowner had the right to appeal this decision to the provincial administration. Very few petitions for compensation were filed under these ordinances, however. About half of the petitions were granted; most awards were less than $1,000, and only a handful were as high as $5,000.

Policies and Programs for Population Distribution and Land Development

Population projections for the Netherlands have strongly influenced development policy. With an anticipated population of 20 million shortly after the year 2000, the density will be 1,500 people per square mile. While this is more people at a higher density than the Dutch think desirable, the projection seems a realistic one. Of the possible choices for future growth—concentration, deconcentration, and concentrated deconcentration—the government has selected concentrated deconcentration. Under the government's plan, there would be four principal urban zones, each linear in nature. All would be in the southern two-thirds of the country, leaving the north less urbanized and less densely settled. One large new city—Lelystad—would develop, a number of existing small cities would increase by up to five times, and some large cities would expand substantially. The Randstad's growth, while inevitable, would be restricted and directed outward in order to preserve its central open space. Other large open areas would be retained to separate the four urban zones and to buffer the city regions within the urban zones. Residential densities for new urban growth are to be only moderately high. An average of twelve dwelling units per acre is the objective for the Randstad, as well as easy access to the countryside and to recreation areas for all.

Policies for the future have been articulated clearly by government and private planners, particularly in the *Second Report on Physical Planning in the Netherlands*, which constitutes a national, indicative physical plan. The report acknowledges that the Netherlands is but one portion of an interdependent metropolitan region and calls for international plan coordination. "A situation of this kind especially creates the need also to base the national physical planning concept on developments across the frontiers.... In the various. countries the national concepts of urban development are largely based on the same fundamental principles (avoiding excessively high concentrations, developing new towns and regional centres), but as regards their implementation they have still little in common."[63]

The awareness of postwar sprawl elsewhere is widespread, and it is feared that the sprawl is incipient in the Netherlands and in the North European conurbation of which the Netherlands forms one part. A consciousness of land shortage, of agglomeration tendencies in the Randstad, and of increasing population pressure has contributed to a high measure of agreement on policies for the future. However, the measures planned to assure realization of these policies may well fall short of those that will be needed, if experience in other rapidly growing urban areas is any guide. National investment in the Delta Works and Yssel Lake polders is an important and critical key to success. In addition, the strengthening of other public programs is likely to be essential. National and municipal purchases of land for open space and development can be of major significance if far more extensive; this in turn implies a greater commitment of public revenues. Public incentives, in differential taxes or in grants, must be increased to spur the industrialization and consequent urbanization of the north. Stronger national controls may be necessary if the government chooses to check the powerful growth pressures in the Rotterdam area.

As the Dutch and their neighbors have more and more time and money for recreation, the mounting demand for beaches, lakes, seashore, and countryside will pose an ever more serious problem of overuse. Protection of land and water, further development of the highway and rapid-transit network, restoration of water quality, and pollution management all will become more critical, and again will require a greater public investment and more stringent controls.

Population Distribution: Concentrated Deconcentration

Given their principal economic dependence on manufacturing and shipping, rather than on agriculture and mineral resources, the Dutch have considerable freedom in the location of new development. Past investment in Botlek and Europort on the New Waterway assures that much future port growth will occur there. Ymond, the Western Scheldt, and some locations on the northern coast also offer excellent opportunities for port expansion. Fortunately, most future industrial growth will be location-free. While agglomeration economies attract industry to the Randstad, in a small country with good transportation and communications and with skilled labor available anywhere, the comparative location advantages for most industries are small enough so that they can be influenced by government incentive programs. With a view to habitability, however, and because of the fact that an ever-extending area of agglomeration is not likely in the long run to offer any advantages with regard to private or public economic costs, a policy aimed at a satisfactory distribution of activity may positively assist the growth of the nation's prosperity and well-being.[64]

The Netherlands enjoys considerable freedom to develop a population distribution policy based on the realization of environmental goals. For the Dutch, environmental goals include adequate housing—preferably in single-family homes—quick and easy access to jobs, shops, and the countryside (see Figure IV-15), clean air and water, diversity of urban land uses, a visually pleasing landscape, and ample opportunities for recreation. These goals would be impossible to realize if most people moved to the Randstad. Living conditions would be crowded and inconvenient, marked by long commuting times and inadequate open space.

... [W]e think we should limit the number of people in the Randstad because we also have to offer them recreation. Until a few years ago we had six working days, now we have five, and in 1980 we expect to have four working days. Our per capita income is rising very much, and I think that, in 1984, we will have double the per capita income we have now. We won't work so long, and we will need more place for recreation. We should limit the size of our city proper so that everybody, by bicycle, can reach a recreation area, because we think that is necessary for a full human life. We were speaking about the size of the individual cities in the conurbation—the pearls of the necklace. We think that they should not be wider than eight kilometers [about 5.5 miles], so that everybody, by bicycle, can get to the border of the city within fifteen minutes.[65]

In 1962 several additional standards for future growth in the Randstad were proposed and were generally accepted. The maximum length of each of the conurbation cities was posited at 14 miles, so that travel time to the center from any point would not be excessive. Each Randstad city would be

Figure IV-15. Expressway Interchange on the Outskirts of The Hague. Note the
clear demarcation of city and country.

separated from its neighbors by a greenbelt of at least 2.5 miles. Individual
cities would not exceed a population of 1.3 million. Because it was, and is,
considered essential to maintain the open core of the Randstad, these standards, when combined with housing density standards and soil limitations,
set a maximum population for the Randstad of about five million.[66]

The attraction of existing industrial development in the Randstad, particularly at Europort and Ymond, means that additional growth is occurring
rapidly and that the area will reach this maximum soon. This raises the question of revising the above specifications. The government, recognizing that
further growth will come, has adopted the policy that development should
occur in directions radiating outward from the Randstad (see Map IV-8).
This is possible in all directions except that of the sea, where, unless additional land is created, the Randstad already has reached its limits.

The location of the Netherlands on the Rhine-Meuse-Scheldt Delta is a
considerable advantage for the Dutch in carrying out a policy of population
distribution. All of the major tributaries of the delta have economic potential
for development, as has been reflected by the rapid growth of the east and
south following only modest government initiative. In the past, the absence
of quick, convenient access by road has isolated both the southwest and the
north. This isolation, and the concomitant reluctance of people or industries
to settle there, should vanish when modern highway links are completed.
Already the new tunnel, dam, and bridges linking Rotterdam and the Western Scheldt have reduced travel time to an hour, and development has begun
to flourish (see Map IV-9). The government's gigantic investments in the

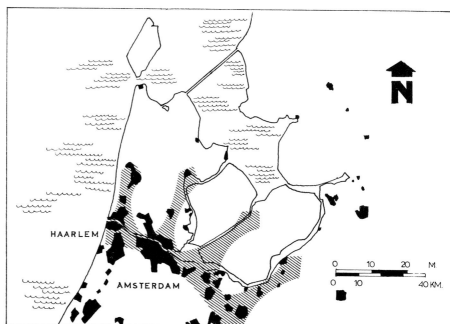

Map IV-8.
Randstad
Expansion to
the Polders

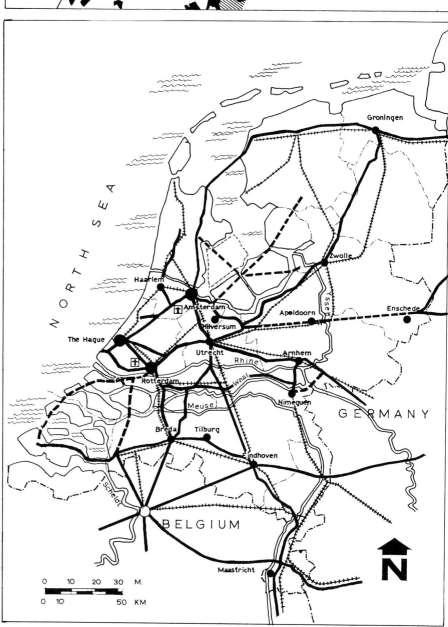

Map IV-9.
Cities and
Transportation

Delta Works, in the reclamation of the Yssel Lake polders, and in the transportation network are the major public mechanisms for carrying out growth policies for those areas. While neither area lies along currently developed corridors, the recreation potential of both coasts and of the newly created fresh-water lakes should prove a strong stimulus to development, once convenient access exists. The southwest also is attractive to industry, and conflict may arise between industrial and recreational demands for land and water there.

Although some planners in the Netherlands have embraced Christaller's theories of urban hierarchical structure, as did their Israeli counterparts, the national planners believe that cities of at least moderate size are necessary to provide sufficient diversity to attract people and industry. As Theo Quené, the director of National Physical Planning, has said:

> The problem of regional concentration and deconcentration of employment and population is a basic issue in Dutch planning policy since 1950.
>
> Up till 1959, the motivation of the financial help for depressed areas was basically economic: trying to tackle the problem of the structural unemployment in agricultural areas by industrial development.
>
> After 1959, the scope of the planning effort was broadened because of the introduction of physical and social-cultural planning elements next to the economic considerations. . . . [T]he planning effort is geared to a better distribution of population over the several parts of the country, in order: to prevent too strong a concentration of population in the West and South; to stimulate the economic and social-cultural conditions in the North.
>
> This stimulation policy is rather strongly oriented towards the main towns within the development areas. We believe that modern industries need concentration in an urban atmosphere; besides we can only reach a high level of social-cultural provisions like schools, libraries, theatres, etc. by virtue of concentration.[67]

In 1956 the Dutch adopted a population distribution policy with the objective of deflecting growth from the Randstad to the rest of the country, particularly to the underdeveloped north and southwest, and of concentrating growth in cities of from medium to large size. At that time, some twenty-five cities were projected to have populations in excess of half a million people, and medium-sized cities were thought to have populations of at least 100,000 people.[68]

By 1966 the population distribution policy had been revised. The evident attraction of large cities, population projections, the continued expansion of the Randstad, the slow growth of the north, and the accelerating shift of employment from agriculture to services all contributed to the recognition of a need to revise the 1956 policy.[69] In 1965, only 3 million people (out of a national population of 12 million) lived north of a line between Alkmaar and Arnhem. The 1966 plan concluded that, even using government powers to direct development, only 5 million of the population of 20 million projected for the year 2000 would live north of this line. Thus the population in the southern part of the country would grow from 9 to 15 million people by 2000. "Moreover, the effort to achieve a harmonious dispersal of the population throughout the country can no longer be the sole main element in the national physical planning policy. . . . With this concentration [in the south] it will be necessary to conduct an organization policy in the urbanized areas, in addition to a stimulation policy directed to expansion of the still little urbanized parts of the country."[70]

After evaluating the implications of concentrated, deconcentrated, and concentrated deconcentrated growth, the government recommended concentrated deconcentration. People would be encouraged to settle in multi-nuclear urban zones, of which there would be four, all in the southern part of the country. There would be urban areas in the north, but these would not be linked together to form linear urban zones.

The projected location and size of the four urban zones reflects the government's confidence in other areas of the south to compete effectively with the existing Randstad for growth. The four urban zones designated in the 1966 plan were as follows: (1) the "north wing" of the Randstad, extending from Alkmaar near the North Sea southeast to Nijmegen and including Amsterdam; (2) the "south wing" of the Randstad, extending from Leiden southwest along the North Sea to The Hague and then southeast through Rotterdam and Dordrecht; (3) a west-to-east chain of cities from the southwest delta area through Eindhoven to Helmond; and (4) a north-south chain of cities along the Meuse in the Netherlands, Germany, and Belgium which would center on Maastricht. Most, but not all, of the large urban areas would be located within the four urban zones. There would be only two urban areas with populations of more than one million: Amsterdam and Rotterdam. Five urban areas would have populations of between 500,000 and one million: The Hague, Utrecht, Eindhoven, Arnhem, and Twente. Eleven other urban areas would have populations of between 250,000 and 500,000. The size and number of other, smaller urban areas are specified in the plan, which demonstrates that the population of 20 million projected for the year 2000 can be located in accordance with the concept of concentrated deconcentration.

The plan gives increased recognition to the people's demand for single-family, lower-density housing by providing more space: from 50 to 70 percent of future urban housing (as compared with from 35 to 40 percent of current construction) can be of the single-family type. Densities in future urban areas would range from six to twenty-five dwellings per acre.

Given the strong preference of many people for single-family housing, the 1966 plan has acknowledged the threat of urban sprawl and has further stressed the importance of retaining major open spaces.

... A third factor of importance is the large amount of space taken up by greatly extended suburbanization. In our flat and densely populated country the value of space is evident: in the first place for the human sphere of life of the present generations, who in this space can find peace and quiet, nature, the counterpart of town life. Moreover, when space is used for housing purposes, this is invariably at the expense of other facilities ... and who can tell what facilities will be required by future generations. Space is one of the most irreplaceable assets and cannot be allowed to be wasted.[71]

The former policy of retaining as open space the central area of the Randstad has been extended to the areas which separate the land designated for the four urban zones. This open space would be determined on a scale comparable to the urban zones; in addition, the urban centers within an urban zone would be separated from one another by smaller open-space buffers.

While maintenance of agriculture in the north and in the open areas of the south is important economically and environmentally, unquestionably the rural population will decline. The 1966 plan proposes that those who do remain on the land be within thirty-five miles of a medium-sized city[72] and close to a rural center able to meet their daily needs. Most rural residents already are so located.

The government's program for implementing its population distribution policy has three major aspects: direct investment, plan enforcement, and incentives. It is important to reiterate that the Netherlands has relied on encouragement and cooperation with private enterprise to implement its policies, eschewing a more forceful government role.

The implementation of the policy in a country like the Netherlands, where the economy is based on private enterprise, can be effective only as a continuous interaction between the activities of the public bodies on the different administrative levels (state, province, municipalities) and the free forces in society. The Netherlands government desires to promote this interaction by positive measures; negative controls have not been put into operation up to now.[73]

Thus far, direct investment has been the most widely used means of implementing government policy and has had the greatest impact. Just as development at Europort has enhanced Rotterdam's position as the world's number one port, so the Delta Works can establish the delta area as a major international recreation area. Providing road access, modern infrastructure, and new schools has stimulated the growth of outlying cities. Now the issue is whether recreation or port-related industrial growth should take priority in the delta. Development of the north, although it lags behind that of the southwest, has been stimulated by policy decisions giving a major road northeast from Amsterdam and reclamation of the Southern Flevoland polder priority over the Markerwaard polder.

Plan enforcement has been more significant for its deterrence than for its incitement to development. The previously cited illustration of the role of the Provincial Planning Board of South Holland in resisting pressures for incursions into the open space of Ysselmonde is characteristic of this role. Without strong government backing through the planning process, the vaunted green core and separators of the Randstad will be overrun by development.

Planning assistance to rural areas has made it possible to establish a continuing program of agricultural land consolidation. Holdings throughout the country are too small for efficient modern farming. Some 65 percent of the agricultural land is in need of consolidation and reparceling, and under the Reallotment Act this is proceeding at an accelerating rate. In 1968, 130,000 acres were included in the consolidation program. Only that land which it is anticipated will remain in agriculture for more than thirty years is included in reallotment plans. The Land Consolidation Service of the Ministry of Agriculture and Fisheries contributes 65 percent of the cost of developing a plan for the reallocation of land, including reparceling for agricultural use, improved water management, the provision of land for urban development and roads, and the conversion of poor agricultural land for public recreation uses. The reallotment plans must be approved by 50 percent of the affected landowners and by 50 percent of the farmers in the area. After approval the Land Consolidation Service assists by relocating willing farmers on new land in the Yssel Lake polders.[74] Farmers wishing to retire are given, in addition to payment for their land, old-age pensions in amounts dependent upon their age, family size, and other conditions.

Incentives for developing the problem areas accounted for 3 percent of the national budget—exclusive of direct grants to the municipalities—for the years 1959–63. These incentives, designed to encourage industry to locate in the problem areas, consisted of: (1) land subsidies for the purchase of industrial sites and the construction of industrial plants; (2) grants to provinces and municipalities for the improvement of infrastructure; (3) early completion of national communications projects; (4) special housing allocations; (5) increased funds for social and cultural programs; (6) additional grants from the Municipal Fund; (7) migration and training-program grants.

The incentive program is the responsibility of the minister for economic affairs and is subject to cabinet approval. The minister designates the overall areas within which the incentives are offered, as well as the nuclei for urban expansion. Currently, the entire north, the province of Zeeland in the southwest, and a portion of the south have been designated as development areas. Twenty-one primary nuclei and twenty-seven secondary nuclei also have been designated. Of these forty-eight nuclei, twenty-nine are in the north, probably more than the area can support, but not as many as have been sought by the northern provinces. "[T]he Government Note to Parliament makes it clear that a further concentration will be necessary for an efficient policy.... For some of the provinces, by the way, this is a rather bitter pill to swallow, the more so, as they have to face also the more awkward problem of the hundreds and hundreds of small villages and hamlets for which there are no chances left in our age of motorization and mechanization."[75]

Under the incentive program, 638 industries received grants for locating or expanding operations in development areas between 1959 and 1968. These industries employed 33,000 people, so one could estimate that, with an equal number of people in service occupations, 200,000 people had been retained in, or drawn to, development areas as a result of the government's industrial incentive program. The over-all figures for net internal migration, however, reveal a somewhat different and less encouraging picture. Table IV-3 showed that outflow—from the north, particularly, but also from the southwest—had been slowed in the 1960s as compared to the totals in the 1950s. The annual figures listed in Table IV-12 show a reversal in trend in 1966 and 1967. The net inflow into the north and south changed to a net outflow, while the substantial outflow from the west dropped considerably. Noting this, the government has moved to increase the incentives.

Table IV-12.
Net Internal Migration per Group of Provinces, 1957–68

Year	North	East	West	Southwest	South
1957	−9,100	1,600	6,600	−1,000	2,100
1958	−5,700	−1,000	4,700	−1,700	3,300
1959	−5,400	2,400	3,200	−2,400	2,200
1960	−6,800	4,100	3,200	−2,500	2,000
1961	−4,700	5,500	−1,300	−2,200	2,900
1962	−3,200	1,800	−2,400	−1,800	4,300
1963	−600	2,700	−5,700	−900	3,700
1964	100	3,200	−9,000	−200	4,300
1965	−300	6,100	−11,900	−300	5,100
1966	800	6,000	−10,400	500	2,000
1967	−700	3,600	−2,900	500	−1,600
1968	−1,200	4,800	−5,800	600	−400

SOURCE: The Netherlands, Government Physical Planning Service, *Annual Report* (The Hague, 1968).
NOTE: These figures include the Northeast polder but exclude the southern Yssel Lake polders.

Between 1959 and 1968 the national government spent $93 million under its incentive program in the north alone. Two-thirds of this sum went toward infrastructure, primarily highways and local roads. The remainder was divided almost equally between industrial incentives and expenditures for social and cultural development.[76]

Government incentives to provinces and municipalities are being employed to stimulate the retention of open space. The program began in 1964 through the granting of subsidies for the protection of buffers in the Randstad. By

1966 the government was considering extending the subsidies to the open space between the urban zones. The subsidies can be used toward public land acquisition or toward the compensation of landowners whose land has declined in value as a result either of plans designating it as open space or of easements placed on the land.

Land Development

While it is agreed that increased incentives are needed for development areas, it is now fully evident that in the Randstad the necessity is for a national decision on whether to limit growth. No decision has been reached, but the certainty is that voluntary measures no longer are adequate, particularly in the Rotterdam area, if plan objectives are to be achieved.

Only in one location—the Yssel Lake polders—has the government sought to control development through national ownership of the land.

... In the polders the government never sells the land. The government has made the polders, built the houses, planned the population, and has given subsidies to get a doctor when there are not enough people. They never sell the land. I think [that] soon, in the whole world, there will be no more private landownership. Land is the only thing in which we have a growing scarcity. With uncontrolled land prices, you can no longer get town planning. As soon as you have no control of land prices, the price of the land goes up.[77]

Since this statement was made, the cabinet has recommended changing the no-sale policy so that some polder land could be bought by the farmers. Parliament concurred, but this policy shift has not been implemented, largely because the farmers prefer moderate lease terms to the opportunity to purchase.[78] In the Randstad the national government has cooperated with cities in an effort to control development, but public ownership has been much more limited and is vested in the municipalities. Nationwide, only 10 percent of the land is publicly owned,[79] and much of this consists of land acquired by municipalities in advance of development. Such acquisition, by voluntary purchase or eminent domain, is customary for municipalities.

The Yssel Lake Polders

The program for the polders is a complex combination of national planning, direct government expenditures, and government incentives designed to contribute toward meeting a number of national development goals—direction of the Randstad's outward expansion, development of the north, creation of large regional cities, rationalization of agriculture, and establishment of new recreation areas. In the polders, much is possible through direct national action because the government owns the land it has created. Entirely new towns and cities are being built. While it still is necessary to attract settlers and industries through incentives, the government has complete flexibility in the design of development, the timing of construction, and the evolution of an administrative structure.

In the late nineteenth century an engineer named Lely developed and promoted a plan for damming the Zuyder Zee and reclaiming the land. He subsequently became minister of transport, water control, and public works and finally saw his proposal adopted by Parliament in 1918. The plan as it is being implemented today is basically Lely's plan, and it is for him that Lelystad, the principal new city of Yssel Lake, is named.[80]

The Yssel Lake dam was completed in 1932, making possible the reclamation of the polders (see Figure IV-16). The sea there was shallow (only about fifteen feet deep) and contained rich alluvium, which would make fertile agricultural land. In fact, in Roman times much of the area had been land, but in ensuing centuries the sea had gouged out the Zuyder Zee. From experience with polder reclamation in earlier centuries, the Dutch knew how to design the dike and drainage system so that no part of the polder would suffer from drought or inadequate drainage. They also had experienced the monotony of a rigid, uniform parceling of the land and were concerned with development that would provide a satisfying environment.

By the 1980s, when reclamation is finished, there will be five Yssel Lake polders: Wieringermeer, the Northeast polder, Eastern Flevoland, Southern Flevoland, and Markerwaard. Together they will total 556,000 acres, or 7 percent of the total land area of the Netherlands. Southern Flevoland begins only ten miles east of Amsterdam; when linked by good roads and commuter railroad, it will be a logical area in which to accommodate part of the planned radial expansion of the Randstad. Lelystad, with a projected population of 100,000, already is under construction along the principal highway and canal leading northeast from Amsterdam. New towns also are being built, and experience is showing that fewer and larger towns are needed. The original plan for Eastern Flevoland, for instance, has been revised to reduce the number of villages. The original plan contemplated a regional city, a principal town, and ten villages; the revised plan has cut the number of villages to four. Dronten, the principal town for Eastern Flevoland, already is inhabited, as is Emmeloord, the principal town in the Northeast polder.

It is expected that the new polders will be incorporated into existing provinces, and there may be some consolidation of the eleven provinces. A private organization called Flevo has recommended that the provinces be combined into three or four larger provinces or districts. One such district would include North Holland, Utrecht, Gelderland, and the Yssel Lake polders. The government has yet to act on this question.

The Wieringermeer polder was the first to be reclaimed. At 50,000 acres, it is the smallest of the five polders. Work progressed simultaneously with construction of the Zuyder Zee enclosure, and, when the polder was ready for development, it was turned over to the newly created Wieringermeer Polder Development and Colonization Board. This board later became responsible for the other Yssel Lake polders.

After the polder was created and drained, the board spent four years preparing the land for farming. During this period the board also sponsored the construction of farm buildings and farm villages and coordinated the building of roads and infrastructure. All utility lines were laid underground in the road right-of-way, and trees were planted adjacent to the roads. The development pattern provided homes for the farmers on the farms, while homes for the hired farm laborers were built in nearby villages. These villages were of a size to meet the farmers' daily needs. Each of three A-level villages covered 100 acres and included three churches and three schools (a catering to the religious schism which has been common to the Netherlands). Evidence of recent mellowing is that, in the newer polders, as well as elsewhere in the country, churches have been built jointly by several faiths.

Farm parcels varied in size and design according to their purpose. Land for pasturage and the cultivation of hay and other grasses was in parcels of 100 and 150 acres, while 50-acre parcels were established for more intensive agriculture. The 50-acre parcels were designed so that a road bounded one side, a canal ran along the opposite side, and small drainage ditches formed the remaining borders (see Figure IV-17). A farm might consist of from half to two of these 50-acre parcels; if as small as 25 acres, the farm usually was used for horticulture.[81]

When the land was ready for occupancy the government offered it on twelve-year lease terms. The entire polder became a single municipality and

Figure IV-16. The Twenty-Mile Enclosure Dam—Wadden Sea on the Left,
Yssel Lake on the Right

Figure IV-17. Farm Parceling in Wieringermeer Polder

one of the villages was designated the administrative center. Initially, the municipality was run by the board; a locally elected council exercised advisory powers only. When development was completed, the board withdrew and the council began to function as any other municipal government. Management of the leases was turned over to an administrator of government property.

The problems encountered in Wieringermeer polder were related to village planning. The villages were poorly located; they provided overlapping service to some areas and inadequate service to others. Also, because of farm mechanization, farm population growth was less than had been projected and shopkeepers had insufficient business.

The Northeast polder was planned for development in immediate succession with the Wieringermeer polder. Unfortunately, World War II interrupted the work, and development of the Northeast polder was not completed until 1960. Because the Northeast polder is much larger (120,000 acres) than Wieringermeer, the planners thought from the start that a larger, B-level central town would be needed. Emmeloord initially was planned for 10,000 people, and ten evenly spaced A-level villages were planned. Each village was to have a resident population of 1,000–2,000 and a service population of 2,000–3,000 within three miles of the village. For the over-all plan, see Map IV-10.

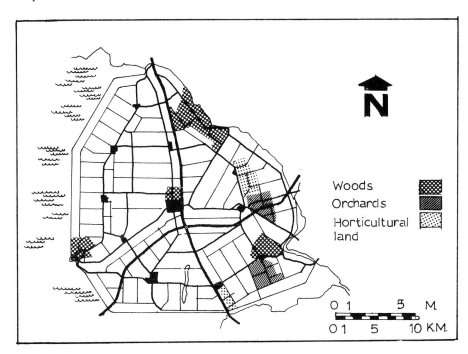

Map IV-10.
Plan for the
Northeast Polder

Emmeloord is a low-density town with a mix of residential and commercial uses. Row houses with private gardens prevail, constituting 80 percent of the housing stock. Of the remaining dwelling units, 15 percent are walk-up apartments, often over shops. Construction is costly, as it is throughout the polders and other reclaimed lands, because of the necessity for pilings or sand fill. When development of the town is completed, 15 percent of the land will be in residential use, 10 percent in institutional use, 18 percent in commercial and industrial use, 3 percent in community facilities, 13 percent in roads and paths, and the remaining 46 percent in open space, including woods, parks, playing fields, and canals. A canal, which serves primarily an aesthetic purpose, parallels the main street, bordering the town center. A large area north of the developed area has been afforested, and a racetrack and swimming pool provide recreation for town and farm residents.

To insure the dominance of Emmeloord, the Wieringermeer Development Board refused to grant building permits in the smaller villages for types of development which it believed should take place at Emmeloord. Because of this and because of the natural attraction of a larger center, Emmeloord is prospering. It even is attracting new industry, and a new master plan is in preparation to provide for a larger population. This attraction of growth does not characterize most of the villages (see Figure IV-18). If it was true several decades ago that farmers preferred the propinquity of a small village to a broader range of services in a more distant town, it is true no longer. In addition, as a result of the mechanization of farming operations, there are fewer people engaged in farming.

The Northeast polder was designed for hierarchies of road networks, drainage systems, and farm parcels (Figure IV-19), as well as hierarchies of settlements. For a general view of land parcelings there, see Figure IV-20.

A major east-west highway will link the Northeast polder with Lelystad and the Randstad. An arterial road runs north-south, bisecting this highway and tying it to Emmeloord. A circumferential road links the villages. Farms are located on the minor roads, which are built on a one-mile grid. The drainage network consists of drainage ditches (1,000 miles), drainage channels (190 miles), minor canals (30 miles), and major canals (26 miles). In addition, there are 25,000 miles of drainage pipes.[82] The basic unit for the farm parcel was increased from the 50 acres of Wieringermeer polder to 60 acres in the Northeast polder. Farms of 30 acres, or half a parcel, are located near the villages, with farm buildings clustered in groups of four at their common boundaries. Larger farms, of 60, 90, and 120 acres, are farther away from the villages. Dwellings for farm laborers are clustered near farms of 120 acres or more; some farm laborers live in nearby villages.

The board turned the Northeast polder over to municipal self-government in 1962, and, with the lessons learned from the first two polders, moved on to Eastern Flevoland. The planning for Eastern and Southern Flevoland was carried out concurrently, and both are part of the same drainage system. Because of the size of the undertaking, it was decided to develop them in two successive stages. Drainage of Eastern Flevoland has been completed, and most of the land is now being used as planned (see Figure IV-21). Drainage of Southern Flevoland began in 1960 and was completed in 1968. The one C-level town, Lelystad in Eastern Flevoland, is intended to serve all four of the southern polders. The original target population of 30,000 was later raised to 100,000. As a result of the experience in the Northeast polder, a B-level town was planned for each polder, and the number of A-level villages was sharply reduced.

Farm parcel size has been increased to a basic unit of 75 acres, but some farms are as large as 500 acres. The ideal size remains an open question. Parcel size is limited by drainage requirements; drain pipes are needed at 30-foot intervals, drainage ditches at 900-foot intervals. Additional new planning considerations are emphasis on recreation and an increased concern for landscape (see Figures IV-22 through IV-26). Planting plans are being related to the ecology of the area—wind direction, microclimate, and soils. The first of a chain of lakes between the mainland and the polders has been built to maintain the level of the water table on the mainland. The lakes also are attractive for recreation and provide fresh-water storage.

There has been extensive discussion as to whether the economically oriented decisions for Eastern and Southern Flevoland (calling for an increase in farm size and a decreased reliance on villages) are compatible with the future

Figure IV-18. The Village of Bant, Northeast Polder

Figure IV-19. Farms in the Northeast Polder

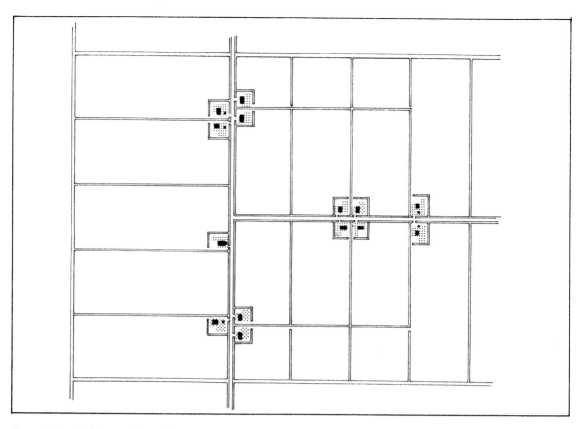

Figure IV-20. Polder Land Parceling

Figure IV-21. Dronten, in Eastern Flevoland. The town greenbelt has not yet been planted; in time, Dronten will look like Bant.

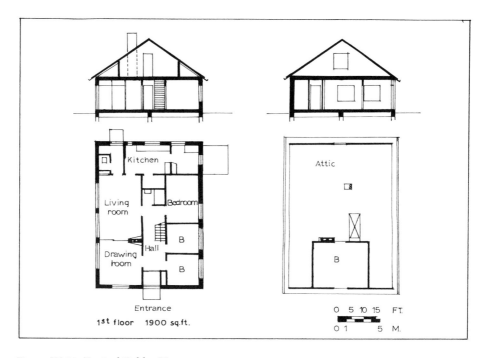

Figure IV-22. Typical Polder House

Figure IV-23. Dronten Housing and Church

Figure IV-24. The Dronten Community Building

Figure IV-25. The Dronten Community Building

Figure IV-26. The Dronten Community Building

Dutch social structure for rural areas. In Southern Flevoland this question may never be answered, for the area is going to be subject to considerable pressure from the urban expansion of the Randstad. Many of the towns will serve as bedroom communities for commuters. It is planned that only the southwest section of the polder will absorb the Amsterdam overspill, while the center of the polder will be devoted to agriculture, the lake border to forest and residential-recreation uses. It is possible that urban development pressures will prove much greater than initially contemplated.

Drainage of the fifth polder, Markerwaard (Figure IV-27), is scheduled for completion in 1980. Markerwaard will cover 150,000 acres and will be easily accessible from the Randstad. Current urban expansion plans describe it as an open wedge between the major development corridors which will serve farm and recreation functions. Because settlement of Markerwaard is more than a decade away, final decisions as to its pattern of land use have yet to be made.

The succession of planning decisions in the years spanned by the development of the Yssel Lake polders reflects the adaptability of the Dutch government to changing economic pressures and changing life styles as well as a respect for cultural and social patterns of the past. The scale and accessibility of towns and farms are increasing. At the same time, concern for size and rate of growth has not dominated a sensitivity to preferences for traditional building styles and materials, to the need to create variety in landscaping, and to improved designs for recreation areas. Offering homes, beaches, woods, and fields to urban Randstad, the Southern Flevoland and Markerwaard polders are destined to serve a far different function than was originally contemplated. Yet there is every reason to believe that the vast national

Figure IV-27. Creating Markerwaard Polder

investment in their development, initially justified as an investment in expanded agricultural productivity, will prove to have been considerably more valuable than could possibly have been foreseen, particularly as a means of drawing development pressure away from the Randstad and diverting it to the polders themselves and, through them, to the north and northeast.

Rotterdam

Despite the success of the Yssel Lake polders and the government incentive programs elsewhere, the growth of the Randstad threatens to exceed greatly the planners' projections. Each of the metropolitan areas of the Randstad is struggling with a set of irreconcilable factors: more people, limited space, moderate-density goals, and a rising demand for more private living space. The Rotterdam area (Rijnmond), with its already stupendous port and industrial growth and its magnetism for further growth, is under the greatest pressure. There are many in Rotterdam who would welcome more people, higher densities, and less open space as the price of economic success; many others, there and elsewhere in the nation, oppose such growth.

The Rotterdam urban area has grown spectacularly, although the city proper has declined in population since 1960. The 640-acre heart of the city, entirely destroyed by bombing in 1940, has been rebuilt. The New Waterway, which links the city to the sea, has been completely built up since the war, and now filling and development of the adjacent seashore have begun in order to provide more space for tankers, refineries, and factories. New towns are underway to house the workers drawn to these new jobs. Southwest of Rotterdam are Hoogvliet and Spijkenisse, each planned for 60,000 people, and, if needed, Hellevoetsluis, which is planned for 100,000 people. Unlike the polders, where the national government finances and carries out new town development, these new towns are municipally sponsored, under the guidance of the provinces. Because the bulk of municipal revenues is derived from the national government, however, the state, through its allocation of funds, largely determines the capacity of Rotterdam to proceed with programs of land acquisition, construction of infrastructure, and new development. Not surprisingly, the funds available are insufficient for the tasks envisaged. Nonetheless, Rotterdam's recent achievements surpass those of most of the world's cities. While many aspects of Rotterdam's postwar development warrant comment, possibly center-city reconstruction, the creation of Europort, and the development of satellite communities are most outstanding.

Center-City Development

Rotterdam's seventy-seven-square-mile area is bisected by the New Maas (Meuse) River. The center city lies just north of the river and, together, they are the focal point of Rotterdam. Although the river is the city's *raison d'être,* its location restricts access to the center city from the south (the left bank). Today there are three tunnels: one for the new subway that opened in 1968; a second near center city—the Maas tunnel—for cars, cyclists, and pedestrians, which opened in 1962; and the third—the new Benelux tunnel—west of the city. The capacity of the Maas tunnel is 80,000 cars per day. In the future, the center-city bridges will be replaced by a six-lane tunnel. A new bridge at the eastern edge of the city has the longest single span in Europe —about 600 feet—with an elevation of 80 feet above the waterline.

A new expressway carries right-bank traffic to the center city, while the center-city railway station provides convenient and speedy access to other Randstad municipalities. As seen in Map IV-11, the new, almost four-mile subway line now joins the right-bank railway station and center city with

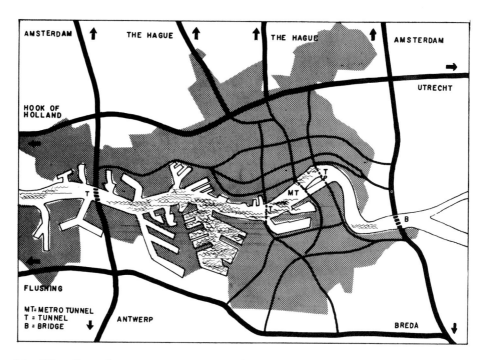

Map IV-11. Rotterdam Transportation Network

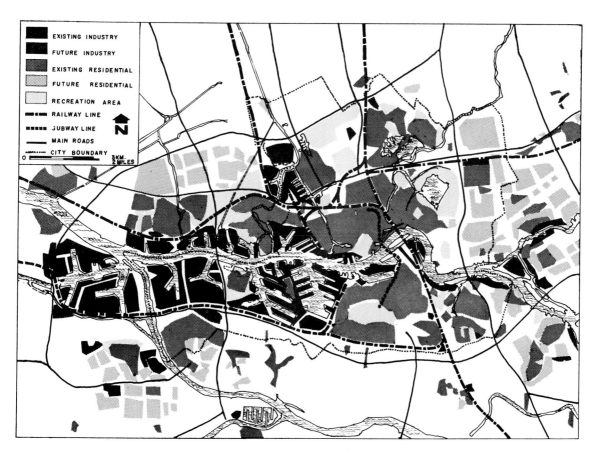

Map IV-12. Rotterdam City Plan

the left bank of the Maas, the area from which much of the center-city labor force of 60,000 is drawn. A typical metro entrance is shown in Figure IV-28. When the subway is extended it will link the newly developed or developing satellite communities of Zuidwijk, Pendrecht, Hoogvliet, and Spijkenisse to center-city Rotterdam. An east-west line from center city to the satellite development at Prince Alexander polder also is planned.

In retrospect, the leveling of center-city Rotterdam was *not* a total disaster. It has made possible the planning and building of an entirely new, efficient, and attractive commercial and cultural center and to reduce residential density (see Map IV-12). Today, only 15,000 people live where there were 100,000 before.

Scarcely had the dust from the bombing settled when Rotterdam's planners began preparing designs for postwar reconstruction. Subsequently, the land —some 425 acres in 12,000 parcels—was acquired by the city through exercise of the power of eminent domain. Because the city then had no money to pay for the land expropriated, it guaranteed the owners pieces of ground equal in value to the ground taken, as that value existed prior to the bombing. However, the guarantees were subject to the owners' obligation to rebuild on these sites. Compensation for destroyed buildings was not paid until an equivalent amount had been spent on new construction. Today, the expressway, the subway, the Lijnbaan—the pedestrian shopping street—new apartments, stores, and cultural facilities all stand as a testimonial to the confidence and determination of those who began to plan again in 1940.

Since its opening in 1953, the Lijnbaan has been a major prototype for shopping-center development in the United States and Europe. The pedestrian street; the human scale of shop buildings, with adjacent high-rise apartments concealed from the pedestrian's line of sight; the warmth and gaiety of the flowers, sculpture, and caged birds; the protection of the pedestrian from inclement weather; and sign controls—all have been emulated and warrant widespread emulation (see Figures IV-29 through IV-32). The City Hall was one of the very few center-city buildings left standing in 1940, and its natural role as a major city landmark has been emphasized in the design of the Lijnbaan. One of the axes of the Lijnbaan gradually widens to form a broad plaza facing the City Hall. As the width of the Lijnbaan increases, so too does the height of the adjacent buildings; the pedestrian experiences a gradual change from the intimate to the monumental scale. Here are the sidewalk cafes, fine restaurants, and shops, and here are the bustle, liveliness, and color which characterize a successful center city.

The Port

The port of Rotterdam also suffered devastation during the war. In 1944, German occupation troops blew up one-third of the piers and destroyed even more of the cranes, elevators, gantrys, and other port facilities. Reconstruction began in 1945, and by the early 1950s the port was handling its prewar load. Several successive plans were developed for the New Waterway between Rotterdam and the sea (see Map IV-13).

At Botlek and Pernis, on the south side of the river, thousands of acres have been developed for piers, refineries, petro-chemical plants, and the transshipment of oil and ore (see Figure IV-33). Industrial sites for lease remain in great demand. Europort, farther west along the New Waterway, has 2,500 acres available for lease. It, too, is being developed as a port for handling and shipping oil, ores, and containers. Construction is well underway to extend Europort into the North Sea. The public costs of this land acquisition and development have in large measure been borne by the city of

Figure IV-28. Metro Entrance

Rotterdam. Some of the land has been annexed, while the rest remains well beyond the city limits.

Satellite Communities

Rotterdam has made extensive use of land acquisition, by voluntary purchase and eminent domain, and of annexation to accommodate its postwar growth. Today, however, the public land supply is being consumed more rapidly than it is being replenished, and the demand for sites is far in excess of the number of building permits authorized by the national government. The municipal government is subject to conflicting demands: from the national government, through its efforts to deflect and limit future growth, and from industries and individuals demanding building sites.

Municipal acquisition of land for future development has a long history in the Netherlands, as it does in the Scandinavian countries. The city of Rotterdam owns more than half of the land within its borders.[83] The merits of public ownership of urban fringe land and of retention of the fee to developed land are beyond question to the Dutch. The problem, once again, is a shortage of public funds. The rate of postwar urban expansion, the burden of reconstruction costs, and the demands for a far higher level of public services all have strained the public exchequer and drained funds away from public land acquisition.

During World War II the city of Rotterdam used the same technique of delayed compensation for acquiring undeveloped fringe land as was used in the center of the city for acquiring bomb-devastated land. In 1941 more than 1,500 acres outside the city limits were expropriated for future development. Compensation, when finally paid, carried a 5 percent interest.[84] Also in 1941, Rotterdam strengthened its development control by annexing several neighboring municipalities where much of the newly acquired land was

Figure IV-29. Lijnbaan

Figure IV-30. Lijnbaan

Figure IV-31. Lijnbaan

Figure IV-32. Lijnbaan

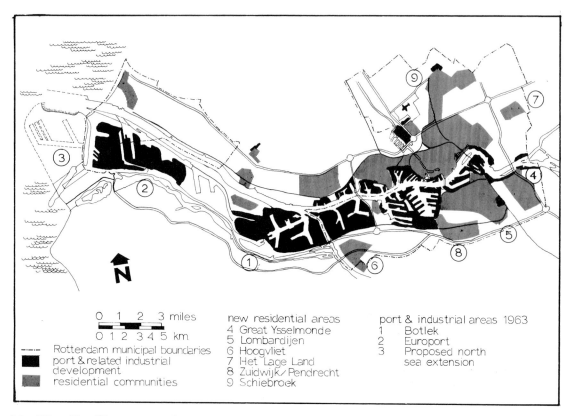

Map IV-13. New Waterway Development

Figure IV-33. The First Petroleum Harbor, Rotterdam

located. Following the war, municipal land acquisition continued, by voluntary purchase and expropriation, although frequently the land acquired was not annexed to the city (see Figure IV-34). Funds for land acquisition customarily are raised through the sale of municipal bonds.

Rotterdam accepts the responsibility of providing an adequate environment for its citizens. In the city's judgment, this requires lowering the prewar center-city density, accommodating natural increase, and decreasing the person-per-room ratio; the result has been municipal development of many large new communities inside and outside the city limits. For instance, the city's stimulation of industrial growth at Botlek and Europort was accompanied by city sponsorship of a new town nearby for the workers drawn to the new jobs.

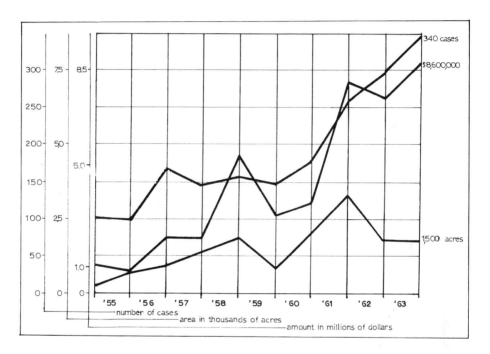

Figure IV-34.
Land Acquisition,
1955–63

... For the members of Council there would be a lack of sense if they would have nothing to do with it. We want to help people there, and we would be happy to have the possibility to build a new town in the other municipality. We don't think it's very important whose money it is; the important thing is that the province, we, and the state all get together and discuss things. We sometimes quarrel about who should pay, but we all agree it should be so.[85]

Despite the city's commitment to provide housing for its residents, it is rapidly running out of land, either within or without the city boundaries. Whereas in 1961 there was enough land available for 5,700 dwelling units, by the start of 1964 the remaining land stock was sufficient for only 1,770 units.[86]

After acquiring new land, the city plans the development, builds the roads and lays the utilities, and then leases or sells the land for development in accordance with the plan. Many cities, including Amsterdam, always lease for development. Rotterdam in some instances sells residential land in order to obtain more revenue, trading a short-term gain for a long-term loss. All of Rotterdam's industrial land is leased.

The municipal government questions the national policy of limiting Rotterdam's growth on several interrelated grounds: Rotterdam's industrial production is essential to the national economy, and the industrial labor force must have an opportunity to acquire adequate housing; further industrial growth cannot occur without accompanying community development; and a large, unmet demand for new construction exists. These arguments are irrefutable so long as one accepts the premise of further industrial expansion along the New Waterway. To some extent the new growth can be directed southward to Ysselmonde and toward the delta, yet there are unresolved conflicts between the national economic objective of enhancing Rotterdam's role as the world's number one port and the development objectives of dispersed growth, limited expansion of the Randstad, and protection of the recreation potential of the delta area.

While the long-term question remains at issue, Rotterdam has been deeply involved in the development of satellite communities for its burgeoning population. Some of these communities have been built on land annexed by the city as early as 1941; some are on land that is owned by the city but is politically a part of another municipality. In size, the new communities range from neighborhoods of 10,000 to a satellite of 200,000 in Prince Alexander polder.

Pendrecht is characteristic of satellite community development immediately after the war and in the 1950s. At that time, formerly independent towns north of Rotterdam—Overschie, Schiebroek, and Hillegersberg—were developed, as were Zuidwijk, Lombardijen, and Groot Ysselmonde on the left bank, south of Rotterdam.

In Pendrecht, as in these other communities, the intent of Rotterdam's planners was to develop a satellite community which would be tied to the whole of Rotterdam for jobs and special commercial and institutional needs, yet would provide major shopping, educational, recreational, and cultural opportunities within the center. Socially, the communities were to be diversified, and sufficient opportunity was to be provided in the choice of housing size and type. Pendrecht and the other south-bank communities would be separated from central Rotterdam by a thin greenbelt in order to reinforce the satellites' sense of separation and to provide recreation opportunities.

Pendrecht was designed for 6,400 dwelling units with a net density of 30 dwelling units per acre. It is subdivided into four "quarters" (see Map IV-14) and is further subdivided into many residential units of 85 dwelling units each. A typical unit includes a few single-family houses for large families with small children, a few one- or two-story row houses for the elderly, a substantial number of three- and four-story gallery apartments, and one or two apartment buildings of eight stories or more, all grouped around an area of community open space and a play area for children. Only collector streets serve these residential units directly. Schools, shops, recreation areas, and churches are grouped in a spacious, centrally located community center which is easily reached by foot or frequent bus service.

Of the housing, 68 percent is in gallery apartments, 24 percent in single-family dwellings, and only 8 percent in high-rise apartments. The Dutch have long opposed high-rise residential construction and only reluctantly accepted it at Pendrecht in order to obtain a higher density while retaining open space (see Figures IV-35 through IV-38). Subsequently, the high-rise apartment has become a standard element of new community development, although the individual preference still is for single-family housing. At Pendrecht, some opportunity to indulge this preference for a detached house with garden is provided by the nearby allotment gardens. A section of the greenbelt separating Pendrecht from central Rotterdam has been set aside for allotment gardens (see Figure IV-39). Plots, with a small cottage on each, are leased to Rotterdam families by the city for about $15 per year. Rotterdam subsidizes the additional costs of the gardens. The families paint and

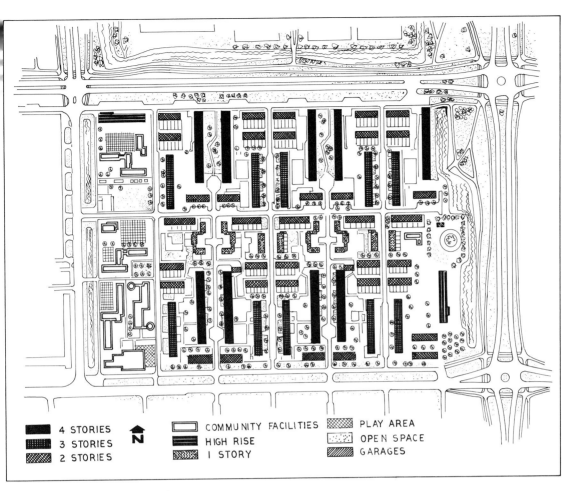

4 STORIES   3 STORIES   2 STORIES   N   COMMUNITY FACILITIES   HIGH RISE   1 STORY   PLAY AREA   OPEN SPACE   GARAGES

Map IV-14. Pendrecht Residential Area

furnish the cottages and plant the plots as they wish, retaining a plot from
year to year. They are not supposed to stay overnight at the cottages, which
are equipped with running water but have no toilet or cooking facilities.
The allotment gardens are beautifully planted and maintained, and the demand for them is heavy. Their color and variety are in marked contrast to
the regular and rather monotonous pattern of development at Pendrecht. The
demand for urban open space for recreation also is great, and this pressure
prevents the city from allocating more of the greenbelt for allotment gardens.

The plans for Pendrecht were made by Rotterdam's planners and architects. Development was carried out by five private corporations. A bridge
between the public planners and private contractors was provided by a
special Pendrecht committee consisting of representatives of the city Departments of Residential Development, Planning and Reconstruction, Public
Works, and the Welfare Board, as well as representatives of the developers.

More recent plans and development—such as at Hoogvliet and Spijken-
nisse, near Botlek and Europort, and at Prince Alexander polder, to the east
of Rotterdam—reflect trends toward increased size, more physical and economic separation from Rotterdam, development around existing village centers, and a greater variety of building types. Hellevoetsluis, a small town,
may become an expanded town with an initial increase in population to
100,000 and an eventual population of 200,000. There are proposals to develop it at a density of fifty persons per acre, retaining half of the island site
in open space. Also, there are plans to attract other industry so that the town

Figure IV-35. Cottages for the Elderly, Pendrecht

Figure IV-36. Residential Area, Pendrecht

Figure IV-37. Residential Area, Pendrecht

Figure IV-38. Pendrecht Shopping Center

Figure IV-39. Rotterdam Allotment Gardens

will not be dependent solely on the port economy. This development would provide another community within a quarter-hour's railway commuting time of Europort. Alternatively, development might occur farther south in the island districts of Goeree and Overflakee. Each of these proposals is subject to considerable controversy.

Rotterdam has long acted responsibly to attempt to design and develop attractive new communities for its residents, both those who wish to move out from old and crowded housing and those who are newcomers, attracted by new job opportunities. Under Rotterdam's plans and the regional plan for Ysselmonde, an effort is being made to retain open space and to direct new growth to large new towns south and east of the existing conurbation. The Rotterdam area continues to seek and to attract further growth. The question —which only the national government can answer—is whether the national policy of limiting growth of the Randstad and stimulating growth in the northeast and southwest is to be put into effect by applying stronger controls to limit the very evident growth pressures in Rotterdam particularly, as well as in the entire Randstad. The issues appear to be those of more national income versus a more agreeable living environment, continued local autonomy versus stronger national controls. It is a choice facing the United States as well, but it is more immediately and clearly presented in the Netherlands, given that nation's small size and current state of urbanization.

Notes

1. The Netherlands, Government Physical Planning Service, *Report on Physical Planning in the Netherlands* (The Hague: Netherlands Printing Office, n.d.).

2. The Netherlands, Ministry of Housing and Building, *Housing in the Netherlands* (The Hague, 1964).

3. Eldert Willems, *Holland Growing Greater* (Amsterdam: De Bezige Bij, 1963).

4. J. J. Hopmans, "The Importance of the River Rhine for the Water Economy of the Netherlands," in *Water Pollution Problems on the Rhine River*, Economic Commission for Europe, GE. 63–8321 (1963).

5. Correspondence with Professor Jacques P. Thysse, 1969.

6. Hopmans, "The Importance of the River Rhine."

7. Willems, *Holland Growing Greater*.

8. Conversation with Professor Jacques P. Thysse, February, 1967.

9. Ministry of Housing and Building, *Housing in the Netherlands*. As has been noted elsewhere, the classification "urban" varies from country to country. Therefore, comparisons may be misleading.

10. Jacques P. Thysse, "The Netherlands: The Most Densely Populated Country of the World" (Speech delivered at People's University, February, 1962).

11. Government Physical Planning Service, *Report on Physical Planning*.

12. Thysse, "The Netherlands."

13. Sjoerd Groenman, "Social Aspects of the Demographic Development in the Netherlands," *Planning and Development in the Netherlands*, 1, no. 1 (1962): 24.

14. Willems, *Holland Growing Greater*, p. 71 ("Second Industrial Note, 1950").

15. *Ibid.* ("Sixth Industrial Note, 1958").

16. "An Unusual Metropolis: The Regional Complex of Cities and Country, Conurbation Holland," mimeographed (1963). Conversion from guldens to dollars was at the then official rate of 1 U.S.\$ = 3.60 guldens.

17. The Netherlands, Ministry of Economic Affairs, "A Summary of the Memorandum on the Growth and Structure of the Dutch Economy" (no. S24 564001), mimeographed (1967).

18. Car ownership per 1,000 population nationwide was 61. "Physical Planning as a Means of Balanced Development in the Netherlands" (Paper presented by the Netherlands to the Economic Commission for Europe, February, 1964).

19. Conversation with Professor Jacques P. Thysse, February, 1967.

20. *New York Times*, January 13, 1969.

21. Peter Hall, *The World Cities* (New York: McGraw-Hill, 1966), and information from Mr. Jasper Vink, former director of the Government Physical Planning Service.

22. Willems, *Holland Growing Greater*.

23. OECD, *OECD: Main Economic Indicators*, June, 1968.

24. *New York Times*, January 13, 1969.

25. Conversation with Mr. Jasper Vink, August, 1964.

26. "Physical Planning as a Means of Balanced Development in the Netherlands."

27. Government Physical Planning Service, *Report on Physical Planning*.

28. Conversation with Mr. J. van Ettinger, director of Bouwcentrum, August, 1964.

29. "Physical Planning as a Means of Balanced Development in the Netherlands."

30. Conversation with Mr. Jasper Vink, August, 1964.

31. Jasper Vink, "Thoughts on National Planning," mimeographed (Paper read in Copenhagen, May 25, 1962), p. 5.

32. "Municipal Finance in the Netherlands," mimeographed (October 14, 1963).

33. Much of the following discussion is derived from "The position of the municipalities in the Netherlands within the general structure of the State," mimeographed (April 13, 1961).

34. Conversation with Professor Jacques P. Thysse, February, 1967.

35. Conversation with Mr. Jasper Vink, August, 1964.

36. Ministry of Housing and Building, *Housing in the Netherlands*.

37. Correspondence with Mr. Jasper Vink, 1970.

38. *Ibid.*

39. Ministry of Housing and Building, *Housing in the Netherlands*, and correspondence with Mr. Jasper Vink, 1970.

40. Conversation with Professor Jacques P. Thysse, February, 1967.

41. Conversation with Mr. Jasper Vink, August, 1964.

42. The Netherlands, Government Information Service, *Physical Planning in the Netherlands* (The Hague, 1961).

43. Ministry of Housing and Building, *Housing in the Netherlands.*

44. *Ibid.*

45. *Ibid.*

46. Correspondence with Mr. Jasper Vink, 1970.

47. The figures for France (5.8%) and Finland (7.8%) were even lower, while Sweden ran 10.1%; see Ministry of Housing and Building, *Housing in the Netherlands.*

48. J. Bommer, *Housing and Planning Legislation in the Netherlands* (Rotterdam, 1967).

49. "Physical Planning as a Means of Balanced Development in the Netherlands," p. 1.

50. Rotterdam has annexed land eleven times in the past century.

51. "An Unusual Metropolis."

52. "Physical Planning as a Means of Balanced Development in the Netherlands," p. 10.

53. Conversation with Mr. Jasper Vink, August, 1964.

54. The Netherlands, Government Physical Planning Service, *Second Report on Physical Planning in the Netherlands* (The Hague: Netherlands Printing Office, 1966), is an abridged version of this report to Parliament.

55. Correspondence with Mr. Jasper Vink, 1970.

56. Vink, "Thoughts on National Planning," p. 19.

57. Conversation with Professor Jacques P. Thysse, February, 1967. Approval of regional plans by the Council of State no longer is required.

58. The following information is derived from Ysselmonde Regional Plan materials as translated by Geert de Koning.

59. The plan was enacted prior to adoption of the 1962 Physical Planning Act, under the 1950 temporary act on national and regional planning. At the time of adoption it was, therefore, a binding plan. In other procedural respects, however, it was characteristic of current regional plans.

60. Dr. Van der Weyde and Mr. Jasper Vink, "Land Use and Land Policy," trans. Geert de Koning (Paper read at a Zurich conference, April 4–6, 1963).

61. The Netherlands, Ministry of Housing and Building, *Municipal Development Plans in the Netherlands* (The Hague, 1963).

62. Van der Weyde and Vink, "Land Use and Land Policy."

63. Government Physical Planning Service, *Second Report on Physical Planning in the Netherlands.*

64. "A Summary of the Memorandum on the Growth and Structure of the Dutch Economy."

65. Conversation with Professor Jacques P. Thysse, February, 1967.

66. Thysse, "The Netherlands."

67. Theo Quené, "Planning Ideas and Ideals in a Small European Country" (Speech delivered to the Citizens' Council on City Planning, Philadelphia, Pa., July 2, 1968).

68. Jacques P. Thysse, "A Spatial Image of the Netherlands in the Year 2000 A.D. with a Population of 20 Million," *Vereniging Voor Demografie* (The Hague), no. 6 (1963).

69. The subsequent discussion is drawn from Government Physical Planning Service, *Second Report on Physical Planning in the Netherlands.*

70. *Ibid.,* p. 24.

71. *Ibid.,* p. 7.

72. Thysse, "A Spatial Image of the Netherlands."

73. "National Planning for the Redistribution of Population and for the Building of New Towns in the Netherlands," mimeographed (March 2, 1964), p. 7.

74. "Physical Planning as a Means of Balanced Development in the Netherlands."

75. Vink, "Thoughts on National Planning," p. 17.

76. Quené, "Planning Ideas and Ideals."

77. Conversation with Mr. J. van Ettinger, August, 1964.

78. Correspondence with Mr. Jasper Vink, 1970.

79. Van der Weyde and Vink, "Land Use and Land Policy."

80. Further discussion of the polder plans is found in A. K. Constandse, N. C. de Ruiter, and L. Wijers's lucid, well-illustrated *Planning and Creation of an Environment*, prepared for the Government Physical Planning Service (The Hague, 1964).

81. Correspondence with Professor Jacques P. Thysse, 1970.

82. Constandse, de Ruiter, and Wijers, *Planning and Creation of an Environment.*

83. Conversation with Mr. Th. Brouwer, August, 1964.

84. City of Rotterdam, Press and Information Services, *Building Rotterdam*, Information Sheet no. 3 (January, 1964).

85. Conversation with Mr. Th. Brouwer, August, 1964.

86. City of Rotterdam, *Annual Report on Construction Activities* (1963).

V | France

A
Synthesis
of
Economic
and
Environmental
Planning

La Grande Motte, a New Resort City

Contents

The National Setting

France is a fascinating and beautiful, yet deceptive and disappointing, country. Its riches—of land, culture, and intellect—are so immense that its failures—of government, economics, and individual well-being—are the more marked. It is as though the very wealth of its endowment had spoiled its capacity for initiative and cooperation.

Why, then, look to France as an exemplar of urban development programs? For two reasons. First, there are many parallels between American and French attitudes and conditions. The hostility of the individualistic Frenchman toward government intervention to influence the use of land or investment of capital will find a ready sympathy in the United States. Second, given broad areas of agreement on the rights of the individual in relation to his government, France's very real commitment to national economic and environmental planning and plan implementation can be seen in a political and philosophical context not antagonistic to American views.

In emphasizing France's natural and historic advantages, it is important not to understate the impact of national catastrophes in recent decades: the devastation of World Wars I and II; the loss of power and pride, and of men and money, in Indochina and Algeria; and the immigrant influx following the loss of former colonies. In addition to crippling national pride, these events have placed severe strains on the French economy. While de Gaulle attempted to restore the former through his stance in international politics, the domestic situation deteriorated. The dominance of Paris and the centralization of decision-making there infuriated and alienated students, workers, farmers, and local government leaders. De Gaulle's resignation and the parlous condition of the franc are manifestations of the current turbulent internal condition of the nation. The situation is not without its parallels in the United States.

Against this setting of challenge and uncertainty, the national government has been proceeding with a series of notable undertakings in economic and environmental planning and regional development. The fifth national economic plan is now in effect, with its projections and proposed allocations subdivided by region. There is a companion national environmental plan. Policy decisions have been made to direct much of the future growth of the Paris region to a series of new cities and expanded old cities extending from the English Channel to Paris. Further policy decisions have been taken to strengthen regional centers throughout the country and to divert growth to them instead of to the Paris region. The failure of the regional decentralization question in the April, 1969, referendum seems to have been essentially a repudiation of de Gaulle rather than an expression of public sentiment on the issue.

Figure V-1. Marseille

Development programs are underway to implement national policy decisions. Funding follows plan priorities to a notable extent. One such program, funded principally by the state, is the Languedoc-Roussillon development of 112 miles of Mediterranean coast. Here, the government has created a national development corporation for land acquisition, planning, financing, and development. Elsewhere, several TVA-like water resource development projects have been initiated to bring power, improved navigation, and irrigation to underdeveloped regions. The national government is an active partner in the development of Marseille (Figure V-1), Bordeaux, Lyon, and five other cities as regional metropolises to balance the attractive force of Paris. Provided that each of these national commitments is fully implemented, the often quoted description of France as "Paris and the French desert"[1] should lose its validity.

The People

If one is to charge the government of France with excessive centralization, disregard of popular will, and bureaucratic rigidity, it is necessary to look first to the French people, for in the final analysis it is they who create the government. Independence, individuality, and intelligence are the dominant national characteristics. Pride, fatalism, and introspection are the imprints of history.

While the educated Frenchman is without peer as an incisive analyst and brilliant conversationalist and stands as an affirmation of his nation's cultural heritage, he too often is a devastating critic of, rather than a forceful participant in, the government of his country. Not only the highly educated few excel as spectator-critics; this activity borders on a national passion rivaling the *Tour de France*. Few elect the role of participant at either the local or the national level, and this reinforces the pattern of centralization of power in an hierarchical bureaucracy. The result is a nation of individuals, each resisting a system all have created by failing to share responsibility for government. Recent events presage a new spirit. If the universities persist in their demands for self-governance, if the farmers are willing to cooperate to solve problems of scale, modernization, and marketing, and particularly if the new regions receive and exercise more decision-making powers, there will be reason to anticipate that the opportunity for all the people of France, not just the elite, to enjoy a future environment of high quality.

Having described France as a nation of individuals, what categories of differences can be discerned? Different parts of France have been subject to different cultural influences since the founding of Marseille by the Greeks in 600 B.C. or since Caesar's invasion in 58 B.C., to choose two early examples. In more recent times, Belgium on the north, Germany and Switzerland on the east, Italy on the southeast, and Spain on the southwest have had varying impacts on the language, work patterns, and leisure preferences of their French neighbors. There are many combinations of the Latin and Northern European temperaments. Climate, topography, and natural resources show vast variations for a comparatively small country and have shaped many different life styles.

Some families have been urban for generations; for most, the shift has been recent and gradual. The young of the family have gone to a nearby city, then to a larger city or to Paris. Half of the people now living in the Paris region were born in the provinces. Notably, 61 percent of this group say that they do not care for Parisian life. They and many Paris-born residents claim that they would move elsewhere, given the same financial, social, and cultural opportunities.[2] So far, however, the same opportunities have not existed elsewhere.

For a technologically advanced nation with a high general level of education, urbanization and large-scale industrialization came late. While industrialization reached northern France, especially, in the late nineteenth century, the rapidity of the move from farm to city in Great Britain, Germany, and the Low Countries was not matched in France. In 1861 one-third of the French population was urban. Not until 1930 was one-half of the population urban. Today the figure is approximately three-quarters, and the acceleration of urbanization is rapid.[3] Urban migration is altering one pattern in which there had been some national consistency, namely, the cohesion of the extended family unit.

Nationally, the total population declined as a result of World War I, then rose gradually. It declined further during World War II, and, in 1946, France's population was less than it had been in 1901. Finally, a postwar resurgence of growth occurred nationwide, stimulated by further industrialization, a higher birth rate, and the return of French citizens from the former colonies. Some two million people have come to France to make it their permanent home, among them one million who arrived from Algeria in 1962 and 1963. There also is a substantial temporary population of laborers from Algeria, Africa, and the poorer nations of Southern Europe, particularly Spain and Portugal. In 1966 there were 250,000 Algerian, 45,000 Portuguese, and 33,000 Spanish workers in France. These new arrivals and non-citizens account for 6 percent of the total population. The current population of almost fifty million[4] makes France the fourth most populous country in Europe,

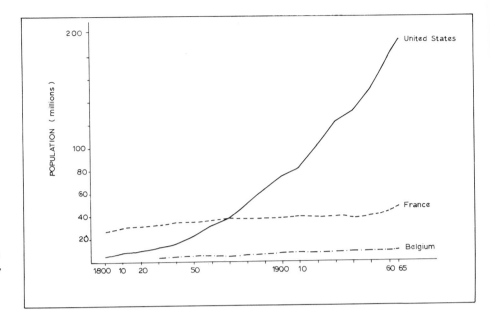

Figure V-2.
Population Growth
in France, Belgium,
and the
United States,
1800–1965

after West Germany, Great Britain, and Italy. For a comparison of France's population growth with that of Belgium and the United States, see Figure V-2.

The natural increase per year has been averaging 300,000 people, with the birth rate ranging from 17 to 18 per 1,000 people. The death rate fell from 13.5 per 1,000 in 1945 to 11.1 per 1,000 in 1965, and the rate of natural increase has risen to 7 per 1,000.[5] A high birth rate since the end of World War II has led to a population distribution in which one-third of the people are under the age of twenty. The low death rate is attributable in part to better health but also in part to the fact that there is an unusually small male population over the age of sixty-five because of the heavy losses suffered in World War I. Life expectancy today is sixty-seven years for men and seventy-four years for women, while the average number of children per family is 2.4.

At 230 people per square mile, population density is low when compared with the 1965 figures of 940 people per square mile in the Netherlands, 615 in West Germany, and 579 in Great Britain.[6] Because the urban three-quarters of the population occupies only 6 percent of the land (see Map V-1), average rural density is very low—87 people per square mile. In contrast, Parisian densities are high for the region—1,794 people per square mile—and extremely high for the city—82,051 people per square mile.[7]

While the provincial cities have been growing rapidly, it is the Paris region which has seen the greatest absolute growth. From the start to the close of the nineteenth century, the Paris region more than doubled its share of the total French population, rising from 5 to 12 percent. Until World War II, Paris continued to grow, and more and more power became concentrated there. Now the city, like many other old, dense cities in the United States and Europe, is declining in population very gradually. The Paris urban area, however, grew from 4.8 million in 1901 to 8.1 million in 1968,[8] and it now has about one-sixth of the total national population. See Figures V-3 and V-4 and Map V-2. The Paris region, with 9.1 million people, has about one-fifth of the national population. Paris, of course, is the capital. It also is the business, educational, and cultural center. Paris employs 25 percent of all government workers (500,000 people) and of all industrial workers (1,600,000 people). One-third of all university students attend school there.[9]

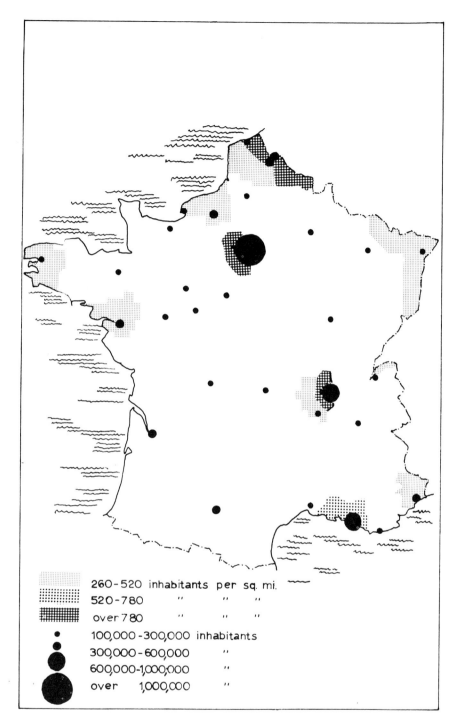

Map V-1. Urban Densities

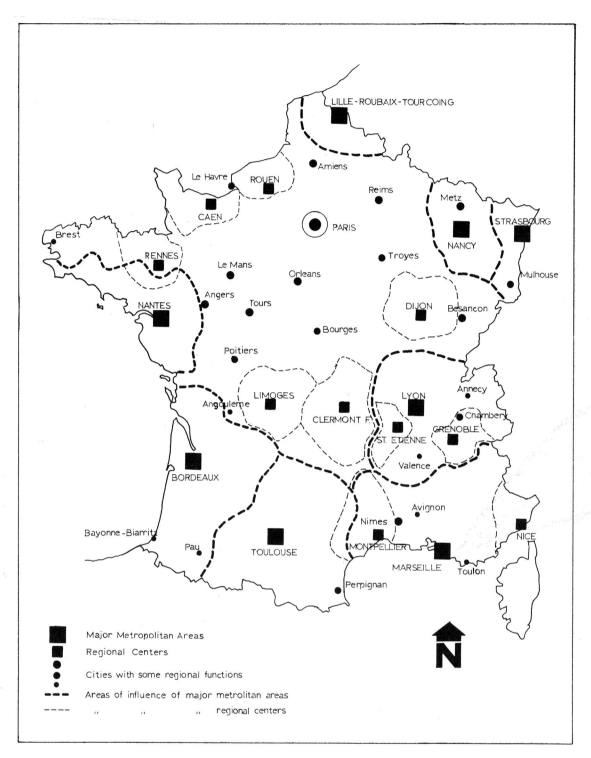

Map V-2. Regional Cities and Their Areas of Influence

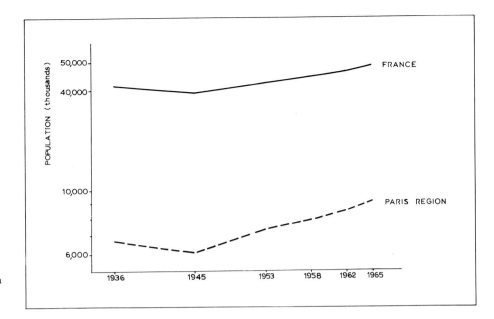

Figure V-3.
Population Growth
in France and the
Paris Region

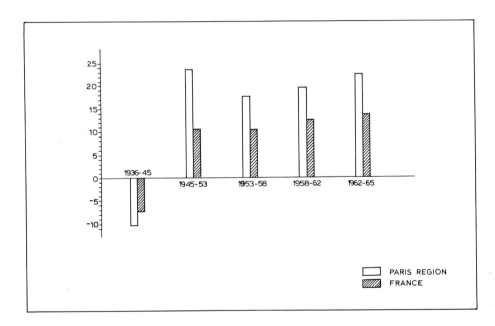

Figure V-4.
Rate of Change in
France and the
Paris Region

**Paris
versus
the Provinces**

There is no other French city which competes with Paris. There is Paris and then there are the rest. Closest in size to Paris are the metropolitan areas of Lyon (1,083,000), Marseille (964,412),[10] and Lille-Roubaix (881,271). They are followed by ten other metropolitan areas with populations of between 300,000 and 600,000: Bordeaux, Toulouse, Nantes, Nice, Rouen, Toulon, Strasbourg, Grenoble, Saint-Étienne, and Lens, in descending order of size. Also, as of 1968, there were seven other urban areas with populations of between 200,000 and 300,000, and twenty-nine with populations of between 10,000 and 200,000. The major urban areas are noted on Map V-3.

Between 1954 and 1962 the urban areas which grew most rapidly were those of between 100,000 and 200,000 population, with a growth rate of 18.6 percent. The largest urban areas, including Paris, grew at rates of between 15 and 16 percent. The rate of growth decreased steadily by size of urban area and rural community for all classes under 50,000, with a negative rate of

Map V-3.
Major Urban Areas

growth for those under 1,000 population. See Figure V-5, which is calculated on the annual rate of change per 1,000 inhabitants. Dividing rural areas into two categories—those small municipalities within commuting range of cities and those outside an urban ambit—the former have 11 percent of the population and gained 5 percent between 1954 and 1962. The truly rural municipalities have 26 percent of the national population but lost 4.5 percent of it during the same period.[11]

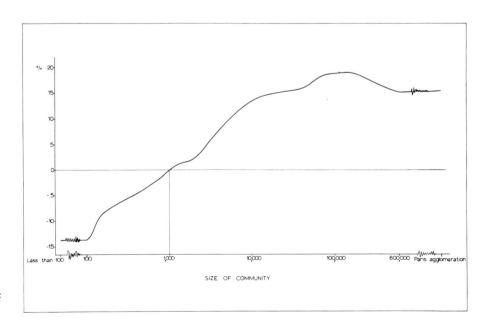

Figure V-5.
Growth Rate,
1954–62, by Size of
Community

By location, the fastest growing areas are the Paris region and the southeast, particularly the Riviera, and the lower Rhône basin (see Maps V-4 and
V-5). Between 1954 and 1962, 895,000 people immigrated to the Paris region,
while 568,000 emigrated, for a regional gain of 327,000 (see Map V-6).
The immigrants were young and came in largest numbers from the Center,
Aquitaine, and Brittany regions. The emigrants were evenly distributed by
age and went, preponderantly, to the Center and Provence–Côte d'Azur
regions.

While mobility is increasing, the increase is relative. As of 1962, about
four out of every ten French adults not living in the Paris region had never
moved beyond the borders of the municipality or city in which they had
lived at the age of fifteen. Another 28 percent had moved only once. Those
who move do so early in their careers and seldom move after the age of forty.
Not surprisingly, the most mobile are those at the bottom and top of the
economic scale—farm laborers and managerial and professional people.[12]

Map V-4.
Immigration to
Paris, 1954–62

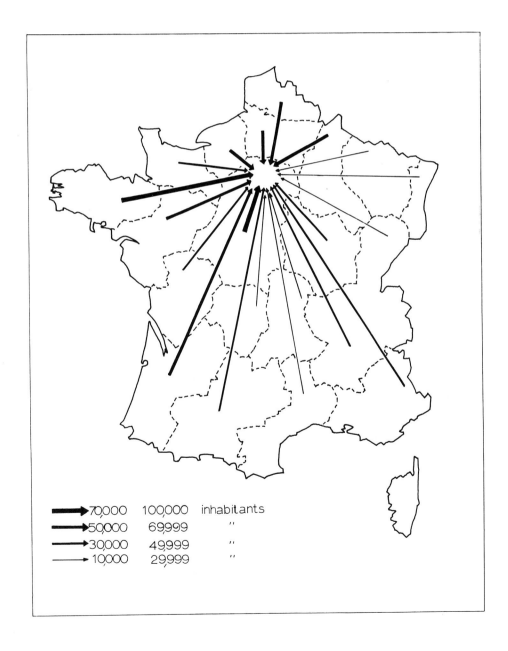

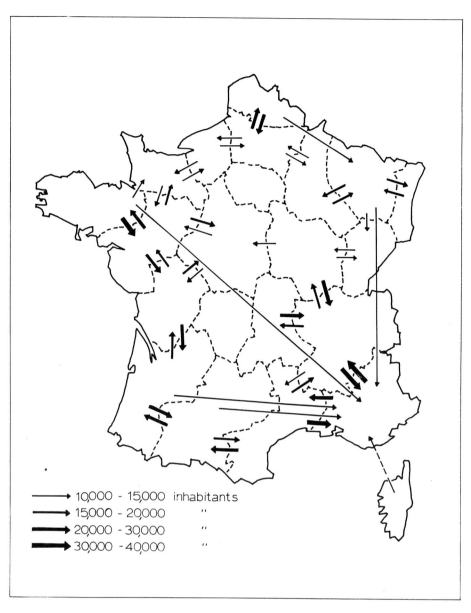

Map V-5.
Interregional
Migration,
Excluding the Paris
Region, 1954–62

**The
Government**

The dominance in the French character of the spirit of independence over the spirit of cooperation is magnified many times in the French government. This is equally true whether one looks to France's recent role on the international political scene, to local or national politics, or even to intraparty politics. Splintering of interest groups and power bases, resistance to change, and choice by non-decision have dominated the political sphere. Meanwhile, the already constituted bureaucracy has continued in the direction in which it was pointed—toward greater centralization of control. Thus an anomalous situation exists: the people, through their chosen representatives, demand a greater role in decision-making, yet, because there is no agreement on the definition of this role, the existing, non-responsive system continues its course.

The current government structure borders on the incredible: there are 38,000 local governments[13] vying for power with one another, with two intermediate levels of government, and with the national government. On the average, there is one municipality per 5.6 square miles. Ten thousand of the municipalities have fewer than 200 residents, while 25,000 have a population of less than 500. Only 2,000 are classified as urban, with a population of 2,000 or more.

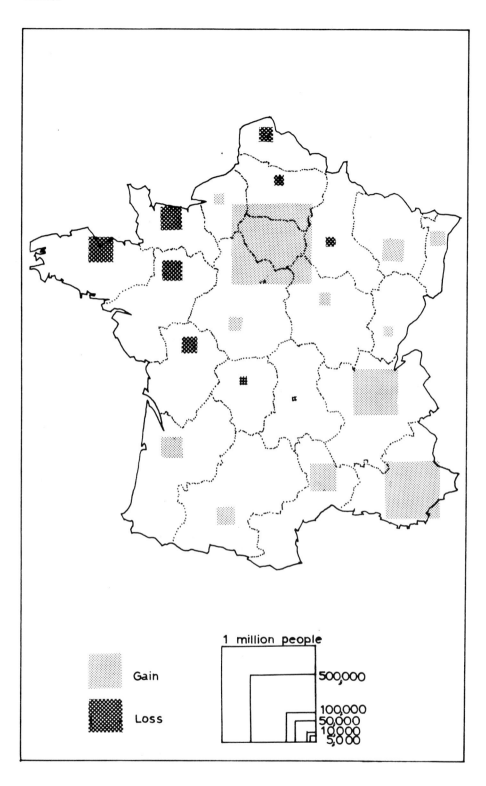

Map V-6.
Regional Growth
or Decline,
1954–62

While each local government is locally elected and nominally independent under the constitution, in fact much local autonomy is illusory. Each municipality is financially dependent on the national government and so is firmly tied to a rigid structure of bureaucratic regulations and requirements. Being small, most of the municipalities are unable to afford competent, paid administrators and, again, the national government steps in, by way of its departmental appointee, the prefect, and his staff.

The national government has moved to improve the efficiency of the intermediate levels of government—the department and the region—and to follow this up by granting greater autonomy to these levels of government. In 1955 the then eighty-nine departments were joined into twenty-one regional units of from two to eight departments each (see Map V-7). Each department retained its boundaries and its political and administrative identity, but a new administrative layer was added, appointed by and answerable to the national government.

Map V-7.
Regions of France

Then, in April, 1969, President de Gaulle called a national referendum on two issues, which he chose to pose as a single question. The first issue was whether the regions should have regionally elected assemblies with legislative powers. The second issue was whether the Senate should become merely an advisory council. Because the polls had indicated strong popular support for the establishment of regional legislative bodies and moderate support for the Senate proposal, defeat of the question is attributed to de Gaulle's announced decision to judge the vote as an affirmation or rejection of his leadership. Despite the defeat of this referendum, expansion of regional power in relation to both local and national power is the most probable future direction for French government structure. Popular rejection of the centralization of decision-making represented by de Gaulle, further depopulation of the rural municipalities and the consequent further growth of urban regions, and the national government's own support of economic decentralization from Paris point to the likelihood that the regions, with their major urban centers, will achieve a more powerful position in the continuing competition for decision-making power in the use of national resources.

Reverting, briefly, to the past, France's present republican system of government was established following the overthrow of the monarchy in the Revolution of 1789. It has, however, undergone many reverses and shifts. The First Republic was established in 1792, then was succeeded from 1804 to 1815 by the empire of Napoleon I. Between 1815 and 1848 the monarchy was restored, then displaced briefly by the Second Republic from 1848 to 1852, which in turn was succeeded by the Second Empire from 1852 to 1870. The Third Republic enjoyed greater longevity than the First and Second, enduring from 1870 until World War II. After the liberation of France from German occupation, a provisional government was established in 1944, and the Fourth Republic came into being in 1946. It was replaced by the Fifth Republic following approval of the constitution of 1958.

Under the 1958 constitution, executive power is lodged in the president, the prime minister, and the other ministers of the cabinet. It was the intent of this constitution to overcome the weakness of government structure prevalent in the Fourth Republic, when principal power had been lodged in the National Assembly. With a multiplicity of parties and uncertain coalitions, this structure had proved unstable.

The president is popularly elected for a seven-year term by direct universal suffrage of all citizens over twenty-one years of age. He selects his prime minister, who in turn and with the accord of the president selects the other ministers. All serve at the pleasure of the president. Together with the president, they constitute the government. The president presides over the cabinet, may require the National Assembly to deliberate further on proposed legislation, may submit draft legislation to the electorate by referendum, and may dissolve the National Assembly. He may exercise exceptional powers in times of national emergency. General Charles de Gaulle served as president of the Fifth Republic from 1959 to 1969, when, although not legally required to do so, he resigned following the referendum defeat of the two laws previously discussed. Georges Pompidou was elected president on June 15, 1969.

The legislature, or National Assembly, is bicameral. According to the 1968 census, the Chamber of Deputies had 487 members—one deputy for each 93,000 people and at least two deputies from each department. The former president of the Chamber of Deputies, Jacques Chaban-Delmas, now is prime minister. He continues to be mayor of Bordeaux. (More than 300 members of the Chamber of Deputies also are part-time mayors. As Prime Minister Chaban-Delmas has said, because most decisions affecting the local governments are made in Paris, these localities need an influential person representing them in the capital.) Voting districts follow departmental boundaries. By majority vote the Chamber of Deputies may overthrow the government in a motion of censure. To be brought to a vote, the motion must have been signed by 10 percent of the deputies. The deputies are elected by direct universal suffrage to five-year terms.

The Senate consists of 287 members, none of whom may also serve in any other private or appointive function for any organization under the control of the national government. Most, however, hold local elective office. More than half are mayors, while many of the rest sit on either departmental or municipal councils. Senators are elected indirectly, through an electoral college of the deputies and municipal officials, to nine-year terms. One-third of the senators stand for election every three years.

Either house of the National Assembly or the prime minister may propose legislation. The National Assembly may authorize the government to act, by ordinance, for purposes normally requiring legislative action.

There are several advisory and judicial bodies at the national level.

The Constitutional Council, consisting of former presidents plus nine persons appointed, three each, by the president, the president of the Senate, and the president of the National Assembly, determines whether laws are constitutional. The council may act only upon the request of the president, prime minister, president of the Senate, and president of the National Assembly. In addition to its role as constitutional interpreter, the council supervises referenda and judges disputed elections.

The Chief Court of Justice hears the case against the president and ministers if they are accused of treason. Half of its judges are elected by the Senate, half by the National Assembly.

The Council of State is the final administrative appeal body and also advises on the drafting of legislation.

The region is the administrative unit immediately subordinate to the national government. Its chief executive is the regional prefect. The capital of the largest department in each region usually is the regional administrative center (see Figure V-6). The prefect of this department also serves as regional prefect. This double role has led to charges of favoritism for the prefect's department over the other departments in the region. Because the prefect does not outrank the prefects of the other departments, it is exceedingly difficult for him to act in the interests of the region, as differentiated from the interests of each department. With the failure of the April, 1969, referendum, there still is no elected government at the regional level. Instead, the regional prefect is advised by the Regional Administrative Conference, which consists of the prefects of the other departments and other state civil servants.

The department is the traditional intermediate level of government and was established at the time of the First Republic as the link between the central government and the people. There are now ninety-five departments in metropolitan France, which includes Corsica. There are four overseas departments (Guadeloupe, Guiana, Martinique, and Réunion) and six overseas territories (Saint-Pierre and Miquelon, French Polynesia, New Caledonia, Wallis and Futuna Islands, Camoro Archipelago, and French Somaliland). While the chief administrative official of the department is the prefect, a civil servant appointed by the national government, there also is a limited measure of self-government. There is an elected General Council which meets twice yearly, approves the department budget and exercises some control over the municipalities. The prefect and his staff of national government civil servants carry out decisions of the General Council, although they have a considerable area of discretion, even to the point of questioning the legality of General Council enactments.

The 38,000 municipalities are the bottom tier of government. They are governed by a Municipal Council of between eleven and thirty-seven members and by a mayor, who is the chief executive. The Municipal Council is elected by the voters of the municipality to a six-year term and meets for at least fifteen days each session, four times yearly. The mayor is elected by and from among the members of council for a six-year term. The Municipal Council is subject to quite strict scrutiny by the prefect and the General Council. The mayor is the local official directly answerable to the prefect and so, through the government hierarchy, to the national government. His responsibility is considerable but he receives no salary. If the municipality is small, the paid staff is negligible or non-existent, and the prefect's staff of national civil servants often steps in to provide necessary administrative services. Local autonomy therefore appears greater on paper than the budgetary situation permits in practice.

Figure V-6. Clermont-Ferrand, population 205,000, is the capital of
Puy-de-Dôme Department and the regional center of the Auvergne region.

Small municipalities may form intermunicipal syndicates for joint administrative services. Since 1959, urban municipalities have been authorized to form urban districts to provide common management for services such as water and electricity. While prime minister, Georges Pompidou voiced his desire for local government to hold more real power, provided that the local government is economically and socially viable. In his terms of reference, local government is far more extensive than the municipal boundary:

... Far from reducing the power of local governments, the government proposes to extend it. But it is necessary that these local governments represent entities having a socioeconomic reality and substance: this is true of the regions where the departments constituted too small a unit for certain economic activities; this is true for urban communities which we will establish or for intermunicipal syndicates where the municipality offers too narrow a base for public services. The government seeks to improve the balance of power, in accordance with the basic principles of the Fifth Republic, namely, the sharing by the French people in the management of their own affairs.[14]

Special administrative provisions exist for Paris. As of 1968 the Paris region was reorganized into eight departments, each with a prefect and General Council, and all, for regional questions, under the jurisdiction of a regional prefect.

The French judiciary system is complex. It suffices to note that there are four categories of courts: civil, criminal, professional (private disputes concerning professional matters and certain labor relations issues), and administrative.

The role of the civil service and its motivations in the decentralization debate should be clearly understood, and its powers must not be underestimated. Only the civil servants of the municipalities are not members of the national civil service. The administrative employees of the departments, the regions, and the state all belong to the same civil service system. This includes the prefects and regional prefects. The ultimate accolade for work well done is promotion to a state job in Paris. One reason why municipal civil servants are so difficult to recruit is that they cannot enter into this promotional stream; another reason is that, by law, they may not be paid more than people of the same competence in the national civil service.[15] Given the transitory nature of governments during the Fourth Republic, the limited legislative role of the municipalities and departments, and the absence of a regional legislative function, it is hardly surprising that the civil service has established a tenacious hold on government administration at all levels. It quite correctly perceives decentralization as a threat to its existing position of power.

There are many political parties representing most shades of the political spectrum, parties which are pro- and anti-church, and parties representing agrarian and urban interests. Since World War II, the parties have undergone reorganization, cleavages, and shifts in allegiance. Few voters belong to a political party—in 1962 only about 3 percent. Many party platforms change with changes in party leadership, and party names undergo frequent alteration. Unlike the other parties, the Communists are well organized, with 500,000 members, and control the General Confederation of Labor, the largest labor union. Their organizational effectiveness was well demonstrated in the June, 1969, presidential election. In the first round, Jacques Duclos, the Communist candidate, received five million votes. In the runoff between Alain Poher and Georges Pompidou, the Communists urged voters to abstain. The number of abstentions rose from 21 percent in the first round to 31 percent in the runoff. One can credit the Communists with the difference in total votes between the two rounds—some 2.5 million.

Representation by party in the National Assembly as of June, 1968, was as follows:[16]

Chamber of Deputies

Independent Republican	61
Union for the Defense of the Republic (Gaullist)	292
Progress and Modern Democracy	33
Federation of the Democratic and Socialist Left	57
Communist	34
Unaffiliated	10
Total	487

Senate

Independent Republican	56
Union for the Defense of the Republic (Gaullist)	36
Socialist Federation of International Workers	51
Progress and Modern Democracy	48
Democratic Left	42
Republican Center for Rural Social Action	19
Communist	18
Unaffiliated	17
Total	287

On the international scene, de Gaulle's vision of France as the holder of the balance of power between West and East and as the dominant voice in the Common Market seems subject to modification by the Pompidou government. The immediate question of British membership in the Common Market has at least been opened and the French price for an affirmative vote will be spelled out more clearly in the months to come. Continued subsidy of French agricultural production by the five other Common Market members and by Great Britain seems certain to be a major demand.

The Natural Environment

France is exceptionally well endowed by nature. There is a climate and a topography for every taste. Some areas are hot and dry, others cool and moist. There are coastal plains, rolling hills, and rugged mountains. There are seas, lakes, and rivers. Good soil and water are plentiful. Coal, gas, water, and a limited oil reserve provide substantial, although insufficient, power and fuel sources. All of this diversity is found in a country of 213,000 square miles, or almost the area of Colorado and Nevada together. France's greatest length and width, respectively, are 601 miles and 583 miles.

As seen in Map V-8, France is roughly hexagonal, bounded on three of its sides by sea and on two by mountains. On the northwest lies the English Channel, on the east the Rhine River and the Alps, on the southeast the Mediterranean, on the southwest the Pyrénées, and on the west the Atlantic Ocean. Only on the northeast is there no natural boundary separating France from neighboring Belgium, Luxemburg, and West Germany. A southwest-northeast axis divides the country into plains and mountains. There are three principal mountain ranges—the Pyrénées, Massif Central, and the Alps (extending to the Jura and Vosges)—and five major river basins which drain these mountains—the Garonne for the Pyrénées; the Garonne, Loire, Seine, and Rhône for the Massif Central; and the Rhône and Rhine for the Alps. Almost all of France's major cities are located either on a coast or on one of the principal rivers.

The mountain climate is cold in the winter, cool in the summer, and high in precipitation. The Atlantic and Channel coasts have moderate rainfall and moderate temperatures, shading from warm to cool as one progresses northward. The inland plains have low rainfall and moderate temperatures. The Mediterranean coast is moderate and rainy in the winter, hot and dry in the summer.

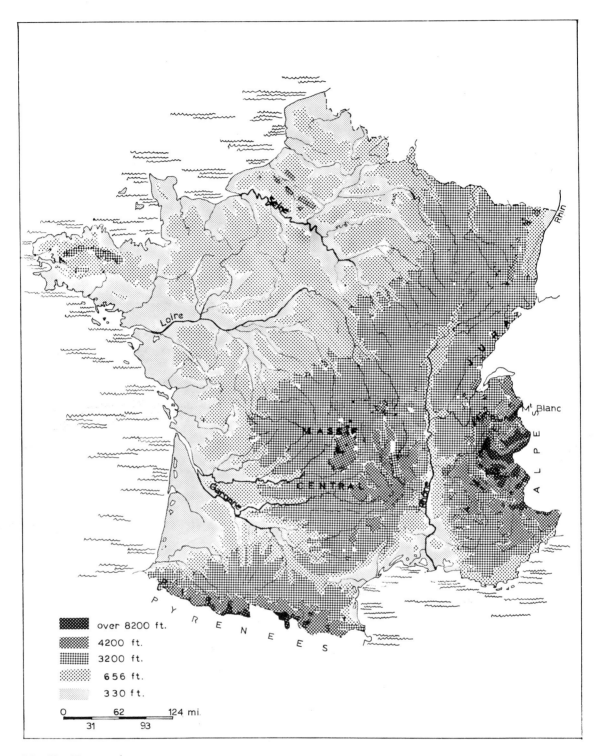

Map V-8. Topography

There are three principal soil types. The plains of the north and west have grey soil, rich in humus and minerals and well suited for field crops. The mountains, where erosion has not stripped the soil cover, have brown soil, and the Mediterranean coastal plain has the red soil characteristic of iron salts. The latter, which also has a high magnesium and limestone content, retains moisture well and thus is suitable for irrigation.

Combining topography, climate, and soils, the areas best suited for crops are Brittany, Alsace, and the north-central and west-central portions of the country. Lower Normandy is excellent for pasturage, while the finest areas for grapes are the Garonne, Dordogne, and Gironde valleys near Bordeaux, the Mediterranean coast in Languedoc, and sections of the Rhône Valley. Thirty-eight percent of the country is suitable for crops, including fruits, vegetables, and wine grapes; 23 percent is in pasture; and 22 percent is forested.

Large deposits of coal are located in the north and northeast, uranium in the Massif Central, natural gas in the southwest, and oil south of Paris and along the Atlantic coast south of Bordeaux. France has enough iron and bauxite ores to meet its needs, as well as substantial deposits of lead, zinc, tin, and copper.

Coal remains the primary source of power (see Table V-1), although its importance is declining. France has an active program of hydroelectric power development. Among the dams built to harness the power of mountain torrents is Serre Ponçon, the largest dam in Europe, with a capacity of 42.3 billion cubic feet. At Rance, in Brittany, is the world's first tidal power plant, producing 350 million kilowatt hours per year. In the Rhône basin a network of dams in the Alps and downstream have provided power for the area reaching from Switzerland to the Mediterranean. The dams have made it possible to irrigate the arid lower Rhône coastal plain, thus vastly increasing the productivity of fruits and vegetables. After 1980 France expects to concentrate on the development of nuclear power plants.

Table V-1.
Sources of Power

Source	1959	1965
Solid fuels	58%	50.0%
Oil	30	34.0
Water	10	11.0
Gas	2	4.6
Nuclear fuels	—	0.4

SOURCE: *France* (Paris, 1967 ed.), p. 72.

Water Quality

Tourism is a major source of revenue for France, and, with the growing attraction to water-related recreation, water quality has become increasingly important. Except along its Rhine border, France's pollution is generated from within and so can be resolved without recourse to international compacts.

With its Water Act of 1964, France took a major step toward a stronger national policy for pollution abatement and the restoration of water quality. Discharge of untreated or inadequately treated municipal and industrial wastes into the seas, lakes, and rivers continues, but there now are clear national directives for the achievement of improved water quality. Given the enactment of new regulations under the 1964 act and more uniform enforcement of the pre-existing congeries of laws, the prospects for cleaner waters look bright.

The administrative and financial aspects of the old and new laws are of particular interest.[17] They provide for representation by the public, the users, and the dischargers on basin planning boards. Although principal enforcement power is lodged in a single agency, other agencies with functional concerns have concurrent rights of investigation and complaint. The enforcement agency is financed principally by those discharging effluent.

The Water Act of 1964 provides a unified national policy statement without repealing prior acts. Its purpose is to establish a framework for the prevention of future pollution and the improvement of existing water quality. The act's scope is comprehensive; it applies to "... any occurrence liable to cause or increase the pollution of water by altering the physical, chemical, biological, and bacteriological properties of surface water, ground water, or sea water within territorial limits." It directs that a national inventory be made of all surface waters, with respect to their current level of pollution, and that, upon completion of this inventory, standards to be attained for each body of water be promulgated and the time for realization of these standards be set. The National Assembly charged the Council of State with issuance of these stream standards and the general regulations under the act.

The act established several administrative bodies for the development of policy and the enforcement of regulations. At the national level, a National Water Committee, answering directly to the prime minister and cooperating with the existing Interministerial Committee for Regional Planning, is to advise on major water problems.

River basin committees have been established to advise on proposed standards or other water control measures, including dams and flood control works. Membership is divided equally among the state government administrators, the local governments, and the water users in the basin.

Water standards are to be enforced by public administrative agencies acting under state supervision throughout a watershed. These agencies are to cover their expenses, including the cost of treatment plants and other pollution abatement facilities, through polluter charges levied against corporations and individuals, "... taking into account the extent to which they have made the provision of the facilities useful or necessary or will benefit therefrom." Pollution abatement works are to be provided for also through loans and grants to corporations and individuals from river basin financial agencies managed by a board composed of persons representing all interests.

Prior legislation, still in force, governs many of the separable aspects of water quality. It provides for administrative enforcement and established civil and criminal procedures. Only a few of the more notable aspects of these pre-existing laws will be mentioned. Under the Civil Code, a riparian owner is entitled to use the water supply as long as he does not impair its quality. Fines from $100 to $1,000 and/or from ten days to one year in prison are fixed for discharging effluent harmful to fish, fish food, or fish reproduction.[18]

In 1963 the Higher Council of Fisheries, a national public body, succeeded in obtaining voluntary abatement of harmful practices by 500 manufacturers. Another 75 improved their effluent standards only after formal abatement proceedings had been instituted.[19]

Over-all responsibility for industrial waste management has rested with the prefects; subject to the new provisions of the 1964 act, it still does to a considerable extent. The Dangerous, Objectionable, and Unhealthy Establishments Act of December 19, 1917, with its implementing decrees, gives a mandate to the prefects to oversee and regulate the effluent quality from industrial and commercial enterprises. Under that act some enterprises must state the nature and volume of their proposed effluent and obtain a permit from the prefect before starting or altering their operations; other enterprises, potentially less damaging, need only file a statement of their intentions. The inspectors of classified establishments act on behalf of the prefects, advising on permit requests, sampling effluent for conformity to authorized pollution levels, and sampling water quality. Other public officials, including agents of the Water and Forestry Division of the Ministry of Agriculture and public health officers of the Ministry of Health, frequently check water quality in relation to their particular concerns. Their findings are reported to and coordinated by the prefect, who has the right at any time, in the public interest, to revoke any permit to discharge industrial wastes or to order the enterprise to achieve a higher standard of treatment. Methods of achieving these higher standards are the option of the entrepreneur.

France still has serious pollution problems from municipal and industrial wastes, as well as from tanker oil spills, but legislation now equips the country to act effectively, and there is every evidence of a national commitment to do so.

The Economy

From a rapid though seriously inflationary postwar recovery and subsequent spectacular growth during the early 1960s, France has slipped into the economic doldrums. French national economic planning was widely credited for the earlier success, while former President de Gaulle's sometimes quixotic decisions have been blamed for the more recent weakness of the franc. It may be that both credit and blame are overstated.

The potential—in natural resources, industrial plants, and a skilled work force—for continued economic growth is strong. However, President Pompidou and Premier Chaban-Delmas first must surmount the present challenges of worker dissatisfaction and regional disequilibrium. The new government inherited a continuing trade imbalance, inflationary conditions, an ossified and centralized bureaucracy, and an alienated populace. As C. L. Sulzberger said following Pompidou's election, "Bourgeois Frenchmen expect the new President to safeguard the franc, personal freedom and national independence—perhaps in that order of preference."[20] To introduce some unity and cohesion of purpose and to enforce economic decisions, possibly at the cost of national face, will prove a severe test. The August, 1969, devaluation of the franc demonstrated the readiness of the government to face economic reality at the cost of popular disenchantment.

As has been noted, the Industrial Revolution came to France later and more gradually than to Great Britain and Germany. Only in the 1960s did France finally catch up. Prior to World War I, industrial and agricultural productivity were low. During that war France suffered devastating losses of men and physical plants. Then, after considerable progress during the 1920s, the country plunged into the depression of the 1930s. The depression was particularly severe and prolonged in France, continuing right into World War II. Between 1913 and 1938 the Gross National Product rose only 6 percent. Over a longer period, from 1870 to 1938, real national income rose only 1.7 times, as compared with a threefold increase in Great Britain and a fourfold rise in Germany.[21]

During World War II, 1.1 million of a population of about forty million French people died as a result of the war. Six hundred thousand were killed on the battlefield, by bombing, or in prisoner-of-war camps, while the remainder of the deaths, including starvation and infant mortality, were attributable to the war. In addition, many men were deported to Germany as slave laborers. With the exception of Paris, French cities suffered extensive damage. Many were virtually obliterated. Railroads, ports, homes, and factories were destroyed, largely by Allied bombs. Industrial production sank to

20 percent of the already low 1938 level. By the termination of the war, France faced a gigantic task of rebuilding confidence and capital.

American, British, and Swiss aid helped enable France to support her people and to undertake the immense tasks of clearance and reconstruction.[22] Immediate recovery was rapid. By 1947, industrial production had risen to the 1938 level. Because of bad weather conditions, agricultural production rose more slowly and did not reach the 1938 level until 1948. By then, the country was well launched on its First Plan.

The Five Plans

During the war, the Gaullists decided that national economic planning was a postwar necessity. In 1946 the General Planning Commission (Commissariat Général du Plan) was created, Jean Monnet was appointed first chairman, and the First Plan, also called the Monnet plan, was prepared.

The First Plan, 1947–53. Initially the First Plan was to cover the years 1947–50; subsequently it was extended to 1953. It established as its principal objective the restoration of the basic sectors of the economy. No annual growth rate was proposed, but targets were set for a number of basic industries and types of agriculture. By 1952 some of these targets had been exceeded, some had not. Targets for coal, steel, electricity, wheat, meat, milk, and sugar were not met, but those for crude oil and cement were exceeded. Housing completions were low, running from 40,000 to 80,000 units per year between 1948 and 1952. The actual allocation of resources to the various sectors showed considerable variance from that which had been projected. The 1948 revision of the First Plan set the pattern for revisions of future plans: when the economy was not proceeding in the direction projected in the plan, the plan was revised to reflect the actual direction. Table V-2, showing investment expenditures for the First Plan, is characteristic. From the time of the First Plan until today, economists have disputed whether the plans are simply projections, revised as new data are available, or whether they are targets toward which expenditures are shaped. Over the years it would seem that there has been a marked shift from the former to the latter.

... French planning is flexible because of its indicative nature. Far from dictating a set of rules for attaining a rigid series of goals, it proposes a future line of action that falls within the limits of the possible while reflecting the country's individual and collective aspirations.

The Plan contains two basic elements: first, forecasts in the form of the nationwide market survey, which serves as a reference for those who have to make long-range economic decisions; second, targets, drawn from the forecasts, which form the Plan's backbone.[23]

Table V-2.
First Plan Investment Expenditures

Investment	1946 Plan	1948 Revision	Actual, 1947–52
Energy	13.1%	22.2%	18.2%
Transportation	10.2	15.6	15.2
Agriculture	15.8	15.2	11.6
Industry and Commerce	15.5	13.6	23.8
Housing	29.3	} 33.4	24.4
Other	16.1		6.8
Total	100.0	100.0	100.0

Despite the First Plan and despite government measures that included price controls, wage controls, subsidies, and rationing, the recovery of productive capacity was accompanied by runaway inflation. There was a long pent-up demand for goods that were still in short supply, a desire for better and more plentiful amounts of food after the deprivations of the war (workers then were spending 60 percent of their income on food), and pressure for wage increases. The sole counter to these pressures was the hefty foreign trade deficit, for at this time France was relying heavily on imports while not yet having recovered adequate capacity to produce for internal consumption or for export. The government expressed the desire to control inflation but only halfheartedly exercised the fiscal controls to achieve that objective. Wholesale prices, for instance, rose twenty-two times between 1937 and 1948, while in most of the rest of Europe they rose only from two to four times during the same period.[24]

The early stages of the First Plan were complicated by further fiscal problems. In 1946 the government began to increase its military budget to support the war in Indochina. Also in 1946 the government passed a law providing for reparations to individuals for housing and industrial structures destroyed during the war. Grants were made for the replacement cost of structures as depreciated. The total estimated amount of these payments, in 1950 currency, was five trillion francs.[25]

Immediate postwar inflation ended in 1948, when consumer goods and food became available in adequate volume, but it had been worse and more prolonged than that in any other country of Western Europe. After a short period of stability, new inflation was touched off in 1950 by the Korean War and lasted until 1952. Again, the government had little success in controlling the inflation, and again the inflation was more severe in France than elsewhere in Europe. The years 1952–54 were a period of recession and recovery.

The Second Plan, 1954–57. The principal objectives of the Second Plan were modernization of selected industries, improvement of agriculture, and increased housing production. Emphasis was placed on technical training and research. Much more than the sought-after rapid rise in industrial productivity was achieved. A growth target of 25 percent more than the 1952 figure was set and exceeded. The Gross National Product rose by an average of 4.6 percent from 1954 to 1957. Again, however, targets for specific industries and agriculture varied markedly from results achieved. Housing exceeded its target by 30 percent, while agriculture as a whole fell well below its combined targets.

Once more the nation underwent a period of inflation. Between 1953 and 1957, consumer prices rose 5 percent annually; the increase in wholesale prices was 8 percent.[26]

On the international trade front, conditions improved early in the period of the Second Plan but then deteriorated, and imports again exceeded exports. In 1954 France had her first favorable postwar balance of payments. Agricultural growth, although below target, was comparable to that of the rest of Europe; industrial growth was slow but improving. The major stimulus for growth had been low-interest government loans. The Economic Commission for Europe stated that, of all non-socialist countries, France was the one "... where the influence of the state in the development of basic industries was the most systematic and most pervasive." Because of this and because of the attributions subsequently granted to "French planning" for France's bursts of growth during the 1950s and 1960s, it is important to view later successes in the context of the limited successes of the First and Second plans in controlling inflation and placing France in a competitive position vis-à-vis other Western European countries. As of 1954, Warren Baum noted: "By European standards, the actual level of investments during the postwar period as a whole has not been high, and the growth of production has not been rapid. The economy has not grown at a pace that has permitted France to maintain its relative standing among European countries, let alone to make up for the interwar stagnation."[27] In 1954, investments were 15 percent of France's Gross National Product, compared with 18 percent in other EEC countries.

The Third Plan, 1958–61. By 1958 the repeated periods of inflation had made currency reform essential. One new franc was issued in exchange for 100 old francs. This reform had no technical effect but did have a psychological impact. Third Plan targets had to be revised downward in 1960; because of inflation and balance-of-payments problems, early targets had not been met. Inflation drove consumer prices up 30 percent, wholesale prices up 22 percent, between 1957 and 1961.[28] In 1960 France enjoyed a sudden upsurge, with a spectacular growth rate of 6.3 percent. During the entire period of the Third Plan, however, annual growth was only 3.8 percent, not the 4.6 percent that had been projected.[29] Nationalized industries reached their targets. Targets for oil, chemicals, and aluminum were exceeded, while those for steel and cement were met. Targets for non-basic industries were not met, nor were those for agriculture. "On the whole, the attempt to solve the agricultural problem—which is France's major socioeconomic problem—has been unsuccessful, and we cannot say that French 'planning' was able to make much of a contribution."[30]

The Fourth Plan, 1962–65. The Fourth Plan set the following targets: (1) an annual growth rate of 5.5 percent accompanied by an over-all 23 percent increase in private consumption; (2) a favorable balance of trade; (3) the maintenance of full employment; and (4) a more equal distribution of income. At last, social as well as economic goals were endorsed, and commitments were made for public investments—in education, culture, health, and research—to support these goals.

In large measure the domestic goals set were reached. The Gross National Product rose 5.6 percent per annum, while private consumption rose 22.2 percent over the four-year period. With an increase in population, the GNP per capita rose more slowly—at an average of 4.1 percent per annum. Income per capita reached $1,800 in 1964 and was as high as that in any European country. Targets for employment did not anticipate either the rapid decline in the farm population or the influx of 700,000 people, including 300,000 workers from Algeria, but jobs were found for these people. Despite these marked successes, agriculture remained an unsolved problem, and the volume of imports rose faster than the volume of exports.[31]

Comparing the percentage rise in the French Gross National Product for the years 1953–63 to that in the United States, the Netherlands, and Sweden for the same period, France appears to have fared comparatively well (see Table V-3).[32] In making such a comparison, however, it is only accurate to note that 1953 was a recession year in France and that France then was lagging behind the other countries. Taking another period—the fifteen years from 1949 to 1964—France's Gross National Product more than doubled. Even given the very low postwar level of production, this increase was notable.

From 1953 to 1963 the rise in residential construction costs was more rapid than the rise in Gross National Product, but other construction costs rose more slowly than the GNP. Taken together, for the years 1953–63 the ratio of the rise in all construction costs to the rise in Gross National Product was 98.7.[33] As a percentage of the Gross National Product, total construction

Table V-3.
Percentage Increase in the Gross National Product
of France, the United States, the Netherlands,
and Sweden, 1953–63

(1953 = 100)

Country	1963
France	159.6
The United States	119.8
The Netherlands	139.6
Sweden	136.4

SOURCE: OECD, *Observer*, no. 21 (1966).

expenditures, as well as residential construction expenditures, rose during the same period (see Table V-4). So, too, did new construction expenditures as a percentage of fixed investment, and housing expenditures as a percentage of all construction. As of 1963 France was spending a higher percentage of her Gross National Product on general construction and housing construction than was the United States. France's gross fixed capital formation invested in housing rose steadily, to almost 7 percent in 1965, while in the United States the percentage declined from 4.7 in 1961 to 3.6 in 1966.[34]

Table V-4.
Construction Expenditures,
1953 and 1963

Expenditures	1953	1963
Total new construction expenditures as percentage of GNP	8.7	11.1
Residential construction expenditures as percentage of GNP	3.6	5.0
Residential construction expenditures as percentage of total new construction expenditures	40.7	44.9
Total new construction expenditures as percentage of fixed investment	53.9	56.0

SOURCE: OECD, *Observer*, no. 21 (1966).

The Fifth Plan, 1966–70. The Fifth Plan provides for the following increases in funds: 55 percent more for schools, hospitals, and other public facilities; 35 percent more for housing construction; and 39 percent more in social allowances. A 4.8 percent annual increase in farm income is another goal, as compared with the goals for annual income increases of 2.8 percent in wages with no upgrading of skills, and 3.3 percent in wages with an upgrading of skills and for non-farm entrepreneurs.

The plan set its highest target for the rate of growth—7.9 percent—of exports. Even if achieved, this would yield only a wafer-thin margin of exports over imports.

With modernization of agriculture still lagging, the highest growth rate target for labor productivity—5.6 percent—was set for agriculture (see Table V-5). This would be achieved despite a projected 3.7 percent decline in agricultural employment (see Table V-6).

Table V-5.
Productivity Growth Rates
per Man Year

Sector	Average Annual Growth Rates	
	1962–65	1965–70
Agriculture	3.7%	5.6%
Industry	3.2	4.4
Construction and Public Works	2.6	3.8
Services	2.8	2.7
All Sectors	3.3	4.4
All Non-agricultural Sectors	2.8	3.6

SOURCES: "The Fifth Plan, 1966–1970," mimeographed (n.a., n.p., n.d.); the figures for 1970 were given to the author by Nice Matin on June 6, 1970.

Table V-6.
Labor Force by Sector

Sector	1965	1970	Projected Annual Rate of Change
Government and Financial Institutions	3,020,000	3,310,000	+1.9%
Services	5,395,000	5,990,000	+2.1
Construction and Public Works	1,765,000	1,850,000	+0.9
Industry	5,895,000	6,160,000	+0.9
Agriculture	3,415,000	2,830,000	−3.7
Total	19,490,000	20,140,000	+0.7

SOURCES: "The Fifth Plan, 1966–1970," mimeographed (n.a., n.p., n.d.); Nice Matin, personal communication, June 6, 1970.

The Fifth Plan adopted a slightly lower annual growth rate than did the Fourth Plan. A goal of 5 percent was set with the intent of stimulating investment and maintaining production while controlling inflationary tendencies. It was estimated that investments in infrastructure would increase at 10 percent per annum, private consumption at 3.5 percent per annum. The Fifth Plan includes several firsts for French planning: (1) it looks ahead to 1985 as a context for the five-year plan; (2) targets have been set by value rather than by volume; and (3) the plan has regional subtargets.

The target for 1970 Gross Domestic Production is $93.6 billion and is divided as follows:

Household Consumption	68.0%
Productive Investment	13.0
Other Investment	2.8
Housing	6.0
Public Facilities	4.6
Military Purchases	3.5
Civilian Government Purchases	2.1

A detailed description of Fifth Plan goals for Gross Domestic Production is given in Table V-7.

Table V-7.
Fifth Plan Goals
for Gross Domestic Production

	Billions of Dollars		Average Annual Growth Rate
	1965	1970	1965–70
Resources			
Gross Domestic Product	73.38	93.63	5.0%
Imports	9.74	13.98	7.5
Total Resources	83.12	107.61	5.3
Uses			
Net Consumption	*54.83*	*69.07*	4.7
Household	51.13	64.07	4.6
Government	3.30	4.52	6.5
Civilian	1.52	1.92	4.9
Military	1.78	2.60	7.8
Financial Institutions	0.40	0.48	3.7
Gross Fixed Capital Formation	*17.84*	*22.63*	4.9
Business	10.10	12.87	5.0
Housing	5.40	6.34	3.3
Government	2.26	3.31	7.9
Financial Institutions	0.08	0.11	5.9
Inventory Accumulation	*0.43*	*1.21*	
Exports	10.02	14.70	7.9
Total Uses	*83.12*	*107.61*	*5.3*
External Account	+0.28	+0.72	

SOURCES: "The Fifth Plan, 1966–1970," mimeographed (n.a., n.p., n.d.); the figures for 1970 were given to the author by Nice Matin on June 6, 1970.

Data now are available for a comparison of the targets of the Fifth Plan with achievements as of 1966 or 1967, as well as for a backward look of more than a decade to determine the direction of change (see Table V-8).

First, looking back to 1959, it is surprising to find only a negligible change in the sources of Gross Domestic Production. Whereas services and industry might have been expected to gain significantly, they did not. The shares of food and forestry, food industries, and services fell 1 percent, while the contributions of industry and construction rose 1 percent. The contribution of duties also rose 1 percent.

Tables V-9 and V-10 show the absolute growth in Gross Domestic Production, the former in current prices, the latter in constant 1959 prices. Between 1959 and 1966, consumption fell from 68 to 65 percent of total resources, gross capital formation rose from 19 to 21 percent, and exports fell from 12 to 11 percent (see Tables V-11 and V-12).

One key concern has been that such a large proportion—more than one-third since 1960—of direct investments has been by foreign companies, many of them American. This is but one aspect of France's continuing inability to compete effectively on European and world markets. A principal motivation

Table V-8.
Sources of Gross Domestic Production,
1959, 1963, and 1966, in Constant 1959 Prices

Source	1959	1963	1966
Internal Production			
Agriculture and Forestry	10%	9%	9%
Food Industries	7	7	6
Other Industries	38	39	39
Construction and Public Works	8	8	9
Services, Commerce, and Transportation	35	34	34
Taxes on External Production			
Duties and Taxes on Imports	2	3	3
Total	100	100	100

SOURCE: Institut National de la Statistique et des Études Économiques (INSEE), *Annuaire Statistique de la France* (Paris, 1967).

Table V-9.
Gross Domestic Production
in Current Prices

(billions of francs)

Source	1959	1963	1966
Agriculture and Forestry	25,034	34,031	37,211
Agricultural Industries	17,469	23,141	28,516
Other Industries	90,741	131,218	157,944
Construction and Public Works	19,426	30,296	44,882
Transportation, Services, and Commerce	82,478	124,922	164,816
Total Value Added	235,148	343,608	433,369
Duties and Taxes on Imports	3,811	8,258	11,802
Gross National Product	238,959	351,866	445,171

SOURCE: INSEE, *Annuaire Statistique de la France* (Paris, 1967).

for the 1969 devaluation of the franc was to stimulate exports, by making them cheaper to the purchasers, and to discourage imports, by making them more expensive to the French.

France remains concerned over its ability to compete within the Common Market as tariffs are lowered. While efficiency has improved, the degree of modernization and the scale of enterprise still lag behind other members of the Common Market, particularly West Germany. France's reluctance to admit Great Britain to the Common Market is economic as well as political.

France's agricultural produce, accounting for one-sixth of its exports, is largely of superior quality. Her wines (1.7 billion gallons in 1965), lamb (21 million head in 1965), cheeses, fruits, fish, and seafood are known

Table V-10.
Gross Domestic Production
in Constant 1959 Prices

(billions of francs)

Source	1959	1963	1966
Agriculture and Forestry	25,034	28,156	29,802
Agricultural Industries	17,469	19,695	22,071
Other Industries	90,741	118,863	139,243
Construction and Public Works	19,426	24,993	31,552
Transportation, Services, and Commerce	82,478	104,096	118,980
Total Value Added	235,148	295,803	341,648
Duties and Taxes on Imports	3,811	8,688	12,237
Gross National Product	238,959	304,491	353,885

SOURCE: INSEE, *Annuaire Statistique de la France* (Paris, 1967).

worldwide as the finest. Much of this produce requires constant cultivation and is labor intensive, making a rise in output per worker difficult to achieve. To produce superior quality food and drink, production necessarily is inefficient and prices are non-competitive with standard quality produce. These explanations of higher costs obviously are not applicable to France's labor-extensive agriculture. Following devaluation of the franc, France was forced to request of the Common Market a suspension for agricultural produce because the country was not ready to accept the domestic repercussions of a 12.5 percent increase in food prices.

The largest share of France's trade today is within the Common Market; the next largest is with the rest of Europe and the United States. Currently, only 6 percent of her exports go to the United States. As trade within the franc zone declined during the 1950s and 1960s, trade within the Common Market increased (see Figure V-7). In 1950 the franc zone received 36 percent of France's exports and was the source of 26 percent of her imports. By 1965 these figures had dropped to 18 and 16 percent, respectively. In 1950, 43 percent of French exports went to EEC countries, while these countries accounted for 28 percent of French imports. In 1967, 67 percent of France's exports were to EEC countries; in 1964, 55 percent of her imports were from EEC countries.

Because she produces only 60 percent of her power requirements, France's principal import is fuel—crude oil, coal, and solid fuels. The principal exports are manufactured goods (including textiles), iron and steel machine goods, automobiles, chemicals, and food. The import-export, or trade, balance improved in the early sixties, then declined again sharply in 1962 and has been unsatisfactory ever since (see Table V-13).[35] There has been a balance-of-payments deficit since 1961 (see Table V-14). In 1968 the deficit passed the $3 billion mark.[36]

In 1966, President de Gaulle could say, "There is no currency in the world stronger than the franc and we can handle, on the international level, all economic, financial, and monetary problems without anyone having a hold on us."[37] At that time French monetary reserves amounted to $6.0 billion; in 1969 they were officially assumed to be $3.6 billion, but it is probable that

Table V-11.
Resources and Uses of Goods and Services,
1959–66, in Constant 1959 Prices

(millions of francs)

Goods and Services	1959	1960	1961	1962	1963	1964	1965	1966
Resources								
Gross Domestic Product	238,959	258,003	269,843	288,355	304,491	323,411	336,795	353,885
Imports	26,289	31,087	33,272	36,993	43,334	48,957	50,306	56,557
Total Resources	265,248	289,090	303,115	325,348	347,825	372,368	387,101	410,442
Uses								
Consumption								
Household	167,627	176,807	186,600	199,736	213,877	223,787	231,960	242,870
Government and Financial Institutions	12,243	12,492	13,009	14,286	15,192	16,970	18,220	19,161
Total Consumption	179,870	189,299	199,609	214,022	229,069	240,757	250,180	262,031
Gross Fixed Asset Formation								
Productive Investments (except housing)	31,449	34,161	38,131	41,029	43,531	46,610	47,544	50,988
Housing	13,297	13,775	14,690	15,577	17,142	20,124	23,061	23,033
Other Investments	6,086	6,345	7,144	8,061	8,886	9,773	10,913	12,457
Total Gross Fixed Asset Formation	50,832	54,281	59,965	64,667	69,559	76,507	81,518	86,478
Change in Business Inventories	1,811	6,980	2,714	5,229	4,227	7,117	1,765	4,407
Exports	29,031	34,082	36,132	36,765	40,086	43,005	48,160	51,806
Balance of Services[a]	3,704	4,448	4,695	4,665	4,884	4,982	5,478	5,720
Total Uses	265,248	289,090	303,115	325,348	347,825	372,368	387,101	410,442

SOURCE: INSEE, *Annuaire Statistique de la France* (Paris, 1967).
[a] In international transactions includes such items as tourism and transportation.

Table V-12.
Resources and Uses of Goods and Services,
1959–66, in Current Prices

(millions of francs)

Goods and Services	1959	1960	1961	1962	1963	1964	1965	1966
Resources								
Gross Domestic Product	238,959	265,720	285,757	317,594	351,866	387,177	413,454	445,171
Imports	26,289	31,377	33,406	36,789	43,539	50,241	51,640	59,209
Total Resources	265,248	297,097	319,163	354,383	395,405	437,418	465,094	504,380
Uses								
Consumption								
Household	167,627	182,921	198,689	221,573	248,402	268,778	285,177	307,146
Government and Financial Institutions	12,243	12,673	13,445	15,139	16,702	19,099	20,848	22,195
Total Consumption	179,870	195,594	212,134	236,712	265,104	287,877	306,025	329,341
Gross Fixed Asset Formation								
Productive Investments (except housing)	31,449	34,834	39,971	44,412	49,049	53,880	56,261	61,631
Housing	13,297	13,977	15,434	17,069	20,409	25,226	30,502	31,257
Other Investments	6,086	6,432	7,465	8,697	10,168	11,640	13,400	15,598
Total Gross Fixed Asset Formation	50,832	55,243	62,870	70,178	79,626	90,746	100,163	108,486
Change in Business Inventories	1,811	7,071	2,846	5,433	4,411	8,050	2,037	4,985
Exports	29,031	34,784	36,641	37,433	41,336	45,673	51,193	55,594
Balance of Services[a]	3,704	4,405	4,672	4,627	4,928	5,072	5,676	5,974
Total Uses	265,248	297,097	319,163	354,383	395,405	437,418	465,094	504,380

SOURCE: INSEE, *Annuaire Statistique de la France* (Paris, 1967).
[a] In international transactions includes such items as tourism and transportation.

Table V-13.
Value of Exports
as Percentage of Value of Imports

| | Prices | |
| | Constant | |
Year	1959	Current
1958	91	—
1959	110	111
1960	109	111
1961	108	111
1962	98	101
1963	93	93
1964	89	92
1965	97	99
1966	92	95
1967	91	95

SOURCE: Services Culturels Français, *Géographie de la France* (New York, n.d.), p. 15.
NOTE: The figures for 1967 are estimates.

Table V-14.
Balance of Payments, 1959–67

Year	Millions of Francs in Current Prices
1959	−207
1960	+532
1961	−16
1962	−528
1963	−3,143
1964	−5,632
1965	−823
1966	−3,901
1967	−4,482

SOURCE: INSEE, *Rapport sur les Comptes de la Nation de l'Année 1967* (n.p., n.d.).

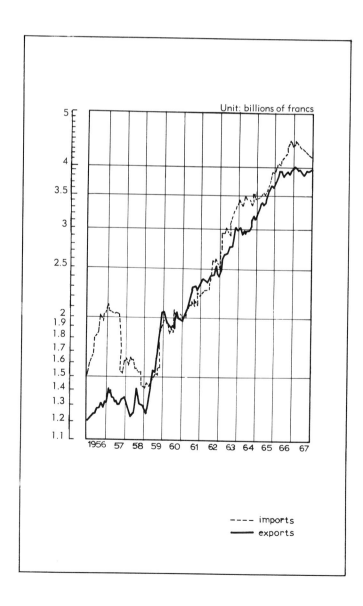

Figure V-7. Foreign Trade outside
the Franc Zone

they were even lower. The student and worker strikes of 1968, continued inflation, and a greater export-import gap led to the loss of reserves. Politically, devaluation was a more palatable choice than wage and price ceilings and even tighter credit restrictions.

The Sixth Plan, 1971–75. The Sixth Plan was debated in the National Assembly for four days in June, 1970. Some one hundred and twenty legislators voiced their opinions, and several cabinet ministers appeared in order to reply to questions. Following this, Prime Minister Chaban-Delmas, having noted the comments and objections, presented the revised final version of the plan for a yes or no vote. It passed, over the opposition of the parties of the left.

The Sixth Plan's prime objective is the increased industrialization of France, which would be accompanied by increased employment at the target rate of from 50,000 to 70,000 jobs per year. A growth rate of almost 6 percent is proposed. Housing construction would receive even greater emphasis, with an annual target rate of ten dwelling units per 1,000 persons. Budget allocations to education, agriculture, and social services would be restricted in order to pour more funds into industrialization, and herein lay the principal source of objection to the plan.

Prime Minister Chaban-Delmas' articulation of the role of the plan is as applicable to the United States as it is to France: "The plan is a rendezvous with ourselves; it permits us periodically to interrogate ourselves about our essential problems, while comparing the desirable to the possible. Furthermore, it obliges us to express our priorities clearly and to order our actions to carry out that which we have expressed. In this sense, more than ever, the plan constitutes the indicator of our economic and social development."[38]

Recent Economic Conditions

Data are available to show the condition of the economy in 1966, as well as the distribution of employment and consumer goods at that time (see Tables V-15 and V-16). The Gross National Product rose 4.9 percent (close to the Fifth Plan's 5 percent target). While the over-all Gross National Product has been rising more or less in accord with the plans, and Gross National Product per capita has risen almost as rapidly, regional and urban-rural disparities are increasing. The growth of technically efficient, large-scale industry diverts attention from the vast number of small, inefficient, and noncompetitive industries.

Traditionally, France has been a nation of small entrepreneurs. The personal relationship between the grocer, the butcher, the baker, the pastry maker, and the housewife is well known and is one of the inefficient but more pleasurable aspects of French life. Less well known is the fact that most other service, commercial, and industrial enterprises have been equally small. In 1960, 60.0 percent of the labor force worked in enterprises employing five people or less, while only 0.1 percent worked in firms of 100 or more employees. The government has acted to encourage mergers and modernization in order to raise productivity.

A cooperative agreement between Renault and Peugeot makes them second only to Volkswagen in European automobile production and fifth worldwide. The French aviation industry ranks second in Europe and fourth in the world. France is third in world production of iron ore, fourth in aluminum. French shipyards rank fifth worldwide. The chemical industry, with the new merger of Rhône-Poulenc with the chemical branches of Saint-Gobain and Pechiney, will rank fifth in Europe. In contrast to these large, modern industries, which are competitive on the world market, there are some three million handicraft industries, one-third of which are not breaking even. Although industrial

Table V-15.
Budget Receipts, 1967

Receipts	Millions of Francs
Direct Taxes	39,489
Documentary Stamps and Operation of the Stock Market	6,638
Customs	13,058
Indirect Taxes	5,430
Tax on the Transport of Goods	386
Special Taxes	2,285
Turnover Tax	40,400
Subtotal	107,686
Revenues from State and Monopoly Enterprises	501
Other	8,952
Total	117,139

SOURCE: INSEE, *Bulletin Mensuel de Statistique*, n.s., no. 11 (1968).

Table V-16.
Key Indicators, 1966

Indicator	1958 = 100	Percentage of GNP
GNP	151	
GNP per Capita	136	
GNP per Member of Labor Force	148	
Gross Fixed Asset Formation	175	21.8
Private Consumer's Expenditure	148	63.7
Current Public Expenditure on Goods and Services	137	13.3
Industrial Production	155	
Exports	198	15.1
Imports	193	−14.8

SOURCE: European Economic Community Commission, *The Economic Situation in the Community* (Brussels: EEC Directorate-General for Economic and Financial Affairs, 1967).

production has been rising 7 percent per annum (1956–66), it still remains behind that of West Germany, Great Britain, and other Common Market countries.[39]

As has been emphasized, agriculture continues to be one of France's most serious economic problems. Although migration from farms to urban areas continues, agriculture still contributes a large share to the nation's employment and a lesser but large share to total production. Some 800,000 farms employ 1.5 million people, yet one-third of these farms—usually the smallest —yield only a marginal return.[40] Eighty-seven percent of the farms are less than 125 acres in size, and 33 percent are smaller than 12 acres. The average farm size is 38 acres. Farm size obviously is one cause of expensive agricultural production. To increase farm size the government has several programs under which it is re-allotting 1,250,000 acres per year. Today 55 percent of French farms are owner-operated, 30 percent tenant-operated, and 15 percent sharecropped (*métayage*). Increasingly, farmland is being converted from crop land to pasturage for cattle, hogs, and sheep. In 1966, animal products accounted for 60 percent of farm revenues. Among them, milk ($21 million), cattle ($14 million), and pigs ($12 million), were the leaders. That year, France was second in world production of cheese, though indubitably first in variety and quality. The production of grain brought $11 million in revenues, that of wine $8 million; vineyards covered 20 percent of the farmland. As with cheese, French wines have no peer.

As a nation of gourmets, rightfully priding itself on the supreme quality of its produce and cooking, France's inclusion of her system of food merchandising in the drive for modernization and efficiency is of questionable benefit. Between 1957 and 1967 the number of supermarkets shot up from 1 to 821. The average size of these supermarkets is 7,500 square feet. On the benefit side, the new retailing system will be cheaper and quicker. For a nation which derives such pleasure from fine food and drink, however, the cost in quality and personal service will be severe.

Rail, air, and water transport technology is ahead of most of the world in speed, reliability, and comfort. The extent of passenger and freight traffic by rail is depicted in Map V-9. However, France's transportation network graphically reflects the role of Paris. All systems radiate out from Paris, and it is difficult to travel from one city to another in the provinces. Road mileage is the densest in Europe, but there are few expressways. Their absence contributes to economic discrepancies between the have and have-not areas. There is no transnational east-west expressway, and the north-south expressway from Lille to Marseille is only about two-thirds completed, with a mileage total of 750. Construction moves forward slowly and is carried out by five public-private companies with financing from the Ministry of Equipment. The ministry now has requested bids from private companies to build and operate toll roads. The companies would provide 25 percent of the cost, the government would lend 25 percent without interest, and 50 percent would be raised through the sale of government-guaranteed bonds.

Motor vehicle production is high and rising, as seen in Table V-17, and urban highways are painfully overcrowded.

In 1966 the work force of twenty million was employed as follows: agriculture, forestry, and fishing, 16.7 percent; industry, 39.9 percent (of which construction accounts for 9.6 percent); and services, 43.4 percent.[41]

While the cost of living in France has risen annually, the rate of increase during the 1960s was slower than that of the prior decade. Between 1960 and 1967 France's rate of increase was the same as Finland's, somewhat higher than Sweden's, the Netherlands', and the United States', but not as high as Israel's. Looking back two decades, however, of these countries, only Israel has experienced a greater increase in the cost of living. The rise in France has tripled that in the United States.

As income and production have risen, more and more households have purchased modern conveniences (see Tables V-18 and V-19), although France remains considerably behind the United States in this regard. Half of all households possess vacuum cleaners, and radios are found in virtually all homes. Seven and two-tenths percent of French families own a second house.

Neither income nor ownership of modern conveniences is evenly distributed (see Table V-20). In 1965 the average annual salary in the Paris region was 15,263 francs ($3,200), as compared with the average for the rest of the

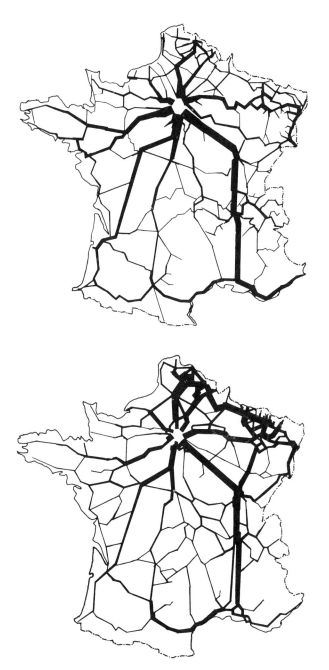

Map V-9. Rail Networks: *Top*, Passenger Traffic; *Bottom*, Freight Traffic

Table V-17.
Production of Motor Vehicles

Year	Cars	Trucks	Buses	Tractors	Special Vehicles	Total
1962	1,277,980	223,460	2,500	3,210	380	1,507,530
1963	1,452,760	247,030	2,760	3,750	430	1,706,730
1964	1,321,080	253,870	2,770	4,050	360	1,582,130
1965	1,315,000	202,910	2,500	3,300	350	1,524,460
1966	1,653,780	255,680	2,860	4,120	210	1,916,650

SOURCE: INSEE, *Annuaire Statistique de la France* (Paris, 1967).

Table V-18.
Percentage of Households
Owning Modern Conveniences

Convenience	1950	1960	1965	1970
Car	14.0	30	46.5	56.2
Television	—	14	41.0	68.6
Refrigerator	3.0	27	54.0	76.9
Washing Machine	2.5	25	38.5	54.0

SOURCE: "The Fifth Plan, 1966–1970," mimeographed (n.a., n.p., n.d.); the figures for 1970 were given to the author by Nice Matin on June 6, 1970.

Table V-19.
Sale of Radios and Televisions

Year	Radios	Televisions
1962	2,672,000	991,000
1963	2,819,000	1,152,000
1964	2,333,000	1,314,000
1965	2,298,000	1,250,000
1966	2,400,000	1,320,000

SOURCE: INSEE, *Annuaire Statistique de la France* (Paris, 1967).

Table V-20.
Average Salary by Region, 1965

Region	Average Salary (francs)
Paris	15,263
Champagne	9,906
Picardy	9,963
Upper Normandy	10,836
Center	9,401
North	10,195
Lorraine	10,263
Alsace	10,574
Franche-Comté	10,166
Lower Normandy	9,387
Loire	9,250
Brittany	9,173
Limousin	8,569
Auvergne	9,754
Poitou-Charentes	8,851
Aquitaine	9,675
Midi-Pyrénées	9,387
Burgundy	9,514
Rhône-Alps	11,103
Languedoc	9,411
Provence–Côte d'Azur–Corsica	11,359
Frontaliers	9,683
National Average	10,076
National Average excluding Paris Region	9,829

SOURCE: INSEE, *Annuaire Statistique de la France* (Paris, 1967).

nation of 10,000 francs ($2,100). The region of Limousin, in south-central France, had the lowest average salary: 8,569 francs ($1,750). If this figure included non-salaried farmers, it would be lower still.

In 1964, residents of the Paris region possessed 22 percent of the cars in France, 39 percent of the telephones, and 42 percent of the total value of bank deposits.[42] Next to the Paris region, the northeast is highest in income and productivity. The area northeast of a line between Le Havre, Paris, and Mulhouse accounts for 46 percent of national agricultural and industrial production.[43] In this area, agricultural employment is lower but productivity higher, and industrial and service employment are greater, than the national average. In Brittany, Auvergne, and the southwest, where farms are small and as much as 64 percent of a department's labor force is employed in agriculture, productivity and incomes are lowest.[44]

Taking the nation as a whole, in 1966 the average allocation of the family budget was as follows:

Food, Alcohol, and Tobacco	40.0%
Health	11.0
Housing	13.5
Clothing	10.0
Transportation and Communication	12.0
Other	13.5

The French drink eighty times more wine than the Dutch, or thirty-one gallons per person per year. However, the French smoke only one-third as much as Americans. Housing expenditures are low in comparison to United States figures.

Housing

The deplorable housing conditions which prevailed in France after World War II resulted from an accumulation of causes: the move to the cities accompanying the Industrial Revolution, destruction during World War I, rent controls, the depression of the 1930s, and further destruction during World War II. Because of the even more urgent postwar demands for restoration of agricultural productivity, industrial capacity, and transportation systems, housing did not receive high priority until the Second Plan. Between 1953 and 1965, except for the years 1960–62, the rate of housing construction exceeded the rate of population growth. Since 1965 the rate of increase of construction has declined. The volume of construction is high, however, and now French housing construction technology is among the most advanced in the world. Upgrading of the size and equipment of housing continues. Nonetheless, today the housing shortage remains acute, particularly in Paris. With postwar babies now marrying and having families, with jerry-built postwar housing already deteriorating, and with over-all housing standards still low, the problem will require an even greater public investment.

During World War I, 400,000 homes were destroyed. Between the two world wars, housing completions averaged only 90,000 per year. As was true of many port cities, Rouen and the coastal strip of Royan were totally destroyed during World War II. Figures V-8 and V-9 show the respective cities as they were rebuilt.

Figure V-8. Rouen during Reconstruction

Figure V-9. Royan Rebuilt

The decline in the birth rate and the initiation of a low-income housing program during the interwar period alleviated bad housing conditions somewhat, but old units continued to deteriorate and little was done to renovate them. World War II brought the total destruction of 450,000 dwellings and the partial destruction of another two million.[45] Immediately after the war, the initial housing effort was to clear or repair the war-damaged buildings. When new construction began, building contractors were small and inefficient, and total housing production rose slowly. In 1948 only 40,000 new dwellings were built; in 1950 the figure was 70,000. Not until 1953 were more than 100,000 units built in a year. The increase in housing construction was rapid after that: more than 200,000 units in 1955, more than 300,000 in 1959, and, finally, more than 400,000 units in 1965. Unfortunately, the rate of increase now has slowed. For 1969 it was estimated that only 425,000 units would be completed, and there is considerable doubt that the 1970 target of 480,000 units will be met. Figure V-10 shows the relationship of housing construction to population growth.

Despite this high volume of construction, as of the 1962 census 84 percent of all dwellings had been built before 1949, 62 percent prior to World War I (see Table V-21).

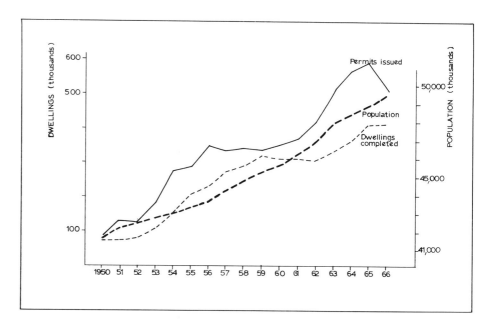

Figure V-10.
Housing
Construction and
Population Growth

In 1964, with 17,096,100 dwelling units, France had 331 units per 1,000 inhabitants. The rate of construction per 1,000 population has risen dramatically—but not sufficiently—since postwar construction began (see Figure V-11). In 1948 only one dwelling unit per 1,000 population was built, while by 1965 and 1966 the rate was 8.4 dwelling units per 1,000. By comparison, in 1963 the rate of construction in the United States was 8.6 per 1,000. See Figure V-12 for a comparison of the types of residential construction undertaken in the two countries.

As in the United States, there is almost no direct government housing construction in France. About one-third of all housing is built by housing associations and cooperatives, mostly under the moderate rent housing program, HLM (see Figure V-13). In 1967 only 22 percent of all dwelling units built did not receive some form of government financial aid (see Table V-22 and Figure V-14). In recent years less than 10 percent of all housing was built without aid.

Table V-21.
Age Distribution of
Principal Residences in 1962

Residences	Number	Percent	
Built before 1871	4,653,931	32.3	
1871–1914	4,294,623	29.8	
1915–39	2,696,589	18.7	
1940–48	430,294	3.0	
1949–51	173,850	1.2	
1952–53	190,344	1.3	
1954–57	760,995	5.3	2,311,981
1958–62	1,159,914	8.1	(16.1%)
Being constructed and partially inhabited	26,878	0.2	
Total	14,387,418	99.9	

NOTE: Figures are based on the 1962 census. Principal residences include ordinary dwellings, rented rooms, and furnished rooms in hotels and rooming houses. At that time, only 16 percent of the housing had been built since World War II.

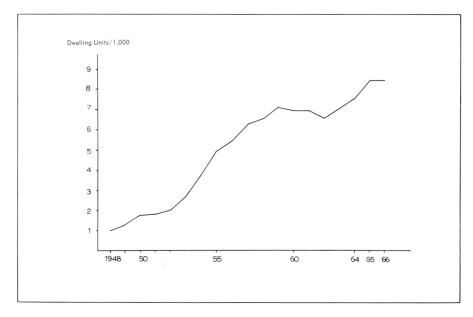

Figure V-11.
Rate of Housing
Construction,
1948–66

Table V-22.
Financial Aid to Housing, 1967

Type of Aid	Number of Dwelling Units
HLM, rental	107,100
HLM, sale	31,100
Subsidized housing, with Credit Foncier loan provisions	121,900
Subsidized housing, without Credit Foncier loan provisions	69,400
Non-subsidized	92,700
Total	422,200

SOURCE: INSEE, *Bulletin Mensuel de Statistique,* n.s., no. 10 (1968).

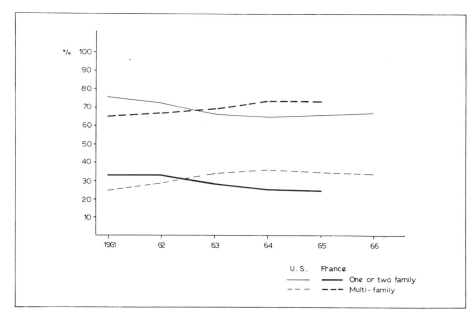

Figure V-12.
Type of Residential
Construction:
France and the
United States

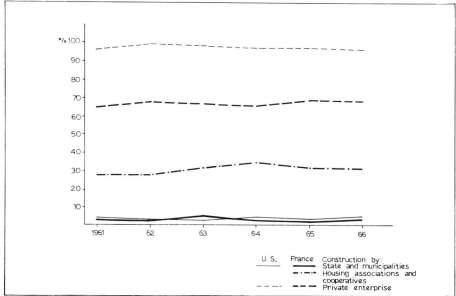

Figure V-13.
Who Builds
Housing: France
and the
United States

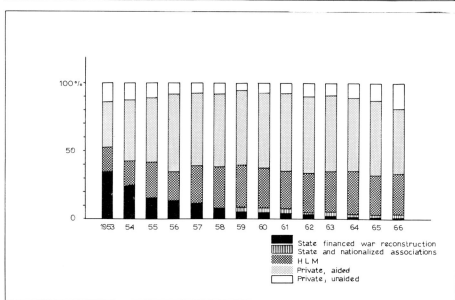

Figure V-14.
Distribution of
Housing
Construction by
Type of Financing

In comparison with the United States, the average French family spends little on housing. This expenditure has shown a radical increase, however, from only 3.7 percent of family income in 1953 to 5.8 percent in 1961, 7.2 percent in 1963, and 13.5 percent in 1967. This comparatively low expenditure is the result of government subsidies and of rent controls on housing built prior to 1948. In addition to direct aid for construction, government subsidies include a housing allowance and a rent allowance. The former is for those eligible for social welfare, the latter for those not covered by social welfare. Rent control has deterred property owners from making needed improvements to older structures. However, it is being removed gradually and already has been lifted from communities where the housing supply is adequate, from the most luxurious housing, and from units with new tenants. In addition, rent increases have been granted at regular intervals for those units still subject to controls; the amount of the increases depends on the level of maintenance required for the units. This lifting of rent controls has contributed to the higher cost of housing, as has the growing stock of new, higher-priced dwelling units.

The cost of residential construction increased somewhat faster than other construction costs between 1953 and 1963. During the same period the ratio of the increase in residential construction prices to the increase in the Gross National Product was 108.6. Land costs ran from 18 percent of the total cost of development in urban areas to 30 percent in low-density residential areas.[46] In the Paris region particularly, the speculation in land has forced new construction of housing for low-income families to take place far from the center city, in outlying communities (see Figure V-15). The rise in land costs has wiped out gains in rates and efficiency of construction.

Housing is crowded, and, despite the high volume of construction in recent years, the situation grew markedly worse between 1954 and 1962, particularly in Paris (see Table V-23). There, 52 percent of all households were crowded or extremely crowded in 1962, while the comparable 1954 figure was only 28 percent. Paris is more than twice as crowded as the rest of France. In 1968, 2.9 million people in the Paris region were living in overcrowded and/or substandard housing.

Table V-23.
Household Crowding, 1954 and 1962[a]

Condition	France 1954	France 1962	Paris Region 1954	Paris Region 1962	Paris 1954	Paris 1962
Extremely undercrowded	10.8%	14.2%	—	7.2%	4.4%	6.1%
Undercrowded	20.7	18.7	—	15.2	16.8	11.7
Normal	39.2	28.4	—	31.5	46.3	29.8
Moderately crowded	12.5	26.0	—	33.9	17.4	40.7
Extremely crowded	13.7	12.7	—	12.2	10.6	11.7

SOURCES: INSEE, Direction Regionale de Paris, Le District de Paris: Structure, Population, Habitat (n.p., n.d.); INSEE, Annuaire Statistique de la France (Paris, 1967).
[a] The index of crowding is calculated by comparing the number of rooms occupied by a household of a given size with the "normal" number of rooms occupied by such a household. The "normal" number of rooms for each household size is determined as follows: (1) one room per couple (legitimate or not); (2) one room for two children from birth to six years of age, whatever their sex; (3) one room for two children from seven to eighteen years old, if they are of the same sex; (4) one room per person, if unmarried, divorced, widowed, or separated from spouse; (5) one room for servants.
    The index is calculated as follows: Extremely undercrowded—The number of rooms exceeds by at least three the "normal" number. Undercrowded—The number of rooms exceeds by two the "normal" number. Normal—The number of rooms exceeds by one the "normal" number. This implies that a normal household should have an extra room; namely, a living room. Moderately crowded—The number of rooms equals the "normal" number. Extremely crowded—The number of rooms is less than the "normal" number.

Figure V-15. Bobigny, Near Le Bourget Airport

The other large cities also are very crowded. As part of the Fifth Plan's policy to encourage growth outside the Paris region, these other urban areas have been granted priority allocations for additional housing construction. To assure that land will be available, the Depository and Consignment Bank (Caisse des Dépots et Consignations) has purchased tracts outside some of the cities.

In 1960, there were 1.04 rooms per person in France, as compared with 1.49 rooms per person in the United States.[47]

As of the 1962 census, 52 percent of all dwelling units had either two or three rooms; 16 percent had five or more rooms (see Table V-24).

Table V-24.
Number of Rooms per Dwelling, 1962

Number of Rooms	Number of Dwelling Units
1	1,675,488
2	3,412,326
3	3,845,745
4	2,748,442
5	1,266,996
6 or more	966,956
Total	13,915,953

SOURCE: INSEE, *Annuaire Statistique de la France* (Paris, 1967).
NOTE: The kitchen is counted as a room only if it measures more than 12 square meters (122 square feet).

During the period of the Fourth Plan the percentage allocation for one-room efficiency dwelling units doubled, while that for two-room units increased modestly. Nonetheless, as seen in Table V-25, more than 60 percent of all residential construction during the Fourth Plan was projected for three- and four-room units.

Residents of urban France have been and continue to be apartment dwellers. Even with many rural residents and many residents of small and medium-sized towns, two-thirds of recent housing construction has been that of apartment buildings (see Figures V-16 through V-19).

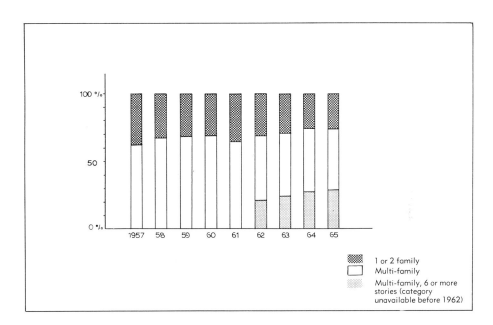

Figure V-16. House and Apartment Construction, 1957–65

Figure V-17. Recent Apartment Development in Marseille: Parc Dromel

Figure V-18. Recent Apartment Development in Marseille: HLM Apartments, La Verdière

Figure V-19. Older Housing, Clermont-Ferrand

Table V-25.
Fourth Plan Authorized Housing
by Number of Rooms

Number of rooms	1961	1962	1963	1964	1965
1	3.7%	4.0%	4.3%	5.3%	6.8%
2	11.3	10.7	10.9	12.4	13.4
3	30.4	29.6	29.5	29.6	28.9
4	35.9	36.9	36.8	35.4	33.5
5	15.3	15.2	15.1	13.8	13.6
6 or more	3.4	3.6	3.4	3.8	3.8

SOURCE: La Documentation Française, "Bilan du IVᵉ Plan," *Notes et Études Documentaires*, no. 3441 (Paris, 1967).

Increasing use is made of various methods of prefabrication (see Table V-26 and Figure V-20). In and around the larger cities, apartment developments (*grands ensembles*) frequently are enormous and include shops, community services, and recreation facilities (see Figures V-21 and V-22).

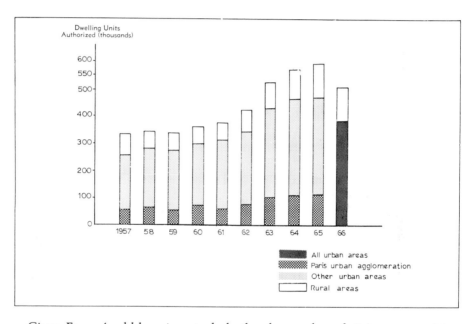

Figure V-20.
Number of
Dwelling Units
Authorized,
1957–66

Given France's old housing stock, both urban and rural, it is not surprising that the distribution of television sets, refrigerators, and washing machines has outstripped the installation of more basic comforts such as bathrooms, running water, or central heat. The enormity of the gap, however, is astonishing. In 1967, 26 percent of all dwelling units had no running water and 89 percent lacked central heat (see Table V-27). Conditions were notably better in Paris, where electricity, gas, and running water were virtually universal. Even there, however, 66 percent of the homes lacked central heat.

Millions live in units without bathrooms. Millions who have running water in their homes still use the kitchen sink in lieu of a washbasin and must rely on public baths. More than one-quarter of all families use toilet facilities "other" than inside or outside toilets belonging to the dwelling unit! These figures, listed in Table V-28, give immediacy to the statement that France is far from meeting its housing problem and must allocate far more of the national budget to this end in order to overcome the enormous backlog of inadequate housing.

Figure V-21. *Grand Ensemble*: Fontenay aux Roses

Figure V-22. *Grand Ensemble*: Marly les Grandes Terres

Table V-26.
Type of Residential Construction Authorized, 1967

Type of Construction	Number of Dwelling Units	Percentage of Dwelling Units
Houses	159,700	35
Apartments	285,000	60
Buildings whose principal use is not housing	4,100	1
Additions to existing dwelling units	17,400	4
Total	466,200	100

SOURCE: INSEE, *Bulletin Mensuel de Statistique*, n.s., no. 10 (1968).

Table V-27.
Basic Household Conveniences, 1967

Convenience	France Number of Dwelling Units	%	Paris Region Number of Dwelling Units	%	Paris Number of Dwelling Units	%
Public water supply	6,871,720	66	931,294	93	81,313	99
Private water supply	803,722	8	14,217	1	199	—
Public gas	2,595,490	25	611,733	60	80,565	98
Electricity	10,098,559	96	988,123	97	81,962	99
Central heating (apts.)	186,077	11	69,051	37	22,169	34
Central heating (houses)	1,060,268		306,677		5,704	
Total	10,465,390		1,024,631		82,949	

SOURCE: INSEE, *Annuaire Statistique de la France* (Paris, 1967).

Government Control of Production

A combination of factors led France to nationalize or take control of a number of enterprises prior to and following World War II. Today the government owns or controls public transportation (air, rail, and ship), communications media (mail, telegraph, radio, and television), fuel (coal, gas, and electricity), and much of the financial community.

Between World Wars I and II France had some experience with combined public and private ownership of corporations (*sociétés d'économie mixte*). During the depression several large enterprises, including France's principal steamship company, the Compagnie Générale Transatlantique, turned to the government for financial aid. In return for money, these enterprises issued stock to the state, although the state usually did not receive majority control. During this era the state also joined in founding the public-private Compagnie Nationale du Rhône to develop and market the hydroelectric potential of the Rhône. The state guaranteed loans to the company and granted it the Rhône development concession in return for two-fifths of the seats on the company's board of directors. Others—several departments and municipalities, the city of Paris, a railroad, corporations, and individuals—held the company's stock and the other seats on its board.

Table V-28.
Bathroom Facilities, 1967

Facility	Number		Percent
Toilet			
Inside toilet	5,894,894		40.5
Outside toilet belonging to household	4,553,559		31.3
Other arrangements	3,868,589		26.5
No reply	248,127		1.7
Total	14,565,169		100.0
Bath, Shower, Sink			
Bath or shower	4,211,544		28.9
No bath or shower, but washbasin	842,686		5.8
No bath, shower, or washbasin	8,833,006		60.6
No running water in dwelling unit		5,800,742	
No running water in same building		237,629	
No reply	677,933		4.7
Total	14,565,169		100.0

SOURCE: INSEE, *Annuaire Statistique de la France* (Paris, 1967).

When the left-wing Popular Front won control of the government in 1936, the government moved to assume majority control of companies in which it already held a majority interest, as well as of additional enterprises. The railroad—Société Nationale des Chemins de Fer—is an example of the former; munitions industries and airplane producers are instances of the latter.

During World War II it was widely thought that a number of large manufacturers cooperated too willingly with the Germans and should be punished by having their companies nationalized. In addition, there was general agreement that higher wages, more representation of the labor viewpoint, and lower prices would result from nationalization of the means of production. Backed overwhelmingly by popular opinion, in 1944–46 the government decided by separate votes of approximately ten to one to nationalize coal production, a majority of insurance companies, the Bank of France and the four largest depository banks, and the Renault automobile company. The objective was to remove control from private entrepreneurs, but, because the public had considerable doubts about the efficiency of government management, the nationalization laws provided that the companies should be managed by government employees under the control of tripartite boards of directors. The government, labor, and consumers were to have equal representation on the boards. This concept did not work as planned. Politics dominated the choice of labor and consumer members (the Communist labor unions often were able to dictate the selection of both), while management decisions increasingly were made by the government. Later, in 1953, the government proposed to add industry as a fourth group on the boards, but socialist members of the National Assembly were able to defeat the proposal.

The preamble to the 1946 constitution stated that "... every good, every enterprise, whose use has or acquires the characteristics of a national public service or of a *de facto* monopoly must become the property of the community." Yet, after 1946 there were no further nationalizations. Instead, the government turned back to acquiring majority control of mixed companies. It was during this period that the shipping companies and Air France came under majority control of the state.

As of December, 1969, the government had endorsed and submitted to the National Assembly a bill which would distribute to employees a percentage of the stock in the nationalized auto and aircraft companies. Renault, with 80,000 employees, would be first to participate. Initially, 10 percent of the company's stock would be distributed, and a maximum distribution of 25 percent might be achieved. Workers' allocations would be made in relation to job and seniority. The stock could not be traded on the market and could be resold only to a company fund.

Government control provides powerful leverage over investment and production. For example, the national Depository and Consignment Bank requires private savings banks and the National Savings Fund (Caisse Nationale d Epargne) to transfer 50 percent of their deposits to it in return for a guaranteed interest of 5 percent. It also receives transfers from the local Savings Banks (Caisses d'Épargne et de Prévoyance) of each department. The Depository and Consignment Bank then places its funds in the Treasury or invests in government-backed enterprises. It was established in 1848 and today is the largest holder of funds in France. Annually it lends $2 billion. It is the major source of funds for plan implementation.

Government control has meant larger and larger government expenditures. Warren Baum notes that government expenditures increased 4,000 times, in constant francs, between 1815 and 1954, and points out that "critics of state intervention relish the opportunity to point out that the government now spends more in a day than it did in an entire year before the first world war."[48] In 1952–53, however, national government expenditures as a percentage of Gross National Product were comparable in France and several other West European countries: France, 30 percent; the United Kingdom, 32.3 percent; and Benelux, 26.8 percent. That same year the figure was 21.1 percent in the United States and 14.5 percent in Denmark.[49]

One of the reasons for a government takeover was the hope of achieving lower prices through more efficient production. This goal has not been achieved. Productivity per worker has lagged far behind that in the United States and also is markedly lower when compared with the other countries of Western Europe.

Planning Organization, Finance, and Powers

Planning is new in France, being largely a post–World War II innovation. It has, however, been adopted with a vengeance. In addition to the Fifth (Economic) Plan, there is a national land-use plan. Economic and land-use plans have been regionalized. Local governments were the last to enter into planning, but pressure from the national government may well serve as the catalyst for local government planning and land-use reforms.

The long-term cleavage between the physical planners and the economic planners is narrowing, and rivalries between graduates of the different *grands écoles* are diminishing somewhat. On the physical side, the past dominance of the engineering graduates of the Corps of Ponts et Chaussees continues, although there now is some dilution of this control through the addition of architects and a sprinkling of geographers, demographers, sociologists, and planners to planning staffs. The engineers, however, remain in charge. The public administrators from the École Nationale d'Administration (National Administration School) and economists of the five-year plan teams are attaining a high degree of sophistication and specialization in regional science and econometrics and are broadening their concern to include land development. In both groups the interdependence of their foci has come to be understood more clearly. In addition, the administrative structure has been altered to provide more overlapping of committee membership so that the nature of problems and approaches to their solutions are seen from the viewpoints of both groups.

In France, there is an unusually close relationship between planning, development programs, and development financing. The relationship also is extraordinarily intricate. In addition to the customary direct ministry funding of development for purposes within the purview of a ministry, finance agencies independent of that ministry, or under the Ministry of Finance, play a major role. The interlocking directorates of these agencies are a reflection of their interrelated functions. Representatives of many of the planning agencies and of ministries charged with development responsibilities sit on the directorates of many of these finance agencies. Similarly, finance agency staff members sit on planning agency boards. Projects are funded in accordance with national planning objectives. Local projects receive no national funds unless the local plans have been approved. While the system is inordinately complex, it may be the best extant operative national program for stating goals and priorities, refining goals into action programs, and channeling funds to programs.

Planning Organization

The administrative organization for planning alone is exceedingly complex and has undergone frequent modification. As of 1969 it took the form shown in Chart V-1, which includes only the major agencies and committees.

Having stated that there is increasing correspondence between physical and economic planning, the dichotomy remains distinct enough so that some agencies or committees serve only one of the two planning functions. Often the structure has been modified so that, for instance, a committee which initially had solely an economic role now has both. To avoid some confusion, much of the past history of planning organization in France has been omitted here, and the focus is on the current functions of the groups shown in Chart V-1.

National Planning

The reasons for, and the nature of, postwar economic planning in France have been described. The General Planning Commission was created in 1946, and responsibility for national economic planning was lodged there. At this time it was recognized that environmental planning[50] would be an essential companion to economic planning.

In the early postwar years, however, it was necessary to equate environmental planning with the programming of clearance, rehabilitation, and reconstruction. These tasks were carried out by the appropriate ministries, with the major burden falling on the then Ministry of Reconstruction and Housing. By 1950 the ministry's spokesman was able to redefine the task of environmental planning more broadly as

... the geographic expression of the country's economic and social policy, and it can be defined as the voluntary redistribution of agriculture, industry and services for a better use of the nation's space, people and reserves.

... the search for a better distribution of the population on the basis of resources and activities—a search made not only for economic purposes, but even more for the well-being and full development of all.[51]

Environmental planning was to regulate the physical manifestations of economic objectives. As economic policies stimulated growth of some areas at the expense of others, new construction of infrastructure, buildings, and transportation would be needed. Communications and services would require reorganization. The scale of this planning was necessarily national, although implementation might be regional or local. Responsibility for preparing national environment plans was lodged initially in the Ministry of Reconstruction and Housing, a ministry then dominated by technicians. A bureau for environmental planning was created within the ministry, but it lacked sufficient power to coordinate related programs of other ministries with its plans. In addition, the ministry was far removed from the thinking of the local governments, the regions, and the economists of the General Planning Commission. Despite these problems of coordination, in 1950 the ministry proceeded to prepare a national environmental plan for the next twenty years. The plan proposed government initiatives to restrict the influx to Paris and some other rapidly growing areas and to stimulate the growth of underdeveloped areas. This has been a constant theme of economic and environmental plans.

At about the same time, regionalization of economic planning was initiated. Long before the final official designation of the regions in 1960, private groups—businessmen, labor leaders, chambers of commerce—recognized the need to plan for economic development on a regional scale. Regional economic expansion committees were formed, privately and voluntarily, to work with the General Planning Commission. In 1954 these committees were given official recognition by the government, and they have served in an advisory capacity ever since. Their role assumed greater importance when in 1955 the General Planning Commission approached the task of translating national economic plans into regional goals and allocations.

CHART V-1.
ORGANIZATION FOR PLANNING

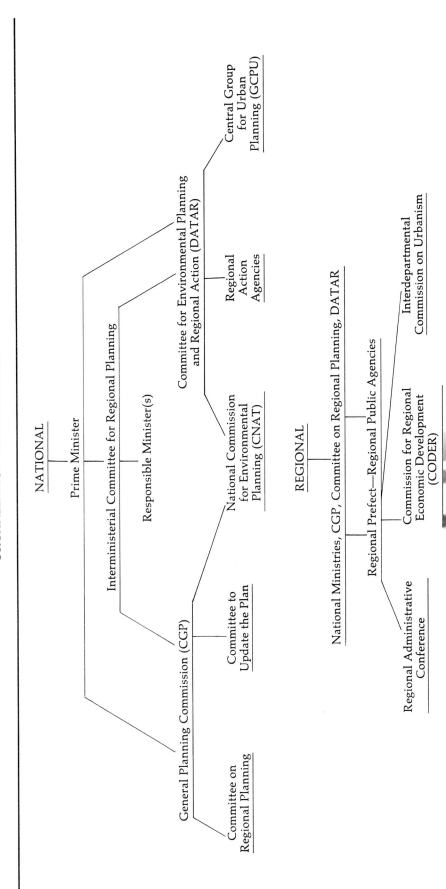

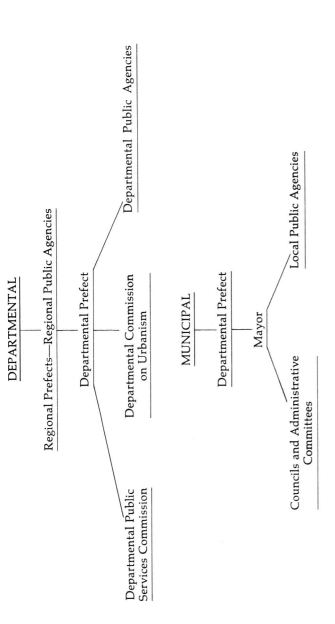

DEPARTMENTAL

Regional Prefects—Regional Public Agencies

Departmental Prefect

Departmental Public Agencies

Departmental Commission
on Urbanism

Departmental Public
Services Commission

MUNICIPAL

Departmental Prefect

Mayor

Local Public Agencies

Councils and Administrative
Committees

By 1958 it was recognized that the coordination of environmental planning with economic planning and with the implementing agencies was inadequate. Organizational changes were instituted then which led to the current planning structure.

The Interministerial Committee for Regional Planning was created in 1960. It is chaired by the prime minister and includes all ministers responsible for some aspect of regional planning and development, including, of course, the ministers of finance, public works and housing,[52] interior, and agriculture. Its chief executive under the present structure also is the chairman of DATAR. The role of the Interministerial Committee is to review all general problems of regional planning and development in order to prepare statements of the government's position on these problems. It is, therefore, the highest policy-making body on regional planning matters.

Until 1963 the General Planning Commission continued to have direct responsibility for national economic planning, while the High Council of the then Ministry of Construction remained responsible for environmental planning. Then, to achieve better coordination and to place environmental planning in a more broadly constituted setting, two new organizations were created. They were the National Commission for Environmental Planning (CNAT), and the Committee for Environmental Planning and Regional Action (DATAR).

The General Planning Commission has approximately forty members, including representatives of all concerned ministries. Among the skills represented on the commission are agronomy, engineering, law, economics, public administration, and geography. Its staff numbers about 150, augmented by the services of thousands of persons who belong to committees and subcommittees for the preparation and revision of commission plans. The commissioner-general is appointed by and answerable to the prime minister. He, by law, is "... the permanent delegate of the prime minister to the ministerial departments for all aspects of the preparation of the plan."[53] The commission serves as the chief conceptual agency for economic and environmental planning. With its earlier history of economic planning, it has greater strength in the economic sphere and remains responsible for preparation of the five-year plans for submission to the Interministerial Committee and then to the National Assembly.

There are three principal subagencies of the General Planning Commission: the Committee on Regional Planning, the Committee to Update the Plan, and the CNAT. The Committee on Regional Planning consists of the commissioner-general as chairman, the director of environmental planning (CNAT), representatives of concerned ministries and of the Economic and Social Development Fund (FDES), and others. Its responsibility is the proposal and coordination of economic and environmental plans at the regional level. When plan regionalization was initiated under the Third Plan, it did not cover the nation. In addition, the Committee on Regional Planning acted solely as a national body, with neither official nor advisory groups in the regions to offer their advice. By 1962, regionalization of the plan was nationwide, and regional groups were participating.[54] In 1964, further organizational changes were made to strengthen the role of the regions. As of now, in the planning process, the staff of the Committee on Regional Planning prepares draft plans for each region. It takes nationally established goals and proposed allocations of funds and subdivides them regionally, recommending the distribution of national funds by region and by sector (construction, agriculture, communications, etc.). Through the regional prefect these draft plans are submitted to the regions, specifically to three regional groups for their advice and recommendations. The three groups are the Regional Administrative Conference, the Commission for Regional Economic Development (CODER), and the Regional Economic Expansion Committee.

The Regional Administrative Conference, whose members are the regional prefect, the departmental prefects, and state civil servants working at the regional level (including an inspector from the Treasury), is responsible for making planning recommendations, particularly with regard to the allocation of funds to the region, and for implementing the regional plan once it has been officially adopted. It is particularly notable that the regional prefect must follow the recommendations of the Treasury inspector regarding the financial soundness of proposals.[55]

CODER was set up in 1964. It is an official advisory body of from twenty to fifty members, one-quarter of whom are local elected officials, one-half of whom are representatives of industrial, commercial, and labor organizations, and the remainder of whom are selected by the prime minister for their technical skills. The chairman of the Regional Economic Expansion Committee is a member of CODER. CODER advises on the economic, social, and locational implications of the regional plan's proposals and participates in translating plan goals into programs.

In 1964 CODER assumed many of the functions that had been exercised since 1960 by the unofficial Regional Economic Expansion committees. The committees remain useful as groups which voluntarily undertake research studies on current and prospective economic development for the region, but their future role is not certain.

Returning to the national level, the Committee to Update the Plan is actually a group of ad hoc committees, appointed anew for the preparation of each five-year plan. The committee's members are representatives of government, management, and labor, and are named by the prime minister on the advice of the commissioner-general; theoretically, they serve as qualified individuals rather than as representatives of particular organizations or interest groups. For the Fourth Plan there were twenty-seven committees, each with from thirty to fifty members and numerous additional volunteer staff members, and for the Fifth Plan there were even more. Twenty-two of the twenty-seven committees were sector groups, one each for fisheries, urban infrastructure, housing, etc. The remaining five were multi-purpose: "general economic and financial aspects; manpower; productivity; research; and regional planning."[56]

After the committees are given preliminary, general forecasts and growth rate targets for the forthcoming plan, they subdivide into sectoral units and refine the forecasts, in light of their knowledge of conditions in their subsector, into forecasts for production, labor utilization, prices, investment required, consumption, etc., for the subsector. When these forecasts have been assembled, the five multi-purpose commissions review them for inconsistencies, and then they are given to the General Planning Commission for final synthesis. Following this, the regional plan goes to the Interministerial Committee for approval and then to the National Assembly for debate on policy and adoption as law.

The third agency of the General Planning Commission, the National Commission for Environmental Planning (CNAT), is France's principal body for environmental planning. CNAT provides detailed and long-term (twenty-year) environmental planning and is responsible for integrating this planning into economic plans by region. It has seventy-seven members, twenty-seven of whom are ex officio representatives of the ministries and financial agencies, and fifty of whom are drawn from all socioeconomic sectors, including union members, industrialists, and professors. The director of DATAR is a vice-chairman of CNAT.[57] CNAT's staff consists of about 170 persons who are divided among six sectors. Its input to the Fifth Plan was prepared in consultation with the regions and somewhat resembles the operation of the Committee to Regionalize the Plan.

DATAR, created at the same time as CNAT, is directly under the prime minister. Some of its tasks are difficult to distinguish from those of CNAT: their directorates overlap considerably, and their staff chiefs serve together as directors of many other commissions, committees, and agencies from the Interministerial Committee on down. DATAR's governing board consists of twenty-seven designees of ministries and other groups, including CNAT. Whereas CNAT is charged with the conceptualization of environmental plans and with relating these plans to economic plans, DATAR's principal functions are to coordinate planning, which includes carrying out interministerial arbitration, to oversee plan implementation, and, on occasion, to undertake implementation. DATAR advises CNAT in its role of conceptualization. As an overseer and coordinator, DATAR arbitrates disputes over funding to the regions and is responsible for seeing that budget allocations accord with environmental planning goals.

Because DATAR is directly under the prime minister, it can exercise greater power over coordination than its predecessor bureau in the Ministry of Construction. DATAR acts as staff for the Interministerial Committee, preparing position papers on questions of environmental planning and regional development, and then is responsible for seeing that the decisions of the Interministerial Committee are carried out. DATAR initiates administrative reforms for more efficient regional action, and is responsible for communicating regional concerns to the General Planning Commission. As previously noted, its director is executive officer of the General Planning Commission and vice-chairman of the Committee on Regional Planning.

DATAR now houses several units transferred from other agencies, such as a water resource group transferred from the Ministry of the Interior, the industrial decentralization activities formerly carried out by the Interministerial Committee, and several interministerial regional development agencies, including those for Languedoc-Roussillon and the Gulf of Fos. It is also the home of the Central Group for Urban Planning (GCPU), created in 1965 specifically to oversee planning in nine large urban areas, including Paris. The GCPU consists of representatives of the Ministries of the Interior, Finance, and Public Works and Housing. Its decisions concerning such questions as a transportation network for Lyon–Saint-Étienne or industrial development for Lille-Roubaix will override local government wishes. As part of its role in regionalizing the national budget, DATAR directs the Action Fund for Environmental Planning (FIAT), and DATAR's director participates in the management of the National Fund for Land Management and Urban Planning (FNAFU).[58]

All in all, DATAR is intended to be a small, responsive, and multi-faceted agency, able to take the initiative for new programs and to offer creative leadership. It advises the government on where development should occur, while the General Planning Commission advises what development should occur and when. In effect, DATAR also is the home of national capital programming for the regions.[59]

The regional planning structure and its relationship to the national planning structure already have been described. The regional planning process is designed so that the regions and the state each will evolve development objectives, re-evaluate these objectives in light of the others' objectives, and then agree on long-term and five-year national plans incorporating regional goals and allocations. Reality, to date, falls somewhat short of this planning concept.

The long-standing centralization of decision-making in Paris and bureau-cratic rigidity remain barriers to the development of coordinated, effective regional planning and implementation. The role of the regional prefect must be strengthened vis-à-vis both the departmental prefects and the civil serv-ants of the national ministries. It has been recommended by the Commission for Regional Economic Development that the regional prefects no longer serve also as departmental prefects. In addition, it has been suggested that the ministries establish decentralized regional offices, whose staffs would answer to the regional prefects.[60] These steps, as well as real control over expenditures in the regions, are essential if France is going to convert the form of her regional planning into substance.

Departmental planning is similar in organization to regional planning but is of far less importance in relation to national planning. Many former plan-ning functions of the departments have been assumed by the regions.

Local Planning

While local planning can be traced back to postwar reconstruction in 1919, it is a recent phenomenon for most French municipalities. Under the Planning Law of 1967, all municipalities of more than 10,000 people must draw up comprehensive plans and district plans by 1972. Planning may be carried out by a single commune or by the urban communities created in 1967 for some of the larger metropolitan areas. Bordeaux, Lille, Strasbourg, and Lyon all have been ordered to plan as urban communities.

The comprehensive plans usually are prepared by Groupes d'Études et de Programmation (GEPs), located in the departmental prefect's office. Only a few of the larger cities have their own planning staffs.

After being available for inspection for three months, the plan is sub-jected to a public hearing. It then is either approved or disapproved by the municipal council. If the council rejects the plan and the prefect wishes it approved, or if 25 percent of the population disapproves it, the plan is sub-mitted to the Council of State for its decision.

The district plan, a detailed land-use plan specifying zoning districts and densities, undergoes similar procedures except that an appeal may not be taken to the Council of State unless the municipality has a population of 50,000. Once approved, the district plan is binding. Its provisions, such as those fixing permitted uses or building density, are applicable without pay-ment of any compensation. Building permits may be issued only for pro-posals that accord with the plan.

Priority Zones for Urbanization (ZUPs)[61] and Deferred Development Zones (ZADs) are the principal local land-use controls for the implementa-tion of local plans. Both are municipally initiated. Approval is obtained at the national level, unless the ZUP or ZAD provides for fewer than 10,000 dwelling units; in that case, approval comes from the departmental prefect.

ZUPs, which date from 1958,[62] are areas designated in the plan for priority development. Once a ZUP has been approved by the Ministry of Public Works and Housing, and its financing has been approved by the appropriate national agencies, national funding for land acquisition and for the national goverment's contribution to streets (30–50 percent), sewerage (40 percent), and water supply (25 percent) is directed there and is refused to non-designated areas. Intensive development occurs only in the ZUPs, which must be large enough to accommodate 500 dwelling units but which may be large enough for several hundred thousand dwelling units.[63] Development occurs under the aegis of a single agency—the municipality, a public-private development company, or an HLM company. Within a ZUP, the municipality may pre-empt development for four years and then extend the pre-emption period for another two years.[64] If the municipality fails to exercise this right, the state may. Whenever an owner wishes to sell, he must give the municipality, or its designee as developer of the ZUP, the first right of refusal at the price of the land one year prior to ZUP approval. The municipality also may expropriate, at the same price.

The purpose of the ZUPs is to make possible the building of entire neighborhoods, districts, or new towns by carefully synchronizing the stages of development and financing in advance. By developing on a large scale with all aspects planned, it is possible to make more efficient use of the nation's development resources. By pre-dating the acquisition price to one year before designation, speculation and its concomitant, high land prices, are lessened. By postponing payment for up to four years after designation, government financial resources are husbanded. By acquiring large tracts of land in advance of development, the best planning and design results can be achieved.[65] As Roger Macé, former director of land development and urbanism for the Ministry of Construction, has said: "[The ZUP and ZAD] make it possible to reconcile two apparently opposite objectives: the creation of land reserves and the lack of financial resources for immediate land acquisition."[66]

A ZUP's powers are extensive. Development elsewhere may be forbidden if a satisfactory infrastructure does not already exist. Alternatively, a municipality may charge some $600 per dwelling unit in order to finance the building of infrastructure.

In the mid-1960s, enough land—65,000 acres—had been designated as ZUPs to meet France's total construction needs for two years. At that time, 45 percent of the ZUP lands had been acquired by public agencies. Designation and acquisition have moved slowly, for reasons which will be familiar to all American planners: (1) center-city land has been used up and suburban municipalities do not want the burdens and costs of development; (2) landowners fight ZUPs because of their loss of the opportunity for land speculation; and (3) the national government failed to allocate enough money to acquire land for 100,000 dwelling units per year.

... The fundamental cause of opposition is the indifference and even the hostility of small municipalities to undertakings whose first effect would be to overturn the life style of the present inhabitants and to impose on them, for the benefit of the newcomers, additional taxes. Two solutions suggest themselves: further government control and financial aid or revision of municipal boundaries. While preferring the former, local elected officials still would insist on defending local self-government against the expanding reach of central control.[67]

ZADs, which date from 1962,[68] are designed to forestall immediate development and halt speculation in land intended for middle-range development. Once designated, the municipality may pre-empt an eight-year option on all land within the ZAD at the value of the land one year prior to the time of pre-emption. Later, if the ZAD becomes a ZUP, the pre-emption period can be extended four more years for a total of twelve years. An owner may sell the land at this fixed price, subject to the option, or he may demand that the municipality exercise its pre-emption right within two years of designation. If the municipality exercises its option, it pays the fixed price corrected for any inflation but without interest. About 250 square miles of land around Paris have been designated ZADs.

Concerted Development Zones (ZACs) are another local planning tool, but they are less widely used than ZUPs and ZADs. These zones are designated after a private group has proposed and gained approval for a plan for intensive development.

Financing the Plan

It is arbitrary and artificial to separate planning from the financing of plans, particularly because the synthesis of these two phases is a major achievement of French planning. It has been emphasized, however, that public funds are allocated in accordance with plans and that there are complex interrelationships between the planning and financing agencies. Chart V-2 provides a simplified outline of the financing agencies; it should be studied with reference to Chart V-1, which outlines the planning structure. Because there are myriad cross-connections between the two structures, the charts cannot, and so do not attempt to, show these linkages. The principal fact is that the financing agencies play a major policy role in plan implementation.

CHART V-2.
ORGANIZATIONS INVOLVED IN FINANCING PLANS

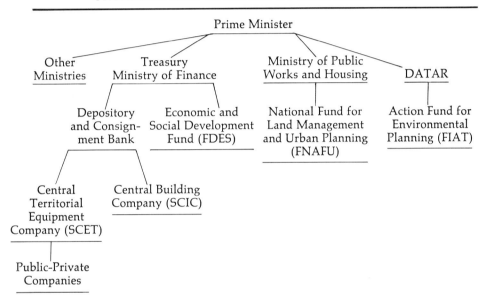

While each ministry has funds for implementing those aspects of plans which fall within its scope, there are in addition four national funding agencies of paramount significance in financing development. They are: the Depository and Consignment Bank and its subsidiaries, the Central Territorial Equipment Company (SCET) and Central Building Company (SCIC); the Economic and Social Development Fund (FDES); the National Fund for Land Management and Urban Planning (FNAFU); and the Action Fund for Environmental Planning (FIAT).

The national Depository and Consignment Bank, whose origin and role have been discussed previously, is headed by a director named by the prime minister on the advice of a committee whose members are half public, half private.

Established in 1955, SCET is a public-private corporation in which 52 percent of the stock is owned by the Depository and Consignment Bank. The bank directs about 45 percent of its annual investment funds to SCET, which employs them to finance local government or departmental public construction or construction by mixed public-private enterprises. Short-term loans are granted for regional infrastructure, industries, farm improvements, and housing. The SCET Board includes the deputy director of the General Planning Commission and directors of FNAFU, the Central Bank for Economic Cooperation, and the Treasury.

SCET takes the initiative in organizing regional and local public-private companies. By law, these companies must receive at least 51 percent, but not more than 65 percent, of their capitalization from public sources. The municipality, the department, HLMs, the chamber of commerce, local builders—all may subscribe to stock in the company. The companies frequently are chaired by a local mayor and employ a director and small staff. Expert advice is provided by SCET, which charges the company for its services. Under its guidance, the company will prepare a plan—possibly for the construction of a ZUP, a highway, or an industrial park. When the plan and the detailed financial prospectus have been approved, the company will contract to buy the land and carry out the construction. SCET then will loan funds for a six-year period, and, during the first three years, only interest will be due.[69] FNAFU also may lend funds for the same operation.

SCET participates in development undertaken by large regional corporations, such as the National Development Company for the Lower Rhône–Languedoc and the Provence Canal Company, and in development overseas, in the Sahara and in several former French colonies.

SCIC receives about 35 percent of the Depository and Consignment Bank's annual investment funds. It was created in 1954 in a reorganization of the bank's housing construction program. SCIC serves local building organizations and in its first eight years was responsible for the construction of 50,000 dwellings. Most were near Paris, in *grands ensembles* offering shopping and social services as well as housing to working-class families. Others were near existing cities urgently in need of new housing. The communities of Mourenx-Le-Neuf, Firminy-Vert, and Épinal are pictured in Figures V-23, V-24, V-25, and V-26.

FDES was created in 1955.[70] It is funded directly by the Treasury and by capital and interest payments on its loans. It has $600 million in capital funds.

FDES is managed by the minister of finance, and its board is drawn from the Treasury, other ministries, principal banks, the Depository and Consignment Bank, the General Planning Commission, and DATAR. It has two roles. In one it operates somewhat like SCET: it provides technical assistance and loans but does not itself undertake construction. For instance, it may carry out the financial planning for ZUPs. It loans money on behalf of the Treasury to public agencies for infrastructure, and to public or private concerns for specified purposes including modernization, conversion, job retraining, and decentralization. The terms of its loans are thirty-three years at 4.5 percent. FDES's other role, presided over by the director of the Depository and Consignment Bank, is to act as the government's principal financial mechanism for regional development. In this phase of its operation, FDES is responsible for translating plan directives into detailed financial programs and for advising the Treasury on priorities for funding development. It then makes loans and grants for regional development, in accordance with its financial recommendations. FDES loans and grants are reviewed by the Court of Accounts (Cour des Comptes) for their conformity with the plan adopted by the government.

Between 1957 and 1964, requests received by FDES for funds for the implementation of aspects of regional plans totaled 2,133. As seen in Table V-29, about two-thirds of these were approved. During this period, grants for the implementation of regional plans totaled 403 million francs, while loans totaled 324 million francs.[71] Firms receiving FDES funds also may be eligible for transfer-tax reductions, building-license reductions or exemptions, and accelerated depreciation. While FDES support has been granted in accordance with the Fifth Plan's policy for strengthening less-developed re-

Figure V-23. Mourenx-Le-Neuf, in the Department of Basses-Pyrénées, was funded through SCI and has 2,882 dwelling units.

Figure V-24. Firminy-Vert, nine miles from the industrial city of Saint-Étienne, was sponsored by the HLM office of Firminy and has 1,070 dwelling units.

Figure V-25. Firminy-Vert

Figure V-26. Épinal

gions, it has been stated that FDES assistance is no match for the external economies offered by Paris and other major metropolitan areas.[72]

Table V-29.
Loan and Grant Requests
for Regional Development

	1957	1958	1959	1960	1961	1962	1963	1964	Total
Requests received	300	183	269	297	356	264	230	234	2,133
Requests approved	127	107	152	229	259	202	174	210	1,460

SOURCE: Niles M. Hansen, *French Regional Planning* (Bloomington: Indiana University Press, 1968).

FNAFU[73] is another Treasury account. Its board includes representatives of several ministries and the director of DAFU (the Directorate of Land Development and Town Planning), an agency within the Ministry of Public Works and Housing. FNAFU makes grants and loans at 2.5 percent for two years, which are renewable for two additional years. On the approval of FDES, the funds go to local communities and public-private companies to acquire land for ZUPs, ZACs, and industrial zones. For infrastructure, communities may receive grants of 25 percent from FNAFU. FNAFU also may invest directly in top priority projects. It has been a contributor in the development of more than 100 industrial zones, covering some 10,000 acres.[74]

FIAT, the financial arm of DATAR, was established in 1963. It is modestly capitalized (at $42 million in 1968)[75] by the Treasury because it is charged only with providing seed money, in the form of loans or grants, for investments that later will be completed by the appropriate ministries. Its investments are proposed by the director of DATAR and approved by the Interministerial Committee for Environmental Planning. Its importance lies in its ability to overcome interagency red tape and to get needed national projects underway. The initial investment at Languedoc-Roussillon came from FIAT, as did that for the aerospace industry at Toulouse and the telecommunications center at Rennes. FIAT funds may be used to buy land, pay for infrastructure, or even to pay industries' moving expenses.

Housing Finance

Housing finance is a separate sphere and a crucial one for the realization of one of the more difficult goals of the current plan. There is a fourfold provision for government financial aid to housing. Two programs—loans and guarantees—assist construction; two—mortgage subsidies and personal subsidies—assist the occupant. In addition to these programs, indirect aid may be given to builders in the form of tax relief.

Some government loans are available only for the HLM program while some are available for all housing construction, including HLM. All HLM companies are non-profit-making and may be organized by a department or municipality to build rental housing, as a cooperative to build either rental or sale housing, or as a building credit company to pass on government loans for housing purchases. The state offers HLM companies long-term low-interest loans. Each year the budget fixes the sum to be granted to HLM companies. Then the Interministerial Committee advises the Ministry of Public Works and Housing on their allocation. The funds are drawn from the Treasury or from the Depository and Consignment Bank. The percentage of government funding varies from 75 to 90 percent of the principal sum, although the companies' obligation to contribute funds is legally fixed at 15 percent.

Loans for rental housing are for HLM, ILN (Normal Rent Housing), and PSR (Social Rehousing Program) construction. HLM construction must meet size, construction, equipment, and cost standards fixed by the government. ILN must meet the minimum construction and equipment standards for HLM, while construction costs may run 20 percent above the HLM maximum; there are no size limitations. PSR size, construction, and equipment standards are the same as those for HLM, while costs cannot exceed the loan plus 20 percent. The principal sum of the loan as a percentage of construction costs is the same for all three programs; it is fixed by law at a maximum percentage of the construction price, which varies only with the number of rooms and geographic location. The terms and interest rates in 1968 were as follows:

Rental Units	Interest	Term
HLM	1%	45 years
ILN	5	30
PSR	0	53 (no principal payment during first three years)

Two additional programs were instituted in 1968, PLR (Reduced Rent Program) and ILM (Middle Rent Housing). In 1969, 21,000 dwelling units were built under PLR, 6,000 dwelling units under ILM.

Funds for sale housing are provided by the government through construction loans from the Depository and Consignment Bank to building loan companies and then to individuals building housing for their own occupancy, or through loans to HLM cooperatives building for sale. The Depository and Consignment Bank is reimbursed by the Treasury for the difference between its interest rate and the going market rate. The families to be housed must be of modest income, while the housing must meet HLM construction and technical standards and may not exceed HLM rental construction costs by more than 30 percent. The principal sum is slightly less than that for the rental programs and also varies according to the number of rooms and geographic location. Currently, the loan is for a maximum of twenty-five years at 4.15 percent.

An alternative to the government loan is a private loan with the interest subsidized by the government. The government sets maxima for computing the principal sums and interests eligible for subsidy.

The government offers construction subsidies to those not eligible under other programs who wish to build housing that meets standards similar to those of HLM. The subsidy amount varies according to the size of the dwelling units and whether the principal sum is to be payable by the builder over ten or twenty years. Alternatively, and under certain circumstances, the builder's subsidy may be converted to an interest rate subsidy.

Those eligible for the interest rate subsidy are eligible for a government guarantee of their loan. The guarantee covers two loans: the middle-term credit of the Contractors Bank (Sous-Comptoir des Entrepreneurs) and the long-term mortgage of the Mortgage Loan Land Bank of France (Crédit Foncier de France). The term and rate of the guaranteed mortgage loan vary with sale and rental housing and with the size and location of the dwelling unit. Under this program the amount of the developer's profit is limited. The guarantee may be refused if the land price is judged to be excessive.[76]

The builder of housing has several sources for the remainder of his financing. An individual wishing to build may open an account in a savings bank and subsequently withdraw his savings and receive a bank loan, the amount of which is determined by the amount of his savings. The builder may receive funds from industries. All industries employing more than ten people are required to establish a housing fund for their employees equal to 1 percent of all salaries paid the preceding year. Family allowance funds, supported by social security and employee contributions, may lend at low interest for land acquisition or construction. Municipalities may offer subsidies, credit guarantees, loans, and/or land for housing construction.

Subsidies are also granted to the family, rather than to the dwelling unit. Young couples and large families meeting specified conditions for income and housing are eligible for subsidies ranging from 45 to 85 percent of their rent to cover the difference between the rent charged and the "correct" rent for their status. The very poor and the elderly are eligible for subsidies covering 75 percent of their rent; two-thirds of this type of subsidy is paid by the state, one-third by the local government.

Land Development Controls

In addition to the regular finance programs of the ministries, the special funds, and the housing programs just discussed, the government has a number of financial and regulatory tools which influence the use of land in accordance with the Fifth Plan.

Tax Incentives

Special interest rates are given for industrial development and modernization. Fiscal relief may be afforded, through reduction of the value-added tax, reduction of the 14 percent transfer tax for industries relocating in accordance with the Fifth Plan, exemption from license fees, and special amortization rates for new construction. Special bank loan rates may be given. Indemnification for the risks of decentralization can be provided.

The range and amount of these financial aids can be varied according to the priority of the area where development is to occur. There are five priority categories; in the fifth, which is the Paris basin, none of these aids may be given, and penalties have been adopted.[77]

In 1955, industrial expansion in the Paris region was limited; in 1958 the limitation was extended to offices of more than 5,400 square feet. In 1960 a tax was imposed on new industrial or office construction and was paralleled by grants for the conversion of former industrial or commercial structures to residential or educational use. Three zones were established in the region: one with no tax or grant; one with a low tax and grant; and one with a high tax and grant.[78] The principal observable effect of these measures was to cause enterprises to move outward but to remain within the Paris agglomeration.[79]

The real property tax offers an important lever for securing land use in accordance with the Fifth Plan and with local plans. After World War II, as construction and birth rates rose, there was a corresponding rise in land values. Little of this rise was captured in taxes, yet the state and local governments bore most of the costs of land improvement and public services to the newly developing areas. After an initial, unsuccessful foray in 1962 with a "registration" tax to capture gains on the sale of unimproved land, the income tax code was amended in 1963[80] to achieve the same objectives.

Under this law—referred to as the value-added tax (TVA)—gains from the sale of unimproved land are classed as a special category of income. Gains include those distributed to shareholders in cooperatives or corporations or those realized on the sale of shares.[81] Unimproved land includes land less than 15 percent of which is covered by buildings. Buildings beyond economic rehabilitation may not be included in calculating this 15 percent. The tax rate is 15 percent, payable upon sale. Several situations qualify for an exemption from or reduction of the tax: profits up to $10,350 are exempt; proceeds from the sale of an owner-occupied house which are invested in another house for the owner or his dependents are exempt; and sales in economically depressed areas, as defined by the government, may qualify for a reduction or waiver. The tax rate is calculated as follows: (1) base value is the declared price at purchase or in gift or estate conveyance; (2) 25 percent of base value is added for capital improvements, the burden being on the seller to establish any amount beyond this; (3) 3 percent of base value per year of ownership multiplied by a legally established index is allowed for depreciation plus currency inflation; and (4) the result of these calculations is deducted from the sale price. This tax has trapped that large number of landowners who habitually recorded the value of their land at somewhere around half of its purchase price in order to hold down other taxes. All sales must be recorded at the Mortgage Office of the department.[82] Formerly, a conveyance tax of up to 20 percent of sale value was levied on land, buildings, and goodwill. By misrepresenting the sale price, an owner could avoid part of this tax. The Frenchman's skill at evading the tax collector often has been noted. In 1954, for instance, to secure cooperation with census takers, the government was forced to promise to destroy all census forms after population data had been transcribed from them so that the forms could not fall into the hands of the taxing authorities.[83]

State and local real estate taxes, collected jointly, are graduated in relation to the rental value of property. A law was passed in 1968 which would tax undeveloped land at its value according to the use indicated on the applicable plan. As of 1970, however, the government had yet to issue regulations for implementing the law. A one-time licensing tax to do business is calculated on rental value. A recording tax of 0.6 percent of the sale price is payable upon recording a sale.

Land Reparceling

The concept of private property in land is of fairly recent vintage in France, but its hold seems quite as tenacious there as in the United States, where the original European settlers took possession under land grants. The opposition of the people to the feudal system was one cause of the French Revolution, and the 1789 Declaration of the Rights of Man and the Citizen declared that, "ownership being an inviolable and sacred right, no one can be deprived of it except when public necessity, lawfully established, so requires, and then on condition of a fair and prior indemnity."

The theory of the right of the individual to own land was established in France under the Napoleonic Code of 1804. Naturally, there was private landownership prior to that time, but in theory the land belonged to the sovereign and was held for the benefit of the people. Having established landownership as a right, the Napoleonic Code continued in a logical, but economically unwise, fashion; it decreed that, on the death of a landowner, each heir should receive an equal share of the land. This led to the repeated subdivision of land until much of it, both urban and rural, was held in parcels of ridiculous and uneconomic size and shape.

By the end of World War II it was evident that the government must be granted powers of land assembly, both to achieve higher agricultural productivity and to make possible large-scale urban development. Expropriation had been allowed for streets, public works, and public buildings. Up to 25 percent of a piece of property could be taken for public streets and squares without compensation, while for all other public uses compensation was required. Now a great expansion in government expropriation powers and in the use of these powers for interim landholding has occurred. Attitudes toward private landownership remain as strong as before, however, and there is little likelihood that the government will assume the role of permanent landowner except in the case of land in public use.

Several mechanisms have been created by law to assist in implementing plans. For both rural and urban land there are landowners' syndicates. These may be formed voluntarily by landowners, formed at the request of the mayor or prefect, or formed at the mayor or prefect's order. The voluntary syndicates may cooperate on projects such as building flood control works or a local sewerage system, but they have no power of eminent domain. Authorized syndicates formed on request come into being if owners of stated percentages of the areas to be affected concur. If this happens, all others in the area must participate, and the authorized syndicate may use the government's power of eminent domain. Compulsory syndicates are created in rural areas only to build works to avert imminent natural catastrophes.

Rural land consolidation may be, but seldom is, carried out by landowners syndicates. Thus power has been given to the prefects to order municipalities to carry out consolidation. The prefect usually acts on the advice of departmental civil servants from the Ministry of Agriculture, although requests sometimes emanate from farmers. Land reallocation programs are developed by a committee which includes the mayor, the magistrate, departmental civil servants, and three landowners actively engaged in farming. The objective is to give each landowner land of the same productive value as his prior holding, but in the largest parcel(s) possible close to his farm buildings. Appeals may be taken to a departmental administrative tribunal and then, only on grounds of abuse of power, to the Council of State.[84]

SAFER,[85] a company for the improvement of rural land, is yet another mechanism for achieving rural land consolidation. SAFERs are non-profit, publicly owned companies which may be created to operate within a department to buy, reparcel, and resell land. SAFERs have the right of pre-emption; in all sales of farmland, except a sale to another family member or farm employee, SAFERs must be notified and given the right to purchase at the price offered. The appeals route is through courts of law.

Yet another agency is the Regional Land Planning Corporation (Société d'Aménagement Régionale), which, with the approval of the regional prefect, may use eminent domain to acquire, reparcel and improve, and then sell rural land.

Urban land consolidation is carried out by voluntary or compulsory landowners' syndicates.[86] When the prefect finds that there is a public need to expropriate and consolidate urban land he may expropriate the land and then transfer it to a syndicate for consolidation and the distribution of rights to the owners.

Upon a finding of need, public bodies have the right to expropriate land for housing, and then to resell the land for housing development in accordance with various plans.[87] All expropriation for public use or public purposes follows the same procedure.[88] A file is submitted to the prefect by the body seeking authorization to expropriate. This must demonstrate the goals, future land use, and estimated cost of the project. A commission appointed by the prefect conducts a public hearing and consults appropriate organizations, such as the chamber of commerce or the farmers' association. The commission then does or does not issue a finding of public purpose; if it does, it also states a period of time within which expropriation may occur. Affirmation at the ministerial level is needed if the project will affect national public works. Otherwise the prefect approves the finding. If the commission fails to find a public purpose, the Council of State may intervene when the project relates to water, gas, or power.

Expropriation of a lease is a recent alternative to fee expropriation.[89] The landowner's right of use is condemned for from eighteen to seventy years, buildings are constructed and rented, and rent is paid to the condemnee according to rental income and construction costs. At the end of the lease term, the landowner becomes the owner of the structures.[90]

Demagnetizing Paris

Paris already holds the pre-eminent position in French economics, politics, and culture. Despite the rapid growth of other metropolitan areas, only a concerted effort by the state can possibly alter the power balance in favor of other cities and other regions. Convinced that a strangling, choking Paris and anemic provinces are contrary to the national interest, the Fifth Plan embodies a commitment to change, for Paris and the provinces. Accepting the inevitability of continued growth for the Paris region, the plan aims at reducing the amount of growth and deflecting much of what occurs to new towns within the Paris basin.

To stimulate provincial growth the plan grants high priority to public incentives to spur growth in eight regional cities—Lyon, Saint-Étienne, Marseille, Lille, Roubaix-Tourcoing, Nancy-Metz, Bordeaux, Toulouse, Nantes–Saint-Nazaire, and Strasbourg. Furthermore, through regional development companies, the government is intervening directly to build a strong economic base in support of regional development. The national company for the Lower Rhône–Languedoc, the industrial development at the Gulf of Fos, the company for the Provence Canal, the development company for the Gascony coast, and the development project for the Aquitaine coast all are examples of this commitment of national talent and funds to regional development. Of this type of endeavor, the interministerial mission for Languedoc-Roussillon is most exciting, given the comprehensiveness and scale of the undertaking.

It still is early to judge the effects of the national effort to deflect growth from Paris and to attract growth to regional centers on population movement and regional disparities. However, the very enthusiasm of leading public officials for these efforts is evidence of an affirmation, rather than a reluctant recognition, of the desirability of continuing and strengthening these national policies. An increase in the dominance of Paris would be at the expense of all, Parisians and non-Parisians alike. The public long has known this; now the cadre of administrators and politicians accepts it and has taken the initiative in programming for change. Next, it is the turn of the rank and file of the civil service to accept new patterns and new alignments.

Plans for the Paris Basin

The magnetism of Paris is nationwide, but its greatest economic influence is exerted within a radius of approximately 130 miles. This area is far larger than either the previously defined Paris agglomeration or Paris region and extends to encompass the cities of Amiens, Reims, Troyes, Orléans, Tours, Le Mans, Caen, Le Havre, and Rouen. Designated the Paris basin, the area is defined by department boundaries and includes parts of six regions—Picardy, Champagne, Upper Normandy, Lower Normandy, Center, and Burgundy. Excluded is the Paris region.

In 1966 the government decided to establish an interministerial group headed by DATAR to prepare a development plan for this area based on three principles: (1) to stimulate growth of the nine medium-sized (100,000–400,000) cities listed above, because each is well separated from Paris and could exert a counterattraction; (2) as far as is feasible, to use the major river valleys as the principal circulation network; and (3) to stimulate the growth of service jobs in the nine cities as the fastest means of increasing employment. With the Seine as a major transportation corridor, linking Caen, Rouen, and Le Havre to Paris, the planning principles for the basin reinforce the direction of growth endorsed in the Paris regional plan. Urban development will be permitted on the hills overlooking the river corridor, with the river valley being held open for recreation and transportation.

This new planning effort was a recognition that past efforts on a smaller scale had, despite limited successes, failed in their over-all objective. Between 1947 and 1962 the Paris region's population grew by 1.8 million. Open space is vanishing and is increasingly inaccessible. The center of Paris is moving toward paralysis. In the city of Paris alone, 800,000 people live in dilapidated and/or unsanitary housing.[91] Half of the sewage goes untreated into the Seine.

The 1960 regional plan, PADOG (Map V-10), was based on the assumption that growth could be contained and lasting greenbelt areas established; but it had been recognized as a vain effort, inadequate in scale and concept. The plan had proposed that no new towns be created and that areas designated for development be limited to the existing centers. Even in these, growth would be severely curtailed so that the scale of expansion would be on the order of doubling centers of 20,000 people. The major change would involve redeveloping Paris as a polycentric city.

The commercial center, La Défense, two and one-half miles from the Arch of Triumph, is one of the new centers proposed in that plan, and the only center now well along in construction. In La Défense, high-density homes are to be provided for 80,000 people, jobs for 100,000. The 1,700-acre center is being linked with the center city by an express extension of the Metro.

Three other high-density nodes were projected for Le Bourget Airport, for a military airport to the southwest, and for one or more locations in the southeast. Instead of allowing additional growth in the Paris region, it would have been diverted to Rouen, Amiens, Le Mans, and the other cities now designated for expansion under the basin plans. The notable difference between the 1960 plan and the principles of the basin planners is that the former endorsed diverting almost all growth to the other basin cities; the latter favors their expansion while accepting the inevitability of growth in the Paris region. The basic premise of the 1960 plan—that the rate of growth in the Paris region could be radically reduced—proved false. In addition, a large body of public administrators, in the national government and the local Parisian administration, bitterly resented the 1960 plan and termed it disastrous for the renovation of the city and its suburbs and for its future competitive position with the other major cities of Europe.

Despite their fears, as of 1964 the Paris region still was receiving, in regional allocations of the national budget, a sum in excess of its 20 percent of the population. Twenty-five percent of education funds, 39 percent of special education funds, 31 percent of health and welfare funds, and 56 percent of cultural affairs funds were allocated to the Paris region that year. It is true that the region received only 17 percent of national funds for infrastructure and 14 percent of funds for communications.[92]

Although the Paris region receives 50 percent more per capita in local tax revenues than the rest of the nation and borrows about this much more from

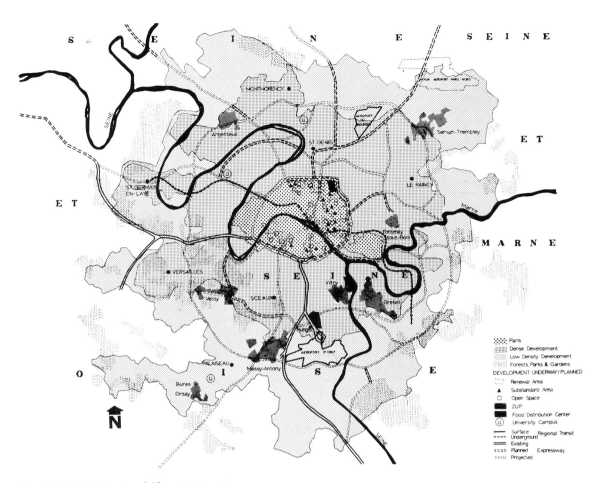

Map V-10. Paris Regional Plan, 1960

the Depository and Consignment Bank, it is not gaining on the rest of the country in capital construction. Its infrastructure, transportation system, and public facilities consume much of the available funds in operating expenses, and there is insufficient money left for expansion or modernization.

In an effort to tie the city more closely to the densely settled agglomeration and to achieve a distribution of funds which would be more efficient for both, an administrative reorganization plan was drawn up which established the District of Paris. The district then was charged with the responsibility of preparing a new master plan for the region (see Map V-11). This plan was published in 1965, and to non-Parisians it seemed but a confirmation of their concern aroused by the 1960 plan—that, despite contrary pronouncements, the national government would concentrate investment in the Paris region at the expense of the provinces.

While endorsing the importance of maintaining the role of Paris as a principal European center, the government realized that it must act to convince non-Parisians that investments there were part of a scheme for shifting the balance of power away from Paris and toward the rest of the country (the French "desert"). Assuredly it is necessary to rebuild dilapidated and inefficient areas in Paris, such as Maine-Montparnasse, and to create new commercial centers, such as La Défense, to relieve pressure at the heart of the city. So, too, are new towns—or satellite cities—needed in the Paris suburbs to deter further sprawl and to provide a broad enough range of jobs, community services, and facilities to bring people there rather than to Paris itself. The eight satellite cities proposed in the 1965 plan would be located along

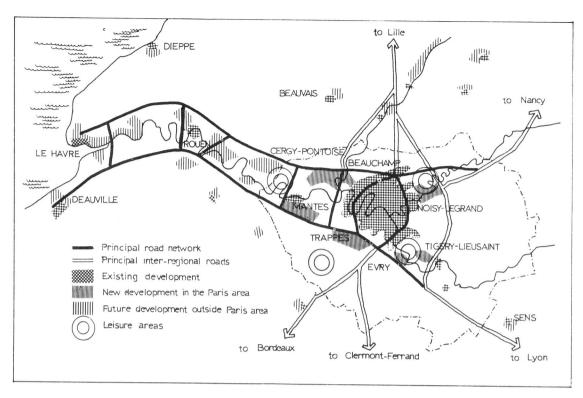

Map V-11.
Paris Region
Master Plan, 1965

parallel corridors of a northwest-southeast axis which corresponds to the orientation of the Seine basin. Growth of the cities to the northwest would be reinforced by construction of the Paris–Rouen–Le Havre expressway and the now-completed electrification of the railroad. These cities would be large enough to influence significantly the growth of Paris proper; their population in the year 2000 would range from four hundred thousand to one million, providing a place for approximately one-third of the fourteen million people who are expected to inhabit the region by then.

The very size of the satellite cities, however, and the evident investment required to create them, is a reasonable ground for concern for those competing for regional development funds. Their growth could well be a new form of Paris' growth at the expense of the rest of the nation. Even within the region, the plan has met with severe criticism. Members of the Paris Municipal Council fear that the strengthening of the region will occur at the city's expense. The prefect of the Paris region may find himself in competition for funds with the administrators of the Paris basin.

The municipalities in which the new cities would be built are hostile because they fear the new burden of municipal costs. Although some agree that the plan may be desirable from a long-term perspective, they do not wish to bear the short-term costs. So criticism abounds, while the Paris region continues to grow. Even if the government succeeds in drawing people to the cities of the Paris basin, the need to accept and implement a plan for the growth of the Paris region itself will remain. This undoubtedly will demand decision-making and financing at the national level.

Languedoc-Roussillon: State Initiative for Regional Development

Languedoc-Roussillon is one visible answer to public allegations that favoritism is being shown to Paris. It is a new type of undertaking for the government, it is in an underdeveloped area, and it has a chance to be highly successful.

The Riviera, the Mediterranean coastal strip which includes such famous resorts as Saint-Tropez, Cap d'Antibes, Nice, Cannes, and Monte Carlo, has long been crowded, affluent, and heavily developed. The half of France's Mediterranean coast west of Marseille has presented a sharp contrast; until recent years it was marshy, mosquito-ridden, poor, and underpopulated. Several factors led the French government to undertake a massive program for development of this coast as a major resort area. First, the Riviera already was overcrowded. With growing leisure time and rising incomes for the French people and a desire to attract more tourist income from foreigners, the Riviera could not possibly satisfy the potential demand. Second, the Languedoc coast, as well as the rest of southwestern France, was seriously underdeveloped, with incomes, services, and jobs far below the national average. Third, studies showed that, given substantial infusions of capital for drainage and landfill, the coast could be made a highly attractive area for resort development. With irrigation the nearby coastal plain could produce fine fruits and vegetables to supply the tourist market. Many historic ruins—the Roman arenas, the medieval fortress at Carcassomme, castles, cathedrals—could become added tourist attractions.

The task of converting miles of swampy, mosquito-ridden coast into beaches alluring to the tourist trade had been under consideration since 1959, but to many the job seemed overwhelming. Two men—Pierre Racine and Pierre Reynaud—were given primary responsibility for the task. Pierre Racine has since remarked: "When in January, 1963, in a helicopter with Olivier Guichard I surveyed for the first time all that wasteland of swamps and shores infested with shanties and tents with no sanitary facilities whatsoever, I was dumbfounded. I thought momentarily that we never could clean up all that."[93] When he first drove to the site of La Grande Motte the mosquitoes were so bad it was impossible to open the car windows, let alone get out.

Once the decision to go ahead was made, once the government was convinced that the undertaking could meet the needs of the local economy and the demands for greater seashore recreation, the question of who should plan and who should develop had to be answered. The necessary investment in land development and infrastructure before towns could be built would be enormous, and returns on the investment would be postponed for about a decade. Private capital could not afford to carry out all parts of the scheme simultaneously. Should small areas be developed on a random, spot basis in line with what the private market could support, rather than as part of an integrated plan for the whole area, there was every likelihood that the coast would become cluttered and unattractive and, therefore, far less productive of revenue in the long run.

With these considerations in mind, the government decided that it would be preferable to have a tripartite structure, with responsibility divided between the state, local governments, and private enterprise. Over-all control for planning the entire development, land acquisition, marsh drainage, beach building, and construction of major roads and ports would be the responsibility of the state. The local governments would install the infrastructure, including sewerage, water supply, and local roads, and then bring in private builders for the resort new towns.[94] In this manner the state hopefully could avoid creating unearned increments in value for local landowners and could capture part of the profits which would accrue from its investment. As the then minister of construction, Pierre Sudreau, said: "The state itself customarily launches speculation by announcing its development projects ahead of time. This is what, this time, it must avoid."[95] Naturally, this attitude of the national government did not increase its popularity with local landowners, many of whom also resented the fact that Paris would plan the development of their land for the benefit of outsiders.

Covering 120 miles of coast, stretching from the western edge of La Camargue almost to the Spanish border, Languedoc-Roussillon was the government's first undertaking as the developer of a major resort area. The first step in implementing the decision was to assign responsibility for planning and land acquisition to the Ministry of Construction, now the Ministry of Public Works and Housing. Preliminary planning, to select sites for future resort new town development, proceeded in the greatest possible secrecy to avoid the speculation in land which would have been inevitable had the public been aware of the government's intentions. Starting in 1961, land purchases were made on behalf of the Ministry of Construction by the National Development Company for the Lower Rhône–Languedoc and by private individuals purportedly acting for themselves but actually buying for the government. In 1961 and 1962, 3,000 acres at the future new town sites were bought at an average price of $880 per acre, and thus the market value for this land was established.

When DATAR was created in February, 1963, responsibility for the project was shifted there. Subsequently, in June of that year, an interministerial mission—the Languedoc-Roussillon Tourist Development Mission—was established[96] and the work of DATAR was placed under its supervision. The prime minister designates the president of the mission and the secretary general, or director. The ministers of the Interior, Finance, Public Works and Housing, and Agriculture, the regional prefect for Languedoc, and the commissioner-general for tourism serve on the mission. Departmental prefects attend mission meetings. The mission's role is one of policy, synthesis, coordination, and synchronization.

The DATAR staff first committed itself to refining the Ministry of Construction's initial development location decisions into a regional master plan. Speed was essential and was forthcoming. The Regional Urbanization Plan of 1963[97] was the responsibility of an eight-man team of architects, planners, and engineers under the direction of Georges Candilis. This private consulting team was hired and supervised by DATAR. In draft form the plan was presented to the councils of the four affected departments and to the Regional Economic Expansion Committee. It proposed: (1) the establishment of six coastal tourist zones in which future development, either of new towns or improvement of existing towns, would be concentrated to provide a complete range of tourist attractions; (2) a complete infrastructure system to make this tourist development feasible; and (3) measures to attract tourists to existing inland communities. Further development of the areas between the six zones would be discouraged, and in this way a natural setting and protection of the habitat of the native flora and fauna would be assured. A new national park would be created as a wildlife refuge. Up to 10,000 acres would be afforested to make the area more scenic, to create shade, and, most importantly, to act as a windbreak for the mistral. The plan proposed that land at the six sites where acquisition had occurred be developed into six resort towns which together would accommodate 1.5 million visitors annually, or 279,000 simultaneously, as well as 15,000 boats in twenty harbors (see Table V-30). One of the towns would adjoin the picturesque and charming old village of Gruissan.

Access to the resort towns would be either by a network of scenic roads or by fast highways linking the towns to the proposed coastal expressway and to the nearby cities of Perpignan, Narbonne, Béziers, and Montpellier. Substantial airports already exist at Perpignan, Montpellier, and Nîmes, and there are a number of smaller airports.

The numerous large coastal ponds would have to be deepened and their water levels stabilized before they would be suitable for marinas and water

Table V-30.
Languedoc-Roussillon Plan:
Proposed Beds and Moorings

At Completion	La Grande Motte	Carnon	Leucate-Barcarès	Cap d'Agde	Gruissan	Aude River Mouth	Saint-Cyprien
Beds	50,000		75,000	50,000	40,000	40,000	24,000
Moorings[a]	1,000	600	7,800	1,000	1,000	800	900

SOURCE: French Embassy, *The Largest Earth-Moving Project in Europe* (New York, 1969).
[a] Plus more than 3,000 moorings in other, established ports along the coast. Moorings can be rented by the day, week, month or year.

sports. This task, along with improvement of the national highway network, afforestation, and mosquito eradication, would be undertaken directly by the national government. Other infrastructure would be installed by public-private companies or by the municipalities with state aid. The plan proposed development priorities by location and type of development.[98]

The Regional Urbanization Plan was further refined into land-use and design plans for each of the six tourist new town areas and into land-use plans and development restrictions for the sixty-six municipalities in the region (see Maps V-12 and V-13). The plans were prepared by private architect-planner consultants under the supervision of Georges Candilis. Plans for the resort towns were prepared by different architects belonging to the initial eight-man team. The Ministry of Construction or the municipalities named the architects for the other plans. All of these plans were submitted to the appropriate municipality or public-private company and to the technical staff of the departments before being approved by the Interministerial Committee.

Simultaneously with the physical design planning, the Interministerial Committee, through its DATAR staff and through the ministries, carried out socioeconomic studies, cultural inventories of the region, tourist-market-demand studies, and technical research preparatory to development. The

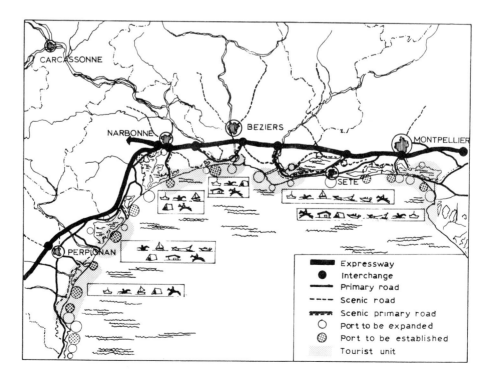

Map V-12.
Sketch Plans for Languedoc-Roussillon

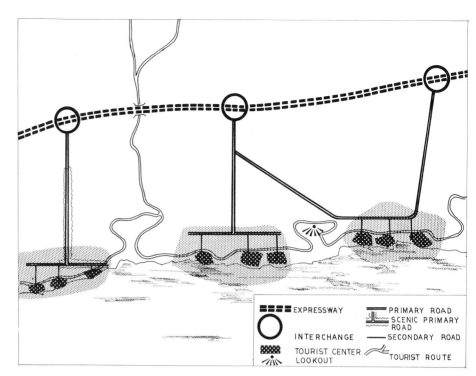

Map V-13.
Sketch Plans for
Languedoc-
Roussillon

Committee met annually with the general councils of the four departments to present its current thinking and to receive the councils' reactions.

With completion and adoption of the 1963 Regional Urbanization Plan, it was time for the government to proceed with further land acquisition. The average price for development land had been established by 1961–62 purchases. In 1963, ZADs were designated, and further purchases were made within the previously established price range. Land acquired after ZADs were established was purchased primarily through negotiated sale, but in part by pre-emption, at an average price of $880 per acre.[99] This was the first large-scale application of the ZAD technique. A total of 10,000 acres was purchased (including the initial acquisitions). FNAFU provided land acquisition funds; by 1968 its allocation totaled $14 million. ZADs covered an additional 60,000 acres and thereby restrained land prices in the area surrounding the six new town development sites.[100]

The development budget prepared by DATAR anticipated a ten-year program costing $141 million:[101]

	Millions of Dollars
Roads	70
Water Supply	10
Ports	25
Mosquito Eradication	20
Afforestation	10
Swamp Drainage	6

Beginning in 1963, funds were allocated to the appropriate ministries to initiate development. By 1968 the national budget, including preliminary studies and aid to existing resort communities ($300,000 annually in 1965 and 1966), had exceeded the 1963 projection and was as shown in Table V-31. If progress continues as envisioned, it should be possible to disband the Languedoc-Roussillon Tourist Development Mission in 1975, and to place all expenditures under the regular ministry accounts for the region. In the Fifth Plan, CNAT recommended and the government agreed to the budgeting of $70 million for Languedoc-Roussillon.

Table V-31.
State Budget for Languedoc-Roussillon

	Millions of Dollars		
	Actual 1964–68	Proposed 1969–70	Projected 1971–75
Over-all Expenses[a]	22.6	11.4	32.9
La Grande Motte	17.4	3.8	11.4
Leucate-Barcarès	11.1	4.1	4.9
Cap d'Agde	1.3	3.4	7.9
Gruissan	1.5	4.1	9.9
Mouth of the Aude River	0.1	—	12.3
Saint-Cyprien	1.9	0.7	11.8
Total	55.9	27.5	91.1

SOURCE: French Embassy, *The Largest Earth-Moving Project in Europe* (New York, 1969).
[a] Afforestation, mosquito eradication, preliminary studies, and aid to existing resorts.

By 1968, background studies were finished, land had been acquired, part of the development was completed, and tourists had begun to arrive. The installation of infrastructure is scheduled for completion in 1975.

Four public-private companies have been created, each with a department and its municipalities as controlling shareholders. The state has given each company the right to carry out detailed planning in accordance with the Regional Urbanization Plan and to contract for construction in one or more of the proposed resort new towns. With state aid, they have installed the infrastructure—gas, electricity, water, and sewers. In 1966 the state decided to guarantee a loan of 60 percent of the companies' expenses, and the departments guaranteed the remaining 40 percent. FNAFU and the Depository and Consignment Bank share equally in the state's loans.

At two of the six sites—La Grande Motte and Leucate-Barcarès—much of the land already has been sold to private developers. Land for building, with roads and infrastructure in place, sells at the fixed prices shown in Table V-32. The financing for each resort area and the resulting proposed sale price for land were approved by the Interministerial Committee. The company may not sell at a profit, but it recoups its investment in the land plus the cost of the infrastructure. Accurate accounts show the per-lot cost of this development, and lot prices are fixed accordingly. The private market apparently has judged the land a good investment, because more than 85 percent of the available parcels have been sold. Thirty developers have bought land planned for apartments, ten have bought land planned for camping, seven have bought hotel sites, and many have bought land for single-family housing. In all cases they must build in accordance with the height, density, parking, use, and other restrictions of the detailed plans. The purchaser must agree to build within five years and in accordance with the plans. He may sell at whatever price he can obtain.

The search for foreign investors has been successful. At La Grande Motte the British have bought or taken options on land planned for 1,635 beds, the Germans have planned for 1,390 beds, and the Belgians have acquired land for 200 beds. At Leucate-Barcarès the figures are 5,889 beds for the British, 7,412 for the Germans, 1,180 for the Swiss, and 200 for the Belgians.[102]

Table V-32.
Land Prices at La Grande Motte and Leucate-Barcarès

Designated Land Use	Land Price
Hotel	$400 per room
Apartment	$2.00 per sq. ft. ± 50% depending on location
Camping	$0.30–$0.40 per sq. ft.
Single-family house	$1.00 per sq. ft.

SOURCE: Mission Interministérielle pour l'Aménagement Touristique du Littoral Languedoc-Roussillon, *Rapport au Gouvernement* (Paris, 1968).

The two first-priority resort new towns, Leucate-Barcarès and La Grande Motte, were evident successes through this stage of their development. Unfortunately, as of 1970, two problems had emerged: high construction costs are pushing prices beyond the budget of the intended middle-income market; and the strong, continuous wind raises clouds of dust and sand.

In addition to supervising the over-all planning, George Candilis was responsible directly for the plan for Leucate-Barcarès (see Map V-14). Development in accordance with this plan is well along. It can be traced in Figures V-27, V-28, and V-29. Leucate-Barcarès has a site of 1,850 acres with a large sand beach, a 9,880-acre lake, and 10 miles of canals. One of its two ports will be used primarily for fishing boats, the other for yachts and small pleasure boats. Already accommodations providing 6,000 beds and 400 boat moorings are available. Furnished efficiency apartments designed by Candilis are selling for $7,000.

La Grande Motte's 1,730 acres of land and 7,900 acres of lakes have seen enormous construction activity mixed with pioneer vacationers (Figures V-30 and V-31). The La Grande Motte plan places intensive development near the water, with 250 acres for hotels, 445 acres for cottages, and 100 acres for camp sites.[103] Land for development to accommodate 22,000 tourists has been sold by the development company.[104] Developers in turn are selling land at $46 per square foot of land for waterfront lots, and from $20 to $36 per square foot for lots inland from the lakes and shore. An additional 400 acres of pine forest were acquired nearby to add to the national forest reserve. The yacht harbor and infrastructure are finished; hotel rooms, apartments, and camp sites are finished and available for thousands of tourists. Single-family housing construction goes on apace. The first restaurants and shops are open. As seen in Figures V-32, V-33, and V-34, the balconied, triangular façades of the hotels and apartments echo the sails and waves in the harbor below, creating a gay scene. La Grande Motte's place in the French firmament was marked in 1969 by an overnight stop by the *Tour de France*.

In its structure and role, the public-private company at La Grande Motte is characteristic of those established for the other resort new towns. The Development Company of (the Department of) Hérault (SADH) was created in June, 1964. It has two classes of stock, A and B. Its capitalization of $50,000 is divided between 1,350 shares of class A stock, which is held by the Department of Hérault and the municipalities of Sète, Palavas, and Mauguia, and 1,150 shares of class B stock, which is held by the Depository and Consignment Bank, SCET, the National Development Company for the Lower Rhône–Languedoc, chambers of commerce, and other public-private companies in the department. The president of this company also is a senator and the president of the Hérault General Council.[105] As of 1968, SADH had received $5 million in loans from FNAFU and the Depository and Consignment Bank. Combined with income from the sale of land, this has made it possible

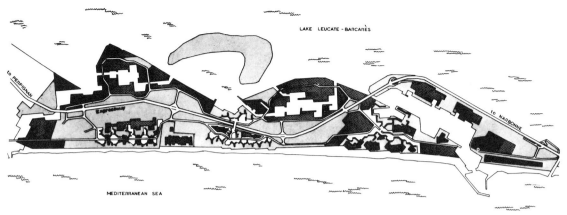

LAKE LEUCATE - BARCARÈS

to PERPIGNAN

to NARBONNE

MEDITERRANEAN SEA

centers (hotels, shops, entertainment)

multi-family housing

single-family housing, vacation villages

open space, camp sites, recreation areas

0   1700   3400 ft.
   850   2550

North ➡

Map V-14. Leucate-Barcarès Plan

to prepare enough land—fill, grading, roads, parking, sewerage systems, water, electricity, gas, and telephone lines—at La Grande Motte to accommodate 22,000 visitors.[106] Now sports facilities and planting are being added.

In 1968 work began at Cap d'Agde and near Gruissan. When the Sixth Plan becomes operative in 1971, construction of the resort town at the mouth of the Aude River will begin.

While there has been some inefficiency caused by inadequate coordination between government bureaus and agencies, on the whole the enterprise has proceeded so satisfactorily that in 1967 the government committed itself to similar ventures for the Aquitaine coast near Bordeaux and for Corsica. The *New York Journal of Commerce* has written of Languedoc-Roussillon: "This project will create the most important tourist area that has ever been planned in the world."[107]

In its 1967 and 1968 annual reports, the Languedoc-Roussillon Tourist Development Mission described its notable progress and acknowledged three problems: control of urbanization outside the designated areas; regulation of camping; and coordination of publicity with available facilities. At this time, plans for each of the sixty-six municipalities were entirely or nearly finished and together constituted a well-coordinated plan for the region. Scenic vistas along highways and large natural and historic areas were designated for preservation. Private development, however, stimulated by public investment, is occurring quite contrary to plans. Strip commercial uses and private camping grounds with no sanitary facilities are springing up.

The main problem, as seen by the interministerial mission, is that the state cannot possibly be held responsible for the detailed surveillance required to assure observance of the plans, and the municipalities generally have ". . . neither the desire nor the means to discipline their own inhabitants."[108]

The next problem, that of 65,500 scattered campers spending an average of three weeks on the beach with no toilets or garbage facilities, is more manageable. As more and more camp sites are made available at the planned locations, unauthorized camping can be prohibited. The mission has requested state funds to enable the four prefects to hire additional staff to police camping.

To deal with the third problem, the mission has undertaken a public relations program and proposes to participate in a long-term plan for improvement of the region's scenic, sporting, and historic attractions, but it notes that the existing municipalities must make a far greater effort to clean up their beaches, install sewage treatment plants, remove shanties, restore monuments, and provide better access to tourist attractions. By 1968, $1.4 million had been made available to thirty-nine municipalities for these purposes.[109]

Figure V-27. Leucate-Barcarès before Development

Figure V-28. Leucate-Barcarès under Development

Figure V-29. Leucate-Barcarès, 1969

Figure V-30. La Grande Motte, 1966

Figure V-31. La Grande Motte under Construction

(right)
Figure V-32.
La Grande Motte,
April, 1969

(far right)
Figure V-33.
La Grande Motte,
April, 1969

Figure V-34. La Grande Motte, Apartments at the Port, 1969

Notes

1. Jean-François Gravier, *Paris et le désert français* (Paris: Flammarion, 1947).
2. François Pasqualini, "French City Planners Ponder Decentralization," *Public Utilities Fortnightly*, July 22, 1965.
3. France, La Documentation Française, *France* (Paris, 1968 ed.).
4. *Ibid.* Actual population as of the 1968 census: 49,850,000.
5. *Ibid.*
6. OECD figures.
7. Niles M. Hansen, *French Regional Planning* (Bloomington: Indiana University Press, 1968). Densities in the ninth arrondissement run as high as 365 people per acre.
8. La Documentation Française, *France* (1968 ed.). This is the agglomeration of Paris as defined by the Institut National de la Statistique et des Études Économiques. There is another, broader definition of the region, for which the 1968 population total is 9.1 million.
9. French Embassy, *France Town and Country Environment Planning* (New York, 1965).
10. La Documentation Française, *France* (1968 ed.).
11. *Ibid.*
12. La Documentation Française, "Les Mouvements de Population en France," *Notes et Études Documentaires*, no. 3377 (Paris, 1967).
13. Called communes in France; here described as municipalities.
14. From a speech at Dijon, June 18, 1966.
15. "L'administration contre la décentralisation," *Partage des Pouvoirs, Partage des Décisions*, no. 9 (1968).
16. French Information and Press Service, New York, 1968.
17. See "France," in *Control of River Pollution by Industry* (n.a., n.p., n.d.), for more details.
18. France, Rural Code, art. 434–I.
19. "France," in *Control of River Pollution by Industry*.
20. *New York Times*, June 20, 1969.
21. Warren C. Baum, *The French Economy and the State* (Princeton, N.J.: Princeton University Press, 1958).
22. *Ibid.* The Marshall Plan made a vital contribution.
23. *Ibid.*
24. United Nations, *Statistical Yearbook*, 1948.
25. Fifty million francs after the 1958 devaluation.
26. Vera Lutz, *French Planning* (Washington, D.C.: American Enterprise Institute for Public Policy Research, 1965).
27. Baum, *The French Economy and the State*.
28. *Ibid.*
29. La Documentation Française, *France*.
30. Lutz, *French Planning*.
31. European Economic Community Commission, *The Economic Situation in the Community* (Brussels: EEC Directorate-General for Economic and Financial Affairs, 1967).
32. OECD, *Observer*, no. 21 (1966).
33. See Appendix, Table A-3, for comparative data on the construction price index.
34. See Appendix, Table A-4, for comparative data on construction and residential construction expenditures.
35. See Appendix, Figure A-5, for a comparison of France's trade balance with that of Finland, Israel, the Netherlands, Sweden, and the United States.
36. *New York Times*, July 17, 1969.
37. Speech of February 21, 1966.
38. Translated by the author from *Le Figaro*, June 16, 1970.
39. See Appendix, Figure A-6, for a comparison of indices of industrial production.
40. French Embassy, *France Town and Country Environment Planning*.
41. European Economic Community Commission, *The Economic Situation in the Community*.
42. Hansen, *French Regional Planning*.
43. French Embassy, *France Town and Country Environment Planning*.

44. Services Culturels Français, *Géographie de la France* (New York, n.d.).

45. Anne Londero, *France's Approach to Social Problems*, supplement to *La Documentation Française Illustrée* (Paris, 1967).

46. M. Freville, "Quelques Traits Caracteristiques de l'Economie et des Finances des Collectivites Locales Françaises au Cours des Dix Dernières Années," *Information Caisse des Dépots: Bulletin de Liaison* (Paris), no. 14 (1966). In the United States, from 1965 to 1968, lot costs for FHA-insured housing averaged 20 percent of total costs.

47. OECD, *Observer*, no. 21 (1966).

48. Baum, *The French Economy and the State*.

49. *Ibid.*

50. Translated literally, *Aménagement du territoire* means "organization of the territory." It also is translated as "integrated development" or as "regional planning." A freer translation (used here) is "national environmental planning."

51. Minister of Reconstruction and Urban Planning, Claudius Petit, quoted in the French Embassy's *France Town and Country Environment Planning*.

52. The Ministry of Construction and Ministry of Public Works were merged on January 8, 1966, to form the Ministry of Public Works and Housing.

53. France, *Journal Officiel*, decree no. 46–2, January 3, 1946, art. 3.

54. The decree of December 31, 1958, called for development of an economic and environmental plan for each region. These plans were prepared but initially resembled inventories rather than statements of goals and programs.

55. La Documentation Française, "L'Aménagement du Territoire en France," *Notes et Études Documentaires*, no. 3461 (Paris, 1968).

56. Lutz, *French Planning*.

57. La Documentation Française, "L'Aménagement du Territoire en France."

58. *Ibid.*

59. Conversation with Mr. Pierre Reynaud of DATAR.

60. Niles M. Hansen, "French National Planning Experience," *Journal of the American Institute of Planners*, November, 1969.

61. France, *Journal Officiel*, decree no. 58–1464, January 4, 1959; *ibid.*, law no. 68–842, July 27, 1962.

62. *Ibid.*, law of August 7, 1957, and decree no. 58–1464, December 31, 1958.

63. Robert Macé, *Techniques et Problèmes d'Urbanisme*, prepared for the Ministry of Construction (Paris, n.d.).

64. France, *Journal Officiel*, law no. 62–848, July 26, 1962.

65. A. Levy-Soussan, "Les Zones à Urbaniser en Priorite," *La Jurisprudence Immobilière*, no. 6 (1962). See David N. Kinsey, "The French ZUP Technique of Urban Development," *Journal of the American Institute of Planners*, November, 1969, for further information on the organization and financing of ZUPs.

66. Macé, *Techniques et Problèmes d'Urbanisme*, p. 15.

67. *Ibid.*, p. 21, translated by the author.

68. France, *Journal Officiel*, law no. 62–848, July 26, 1962.

69. Conversation with Mr. M. Guérin of SCET.

70. France, *Journal Officiel*, decree no. 341, June 30, 1955; *ibid.*, decree no. 1010, October 18, 1955.

71. FDES Council, *Tenth Report* (n.p., n.d.)

72. Hansen, *French Regional Planning*.

73. FNAFU was formed in 1963 from FNAT (National Fund for Environmental Planning).

74. Pierre Bauchet, "Regional Development Policies in France," prepared for the U.S. Department of Commerce, *Area Redevelopment Policies in Britain and the Countries of the Common Market* (Washington, D.C.: GPO, 1965).

75. La Documentation Française, *France* (1968 ed.).

76. Louis Gregoire, *L'Aide à la Construction en France*, prepared for the Ministry of Construction (Paris, 1964), provides much greater detail on the operation of these programs. Its appendix sets forth the standards for the various programs.

77. La Documentation Française, "L'Aménagement du Territoire en France."

78. France, *Journal Officiel*, decree of January 5, 1955; decree no. 58–1464, December 31, 1958, and law of August 2, 1960.

79. Bauchet, "Regional Development Policies in France."

80. France, *Journal Officiel*, law of March 13, 1963, as incorporated into the Finance Act of December 19, 1963.

81. These shares formerly escaped taxation. See British Institute of International Comparative Law, *Land Development in France and Belgium: Law and Practice*, Special Publication no. 5 (London, 1964).

82. Deeds of sale must have attached to them copies of all local plans and planning restrictions relating to the land, as well as all easements and other restrictions (*ibid.*).

83. Baum, *The French Economy and the State*.

84. "The Role of Public Authorities," in *Land Development in France and Belgium*.

85. France, *Journal Officiel*, law of August 5, 1960, as modified by the law of August 8, 1962.

86. France, Urbanization Code, July 26, 1954, arts. 74–78, as amended on December 31, 1958.

87. France, Land Act, August 6, 1953.

88. France, *Journal Officiel*, ordinance no. 58–997, October 23, 1958, as modified on May 19, 1959, June 6, 1959, and December 14, 1964.

89. *Ibid.*, law no. 64–1247, December 16, 1964.

90. Jacques Saindon, "Régimes de l'Appropriation du Sol et de la Construction," in *La Vie Urbaine* (n.p., n.d.).

91. La Documentation Française, "L'Aménagement du Territoire en France."

92. Hansen, *French Regional Planning*.

93. *L'Express*, July 7–13, 1969. Guichard was then head of DATAR. Racine was chairman of the Interministerial Committee for Languedoc-Roussillon, and Reynaud was chief of staff and DATAR inspector general.

94. *L'Express*, July 7–13, 1969.

95. See the numerous government publications cited in the bibliography for more details on the Languedoc-Roussillon project, including mission reports and texts of decrees.

96. France, *Journal Officiel*, decree no. 63–580, June 18, 1963.

97. Approved by decree no. 64–275, March 26, 1964.

98. Conversation with Mr. Pierre Reynaud.

99. Pierre Racine, "Rapport de la Mission Interministérielle pour l'Aménagement Touristique du Littoral Languedoc-Roussillon," extract from DATAR, *Administration*, no. 56 (1966).

100. Conversation with Mr. Pierre Reynaud.

101. La Documentation Française, "L'Aménagement du Territoire en France."

102. *Ibid.*

103. French Embassy, *The Largest Earth-Moving Project in Europe*.

104. *Urbanisme* (Paris), no. 106 (1968).

105. La Documentation Française, "L'Aménagement Touristique du Littoral Languedoc-Roussillon," *Notes et Études Documentaires*, no. 3326 (Paris, 1966).

106. Mission Interministérielle pour l'Aménagement Touristique du Littoral Languedoc-Roussillon, *Rapport au Gouvernement* (Paris, 1968).

107. *L'Express*, July 7–13, 1969.

108. Mission Interministérielle pour l'Aménagement Touristique du Littoral Languedoc-Roussillon, *Rapport au Gouvernement* (Paris, 1967).

109. Mission Interministérielle, *Rapport au Gouvernement* (1968).

Appendix

Table A-1.
Natural Population Increase, 1962 and 1967

| | Per 1,000 Population | | | | | |
| | Births | | Deaths | | Increase | |
Country	1962	1967	1962	1967	1962	1967
The Netherlands	20.8	18.9	7.9	7.9	12.9	11.0
Sweden	14.2	15.5	10.1	10.1	4.1	5.4
France	17.8	16.8	11.5	10.8	6.3	6.0
The United States	24.8	17.9	9.4	9.4	15.4	8.5

SOURCE: The Netherlands, Government Information Service, *Physical Planning in the Netherlands* (The Hague, 1961), and information received from the Ministry of Housing and Physical Planning, The Hague.

Table A-2.
Population Density, 1966

| | People | |
Country	per Square Mile	per Square Kilometer
Finland	36	14
France	233	90
Sweden	44	17
The Netherlands	948	366
The United States	54	21

SOURCE: Stockholms Enskilda Bank, *Some Data About Sweden* (Stockholm, 1968).

Figure A-1. Housing Construction Rates and Subsidies

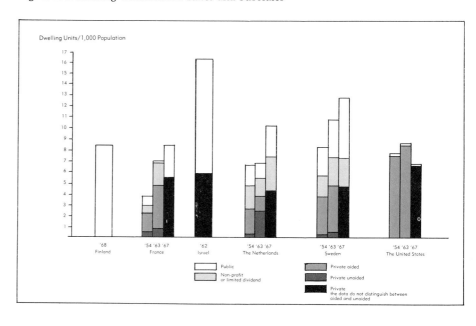

Table A-3.
Residential Construction, 1948–68
(Monthly Averages)

Year	Finland Residential Bldgs. Completed (1,000 cu. m. floor area)	France Residential Bldg. Permits Issued (no. of dwelling units)	Israel Residential Bldgs. Completed (1,000 sq. m. floor area)	The Netherlands Residential Bldgs. Completed (no. of dwelling units)	Sweden Residential Bldgs. Completed in Cities and Urban Districts (no. of dwelling units)	The United States Non-Farm Dwelling Units Started (no. of dwelling units)
1948	—	—	—	3,033	2,881	77,600
1949	—	—	—	—	—	—
1950	630	7,700	94	3,942	2,761	116,300
1951	740	11,500	162	4,889	2,527	90,900
1952	700	10,700	151	4,550	3,012	93,900
1953	780	15,400	70	4,966	3,413	92,000
1954	790	23,300	89	5,707	3,717	101,700
1955	740	24,400	146	5,068	3,461	110,700
1956	800	29,500	146	5,690	3,458	93,200
1957	700	27,900	134	7,366	4,057	86,800
1958	700	28,800	161	7,420	3,926	100,800
1959	720	28,600	170	6,969	4,362	127,600
1960	860	29,800	165	6,985	4,286	105,100
1961	880	31,176	169	6,891	6,148[a]	111,400
1962	1,070	35,597	228	6,531	6,260	122,400
1963	890	43,758	243	6,627	6,784	134,500
1964	920	47,861	247	8,415	7,264	128,000
1965	950	49,505	260	9,586	8,070	124,000
1966	1,040	42,480	260	10,142	7,447	97,700
1967	—	39,116	196	10,619	8,351	108,200
1968	—	45,900	—	10,231	8,853	—

SOURCE: U.N., *Bulletin of Statistics* (issued monthly).
[a] All dwellings.

Table A-4.
Construction Price Index, 1963

(1953 = 100)

	France	The Netherlands	Sweden	The United States
Gross National Product	159.6	139.6	136.4	119.8
Residential Construction	173.4	159.5	135.0	118.1
Other Construction	146.6	159.1	138.5	126.1
Total Construction	157.5	159.3	137.1	122.7
Construction Prices ÷ GNP Prices	98.7	114.1	100.5	102.4
Residential Construction Prices ÷ GNP Prices	108.6	114.3	99.0	98.6

SOURCE: OECD, *Observer*, no. 21 (1966).

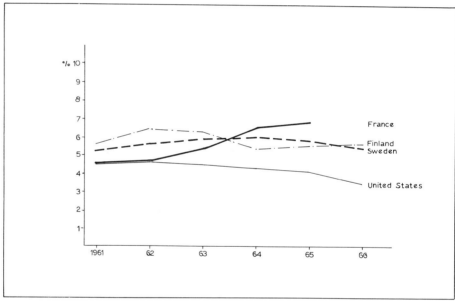

Figure A-2.
Gross Fixed
Capital Formation
in Housing

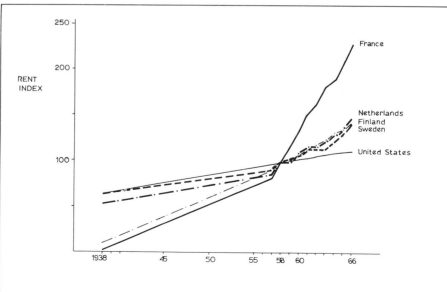

Figure A-3.
Rent Index,
1938–66

Table A-5.
Construction Expenditures, 1953–63

	Total New Construction Expenditure as Percentage of GNP			
	France	Sweden	The Netherlands	The United States
1953	8.7	12.9	11.5	9.9
1963	11.1	15.5	12.5	10.9
	Total New Construction Expenditure as Percentage of Fixed Investment			
	France	Sweden	The Netherlands	The United States
1953	53.9	62.4	55.2	61.9
1963	56.0	66.5	50.5	67.2
	Total New Housing Expenditure as Percentage of Total New Construction			
	France	Sweden	The Netherlands	The United States
1953	40.7	38.7	37.5	41.7
1963	44.9	36.6	32.9	42.1
	Expenditure on Residential Construction as Percentage of GNP			
	France	Sweden	The Netherlands	The United States
1953	3.6	5.0	4.3	4.1
1963	5.0	5.7	4.0	4.6
	Rent as Percentage of Consumer Expenditures			
	France	Sweden	The Netherlands	The United States
1953	3.7	8.3	6.3	11.9
1963	7.2	9.3	8.1	13.3
	Average Number of Rooms per Person			
	France	Sweden	The Netherlands	The United States
1960	1.04	1.21	1.30	1.49
	Housing Completions per 1,000 Population			
	France	Sweden	The Netherlands	The United States
1954	3.8	8.2	6.6	7.6
1963	7.0	10.7	6.7	8.6

SOURCE: OECD, *Observer*, no. 21 (1969).

Table A-6.
Cost of Living Index, 1948–67

Year	France	Sweden	The Netherlands	Israel	Finland	The United States
1948	49	65	66	35	65	83
1949	57	66	70	36	70	82
1950	63	66	77	33	61	83
1951	74	77	85	36	73	90
1952	83	83	85	56	76	92
1953	83	84	85	72	78	93
1954	82	85	89	81	78	93
1955	83	88	91	85	76	93
1956	85	91	92	91	84	94
1957	87	95	98	97	94	97
1958	100	100	100	100	100	100
1959	106	101	102	101	102	101
1960	110	105	103	104	105	102
1961	114	107	105	111	107	103
1962	119	112	108	121	111	105
1963	125	115	113	129	117	106
1964	129	119	119	136	129	107
1965	132	125	126	146	135	109
1966	136	133	133	158	140	112
1967	140	124	—	—	—	116

SOURCE: International Monetary Fund, *International Financial Statistics* (Washington, D.C.), 1968.

Figure A-4.
Cost of Living
Index, 1948–67

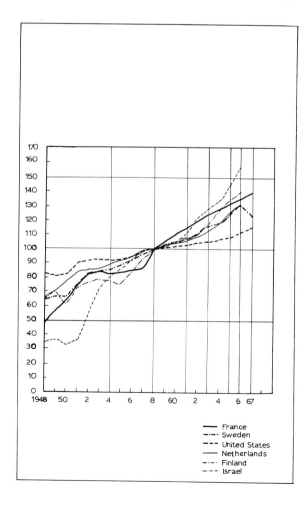

Table A-7.
National Income and Income per Capita, 1967

Country	National Income (in millions of U.S. dollars) 1967	National Income per Capita (in U.S. dollars)	
		1958	1967
Finland[a]	5.6	725	1,207
France	82.1	1,005	1,645
Israel[a]	2.7	455	1,010
Sweden	18.1	1,200	2,300
The Netherlands	18.5	695	1,465
The United States	652.9	2,115	3,280

SOURCE: International Monetary Fund, *International Financial Statistics* (Washington, D.C.), 1968.
[a] Figures for 1967 are post-devaluation.

Table A-8.
Exchange Rates, 1948–70

Year	Finland (Markkaa/U.S.$)	France (Francs/U.S.$)	Israel (Pounds/U.S.$)	The Netherlands (Guldens/U.S.$)	Sweden (Kronor/U.S.$)
1948	136.0		0.248	2.653	3.600
1949	231.0	349.0	0.357	3.800	5.180
1950	231.0	349.9	0.357	3.800	5.180
1951	231.0	350.0	0.357	3.800	5.180
1952	231.0	350.0	0.357 / 1.000	3.800	5.180
1953	231.0	350.0	1.000 / 1.800	3.786	5.180
1954	231.0	350.0	1.800	3.794	5.180
1955	231.0	350.0	1.800	3.829	5.180
1956	231.0	350.0	1.800	3.830	5.180
1957	321.0	419.9	1.800	3.791	5.180
1958	320.4	490.6	1.800	3.775	5.180
1959	320.2	490.9	1.800	3.770	5.185
1960	320.5	4.903[b]	1.800	3.770	5.180
1961	321.9	4.900	1.800	3.600	5.185
1962	322.3	4.900	3.000	3.600	5.188
1963	3.22[a]	4.902	3.000	3.600	5.200
1964	3.22	4.900	3.000	3.592	5.148
1965	3.22	4.902	3.000	3.611	5.180
1966	3.22	4.952	3.000	3.614	5.180
1967	4.20	4.908	3.500	3.596	5.165
1968	3.22	4.948	3.500	3.606	5.180
1970	4.16	5.554	3.500	3.620	5.173

SOURCE: International Monetary Fund, *International Financial Statistics* (Washington, D.C.), various issues.
[a] January 1, 1963: 1 new markkaa = 100 old markkaa.
[b] January 1, 1960: 1 new franc = 100 old francs.

Table A-9.
Value of Exports and Imports on a Per Capita Basis, 1967

Country	$ Value
Finland	709
France	486
The Netherlands	1,271
Sweden	1,194
The United States	312

SOURCE: K. W. Gullers, and Robert Skole, *USA/Sweden* (Stockholm: Gullersproduktion AB, 1969).

Table A-10.
Gross National Product, 1948–67

Year	Finland (billions of new markkaa)	France (billions of francs)	Israel (millions of Israeli pounds)	The Netherlands (billions of guldens)	Sweden (billions of kronor)	The United States (billions of dollars)
1948	3.69	—	—	15.05	25.68	257.6
1949	—	—	—	17.08	26.96	256.1
1950	4.97	—	475	19.04	28.80	284.8
1951	7.27	123.0	690	21.73	35.20	328.4
1952	7.40	145.6	1,064	22.69	38.71	345.5
1953	7.51	151.9	1,327	24.20	39.58	364.6
1954	8.94	160.8	1,754	27.00	42.15	364.8
1955	9.90	172.2	2,117	30.28	45.32	398.0
1956	11.00	191.3	2,526	32.57	49.15	419.2
1957	11.99	213.0	2,930	35.36	52.90	441.1
1958	12.91	244.7	3,357	25.93	55.21	447.3
1959	14.06	267.4	3,824	34.88	58.77	483.7
1960	15.80	296.2	4,311	42.73	63.81	503.8
1961	17.59	319.7	5,479	45.29	71.04	520.1
1962	18.81	356.3	6,585	48.52	79.02	560.3
1963	20.47	396.0	7,935	52.86	86.02	590.5
1964	23.45	435.2	9,252	62.15	95.76	632.4
1965	25.70	464.7	10,934	69.24	105.59	684.9
1966	27.62	500.5	11,862	74.81	115.01	747.6
1967	29.90	537.7	12,171	82.27	123.77	789.7

SOURCE: International Monetary Fund, *International Financial Statistics* (Washington, D.C.), 1968.

Table A-11.
Taxation as a Percentage of Gross National Product, 1953 and 1966

Country	Total Taxes and Fees 1953	1966	Direct Taxes 1953	1966	Indirect Taxes 1953	1966	Fees for Welfare Programs 1953	1966
France	32.9	38.5[a]	5.5	6.7[a]	17.0	17.6[a]	10.4	14.2[a]
Sweden	26.8	41.1	17.4	20.4	8.8	14.1	0.6	6.5
The United States	25.9	28.2	15.1	14.3	8.4	8.9	2.4	5.0

SOURCE: Stockholms Enskilda Bank, *Some Data About Sweden* (Stockholm, 1968).
[a] Figures are for 1965.

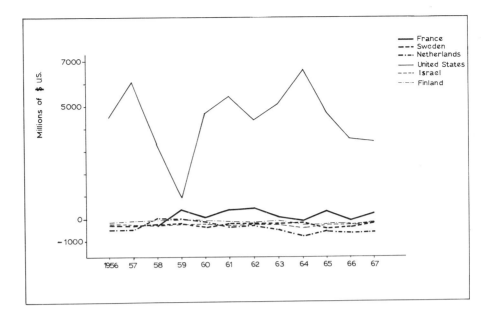

Figure A-5.
Trade Balance:
Exports minus
Imports, 1956–67

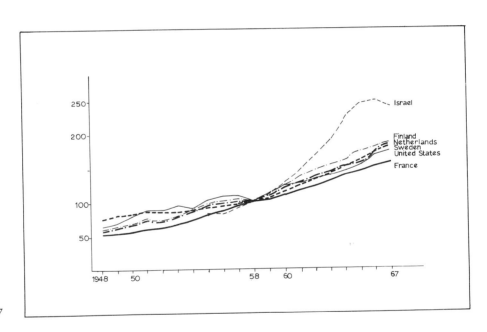

Figure A-6.
Index of Industrial
Production, 1948–67

Bibliography

Sweden

AB Stockholms Spårvägar. *SS Facts and Figures 1965*. Stockholm, 1965.

———. *T-Bana—The Stockholm Underground Railway*. Stockholm, 1965.

Atmer, Thomas. "City Planning and Construction in Stockholm." *Arkitekten* (Stockholm, journal of the National Association of Swedish Architects), 1967.

Bernhard, Harry. *Swedish Housing Policy*. National Housing Board, Stockholm, 1965.

Denmark, National Housing Board. *Housing in the Northern Countries: Sweden*. Copenhagen, 1960.

Dergalin, I., and Stäck, J. M. "General Plan for Vinkeby, Spånga, Kyrka, och Tensta." *Santryck ur Arkitektur*, no. 5 (1964).

Esping, Lars-Erik. "Preserving a Pleasing Landscape." Paper presented at the Fifth World Forestry Congress, 1960. Mimeographed.

"Extracts from the Directions of the Government and the National Housing Board Concerning the Housing Loan." Mimeographed (n.p., n.d.).

Gentili, Giorgio. "The Satellite Towns of Stockholm." *Urbanistica*, no. 24–25 (1958). Reprinted by the Stockholm Department of Planning and Building Control, February, 1960.

Gottfeld, Gunther M. "The Stockholm Underground Railway." *Stadsbyggnad*, no. 3 (1964).

Gustavsson, Just. "The Organizational Structure of Swedish Housing Administration, Financing of Housing, and the Role of Physical Planning in Housing Programmes in Sweden." Prepared for the National Housing Board. Stockholm, 1964. Mimeographed.

Hamrin, Eva, and Wirén, Erik. *Town and Country Planning in Sweden Today*. Prepared for the Swedish Institute. Stockholm, 1964.

Hernbäck, O. "Memorandum Relating to the Allocation of Land and the Control of Land Prices for Housing in Sweden." Report prepared for the National Housing Board, Stockholm, September 25, 1963. Mimeographed.

Holm, Per. "Sweden: Balance of Resources, 1964." Stockholm, 1965. Copy obtained from the author.

International Union for Conservation of Nature and Natural Resources. "Sweden: Checklist of Conservation Organizations and Information." 1961. Mimeographed.

Jensfelt, Simon. *Modern Swedish Housing*. Prepared for The Swedish Institute. Stockholm, 1962.

Jonsson, Ivar, and Odmann, Ella. "Memorandum Relating to Standards and General Guidelines Which Are Applied in Swedish Planning of Different Kinds of Development." Report prepared for the National Board of Building and Town Planning, Stockholm, February 22, 1964. Mimeographed.

———. "The Relationship between Urban Renewal and National, Regional, and Municipal Planning." Report prepared for the National Board of Building and Town Planning, Stockholm, July, 1961. Mimeographed.

Källenius, Sten. "The Financing of Swedish Housing Building." *Byggnadsindustrin*, July, 1965.

Keene, John C. "Urban Development in Sweden." Report prepared for the Institute for Environmental Studies, University of Pennsylvania, Philadelphia, July, 1965. Mimeographed.

Michanek, Ernst. *Housing Standards and Housing Construction in Sweden*. Prepared for The Swedish Institute. Stockholm, 1965.

———. *Old Age in Sweden*. Prepared for The Swedish Institute. Stockholm, 1963.

National Board of Building and Planning. "On the Possibilities for a Commune to Acquire by Force Ground for Dense Development." Stockholm, 1956. Mimeographed.

National Road Board. *The Question of Pure Water in Sweden*. Water and Sewerage Series, Pu 8.3. Stockholm, 1964.

Pontin, H. "Private Land-owners' Contribution to the Exploitation Costs in Sweden." Stockholm, 1963. Mimeographed.

————. "The Right of the Municipality to Use Private Ground." Stockholm, 1963. Mimeographed.

Quraishi, Gulam M. "Municipal Water Demand in Sweden." *Stadsbyggnad*, no. 3 (1964).

Sidenbladh, Göran. "Urban Planning in the Nordic Countries." Address to IFHP Conference, Orebro, Sweden, June 29, 1965. Printed in *IFHP Bulletin* (The Hague), 1965–66.

Smith, Åke. "National Report from Sweden." Report to the Town Planning and Land Development Section of the Eleventh International Congress of Surveyors, Rome, 1965.

Soderman, Bror. "Growing Space Needs in the Urbanized Region." Paper presented at the University of Pennsylvania New Towns Seminar, Tapiola, August, 1965.

Statens Offentliga Utredningar. *Konsumtionsmönster På Bostadsmarknaden*. Stockholm, 1964.

Stockholm Chamber of Commerce. *Swedish Shopping Centres*. Stockholm, 1965.

Stockholm Planning Commission. *Stockholm Regional and City Planning*. 1964.

The Swedish Institute. *Facts About Sweden*. Stockholm, 1964.

Wannfors, Erik. "Planning in Sweden." Lecture given at the Reed College Conference on Urban Development, Portland, Oregon, May 3, 1963. Mimeographed.

Westerman, Allan. *Swedish Planning of Town Centres*. Prepared for The Swedish Institute. Stockholm, n.d.

William-Olsson, W. *Stockholm Structure and Development*. Uppsala, 1960.

Finland

Aalto, Alvar. *Le Nouveau Centre de la Ville de Helsinki*. Helsinki, n.d.

Aaltonen, Jorma, comp. *Tapiola 62*. Tapiola, 1963.

Bjorkenheim, Haaken. "ARAVA—The National Housing Board." Helsinki, May 22, 1963. Mimeographed.

Bryant, R. W. G. "Finland: Organization of the Environment." Paper delivered at the Institut d'Urbanisme, Université de Montréal, 1965.

Bureau of Social Research. *Sosiaalinen aikakauskirja, 7–8/1965*. Helsinki, n.d.

Denmark, Ministry of Housing; Finland, National Housing Board; Norway, Housing Directorate; and Sweden, National Housing Board, *Housing in the Northern Countries*. Copenhagen, 1960.

Finnish ECE Housing Committee. *Monograph on the Housing Situation in Finland*. Helsinki: ARAVA, n.d.

Hannus, Arno. "Condensed Proposals and Opinions of the Finnish Governmental Committee on Land Supply and Land Prices." Report prepared for the Ministry of the Interior, Helsinki, August 27, 1965.

————. "Government Organization, Land Use Controls, Financing, and Taxation as Related to New Town Development." Paper presented at the University of Pennsylvania New Towns Seminar, Tapiola, August, 1965.

"Helsingin Yleskaavaehdotus" [Helsinki City Plan]. *Helsingin Kaupungin Julkaisuja N:09*. Helsinki, 1960. English summary.

"Helsinki-Présentation d'une Capitale." Edité par la Ville de Helsinki.

Iharvaara, Lassi. "Principles and Policies of Regional Planning." Paper presented at the University of Pennsylvania New Towns Seminar, Tapiola, August, 1965.

————. "Views on the Development of the Uusimaa Region and on the Role of the Porkkala Seaside Town in this Scheme." Paper presented at the University of Pennsylvania New Towns Seminar, Tapiola, August, 1965.

Kaupunki, Tehokas. *The Smooth-Running Town* [Olavi Laisaari]. Distributed by Turun Kansallinen Kirkjakauppa Oy, Finland. English and Finnish.

Koskelo, Heikki. "Economic Activities in New Towns." Paper presented at the University of Pennsylvania New Towns Seminar, Tapiola, August, 1965.

Modern Architecture in Finland. Finnish Travel Information Center.

Monograph on the Supply and Allocation of Land for Housing and Related Purposes. Helsinki, 1965.

National Housing Board. *Official Statistics of Finland: General Census of Population, 1960*. Helsinki, 1960.

Paavilainen, Väinö. *National Planning in Finland.* National Planning Office Series, A:14.3. Helsinki, 1963.

———. *Population Trends in the Helsinki Region and Problems Related to Them.* National Planning Office Series, A:13. Helsinki, 1963.

———. *Problems Connected with the Growth of Towns in Finland.* Helsinki, 1956.

Soderman, Bror. "Growing Space Needs in the Urbanized Region." Paper presented at the University of Pennsylvania New Towns Seminar, Tapiola, August, 1965.

Suomi—Certain Facts about Finland. Helsinki: Kansallis-Losake-Pankki, 1965.

"Tapiola." *Town and Country Planning,* 25, no. 3 (1957).

Tapiola Garden City. Tapiola: Asuntosäätiö (Housing Foundation), n.d.

"Tapiola Garden City." *Town and Country Planning,* 25, no. 3 (1957).

Tapiolan Puutarhakaupunti, [Tapiola Garden City, 1951–65]. Tapiola: Asuntosäätiö (Housing Foundation), 1965. English summary.

Uusimaa 2010 [Uusimaa Plan]. Helsinki: Asuntosäätiö (Housing Foundation), 1966.

Von Hertzen, Heikki. "Planning, Design and Management of Tapiola." Paper presented at the University of Pennsylvania New Towns Seminar, Tapiola, August, 1965.

———. "Planning Problems in the Province of Uusimaa: Seven Towns' Plan and its Underlying Principles." Paper presented at the University of Pennsylvania New Towns Seminar, Tapiola, August, 1965.

———. "Practical Problems of New Town Development." Paper presented at the University of Pennsylvania New Towns Seminar, Tapiola, August, 1965.

Israel

Brutzkus, Eliezer. *Physical Planning in Israel.* Jerusalem, 1964.

———. "Planning for a New Settlement Structure in Israel." *IFHP Bulletin,* 1964, no. 4.

Dafni, Rinna. *The Negev.* Israel Today no. 6. Jerusalem: Israel Digest, 1960.

Darin-Drabkin, H. *The Nature of the Urban Land Market and Methods of Compensation.* Prepared for the Ministry of Housing. Jerusalem, 1965.

Dash, Jacob. "National Physical Planning in Israel." Paper presented to the First World Congress of Engineers and Architects, Israel, 1967.

Dash, Jacob, and Efrat, Elisha. *The Israel Physical Master Plan.* Prepared for the Ministry of the Interior. Jerusalem, 1964.

Freudenheim, Yehoshua. *Government in Israel.* Dobbs Ferry, N.Y.: Oceana Publications, 1967.

Ginzberg, Eli. "The Manpower Problem." *The Reporter,* November 16, 1967.

Gouldman, M. D. *Legal Aspects of Town Planning in Israel.* Jerusalem: Hebrew University, 1966.

Halevi, Nadav, and Klinov-Malul, Ruth. *The Economic Development of Israel.* New York: Praeger, 1968.

Harman, Avraham. *Agricultural Settlement.* Israel Today no. 2. Jerusalem: Israel Digest, 1965.

Housing and Development for Israel Ltd. Government publication (n.p., n.d.).

Hovne, Avner. *The Economy.* Israel Today no. 23. Jerusalem: Israel Digest, 1965.

The Jewish Agency for Israel. Israel Today no. 16. Jerusalem: Israel Digest, 1962.

Krivine, David. *Housing.* Israel Today no. 17. Jerusalem: Israel Digest, 1965.

Lankin, Doris. *The Legal System.* Israel Today no. 19. Jerusalem: Israel Digest, 1964.

Ministry for Foreign Affairs, Information Division. *Facts About Israel, 1967.* Jerusalem: Jerusalem Post Press, 1967.

Ministry of Housing. *Abstracts of Seven Sociological Studies on Housing and Urban Settlements.* Jerusalem, 1967.

———. *For Better Living.* Jerusalem, 1964.

———. *Housing and Integration of Immigrants.* Jerusalem, 1964.

———, Planning Department. *Housing Policy in Regions of Rapid Population Growth in Israel.* Jerusalem, 1964.

Ministry of the Interior, Planning Department. *National Planning for the Redistribution of Population and the Establishment of New Towns in Israel.* Jerusalem, 1964.

National Immigrants Housing Company Ltd. *Amidar.* Tel Aviv, 1964.

Orni, Efraim. *Reclamation of the Soil.* Israel Today no. 26. Jerusalem: Israel Digest, 1963.

RASSCO Organization in Israel. *RASSCO.* Tel Aviv, n.d.

Rokach, Avshalom. *Regional Rural Development.* Israel Today no. 32. Jerusalem: Israel Digest, 1964.

Shaked, S. "Israel Builds." In *Rural Planning in Israel*, Jewish Agency for Israel and Ministry of Housing. Jerusalem, 1964.

Shikun Ovdim Ltd. *Histadruth Cooperative Housing*. Tel Aviv, 1964.

Spiegel, Erika. *New Towns in Israel*. New York: Praeger, 1967.

Super, Arthur S. *Absorption of Immigrants*. Israel Today no. 18. Jerusalem: Israel Digest, 1963.

The Netherlands

Angenot, L. H. J. "Age, Structure and Number of Dwellings in the Netherlands." Report to the U.N. World Population Conference, Belgrade, Yugoslavia, 1965 (WPC/WP/84).

Bommer, J. *Housing and Planning Legislation in the Netherlands*. Rotterdam: Bouwcentrum (in cooperation with the Ministry of Housing and Physical Planning), 1967.

City of Rotterdam. *Annual Report on Construction Activities*. 1963.

City of Rotterdam, Press and Information Services. *Building Rotterdam*. Information Sheet no. 3, January, 1964.

————. *Rotterdam in a Nutshell*.

City of Rotterdam, Public Works. *Metro Rotterdam*.

Constandse, A. K.; de Ruiter, N. C.; and Wijers, L. *Planning and Creation of an Environment*. Prepared for the Government Physical Planning Service. The Hague, 1964.

Government Information Service. *Physical Planning in the Netherlands*. The Hague, 1961.

Government Physicial Planning Service. *Report on Physical Planning in the Netherlands*. The Hague: Netherlands Printing Office, n.d.

————. *Second Report on Physical Planning in the Netherlands*. The Hague: Netherlands Printing Office, 1966.

Hall, Peter. *The World Cities*. World University Library. New York: McGraw-Hill, 1966.

Hopmans, J. J. "The Importance of the River Rhine for the Water Economy of the Netherlands," in *Water Pollution Problems on the Rhine River*. Economic Commission for Europe, GE. 63–8321, 1963.

Koning, Geert de, trans. *Advice of the Permanent Commission of the Planning Board of the Province of South Holland*, Report no. 5; *Presentation of the "State Deputies" to the Council of the Province of South Holland to Rectify the Regional Plan Ysselmonde*, Report no. 8; *Revised Ordinance of the Regional Plan Ysselmonde*, Report no. 10. Excerpts (n.p., n.d.).

Ministry of Housing and Building. *Housing in the Netherlands*. The Hague, 1964.

————. *Municipal Development Plans in the Netherlands*. The Hague, 1963.

"Municipal Finance in the Netherlands." October 14, 1963. Mimeographed (n.a., n.p.).

"National Planning for the Redistribution of Population and for the Building of New Towns in the Netherlands." March 2, 1964. Mimeographed (n.a., n.p.).

The Netherlands Universities Foundation for International Cooperation. *Planning and Development in the Netherlands*, 1, no. 1 (1962).

"Physical Planning as a Means of Balanced Development in the Netherlands." Paper presented by the Netherlands to the Economic Commission for Europe, February, 1964.

"The Position of the Municipalities in the Netherlands within the General Structure of the State." April 13, 1961. Mimeographed (n.a., n.p.).

Quené, Theo. "Planning Ideas and Ideals in a Small European Country." Speech to the Citizens' Council on City Planning, Philadelphia, Pennsylvania, July 2, 1968.

"Recent Housing Developments in the Netherlands." February 18, 1965. Mimeographed (n.a., n.p.).

Rutgers, Ir. J. "Municipal Real Estate Policy in the Netherlands." Paper read at the National Institute for Housing, Brussels, November 13, 1959.

Spits, A. *The Delta Works*. Amsterdam: The Society for Making Holland Better Known Abroad, 1964.

Stam-Beese, L. "Planning and Design Considerations." Report prepared for the City of Rotterdam, Department of Planning and Reconstruction. Mimeographed (n.d.).

Thysse, Jacques P. "The Netherlands: The Most Densely Populated Country of the World." Speech delivered at Peoples' University, February, 1962.

————. "Rim City Holland: Problems of the Metropolis in the Making." 1963. Mimeographed.

————. "A Spatial Image of the Netherlands in the Year 2000 A.D. with a Population of 20 Million." *Vereniging Voor Demografie* (The Hague), no. 6 (1963).

Toebes, G. W. "Centralization and Decentralization in the Field of Public Finance in the Netherlands." July 12, 1963. Mimeographed.

"An Unusual Metropolis: The Regional Complex of Cities and Country, Conurbation Holland." 1963. Mimeographed.

Van der Weyde, Dr., and Vink, Jasper. "Land Use and Land Policy," translated by Geert de Koning. Paper read at a Zurich Conference, April 4–6, 1963.

Vink, Jasper. "Thoughts on National Planning." Paper read in Copenhagen, May 25, 1962. Mimeographed.

Willems, Eldert. *Holland Growing Greater*. Amsterdam: De Bezige Bij, 1963.

France

Bauchet, Pierre. *Economic Planning: The French Experience*. Translated by Daphne Woodward. New York: Praeger, 1962.

———. "Regional Development Policies in France." In *Area Redevelopment Policies in Britain and the Countries of the Common Market*, U.S. Department of Commerce. Washington, D.C.: GPO, 1965.

Baum, Warren C. *The French Economy and the State*. Princeton, N.J.: Princeton University Press, 1958.

British Institute of International Comparative Law. *Land Development in France and Belgium: Law and Practice*. Special Publication no. 5. London, 1964.

Bureau Régional d'Industrialisation. *Languedoc-Roussillon-Flash-Informations*, no. 9. Montpellier, 1967.

La Caisse des Dépots. *Les Filiales Techniques de la Caisse des Dépots*. Paris, n.d.

DATAR. *Languedoc-Roussillon*. Paris, 1967.

———. *Rapport au Gouvernement sur l'Aménagement Touristique du Littoral du Languedoc-Roussillon*. Paris, n.d.

Denton, Geoffrey; Forsyth, Murray; and Maclennon, Malcolm. *Economic Planning and Policies in Britain, France, and Germany*. London: PEP, 1968.

La Documentation Française. "L'Aménagement du Territoire en France." *Notes et Études Documentaires*, no. 3461. Paris, 1968.

———. "L'Aménagement Touristique du Littoral du Languedoc-Roussillon." *Notes et Études Documentaires*, no. 3326. Paris, 1966.

———. *France*. Paris: 1967, English edition; 1968, French edition.

———. "Les Mouvements de Population en France." *Notes et Études Documentaires*, no. 3377. Paris, 1967.

European Economic Community Commission. *The Economic Situation in the Community*. Brussels: EEC Directorate-General for Economic and Financial Affairs, 1967.

Falque, Max. "L'Aménagement du Cadre de Vie des Français." *La Revue de la Chambre de Commerce et d'Industrie de Marseille*, no. 799 (1968).

French Embassy. *France Town and Country Environment Planning*. New York: Service de Presse et d'Information, 1965.

———. *The Largest Earth-Moving Project in Europe*. New York, 1969.

Freville, M. "Quelques Traits Caracteristiques de l'Economie et des Finances des Collectivités Locales Françaises au Cours des Dix Dernières Années." *Information Caisse des Dépots: Bulletin de Liaison* (Paris), no. 14 (1966).

Gentot, Michel, and Dondoux, Philippe. *France*. Brussels, 1965. On file at the International Institute of Administrative Sciences.

Germain, P., and Chambraud, R. *La Mission de la Société Centrale pour l'Equipement du Territoire*. Versaille, 1962.

Gregoire, Louis. *L'Aide a la Construction en France*. Prepared for the Ministry of Construction. Paris, 1964.

Hall, Peter. *The World Cities*. New York: McGraw-Hill, 1966.

Hansen, Niles M. "French National Planning Experience." *Journal of the American Institute of Planners* (Baltimore, Md.), November, 1969.

———. *French Regional Planning*. Bloomington: Indiana University Press, 1968.

Institut National de la Statistique et de Études Économiques. *Annuaire Statistique de la France*. Paris, 1967.

International Federation for Housing and Planning and Centre de Recherche d'Urbanisme. *Urbanization and Planning in France*. Paris, 1968.

Kinsey, David N. "The French ZUP Technique of Urban Development." *Journal of the American Institute of Planners* (Baltimore, Md.), November, 1969.

Lerouge, J. *La Planification Régionale du Territoire en France*. Prepared for the Ministry of Construction. Paris, 1964.

Levy-Soussan, A. "Les Zones à Urbaniser en Priorité." *La Jurisprudence Immobilière*, no. 6 (1962).

Londero, Anne. *France's Approach to Social Problems*. Supplement to *La Docoumentation Française Illustrée*. Paris, 1967.

Lutz, Vera. *French Planning*. Washington, D.C.: American Enterprise Institute for Public Policy Research, 1965.

Macé, Roger. *Techniques et Problèmes d'Urbanisme*. Prepared for the Ministry of Construction. Paris, n.d.

Ministry of Construction. *La Construction dans le Budget de la Nation*. Paris, 1964.

Mission Interministérielle pour l'Aménagement Touristique du Littoral Languedoc-Roussillon. *Rapport au Gouvernement*. Paris, 1967.

———. *Rapport au Gouvernement*. Paris, 1968.

OECD. *OECD General Statistics*. 1964.

Partage des Pouvoirs, Partage des Décisions, no. 9. Special Issue of *2000* (Paris), 1968.

Pasqualini, François. "French City Planners Ponder Decentralization." *Public Utilities Fortnightly*, July 22, 1965.

Racine, Pierre. "Rapport de la Mission Interministérielle pour l'Aménagement Touristique du Littoral Languedoc-Roussillon." Extract from *Administration*. DATAR no. 56. Paris, 1966.

Saindon, Jacques. "Régimes de l'Appropriation du sol et de la Construction." In *La Vie Urbaine*. N.p., n.d.

Services Culturels Français. *Géographie de la France*. New York, n.d.

U.N. Economic Commission for Europe. *Annual Bulletin of Housing and Building Statistics for Europe*. 1958 and 1966.

———. *European Housing Trends and Policies in 1961 and 1962*. 1963.

U.S. Department of Commerce. *Statistical Abstract of the United States*. Washington, D.C., 1967.

Illustration Credits

Introduction
Figures 1 through 5. Photos by Michael L. Strong.
Figure 6. Courtesy of Bryan and Shear Ltd., Glasgow.
Figure 7. Photo by Michael L. Strong.
Figure 8. Photo by Douglas Scott.
Figure 9. Courtesy of Bryan and Shear Ltd., Glasgow.
Figure 10. Photo by Michael L. Strong.

Map 1. From Jean Gottmann, *Megalopolis* (New York: Twentieth Century Fund, 1961), by permission.
Map 2. From U.S. Department of the Interior, Bureau of Land Management, *What Are "The Public Lands"?* Information Bulletin no. 1 (Washington, D.C., 1968), by permission.

Sweden
Frontispiece. Photo by Michael L. Strong.
Figures I-1 and I-2. Derived from Gulum M. Quraishi, "Municipal Water Demand in Sweden," *Stadsbyggnad*, no. 3 (1964).
Figure I-3. Derived from data in W. William-Olsson, *Stockholm Structure and Development* (Uppsala, 1960), and C. F. Ahlberg, "The Regional Plan for the Stockholm Area," in *Stockholm Regional and City Planning*, Stockholm Planning Commission (1964).
Figures I-4 and I-5. Derived from Sten Källenius, "The Financing of Swedish Housing Building," *Byggnadsindustrin*, July, 1965.
Figure I-6. Derived from Swedish National Road Board, *The Question of Pure Water in Sweden*, Water and Sewerage Series, Pu 8.3 (Stockholm, 1964).
Figures I-7 and I-9 through I-14. Photos by Michael L. Strong.
Figures I-15 and I-16. Drawn by Ashgar Minai; from Allan Westerman, *Swedish Planning of Town Centres* (Stockholm, n.d.), by permission of the author.
Figures I-17 through I-23. Photos by Michael L. Strong.
Figure I-24. Drawn by Ashgar Minai; from Allan Westerman, *Swedish Planning of Town Centres* (Stockholm, n.d.), by permission of the author.
Figure I-25. Drawn by Ashgar Minai; from Stockholm Chamber of Commerce, *Swedish Shopping Centres* (Stockholm, 1965), by permission.
Figures I-26 through I-29. Photos by Michael L. Strong.
Figure I-30. Drawn by Ashgar Minai; from Allan Westerman, *Swedish Planning of Town Centres* (Stockholm, n.d.), by permission of the author.
Figures I-31 and I-32. Photos by Michael L. Strong.
Figure I-33. Drawn by Ashgar Minai; from *Grindtorp Täby* (n.a., n.d.), a promotional folder.

Finland
Frontispiece. Copyright © by Lehtikuva Oy; courtesy of Asuntosäätiö (Helsinki Housing Foundation).
Figure II-2. Photo by Valok Matti Poutvaara.

Figure II-3. Photo by Karhumaki.
Figure II-4. Courtesy of the Museum of Finnish Architecture.
Figures II-5 and II-6. Courtesy of Asuntosäätiö.
Figures II-7, II-8, II-10, and II-11. Photos by Michael L. Strong.
Figure II-12. Courtesy of Asuntosäätiö.
Figures II-13 through II-16. Photos by Michael L. Strong.
Figure II-17. Courtesy of Asuntosäätiö.
Figure II-18. Photo by Michael L. Strong.
Figures II-19 and II-20. Courtesy of Asuntosäätiö.
Figure II-21. Photo by Michael L. Strong.
Figure II-22. Courtesy of Asuntosäätiö.
Figures II-23 and II-24. Photos by Michael L. Strong.
Figure II-25. Courtesy of Asuntosäätiö.
Figures II-26 and II-27. Photos by Michael L. Strong.

Israel

Frontispiece. Courtesy of Michael L. Strong.
Figure III-1. Courtesy of Gabriele Gutkind.
Figure III-2. Photo by Michael L. Strong.
Figures III-3 and III-4. Photos by Martin Katz.
Figures III-5 and III-6. Derived from Ministry of Foreign Affairs, Information Division, *Facts About Israel, 1967* (Jerusalem: Jerusalem Post Press, 1967).
Figures III-7 through III-10. Courtesy of Gabriele Gutkind.
Figure III-11. Photo by Michael L. Strong.
Figure III-12. Derived from Ministry of Foreign Affairs, Information Division, *Facts About Israel, 1967* (Jerusalem: Jerusalem Post Press, 1967).
Figures III-13 and III-14. Photos by Martin Katz.
Figures III-15 through III-20. Courtesy of Gabriele Gutkind.
Figures III-21 through III-23. Photos by Michael L. Strong.
Figure III-24. Derived from S. Shaked, "Israel Builds," in *Rural Planning in Israel*, Jewish Agency for Israel and Ministry of Housing (Jerusalem, 1964).
Figure III-25. Photo by Michael L. Strong.
Figure III-26. Derived from S. Shaked, "Israel Builds," in *Rural Planning in Israel*, Jewish Agency for Israel and Ministry of Housing (Jerusalem, 1964).
Figures III-27 through III-29. Photos by Michael L. Strong.

The Netherlands

Frontispiece. Copyright © by Luchtfoto Bart Hofmeester, Rotterdam; courtesy of the Netherlands Government Information Service.
Figure IV-1. Copyright © KLM Aerocarto, Amsterdam; courtesy of the Netherlands Government Information Service.
Figure IV-2. Derived from the Netherlands Universities Foundation for International Cooperation, *Planning and Development in the Netherlands*, 1, no. 1 (1962).
Figures IV-3 through IV-5. Copyright © by Luchtfoto Bart Hofmeester, Rotterdam; courtesy of the Netherlands Government Information Service.
Figures IV-6 and IV-7. Derived from the Netherlands Universities Foundation for International Cooperation, *Planning and Development in the Netherlands*, 1, no. 1 (1962).
Figure IV-8. Derived from Peter Hall, *The World Cities* (New York: McGraw-Hill, 1966), by permission.
Figures IV-9 and IV-10. Copyright © by Luchtfoto Bart Hofmeester, Rotterdam; courtesy of the Netherlands Government Information Service.
Figure IV-11. Derived from "Physical Planning as a Means of Balanced Development in the Netherlands" (Paper presented by the Netherlands to the Economic Commission for Europe, February, 1964).
Figure IV-12. From the *New York Times*, January 13, 1969.
Figure IV-13. Derived from Ministry of Housing and Building, *Housing in the Netherlands* (The Hague, 1964), and "Recent Housing Developments in the Netherlands," mimeographed, February 18, 1965 (n.a., n.p.).
Figure IV-14. Derived from "Physical Planning as a Means of Balanced Develop-

ment in the Netherlands" (Paper presented by the Netherlands to the Economic Commission for Europe, February, 1964).

Figures IV-15 and IV-16. Copyright © by Luchtfoto Bart Hofmeester, Rotterdam; courtesy of the Netherlands Government Information Service.

Figure IV-17. Copyright © by and courtesy of KLM Aerocarto, Amsterdam.

Figure IV-18. Copyright © by Mastboom Vlieghedrijf, Rotterdam; courtesy of the Netherlands Government Information Service.

Figure IV-19. Courtesy of Vliegveld Zestienhoven.

Figure IV-21. Copyright © by Mastboom Vlieghedrijf, Rotterdam; courtesy of the Netherlands Government Information Service.

Figure IV-23. Copyright © by Doeser Fotos; courtesy of the Netherlands Government Information Service.

Figures IV-24 through IV-26. Courtesy of the Netherlands Government Information Service.

Figure IV-27. Copyright © by and courtesy of KLM Aerocarto, Amsterdam.

Figure IV-28. Photo by Stephen Chamberlin.

Figures IV-29 and IV-30. Photos by Michael L. Strong.

Figures IV-31 and IV-32. Photos by Stephen Chamberlin.

Figure IV-33. Copyright © by Luchtfoto Bart Hofmeester, Rotterdam; courtesy of the Netherlands Government Information Service.

Figure IV-34. Derived from City of Rotterdam, *Annual Report on Construction Activities* (1963).

Figures IV-35 through IV-39. Photos by Michael L. Strong.

France

Frontispiece. Photo by Claude O'Sughrue.

Figure V-1. Photo by Michael L. Strong.

Figure V-2. Derived from INSEE, *Annuaire Statistique de la France* (Paris, 1967), and U.S. Department of Commerce, *Statistical Abstract of the United States* (Washington, D.C.: GPO, 1967).

Figures V-3 and V-4. Derived from INSEE, *Annuaire Statistique de la France* (Paris, 1967).

Figure V-6. Photo by Léon Gendre.

Figures V-8 and V-9. Courtesy of the Ministry of Public Works and Housing.

Figure V-10. Derived from OECD, *Annual Bulletin of Housing and Building Statistics for Europe,* 1967.

Figure V-11. Derived from OECD, *Observer,* no. 21 (1966).

Figures V-12 and V-14. Derived from OECD, *Annual Bulletin of Housing and Building Statistics for Europe,* 1958 and 1966.

Figure V-15. Courtesy of the Ministry of Public Works and Housing.

Figure V-16. Derived from OECD, *Annual Bulletin of Housing and Building Statistics for Europe,* 1966.

Figures V-17 and V-18. Photos by Michael L. Strong.

Figure V-19. Photo by Léon Gendre.

Figures V-21 through V-26. Courtesy of the Ministry of Public Works and Housing.

Figure V-27. Photo by Alain Perceval.

Figures V-28 and V-29. Photos by Claude O'Sughrue.

Figures V-30 and V-31. Photos by Alain Perceval.

Figures V-32 and V-33. Photos by Léon Loschetter.

Figure V-34. Photo by Michel Moch.

Appendix

Figure A-1. Derived from OECD, *Annual Bulletin of Housing and Building Statistics for Europe, 1967,* and updated by the author.

Figure A-3. Derived from U.N. Economic Commission for Europe, *Annual Bulletin of Housing and Building Statistics for Europe,* 1966.

Figures A-4 through A-6. Derived from International Monetary Fund, *International Financial Statistics* (Washington, D.C.), 1968.

Index